Continuous Authentication Using Biometrics:

Data, Models, and Metrics

Issa Traoré
University of Victoria, Canada

Ahmed Awad E. Ahmed
University of Victoria, Canada

Senior Editorial Director:	Kristin Klinger
Director of Book Publications:	Julia Mosemann
Editorial Director:	Lindsay Johnston
Acquisitions Editor:	Erika Carter
Development Editor:	Myla Harty
Production Editor:	Sean Woznicki
Typesetters:	Deanna Jo Zombro
Print Coordinator:	Jamie Snavely
Cover Design:	Nick Newcomer

Published in the United States of America by
Information Science Reference (an imprint of IGI Global)
701 E. Chocolate Avenue
Hershey PA 17033
Tel: 717-533-8845
Fax: 717-533-8661
E-mail: cust@igi-global.com
Web site: http://www.igi-global.com

Library of Congress Cataloging-in-Publication Data

Continuous authentication using biometrics: data, models, and metrics / Issa Traoré and Ahmed Awad E. Ahmed, editors.
    p. cm.
  Includes bibliographical references and index.
  ISBN 978-1-61350-129-0 (hardcover) -- ISBN 978-1-61350-130-6 (ebook) -- ISBN 978-1-61350-131-3 (print & perpetual access) 1. Biometric identification. 2. Authentication. 3. Computer networks--Security measures. I. Traoré, Issa, 1965- II. Ahmed, Ahmed Awad E., 1971-
  TK7882.B56C66 2012
  006.2'4--dc23
                          2011023573

British Cataloguing in Publication Data
A Cataloguing in Publication record for this book is available from the British Library.

All work contributed to this book is new, previously-unpublished material. The views expressed in this book are those of the authors, but not necessarily of the publisher.

Table of Contents

Foreword vii

Preface ix

Acknowledgment xii

Section 1
Fundamentals

Chapter 1
Introduction to Continuous Authentication 1
 Issa Traoré, University of Victoria, Canada
 Ahmed Awad E. Ahmed, University of Victoria, Canada

Chapter 2
Performance Metrics and Models for Continuous Authentication Systems 23
 Ahmed Awad E. Ahmed, University of Victoria, Canada
 Issa Traoré, University of Victoria, Canada

Chapter 3
Continuous Authentication in Computers 40
 Harini Jagadeesan, Virginia Tech, USA
 Michael S. Hsiao, Virginia Tech, USA

Section 2
Continuous Authentication Based on Physiological and Cognitive Biometrics

Chapter 4
Multimodal Biometric Hand-Off for Robust Unobtrusive Continuous Biometric
Authentication 68
    P. Daphne Tsatsoulis, Carnegie Mellon University, USA
    Aaron Jaech, Carnegie Mellon University, USA
    Robert Batie, Raytheon Company, USA
    Marios Savvides, Carnegie Mellon University, USA

Chapter 5
Low Level Multispectral Palmprint Image Fusion for Large Scale Biometrics Authentication 89
    Dakshina Ranjan Kisku, Asansol Engineering College, India
    Phalguni Gupta, Indian Institute of Technology Kanpur, India
    Jamuna Kanta Sing, Jadavpur University, India
    Massimo Tistarelli, University of Sassari, Italy
    C. Jinsong Hwang, Texas State University, USA

Chapter 6
Cognitive Biometrics: A Novel Approach to Continuous Person Authentication 105
    Kenneth Revett, British University in Egypt, Egypt

Chapter 7
Sitting Postures and Electrocardiograms: A Method for Continuous and Non-Disruptive
Driver Authentication 137
    Andreas Riener, Johannes Kepler University Linz, Austria

Section 3
Continuous Authentication Using Behavioural Biometrics

Chapter 8
Towards Continuous Authentication Based on Gait Using Wearable Motion
Recording Sensors 170
    Mohammad Omar Derawi, Gjøvik University College, Norway
    Davrondzhon Gafurov, Gjøvik University College, Norway
    Patrick Bours, Gjøvik University College, Norway

Chapter 9
Keystroke Analysis as a Tool for Intrusion Detection 193
    Daniele Gunetti, University of Torino, Italy
    Claudia Picardi, University of Torino, Italy

Chapter 10
Personal Identification and Authentication Based on Keystroke Dynamics in Japanese
Long-Text Input 212
    Toshiharu Samura, Akashi National College of Technology, Japan
    Haruhiko Nishimura, University of Hyogo, Japan

Chapter 11
Continuous User Authentication Based on Keystroke Dynamics through Neural Network
Committee Machines 232
    Sérgio Roberto de Lima e Silva Filho, Bry Tecnologia S.A., Brazil
    Mauro Roisenberg, Federal University of Santa Catarina, Brazil

Compilation of References 253

About the Contributors 270

Index 276

Foreword

Conventional security systems check the identity of an individual only once at the entry point (i.e. login) before granting them access to protected resources. This is not enough in high-security environments where access to sensitive resources needs to be constantly monitored to ensure that the authorized user is always the one using the resources. Conventional systems permit session hijacking, in which an attacker takes control of a post-authenticated session and performs unauthorized activities. Continuous authentication (CA) systems arose to prevent such occurrences, and represent a new generation of security systems that require the user to re-authenticate themselves repeatedly (and as frequently as desired) for continued access to sensitive resources.

The idea of continuous authentication emerged in the early 2000s, in part due to heightened security concerns brought about after Sept. 11. Interest in this technology has been increasing since then, both in academia and industry. Continuous authentication may be applied in various environments where high-security is needed. Although most of the systems proposed in the literature have targeted the protection of computing environments, other proposals make the case for safeguarding the aircraft cockpit against unauthorized control, or for ensuring driver identity while he/she is operating the vehicle.

Many different types of technologies (e.g. RFID, tokens) may be used to achieve continuous authentication, but systems based on biometrics have emerged as the most popular. Biometrics are ideal for continuous authentication because they cannot be misplaced (unlike tokens), forgotten (unlike passwords), and are difficult to forge by an imposter. This is especially true when multiple biometrics are used.

Although much has been written about continuous authentication in the past decade, this book on "Continuous Authentication using Biometrics," edited by Dr. Issa Traoré and Dr. Ahmed A. Ahmed, is the first effort at bringing together several representative pieces of work on this important topic. This book is a significant undertaking because it contributes to raising the awareness of the research and industry communities about this emerging area. The book involves 11 double-blinded peer-reviewed chapters contributed by 23 different researchers from around the globe spanning various aspects of continuous authentication. The contributors are among the leading experts in the field, and they cover topics ranging from authentication metrics and fundamental concepts, to practical applications using various types of biometrics (e.g. keystroke, mouse, iris scan, cognitive biometrics, palmprint), to different architectures (e.g. uni-modal and multi-modal).

Researchers and students in academia, as well as security professionals in industry and government will no doubt find this book helpful in advancing the security landscape. The depth of knowledge brought in by the contributors to this endeavour ensures that this book will serve as a professional reference, and provide a comprehensive and insightful view of this emerging field. I congratulate all the authors, as well as the editors, for marking an important milestone in the development of continuous authentication.

Terence Sim
School of Computing National University of Singapore, Singapore

Terence Sim *received the PhD degree in Electrical and Computer Engineering from Carnegie Mellon University in 2002, the MS degree in Computer Science from Stanford University in 1991 and the BS degree in Computer Science and Engineering from the Massachusetts Institute of Technology in 1990. He is an Assistant Professor at the School of Computing, National University of Singapore. His research interests are in biometrics, face recognition, computer vision, computational photography, and music processing. He also serves as Vice Chairman of the Biometrics Technical Committee, Singapore, and as Vice President of the Pattern Recognition and Machine Intelligence Society, Singapore. He has contributed several influential papers in continuous biometrics authentication.*

Preface

User authentication is the process of verifying whether the identity of a user is genuine prior to granting him access to resources or services in a secured environment. Traditionally authentication is performed *statically* at the point of entry of the system (e.g. login); this is referred to as *static authentication*. A popular form of a static authentication technique widely used in computer networks is password-based authentication. It is a well-established fact that traditional passwords are unsafe. Passwords may be stolen or may be cracked using the so-called dictionary attack. Generally speaking there are at least two main issues with static authentication techniques. Firstly, in the case where the authentication process fails to genuinely verify the identity of a user — as may happen, for instance, with password-based authentication schemes — there is no other opportunity to get things right in the rest of the login session or to establish after the session that some malicious activity occurred. Secondly, a successful authentication at the beginning of a session does not provide any remedy against the session being hijacked later by some malicious user.

One of the solutions proposed to address these shortcomings is *continuous authentication* (CA). CA consists of the process of positively verifying the identity of a user in a repeated manner throughout a login session. CA departs from the traditional (static) authentication schemes by repeating several times the authentication process dynamically throughout the entire login session; the main objectives being to detect masqueraders, ensure session security, and combat insider threat. Although CA can be effective in detecting session hijacking, it requires special data sources to detect masqueraders. Such data source should allow the system to discriminate reliably legal users from imposters. Although non-biometric data sources such as user commands sequences and RFID may be used, biometrics technologies are the most suitable for this purpose. This book presents a selection of 11 chapters on continuous authentication using biometrics contributed by the leading experts in this recent, fast growing research area. These chapters provide collectively a thorough and concise introduction to the field of biometric-based continuous authentication. The book covers the conceptual framework underlying CA and presents in detail processing models for various types of practical CA applications.

This book is primarily intended for researchers, developers, and managers who are interested or are currently working in the emerging field of continuous authentication. The book is also of relevance to students of computer science and engineering, in particular, graduate students at the Master's or PhD levels.

The book consists of 11 chapters organized in three sections as follows:

1. Section 1: Fundamentals
2. Section 2: Continuous Authentication Based on Physiological and Cognitive Biometrics
3. Section 3: Continuous Authentication Using Behavioral Biometrics

A brief outline of the book is as follows.

As in any emerging area, the field of continuous authentication requires establishing some common ground regarding the basic aspects and entities as well the characteristics of a standard continuous authentication system. Section 1 of the book involves three chapters (i.e. Chapters 1-3) covering fundamental concepts and generic models for CA systems design, implementation, and evaluation.

Traoré and Ahmed presents in Chapter 1, a conceptual framework outlining basic concepts and entities underlying CA systems. They also introduce a generic architecture for CA systems and discuss various applications of the technology.

In Chapter 2, the same authors identify a set of metrics and models for the design and evaluation of CA systems. The chapter introduces several empirical guidelines that can be used to design high-performance CA systems.

In Chapter 3, Jagadeesan and Hsiao make a significant contribution in outlining CA fundamentals by identifying and discussing the factors and steps involved in building a good continuous authentication system. They illustrate the introduced factors and steps by presenting the case study of a multimodal CA system based on mouse and keystroke dynamics biometrics technologies.

Section 2 involves 4 chapters (i.e. Chapters 4-7) covering the use of physiological and cognitive biometrics for continuous authentication.

The typical trend in continuous authentication research is to establish a clear separation line between static log-on phase and the repeated authentication occurring in the rest of the session. However, the static log-on can influence the rest of the verification activities taking place in the rest of the session to a large extent.

In this regard, Tsatsoullis and colleagues propose, in Chapter 4, to use a robust biometric technology for static log-on combined with a less computationally expensive biometric technology for the continuous verification.

While Tsatsoullis and colleagues are proposing a multi-biometric system involving two biometrics technologies operating independently, Kisku and colleagues discuss the merits of intra-modal biometric systems over uni-modal systems. Likewise, in Chapter 5, they propose a low-level multispectral palmprint biometric fusion scheme, which enhances the accuracy of the palmprint biometric technology by using Gabor wavelet transformation. The authors argue that the proposed multispectral palmprint biometric system can be used to continuously authenticate individuals (when required) in high security zones such as border control as well as low security ones such as home computing environments.

In Chapter 6, Revett discusses a novel approach for continuous authentication based on cognitive biometrics which uses signals based on the response(s) of nervous tissue such as the electrocardiogram (ECG) or the electroencephalogram (EEG). Although the discussion remains at a high level, it provides interesting and useful insight into the background work and foundational technologies underlying cognitive biometrics.

In Chapter 7, Riener discusses the need for continuous authentication for drivers, and then present a system that uses wireless ECG to continuously verify user identity while they are sitting in the car.

Section 3 involves 4 chapters (i.e. Chapters 8-11) covering the use of behavioural biometrics technologies for continuous authentication.

In Chapter 8, Derawi and colleagues discuss the use of gait biometric for continuous authentication and then introduces a continuous authentication system based on wearable gait recognition technology.

The remaining 3 chapters of Section 3 cover continuous authentication based on keystroke dynamics. Keystroke dynamics, along with a few other biometric technologies, exhibit a number of key characteristics ideal in continuous authentication: the data comes as stream which is readily available throughout the session; data collection and analysis can be conducted unobtrusively and do not require any special purpose hardware.

In Chapter 9, Gunetti and Picardi discuss and investigate the use of keystroke analysis for computer intrusion detection, which is one of the key applications of continuous authentication. They also briefly discuss other interesting applications of keystroke analysis relevant to continuous authentication such as identity tracing in the cyberspace.

In Chapter 10, using a hybrid keystroke analysis model based on the combination of the array disorder distance metrics (introduced by Gunetti and Picardi), and the Euclidian distance, Samura and Nishimura establish that the effectiveness of keystroke analysis might be proportional to the skill levels of the typists. In the same vein, in Chapter 11, Silva Filho and Roisenberg discuss the efficiency and cost-effectiveness of using keystroke analysis for continuous authentication, and introduce an approach based on neural networks committee machines.

The above chapters represent a broad coverage of the state of the art which we believe will lead the readers to a deeper understanding of the art and science underlying the emerging field of continuous authentication.

Issa Traoré
University of Victoria, Canada

Ahmed Awad E. Ahmed
University of Victoria, Canada

Acknowledgment

We would like to thank all the authors who have contributed quality chapters to this book. Special thanks to Terence Sim, who provided an excellent foreword for the book, to all our editorial advisory board members and the reviewers who invested a lot of efforts and time in selecting the highest quality chapters possible. We would like also to thank the IGI Global team, who helped and advised us in conducting this book project to term.

Finally, we would like to thank our families for their tireless support throughout this project.

Issa Traoré
University of Victoria, Canada

Ahmed Awad E. Ahmed
University of Victoria, Canada

Section 1
Fundamentals

Chapter 1
Introduction to Continuous Authentication

Issa Traoré
University of Victoria, Canada

Ahmed Awad E. Ahmed
University of Victoria, Canada

ABSTRACT

Continuous Authentication (CA) systems represent a new generation of security mechanisms that continuously monitor user behavior and use this as basis to re-authenticate periodically throughout a login session. CA has been around for about a decade. As a result a limited amount of research work has been produced to date, and the first commercial products have only recently started reaching the market. We attempt, in this chapter, to provide some general perspectives in order to help achieve some common and better understanding of this emerging field. The chapter introduces basic CA concepts and terminologies, discusses the characteristics of CA data sources, and identifies major areas of application for CA systems.

INTRODUCTION

Identity Assurance (IA) is a set of mechanisms and strategies allowing an organization to minimize the business risk related to identity impersonation and misappropriation of authentication credentials. Some of the most serious threats to IA include session hijacking and masquerade attacks (Garg et al., 2006). A successful authentication at the beginning of a session, also referred to as *static*

authentication, does not provide any remedy against the session being hijacked later by some malicious user, even when a strong authentication mechanism such as a biometric technology is used. Session hijacking involves an intruder seizing control of a legitimate user session after successfully getting a valid authentication session identifier while that session is still in progress. A possible remedy against such a scenario, referred to as *continuous authentication (CA)*, consists of re-authenticating the user repeatedly throughout the lifetime of the session (de Lima and Roisen-

DOI: 10.4018/978-1-61350-129-0.ch001

berg, 2006; Calderon et al., 2006; Liu et al., 2007; Azzini and Marrara, 2008). By repeatedly checking the authentication credentials of the user while the session is still in progress, CA has inherently the capability to detect misappropriation of these credentials resulting from session hijacking.

Continuous authentication represents a subclass of activity monitoring. The field of activity monitoring was originally investigated by Fawcett and Provost (1999) as a new class of Knowledge and Data Discovery (KDD) problems, which consists of observing the behavior of a large number of entities or individuals with the purpose of detecting unusual events requiring immediate actions. Activity monitoring applications greatly vary in terms of the kinds of data streams involved. Nonetheless, Fawcett and Provost have attempted in their study to provide a general and common representation for activity monitoring tasks. These tasks vary from fraud detection to intrusion detection, or news story monitoring systems. As a subclass of activity monitoring, the field of application of CA is narrower and broadly fall under the category of intrusion detection.

This chapter provides some general perspectives on CA as an emerging discipline by defining fundamental concepts, discussing the characteristics of underlying data sources, and outlining some major applications. The goal of this chapter is less about presenting some concrete research results and more about providing some insight and laying down some ground for a better understanding of this emerging discipline. The rest of the chapter is articulated around four main sections as follows.

Firstly, we present a conceptual framework for CA where basic concepts and terminologies are introduced. We also outline a generic architecture for CA as part of this framework.

Secondly, we present the characteristics of the data needed for continuous authentication. Although this is not an absolute requirement, most of the data sources that exhibit such characteristics can be classified as biometrics. We give an overview of biometrics technologies, in general,

and present examples of suitable biometrics technologies for continuous authentication.

Thirdly, we identify and discuss major application areas for CA systems, and finally, in the last section, we make some concluding remarks.

CONCEPTUAL FRAMEWORK FOR CONTINUOUS AUTHENTICATION

Terminologies and Concepts

In this section, we present and discuss the fundamental characteristics of CA systems. More specifically we consider CA systems from different perspectives and outline key terminologies and concepts that characterize CA activity and mechanism.

Static vs. Continuous Authentication

Static authentication is a binary decision process consisting of three sub-processes: *enrollment, presentation*, and *evaluation* (see Figure 1). During the enrollment sub-process information is collected about the individual, processed and stored as a template or a profile to be used subsequently as basis for authentication. The presentation sub-process is executed when an individual wants to use the system. When prompted by the system, the individual presents their identity and an authentication factor to the system. The evaluation sub-process which is then triggered consists of comparing the presented authentication information against the stored profile for the claimed identity. The outcome of this process will be a match or non-match.

Continuous authentication is a mechanism that checks the identity of an individual repeatedly for the entire duration of an authorized session.

Static authentication provides assurance of the individual's identity only at the point of entry of a session. As the session progresses, assurance

Figure 1. Static authentication process

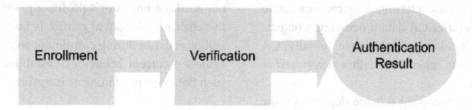

that the individual is who she claims to be can be given only through CA process.

The CA process dynamically iterates the three steps involved in the static authentication process repeatedly throughout the session (see Figure 2). Iterations can be performed randomly or at fixed time interval, or according to the occurrence of specific event.

Establishing an accurate user profile is a key prerequisite for successful continuous authentication. User profile in globally distributed networked environments may involve user knowledge and characteristics, access location, job characteristics, resources used, workstations and transaction profiles. A key challenge is that the user profiles may be subject to constant changes over time in networked environments. This is referred to as

behavior drift and may be dealt with using appropriate artificial intelligence techniques.

CA Entities

A CA system can be characterized primarily by two major entities: the sensor which is linked to a data source and the *controller* which implements the underlying data processing scheme. A typical CA system may involve one or several data sensor/controller pairs. Although the data source needs not be a biometric, it is expected that it should have strong discriminative capability. So ideally, biometric data sources would be more appropriate.

Desirable characteristics for the data processing component include adaptive learning and the capability to handle behavior drift, noisy and incomplete data and so on. Since such character-

Figure 2. Continuous authentication process

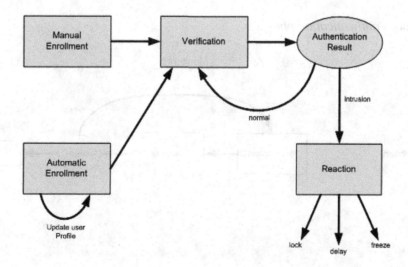

istics are typically in artificial intelligence (AI) techniques, we use a terminology reminiscent to AI to characterize CA data processing schemes. More specifically, we categorize broadly CA data processing schemes as either *supervised* or *unsupervised*.

The data processing scheme depends on the particular type of data (i.e. keystroke, voice, mouse, fingerprint, etc.), but in any case, it must allow extracting from the data a profile for the user that uniquely characterizes her behavior. In the supervised model, the derivation of a user profile requires using sample data from both the individual (*self*) and other people (*nonself*), while in the unsupervised model, only sample data from self is needed when building a user profile.

Using a supervised or unsupervised model will have a significant impact on the scope of the CA system. A supervised model may be used to discriminate between users in a closed setting, where CA data can be collected for all the users. The main weakness of a supervised approach, however, is that all users' data must be collected before CA activity monitoring can proceed and even so the approach may be hindered by the non-uniform class problem as the number of classes or users increases. When public access to hosts is not restricted, as is the case in many operational environments, the unsupervised model is more

suitable for the CA process. In this case, we do not need the impostor's profile a priori in order to detect her. A normal profile is built for each authorized user during enrollment and compared against a current behavior to establish whether such behavior is genuine or intrusive.

CA Phases

A CA system can also be characterized in terms of the major phases involved in the CA process. There are two major phases in a typical CA process: *enrollment* and *monitoring* (see Figure 3).

Enrollment Phase

The enrollment always precedes the monitoring phase. It is a critical phase during which individual user profiles also referred to as signatures are built from sample data collected from the user. The key questions that need to be answered prior or during this phase are the following:

1. What is the minimum amount of data needed to enroll a user?
2. How sound are the enrollment samples?
3. Do the enrollment process and sample collections require active participation of the user or are those transparent?

Figure 3. Continuous authentication phases

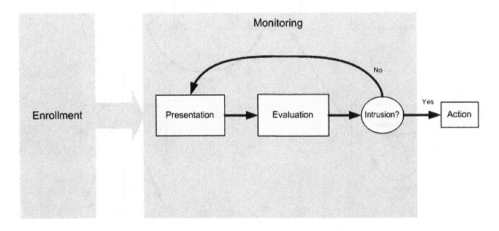

4. What is the level of automation of the enrollment process?
5. How does the process adapt to changes?

The answer to the first question has a direct impact on the length of the enrollment process. The larger the required sample, the longer the enrollment phase will be. Obviously, systems with shorter enrollment phase are preferred over those with longer enrollment phase. But since the enrollment may be considered as part of the general setup phase, a delay in the process could have been considered as a minor inconvenience if there was no underlying security implication. This leads us to the answer to the second question.

The enrollment phase is a fundamental aspect of the provisioning of a CA system, which if not conducted rightfully will inevitably conduct to the failure of the entire system. The monitoring phase relies on the quality of the profiles produced during the enrollment for proper decision-making. To ensure that the profiles are reliable representation of the user behavior, a minimum amount of representative samples must be collected. The size of such minimum amount of data depends on the data processing technique used. On the other hand during the enrollment phase, the system is more vulnerable, specifically in the setup phase where the CA activity monitoring per se has not been triggered yet. Ensuring the security of this phase using alternative means is essential. Otherwise there is no guarantee that the samples used as part of *self* to build the user profile were actually not provided by an intruder masquerading as the legitimate user.

The answer to the third question makes the distinction between *passive enrollment* and *active enrollment*. In a passive enrollment, the data is collected and the profile is derived without any active involvement of the user; the entire process is transparent to the user. In contrast, in active enrollment, the user may be asked to perform specific tasks or exhibit specific behaviors in order to generate her profile. In practical CA environ-ment, passive enrollment is preferred over active enrollment. Active enrollment can be cumbersome because it imposes some burden on the users, in particular in public access networks.

Furthermore, active enrollment can limit the level of automation of the enrollment process. This leads us to the answer to the fourth question.

Ideally, the enrollment phase should complete-ly be automated; this is necessary for scalability purpose, and to limit initial setup and administra-tive efforts and costs. However, according to how complex the user profile derivation and tuning is, the enrollment process may be subject to more or less automation or no automation at all. Manual enrollment is the worst case scenario, and should exist only as an option along with some automated form of enrollment in globally distributed network environments.

The answer to the last question depends on whether the enrollment is static or continuous.

Static enrollment is inherently a manual process designed explicitly to match an entity's identi-fier with some authentication profile, signature or template. In contrast, *continuous enrollment*, which is implicit to users, consists of updating continuously the users' profiles as they use the organization resources over time. In some quar-ters, continuous enrollment is also equated with *adaptive enrollment*.

Continuous enrollment is necessary or use-ful for many of the current CA data sources. In particular, with CA data sources related to human behavioral characteristics, it is necessary to update or adapt the user profile on a regular basis to re-flect changes in user behavior and environmental conditions. Continuous enrollment is inherently an automatic process, in which the human supervisor intervenes only occasionally. The intervention may consist for instance of overriding the system or re-enrolling a user under particular conditions such as illness or an accident causing significant changes in the user profile. In some cases, the human operator may also need to label manually the sample data being used or in re-enrolling the user. In the labeling process, the role of the human operator is to check on one hand whether a session flagged by the CA system as normal is indeed a normal session or a false negative, and on the other hand, whether a session reported as intrusion corresponds either to a real intrusion or a false positive.

Monitoring Phase

The monitoring phase relies on the outcome of the enrollment phase to carry out the actual function of the CA activity. At the beginning of this phase, the user claims specific identity, for instance, by providing some user identification and/or password. The profile of the claimed identity is considered the reference profile. The monitoring phase simply consists of comparing on a regular basis the monitored sample or data (received from the user) against the reference profile. In case of a non-match, an intrusion is reported, otherwise, the user behavior is considered as normal. The following two important questions need to be answered for this phase:

1. What is the length of the verification period?
2. Do the verification process and sample collections require active participation of the user or are those transparent?

The answer to the first question lies at the heart of the main tension that characterizes CA system. The performance of a CA system is inversely proportional to the length of the time interval between consecutive identity verifications.

The shorter the verification period the better as this means quick decision-making and fast response time. Quick decision-making is important mainly from security perspective since this means limited window of opportunity for an attack. On the other hand, short verification period means fewer monitored samples which typically tend to have adverse effect on detection accuracy. So

trade-offs must be made when deciding the length of the verification period.

Similar to the enrollment process, the monitoring process can be active or passive. For instance, in user re-authentication scheme where the user is asked to re-enter his password during a session, the monitoring is an active process. The downside of an active monitoring process is potentially low user acceptability due to its intrusive nature. In contrast, passive monitoring which is conducted transparently has negligible impact on the user activity.

Different categories of CA systems can be considered according to how enrollment and verification are conducted. More specifically the following categories may be considered:

1. Active Enrollment/ Active Monitoring
2. Passive Enrollment/ Active Monitoring
3. Active Enrollment/ Passive Monitoring
4. Passive Enrollment/ Passive Monitoring

In principle, only the last two categories should be considered as practical CA systems, with the latter being the most attractive one. Passive monitoring should be the minimum standard to be expected from a CA system. Passive enrollment can be considered as an important enhancement as discussed above.

The primary outcome of a CA monitoring process is the *authentication confidence level*, which serves as basis for final authentication decision-making. The authentication confidence level intends to provide a measure of the correctness of a claimed identity. It can be expressed as a number between [0, 1] or as a percentage. The final authentication decision is made by comparing the authentication confidence level to a pre-specified threshold. The threshold must be tuned to provide various levels of assurance.

The final authentication decision spawns an authorization level which is used as basis for user access control.

Generally speaking, there are two types of authorization, namely, *static authorization* and *continuous authorization.*

Static authentication leads to *static authorization.* In static authorization, the resources and processes that authorized entities can use are predefined. Static authorization may be acceptable in situations where user activity patterns, roles and job characteristics remain stable. However, in more dynamic and less predictable environments, with changing user profiles, *continuous authorization* is a necessity. Continuous authorization permanently monitors information resource usage patterns and adapt privileges to changes in these patterns. Continuous authentication leads to continuous authorization.

CA Quality

There are two quality attributes of high importance for CA systems, namely *effectiveness* and *efficiency.*

Efficiency refers to the run-time efficiency of the CA detector, specifically its scalability and the extent to which it achieves timely detection. Effectiveness refers to the degree to which the system accurately detects intrusions in the system, while maintaining an acceptable level of false alerts.

The above quality attributes can be measured objectively using performance metrics. We discuss examples of performance metrics and models later in this chapter.

CA Validation

CA systems may be evaluated through two different types of experiments: *controlled* experiments and *free* experiments.

Although controlled experiments are necessary to study the impact of confounding factors on the data sources and models underlying CA systems, these are not enough to validate their operations, in particular if we take the view that CA should be based on a passive monitoring process. By

taking such view, the evaluation of the CA system should investigate the passive characteristic of the system. This can be carried only through a free or uncontrolled experiment. So, the evaluation of a standard system must involve both controlled and free experiments; evaluating the system using only one or the other form of experiment is not enough. The free experiment will consist of at least collecting samples in an environment and through a procedure with as limited constraints or restrictions as possible, without any active involvement of the user. Since a free experiment typically involves a lot confounding factors, the role of the controlled experiment will be to assess the impact of these confounds on the obtained results.

CA Privacy

Legal concerns for CA systems may vary according to the country where the system is being used. But in general, no matter what the country is, three types of legal concerns may arise, namely *consent, notification* and *privacy.*

Consent may be needed when evaluating the CA system, in particular the data source and data processing components. Since these typically may involve human elements, it is necessary to let the participants know what the purpose of the evaluation experiments is, how the collected data will be used and disposed of (when not needed anymore), and more importantly to obtain informed consent for their participation. Obtaining informed consent does not lessen the scope of the experiment and does not contradict whatsoever the transparency requirement outlined in the above discussion for CA experiments.

Notification may consist of posting on the premise a notice informing the users that access to the devices deployed in the corresponding site are being monitored continuously. The proper wording of the notice will depend on the laws of the hosting country.

Privacy is a more complex issue because it may involve, beyond legal considerations, technical challenges which may be difficult to overcome for many CA data sources. Here, the goal is to ensure that the privacy of the user is preserved when collecting and processing CA data. For instance, a data source like mouse dynamics protects the privacy of the user to a large extent because other than the usage pattern of the user no other personal information is collected or can be derived from the data. In contrast, most keystroke dynamics biometric systems collect, along with the dynamics, the key codes which carry private information. In particular, in client/server environments, possible solution may consist of integrating in the client software, privacy-preserving features which may scramble or jam the collected information prior to sending it to the server.

CA Architecture

The basic software architecture for continuous authentication is based on the client/server model, where typically a thin client dealing with CA data collection and preprocessing is deployed on monitored machines or devices, and a server dealing with CA data analysis and decision-making is located in a secure location. Figure 4 depicts generic software architecture for CA systems.

The client involves two types of modules, namely sensor and enforcer. The sensor module which may interface with one or several different types of CA data sensors is in charge of collecting and preprocessing the data, and then sending it to the server. The enforcer is optional and depends on the type of CA application as discussed in the next section. As the name indicates, the enforcer is in charge of ensuring that the CA decision made by the server is enforced on the monitored machine typically in case of intrusion. This may consist, for instance, of locking the machine or logging the user out and asking them to login using an alternative authentication medium (e.g. using a token if a password was used during the initial authentication at the point of entry).

The integration of a locking mechanism into the operating system must balance several conflicting requirements. These include detection accuracy, computational overhead, and reaction time; the reaction time refers to the time used to respond when an intrusion is reported.

On the server side the controller is the brain of the system, in the sense that it implements the CA data analysis and decision-making algorithms as well as the enrollment mechanism used to extract user profiles. The controller interfaces with a log,

Figure 4. Generic architecture for continuous authentication

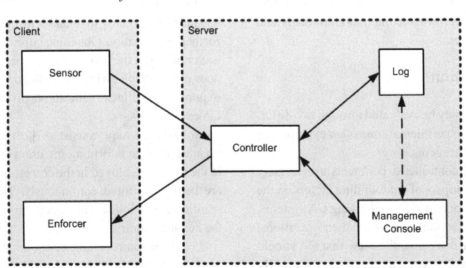

typically a database, where collected CA data along with user profiles are stored. The management console allows the human operator to interact with the system to perform basic management function such as initializing or updating the settings, manually enrolling users (when necessary), viewing and analyzing CA events etc.

Note that the above architecture provides only a basic skeleton on top of which more sophisticated or specialized CA systems can be built. Additional or specific types of modules may be needed according to which application area the emphasis is placed on when designing the system.

CA Application Levels

Calderon et al. (2006) identified four CA levels offering varying degree of protection for information systems. The following CA levels were identified:

1. Level 1 CA: user authentication
2. Level 2 CA: user-resource authentication
3. Level 3 CA: user-resource-system authentication
4. Level 4 CA: user-resource-system-transaction authentication

Level 1 CA provides the basic CA functionality, which consists of challenging and verifying constantly and transparently the user identity throughout a login session, by ensuring that the authentication confidence level remains greater than a set threshold: $P(User) \geq Thr$.

Level 2 CA consists of checking continuously that a claimed identity is genuine when the user accesses a particular resource. This involves checking that the authentication confidence level is greater than the set threshold: $P(User/Resource) \geq Thr_R$.

Level 2 CA encompasses Level 1 CA and provides comparatively a finer grain of authentication. Level 2 CA limits the risk for an authenticated user to access a resource while she is not authorized to do so.

Level 3 CA ensures that the user's claimed identity is genuine when accessing and using the organization's resource from a machine or device which is not under the administrative control of the organization, for instance, through remote login. This will involve checking that the authentication confidence level is greater than the set threshold:

$P(User/Workstation) \geq Thr_W$

Level 3 CA encompasses Level 2 CA

Level 4 CA ensures that the user's claimed identity is genuine when corresponding identity is being used to initiate and execute a particular type of transaction. This involves checking that the authentication confidence level is above the threshold: $P(User/Transaction) \geq Thr_{Tr}$.

Level 4 CA encompasses Level 3 CA. Level 4 CA provides the strongest level of protection, by continuously monitoring user identity and ensuring their actions are authorized across the network, regardless of which machine or location they operate from.

CA DATA SOURCES

In this section, we present the characteristics of the data needed for continuous authentication. Although this is not an absolute requirement, most of the data sources that exhibit such characteristics can be classified as biometrics. We give an overview of biometrics technologies, in general, and present examples of suitable biometrics data sources for continuous authentication.

CA Data Requirements

The two most important requirements for CA data source are the following:

1. It must be possible to extract from the data sufficient information to discriminate reliably different users

2. It must be possible to collect and process the data transparently (or unobtrusively) with respect to the user.

In the last decade, various data sources that fit the above criteria have been used in user behavior monitoring applications which basically can be viewed as early CA systems. These include user command sequence monitoring (Lane & Brodley, 1999, Lane & Brodley, 2003; Maxion and Townsend, 2004), free-text detection of keystrokes dynamics biometrics (Guneti & Picardi, 2005), and mouse dynamics biometrics recognition (Ahmed & Traoré, 2007a). Learning user profiles based on command line strings is one of the earliest types of CA systems proposed in the literature (Lane & Brodley, 1999; Maxion & Townsend, 2004). The basic assumption underlying such systems is that illegitimate activity can be discriminated from normal user behavior when based on command usage. In this case, the recognition tasks will consist of classifying sequences or blocks of user commands as pertaining to *self* (i.e. legitimate user), or *nonself* (i.e. unauthorized user). Distinction must be made between these approaches where user profiles are learnt at the user interface level and approaches based on learning system call traces. Data like system call traces or network packet traces are machine-generated, while user command line strings are human-generated. A common and distinctive characteristic of CA systems is that they use human-generated data for user recognition. As argued in (Lane & Brodley, 2003), machine-level data are generated by automated mediums and exhibit more repetitions and extremely low amount of noise compared to human-generated data. Biometrics technologies, by definition, are based on human-generated data and more importantly they fulfill the first CA data requirement outlined above. However, only a few existing biometrics technologies fulfill the second CA data requirement because they require special purpose hardware devices and active participation of the user in the data collection process.

In the next two sections, we give an overview of biometrics technologies, in general, and then focus our attention on suitable biometrics data sources for CA.

Biometrics Technologies

Overview

Recent years have seen an increasing interest in biometric systems; the underlying technology has improved and the costs involved have been reduced considerably. Biometrics technologies are widely used in various security applications, and are considered among the most accurate and efficient security systems on the market.

Biometrics can be defined as a set of distinctive, permanent and universal features recognized from human physiological or behavioral characteristics. In the Oxford dictionary, the definition of the noun "biometrics" is given as "the application of statistical analysis to biological data" (Pearsall & Trumble, 2001). In the particular field of computer security, biometrics is defined as the automated use of a collection of factors describing human behavioral or physiological characteristics to establish or verify a precise identity (Matyas & Riha, 2003).

Biometrics recognition systems form part of the surveillance technologies deployed in many organizations. Biometrics is commonly used for access control to secured facilities or in conjunction with monitoring systems such as closed circuit television. These allow employers to verify employees work time and attendance, but at the same time to protect employees against employers' manipulations or mistakes in maintaining such records.

Biometrics technologies are commonly categorized into two different classes: physiological and behavioral. Examples of physiological characteristics include hand or finger images, facial characteristics, speaker verification, and iris recognition. Behavioral characteristics are traits that are learned or acquired based on human actions. Dynamic signature verification and keystroke dynamics are two examples of behavioral characteristics. Due to their strong variability over time, so far, behavioral biometric systems have been less successful compared to physiological ones (Bergadano et al., 2002). Despite such limitation, behavioral biometrics such as mouse dynamics and keystroke dynamics, carry the greatest promise in the particular field of online computer user monitoring (Ahmed & Traoré, 2005a). For such application, passive or non-intrusive monitoring is essential. Unfortunately most biometrics systems require special hardware devices for biometrics data collection, restricting their uses to only networks segments where such devices are available. Behavioral biometrics such as mouse dynamics and keystroke dynamics are appropriate for such context because they only require standard human-computer interaction devices.

Biometric Recognition Process

Biometric recognition involves comparing an enrolled biometric sample (biometric template) against a newly captured biometric sample (for example, finger scan provided at an access attempt). A three-step process (*Acquire, Process, and Store*) should be executed every time the user presents his or her biometric sample to the system as follows:

1. **Acquire:** Raw biometric data is acquired by a sensing device, such as the image produced by a fingerprint scanning device, or the data collected by a keystroke event logger. Raw biometric data usually contains noise and cannot be used as is to automatically compare between users.
2. **Process:** The raw data is processed to build a biometric model (template). This model consists of a number of extracted distinguishing features which are represented in a mathematical format.

3. **Store:** The biometric template is stored in a database with all other collected information, (like claimed identity, date, time). This process is required in order to secure enough data for the user enrollment process. Some of the biometric systems implementations do not permanently store the generated template during the recognition process. This is usually the case for non-audited access control systems. However storing such data increases the accountability of the system. Since the biometric template contains all the data representing the user biometric characteristics to the system there is no need to store the raw data. It is also not possible to reconstruct the raw data from the generated biometric template.

Biometrics Modes

Biometric systems operate in one of three modes: *Enrollment, Verification,* and *Identification* modes. In most of the implementations the same hardware is used for the three modes.

Figure 5 shows a generic architecture, which covers the components involved in the implementation of a biometric recognition system. The flow of control and data are shown for the three possible scenarios: enrolling a user, verifying his or her identity, and identifying an unknown user.

During the enrollment mode, a reference biometric model is generated for the user. This model can be developed using number of the templates already stored in the database for the same user or it can be based only on one template. The reference model is stored in the database for future comparisons. Enrolled data should be free of noise and any other defects that can affect its comparison with other samples.

In the two remaining modes, biometric data is captured, processed and compared against the stored enrolled sample. According to the type of application, a verification or identification process will be conducted on the processed sample.

Figure 5. Generic architecture of a behavioral biometric system

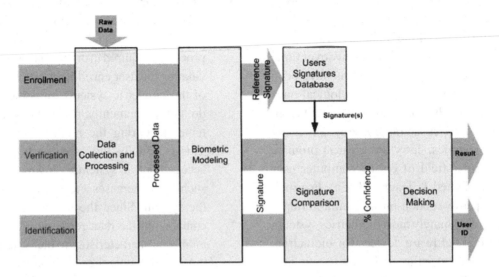

In the verification mode, a 1-to-1 matching process is performed by comparing the calculated biometric template to the enrolled user reference model. In this mode the user will provide other information to the system to claim a specific identity. The decision will be made based on the comparison result. If the two samples are highly deviated from each other, this will indicate that the user is not who she claimed to be.

In identification mode, a 1-to-*n* matching process is performed by comparing the calculated biometric template to the reference models for all of the enrolled users. The matching process should be able to detect the similarities in the compared models and select the closest reference model to the collected sample. The result of this process is either an identity confirmation or a non-match. This mode is mainly used in forensic applications where a proof of the identity of a suspect is not known in advance.

Biometrics-Based CA Sensors

A common limitation of most biometric systems is the need for special hardware devices for biometric data collection. A system's scope is restricted to the networks or organizations where these devices are available. Thus, they are insufficient for securing organizations that conduct business with a large and varied population. Passive sensors represent the answer as they allow capturing the data unobtrusively and in many cases are inexpensive.

Different behavioral and physiological sensors may be used to collect passive measures from a user for the purpose of continuous authentication. Passive sensors can be hidden and used to collect the data transparently, and as a result they lead to more user acceptability.

Examples of passive behavioral measures for continuous authentication include mouse dynamics, keystroke dynamics, and gait.

Examples of physiological measures that can be collected using passive biosensors for the purpose of continuous authentication include eye position tracking, pupil size, skin conductivity, peripheral temperature (finger, wrist), relative blood flow, and body movement.

While some of the above measures may be categorized as strong biometrics, others may provide weak biometrics information for many people, but can be very discriminative for others. An example of such measure is the relative blood flow; many people may have similar finger-tip blood flow wave forms, while a number of people may have a unique wave form that can be used as a strong discriminator.

Whether an individual sensor is strong or weak, combining several sensors tend to improve the performance of continuous authentication.

Using multiple biosensors make it harder for intruders to circumvent the protection mechanism. Multiple biosensors may be deployed through a multi-sensor or a multimodal scheme or a combination of the above.

A multi-sensor biometric system uses several instances of the same type of sensor, for instance several facial recognition cameras or fingerprint readers. The downside in this case is that the occurrence of environmental problem in one sensor is most likely to affect or spread to the other sensors. In contrast, a multimodal biometric system, which involves different modes of sensing biometric data, would be less affected by the occurrence of an environmental flaw in one of the sensors, as independent sampling is presupposed in this case.

We provide, in the following, an overview of some examples of sensors currently being used in existing CA applications.

Face Biometric

Face biometric system extracts and processes the unique shape, pattern and positioning of facial features. The main challenge underlying face recognition is that over time human face tends to change with, for instance, the appearance of beard or wrinkles, and this may impact the performance considerably. To improve the performance of the recognition system, some form of machine learning may be used to simulate human interpretation of faces and adapt to anticipated or unanticipated changes.

Two main types of face biometric sensing devices may be used, namely video or thermal imaging. Video camera is more common and cheaper but provides less accuracy compared to thermal camera. Video data capture simply consists of using standard video cameras to obtain the complete facial image. From the obtained image, a number of points on the face, such as the position of the eyes, mouth and nostrils, are mapped. Accuracy, however, is impacted when the user fails to look directly into the camera, or when the surrounding light is poor, such as in darkness situation.

Thermal cameras capture facial temperature variations caused by vein structure as the distinctive feature. As the source of the heat pattern is the face itself rather than some external heat source, these sensors can capture images despite adverse environmental conditions (e.g. lighting), and as a result they provide better accuracy compared to video cameras.

An example of continuous authentication application using face biometric consists of using live video feed to ensure strict file access control. The system monitors the user in a secure room by ensuring through the video stream from the camera that the legitimate user's face is on the sight all the time when classified information is manipulated onscreen. If the user turns away or goes away from the screen the secret files are hidden from the screen.

For face biometric to be considered as a passive measure, the data capture camera must be hidden; otherwise although the data capture does not require any action from the user it is difficult to claim that the process is unobtrusive. Using hidden camera can raise serious privacy issue and limit the scope of who can be monitored. This is an important limitation in globally distributed networked environments. Mouse and keystroke dynamics, in addition to be far cheaper, are not affected by the above limitation of face biometrics.

Gait Biometric

Gait is defined as "the coordinated, cyclic combination of movements that result in human locomotion", and Gait biometric biometrics is aimed at recognizing individuals by the way they walk.

According to how data is captured, Gait recognition techniques can be divided into three different categories: video sensor-based, floor sensor-based and wearable sensor-based approaches (Gafurov & Snekkeness, 2009). Video sensor-based approaches represent by far the most common form of gait recognition. In these approaches, data is collected using a video-camera and then processed using image processing techniques.

With floor sensor-based approaches, sensors are deployed on the floor and data is collected when people walk on them. Floor sensor-based approaches allow capturing gait-related information which is impossible to capture using video sensors such as ground reaction force, heel to toe ratio etc.

Wearable sensor-based approaches are relatively more recent compared to the above two categories. Wearable sensors are worn or attached to the body of the individual. For instance, the sensor may be attached to the waist of the person or integrated in his shoe or cell phone. The main advantage of wearable sensors is their close proximity to the users allowing the collection and analysis of gait related data anywhere at any time.

Gait biometric can be appropriate for continuous authentication, because unlike traditional biometrics technologies such as iris and fingerprint scans, it does not require close proximity with the human subject for data capture. Data capture may be conducted unobtrusively without any subject cooperation or contact for data acquisition. Continuous authentication based on gait biometric can be applied in surveillance activities and critical infrastructures protection as it involves keeping track of all the activities carried by an individual accessing these infrastructures, and reporting immediately any discrepancy in the identity as soon as discrepancy arises or is noted.

Keystroke Dynamics Biometric

Keystroke dynamics biometric is a passive behavioral measure which is readily available at standard computing stations, since it can be captured using regular keyboards (Bleha et al.,

1990; Bergadano et al., 2002). Keystroke dynamics recognition consists of measuring the dwell time and the flight time for keyboard actions, and then using the computed information to construct a set of digraphs, tri-graphs or *n*-graphs producing a pattern identifying the user.

Traditionally, during the enrollment process, the user is asked to type a pre-defined word or set of words in order to build a reference profile. During the authentication process, the user is also required to enter the same fixed text which is compared against the stored profile. This recognition scheme is referred to as fixed-text detection. Fixed-text detection is unsuitable for CA because it requires the active cooperation of the user, and this is against the goals of CA. In effect, to achieve user acceptability CA activity monitoring must be conducted transparently and unobtrusively. An alternative to fixed-text detection that is more appropriate for CA is free-text detection. Free-text detection consists of recognizing the user based on text freely entered by the user; the user is not required to type a pre-defined message or text (Guneti & Picardi, 2005; Monrose & Rubin, 1997; Ahmed & Traoré, 2008a; Ahmed & Traoré, 2007b). Accurate detection of free text is very challenging; as a result only a handful of free text analysis models have been proposed to date.

Mouse Dynamics Biometrics

Mouse dynamics biometric consists of extracting unique pattern from user mouse movements (Ahmed & Traoré, 2007a; Pusara & Brodley, 2004). Similar to keystroke dynamics, mouse dynamics does not require a special hardware device for data collection. Furthermore, mouse dynamics are collected and verified passively throughout the session. Consequently, mouse dynamics biometrics may be suitable for CA.

Mouse dynamics biometrics can be used for various activity monitoring applications including computer intrusion detection, network forensics analysis and user re-authentication. The data stream involved in mouse dynamic monitoring correspond to a sequence of mouse actions collected over a computing session for a particular user. The collected data are used to build a profile that is compared against a reference profile that is pre-computed and stored in a database for each known or legitimate user. Unusual behavior is reported if there is deviation between the monitored and reference profiles.

Non-Biometric CA Sensors

Examples of non-biometric sensors used for CA include user command data and RFID sensors. We discuss in the following user command data and refer the interested reader to the literature for more details about RFID sensors.

Several studies have been conducted in the last decade on using user command lines data for masquerade attack detection, which is one of the main focuses of CA systems. The command line data can be extracted, for instance, from audit trails like the UNIX *acct* auditing mechanism. For privacy reasons, typically only truncated command lines are used, which consist of the command name and the user name. Examples of commands used, for instance in the case of the UNIX environment, include *sed, troff, dpost, echo, sh, cat, netstat, sh, eqn,* and *sed*.

The data consists of a sequence of adjacent commands, at the end of which verification takes place by matching the monitored sequence against the user profile using various techniques.

Although a variety of artificial intelligence techniques have been used to analyze command line data, the performance achieved in masquerade detection has been very low compared to what can be obtained with biometrics technologies such as mouse and keystroke dynamics. A study conducted by Schonlau et al. (2001) comparing six masquerade detection techniques on the same dataset including the Bayes 1-Step Markov, Hybrid Multi-Step Markov, Incremental Probabilistic Action Model (IPAM), Uniqueness, Sequence-

Match, and Compression, did underscore this limitation. In the study, the hit rates ranged from 39.4% to 69.3% while the false alarm rates ranged from 1.4% to 6.7%. Using this study as their starting basis, and by conducting some thorough error analysis, Maxion and Townsend (2004) were able to achieve 56% improvement in masquerade detection with a hit rate of 61.5% and a false-alarm rate of 1.3%, when using a new detection technique inspired from Naives Bayes classification algorithm (Maxion & Townsend, 2003). Although encouraging, the obtained performance remains unsatisfactory for the level of accuracy that should be expected for effective continuous authentication. By adapting sequence alignment algorithms used in bioinformatics to discover similarities between two sequences of biological data, Coull and Szymanski (2008) were able to improve the Maxion-Towsend results by obtaining a hit rate of 66.5% with a false-alarm rate of 1.8%. This performance, however, still remains very low compared to what can be obtained with biometrics-based CA sensors.

The main advantage of user command line data is the fact that it is a passive data source which is helpful when addressing the transparency requirement. However, its relatively low accuracy can represent a serious limitation in achieving effective continuous authentication. Possible solution may consist of using user command data as part of a multi-modal CA system, by combining it judiciously with other CA sensors which may compensate for its low accuracy.

APPLICATIONS OF CONTINUOUS AUTHENTICATION

We identify four major types of application for CA, namely intrusion detection, network forensics, insider detection, and session security. Some of these applications overlap, and although several or all of them may be provided by the same system, the challenge is how to address the conflicting demands of each application area. For instance, different trade-offs must be made in terms of acceptable levels of FRR and FAR according to different application area; this complicates the tuning process when a system targets several applications at the same time.

Intrusion Detection

When used for intrusion detection, CA augments existing detection capabilities by providing a user centered perspective. This perspective is missing in existing intrusion detection model, or when it is available like in some anomaly detection models, it is still unsatisfactory (Ahmed & Traoré, 2005a; Ahmed & Traoré, 2005b).

In CA-based intrusion detection, the focus is on intrusive events rather than normal events. Each intrusion must further be investigated by the security officer or analyst. Such investigation can be costly in time and effort. Therefore, when tuning the system for intrusion detection, although one may prefer a highly accurate system which means low FAR, the impact of false positives (i.e. FRR) can be very damaging beyond a certain number. Beyond certain number of false positives, the system starts losing credibility, which means that serious intrusive events may be ignored. So proper balance should be made when tuning the system; for instance, an extremely low value of FRR (0-1%) with a slightly higher value of FAR (5-15%) could be considered acceptable.

Another important decision to be made for CA-based intrusion detection is whether alarms should be reported in real-time as they are generated or can be reported in bulk after certain time period, for instance, at the end of the day. For real-time reporting, a suitable mechanism should be designed to achieve this purpose without overloading or annoying the human operator. This may consist, as alarms occur, of displaying them through a console, sending an email or paging the security officer. The mechanism may be selective by reporting immediately only alarms fitting certain categories or criteria.

Real-time reporting provides the benefit of quick reaction or response, which is important for serious events. However, it is expensive as it requires having a human operator always on call.

Bulk or delayed reporting represents a far less expensive alternative compared to real-time reporting. A simple reporting mechanism that generates an incident after specified period (e.g. daily, weekly) may be used.

The potential for reacting lately is, however, greater for bulk reporting, which could have damaging consequences in some organizations. In organizations where the impact of late reaction cannot be undone, bulk reporting is not an option. For instance, when the intrusion may lead to the theft of sensitive information, it is essential to stop the intruder as quickly as possible. On the other hand, in the case of a fraudulent bank transfer between accounts at the same bank, the transfer operations can be reverted back when reporting is done, for instance, on a daily basis. Note also that in the first scenario, the organization might consider putting more emphasis on lowering FAR at the expense of FRR, for instance, with FAR close to 0% and FRR ranging between 5 and 15%.

Network Forensics

Network forensics consists of investigating the aftermath of a reported intrusion, with the purpose of understanding the attack methods and motives, improving the existing protection schemes, and taking appropriate action against the perpetrators such as legal action when sufficient evidence is available. While ideally intrusion detection must be carried in real- or near real-time in some circumstances, network forensics analysis will always typically be conducted offline.

Like in the intrusion detection field, CA-based network forensics fill a missing link in the general network forensics area by introducing the human element. The human element is an essential aspect of physical forensics, while it has been ignored or insufficiently dealt with in network forensics research mainly because of the challenges involved.

CA enables an important aspect of network forensics analysis, namely, *attack attribution*, which consists of identifying reliably the human perpetrator of a reported incident (Ahmed et al., 2008a). In general, this is easily said than done.

In a CA context, the network forensics process is triggered in case where an intrusion is reported either by the CA intrusion detection module or by an external intrusion detector like a network intrusion detection system. The second scenario means that the CA system has reported corresponding event as normal which may either be a false negative or an insider attack. We discuss this scenario later when covering insider detection application. The first scenario means either a false positive or some real attack has occurred such as masquerading or session hijack. The false positive can be ruled out by checking the whereabouts of the target user during the timeline of the incident. In case of a true positive, the investigation will continue by trying to match the intrusive session data against existing user profiles. Unlike intrusion detection, where user identity verification is based on 1-to-1 matching, network forensics uses 1-to-n matching for attack attribution, which is far more challenging in terms of performance.

The matching will be carried out primarily against the known or legitimate database, in which case a hit will correspond to an inside attack.

We recommend, maintaining a profile database for past offenders, although effective use of such database involves significant and sometimes unresolved challenges. The past offenders database has two main purposes: maintaining historical record of intrusive activities conducted over time by specific offender and keeping track of outsiders or unknown offenders.

In case the legitimate users database returns a match, the record of the insider is updated in the past offender database or a new entry is created if this corresponds to his first offense.

In case where there is no match in the legitimate users' database, the intrusive session data can be matched against the outsiders in the past offender database. If a match is found the corresponding record is updated accordingly; otherwise a new entry will be created for the intruder. Historical information about the intruder helps establishing a better picture of his methods, motives, and objectives.

Insider Detection

Insider detection is a special case of intrusion detection which focuses essentially on internal misuse of the system by authorized users. Authorized users can abuse their privileges, and pretend when caught that the malicious activity was perpetrated by some external intruder. Through continuous authentication, it is possible to establish with reasonable level of certainty whether the authorized user is a victim or a liar. While intrusion detection focuses on intrusive events, the primary targets of insider detection are normal events. From the perspective of the CA detector an inside job will be perceived as a normal activity. Therefore the malicious activity must first be reported through an external medium, entity, or event. This will trigger an investigation by checking the event log. The underlying assumption in case of normal event is that the authorized user is the real originator of the malicious activity. For such claim to withstand scrutiny, the CA system must have an extremely low FAR. Actually, for a CA-based insider detector FAR=0% will be a safe choice regardless of how high the FRR is. Otherwise, the alleged insider can argue that the reported normal event was a false negative.

Session Security

Session security consists of preventing a user session from being hijacked. This may happen, for instance, when a user leaves their machine unattended or when a fraudster inserts herself between the source and destination of a communication after initial (static) authentication has been established. In this case, after reporting an intrusion the CA system follows through by locking the client machine, which is the extreme case or by logging the user out and requiring him to re-authenticate using alternative medium. For instance, if initial authentication took place using a traditional password, the user may be invited to provide a one-time password generated by a token or to answer to some challenge questions etc.

One of the benefits of CA-based session security scheme is that it represents a nice alternative to traditional session security approach which consists of locking systematically the system after a period of inactivity. In this case every time the user moves away from her computer for a relatively short period of time, she will need to re-authenticate using, for instance, a password. This can quickly become cumbersome and affect productivity, especially in work environments where the user needs to move back and forth several times during the day. Continuous authentication removes the need for the legitimate user to re-login explicitly after the initial authentication. In this case, the CA system continuously monitors the user activity, and will require explicit login only in case where an intrusion is reported.

When deploying CA-based session security scheme, the need for securing the session must be weighed against productivity concerns. In this case, high FRR value means that legitimate users may be interrupted unnecessarily multiple times in their work, which will impact productivity. On the other hand high FAR will mean more risk exposure to security breach. In practice, unless there are special security concerns, it makes sense to tune the system by targeting FRR value close to 0%.

CONCLUSION

Summary

We have laid down, in this chapter, the ground for a conceptual framework for CA systems, and discussed several related issues such as data sources and major application areas.

First generation security systems such as access control and password-based authentication systems have emphasized prevention by attempting to keep out unauthorized users from the protected security perimeter. The weaknesses of such models have widely been publicized, and given rise to the second generation of security systems. Second generation systems such as intrusion detection systems (IDS) assume that no matter how strong a security defense is, malicious users will always find some way around. Second generation systems emphasize detection. Third generation security systems emphasize reaction; these include forensics and network trace-back tools.

CA systems can be considered as part of the fourth and new generation of security systems, which provide essential ingredients for both detection (2nd generation) and reaction (3rd generation).

CA systems represent a reinforcement of existing strong authentication, not a replacement. They allow dealing with several threats which may be beyond the scope or coverage of traditional authentication systems which are inherently static. These include masquerade attacks and session hijacking.

When developing a CA system, the quality of the authentication data sources and processing techniques is the most important factor to take into account. Although non-biometric data sources may be used, the best CA authenticators available are biometrics-based. However, not all biometrics data source are adequate for CA. The required infrastructures, transparency of data capture, accuracy are important characteristics that eliminate many traditional biometrics

Challenges and Perspectives

As an emerging technology, CA faces several challenges for which appropriate solutions must be found. We briefly summarize some of these challenges in the following.

Typical CA system implementation is based on distributed architecture, and as such it is subject to traditional security attacks faced by distributed systems, such as eavesdropping, denial of service, tampering and so on. In addition the CA system can be subject to targeted attacks during which the attacker may try to take control of the CA system, modify existing user profiles or insert new ones, evade detection, or foul the authentication function using forgery. Therefore, the CA system must be developed with robust built-in protection mechanisms against these potential threats.

Distributed network environments are characterized by their heterogeneity and complexity of the entities and devices involved. This represents a significant challenge when addressing transparency requirement for CA system. The current solution is to derive for each individual multiple profiles, each to be used under particular circumstance or configuration. Maintaining such diverse profiles increase the complexity of the system and may have adverse effect on the system performance. Therefore, there is a need to investigate or develop new profiling and processing techniques that can minimize or offset the impact on user profiles of the heterogeneity in networked environments.

The proliferation of mobile devices not only increases the inherent heterogeneity of distributed networked environments, but it also brings its own set of security challenges that potentially may complicate the CA process. The CA must be robust enough to handle the variations and security risks inherent to these devices and their underlying networking infrastructures.

CA systems are also characterized by the massive amount of data generated, processed and stored. The storage of the CA data plays an important role in network forensics, which besides intrusion detection is another major application of CA. However, storing a record of every single event generated by a CA will inevitably lead to voluminous audit trails, which not only will be unmanageable but will create severe performance penalty. Therefore, it is necessary to establish standards for CA audit trails design and management. Such standards should specify what types of data need to be stored, in which format, for how long and so on.

In globally networked business environment, the integration of CA in an existing security architecture possibly deploying other security systems with overlapping functions raises challenges such as interdependencies and management that need to be considered. How the CA system fits within an organization's internal control structure and how it is perceived from security compliance and auditing perspectives are still unclear.

The above represent some of the challenges that must be tackled by the research community in order to enable large-scale of this emerging technology.

REFERENCES

Ahmed, A. A. E., & Traoré, I. (2005a). Detecting computer intrusions using behavioral biometrics. *Proceedings of 3rd Ann. Conf. on Privacy, Security, and Trust* (pp. 91-98). St. And. NB, Canada.

Ahmed, A. A. E., & Traoré, I. (2005b). Anomaly intrusion detection based on biometrics. *Proceedings of 6th IEEE Information Assurance Workshop, 15-17 June*. West Point, New York, USA.

Ahmed, A. A. E., & Traoré, I. (2007a). A new biometrics technology based on mouse dynamics. *IEEE Transactions on Dependable and Secure Computing, 4*(3), 165–179. doi:10.1109/TDSC.2007.70207

Ahmed, A. A. E., & Traoré, I. (2007b). Behavioral biometrics for online computer user monitoring. In Yanushkevich, S. (Eds.), *Image pattern recognition: Synthesis and analysis in biometrics* (pp. 141–161). World Scientific Publishing. doi:10.1142/9789812770677_0010

Ahmed, A. A. E., & Traoré, I. (2008a). Employee surveillance based on free text detection of keystroke dynamics. In Gupta, M., & Sharman, R. (Eds.), *Handbook of research on social and organizational liabilities in information security* (pp. 47–63). Hershey, PA: Idea Group Publishing. doi:10.4018/978-1-60566-132-2.ch003

Ahmed, A. A. E., Traoré, I., & Almulhem, A. (2008b). *Digital fingerprinting based on keystroke dynamics*. International Symposium on Human Aspects of Information Security & Assurance (HAISA 2008) (pp. 94-104). Plymouth, UK.

Azzini, A., & Marrara, S. (2008). Impostor users discovery using a multimodal biometric continuous authentication fuzzy system. In Lovrek, I. (Eds.), *KES 2008, Part II, LNAI 5178* (pp. 371–378). Berlin/Heidelberg, Germany: Springer-Verlag.

Bergadano, F., Guneti, D., & Picardi, C. (2002). User authentication through keystroke dynamics. *ACM Transactions on Information and System Security, 5*(4), 367–397. doi:10.1145/581271.581272

Bleha, S., Slivinsky, C., & Hussein, B. (1990). Computer-access security systems using keystroke dynamics. *IEEE Transactions on Pattern Analysis and Machine Intelligence, 12*(12), 1217–1222. doi:10.1109/34.62613

Calderon, T. G., Akhilesh, C., & Cheh, J. (2006). Modeling an intelligent continuous authentication system to protect financial information resources. *International Journal of Accounting Information Systems, 7*(2), 91–109. doi:10.1016/j.accinf.2005.10.003

Coull, S. E., & Szymanski, B. K. (2008). Sequence alignment for masquerade detection. *Computational Statistics & Data Analysis, 52*(8).

de Lima e Silva Filho. S. R., & Roisenberg, M. (2006). Continuous authentication by keystroke dynamics using committee machines. In S. Mehotra, et al. (Eds.), *ISI 2006, LNCS 3975* (pp. 686-687). Berlin/Heidelberg, Germany: Springer-Verlag.

Fawcett, T., & Provost, F. (1999). Activity monitoring: Noticing interesting changes in behavior. *Proceedings of the Fifth International Conference on Knowledge Discovery and Data Mining* (pp. 53-62).

Gafurov, D., & Snekkeness, E. (2009). Gait recognition using wearable motion recording sensors. *Eurasip Journal on Advances in Signal Processing*, vol. 2009, Article ID 415817 (16 pages), Hindawi Publishing Corporation.

Garg, A., Rhalkar, R., Upadhyaya, S., & Kwiat, K. (2006). Profiling users in GUI based systems for masquerade detection. *Proceedings of the 2006 IEEE Workshop on Information Assurance* (pp. 48-54). West Point, NY.

Guneti, D., & Picardi, C. (2005). Keystroke analysis of free text. *ACM Transactions on Information and System Security, 8*(3), 312–347. doi:10.1145/1085126.1085129

Lane, T., & Brodley, C. E. (1999). Temporal sequence learning and data reduction for anomaly detection. *ACM Transactions on Information and System Security, 2*(3), 295–331. doi:10.1145/322510.322526

Liu, J., Yu, F. R., Lung, C.-H., & Tang, H. (2007). *Optimal biometric-based continuous authentication in mobile ad hoc networks*. 3rd IEEE International Conference on Wireless and Mobile Computing, Networking and Communications (WiMob 2007).

Matyas, V. Jr, & Riha, Z. (2003). Toward reliable user authentication through biometrics. *IEEE Security & Privacy Magazine, 1*(3), 45–49. doi:10.1109/MSECP.2003.1203221

Maxion, R. A., & Townsend, T. N. (2004). Masquerade detection augmented with error analysis. *IEEE Transactions on Reliability Analysis, 53*(1), 124–147. doi:10.1109/TR.2004.824828

Monrose, F., & Rubin, A. (1997). Authentication via keystroke dynamics. *Proceedings of the Fourth ACM Conference on Computer and Communications Security*, (pp. 48-56).

Pearsall, J., & Trumble, B. (2001). *The Oxford English reference dictionary*. Oxford University Press.

Pusara, M., & Brodley, C. E. (2004). User re-authentication via mouse movements. *Proceedings ACM*

Schonlau, M., DuMouchel, W., Ju, W.-H., Karr, A. F., Theus, M., & Vardi, Y. (2001). Computer intrusion: Detecting masquerades. *Statistical Science, 16*(1), 58–74. doi:10.1214/ss/998929476

Swets, J. A., & Pickett, R. M. (1992). *Evaluation of diagnostic systems: Methods from signal detection theory*. New York, NY: Academic Press.

VizSec/DMSEC'04. Washington, DC, USA.

ADDITIONAL READING

Al solami, E., Boyd, C., Clark, A., & Khandoker, A. I. (2010). Continuous biometric authentication: can it be more practical?. *12th IEEE International Conference on High Performance Computing and Communications*, (pp. 1-3), Melbourne.

Bours, P., & Barghouthi, H. (2009). Continuous Authentication using Biometric Keystroke Dynamics. *The Norwegian Information Security Conference (NISK)* (12 pages)

Furnell, S. M., Dowland, P. S., & Singh, H. (2001). A preliminary investigation of user authentication using continuous keystroke analysis. *Proceedings of the IFIP 8th Annual Working Conference on Information Security Management & Small Systems Security*.

Ikehara, C. S., & Crosby, M. E. (2010). Physiological Measures Used for Identification of Cognitive States and Continuous Authentication. *ACM CHI 2010*, Atlanta, Georgia, USA. (4 pages)

Kurkovsky, S., & Syta, E. (2010). Approaches and Issues in Location-Aware Continuous Authentication. *13th IEEE International Conference on Computational Science and Engineering* (pp. 279-283)

Liu, J., Yu, F. R., Lung, C., & Tang, H. (2009). Optimal combined intrusion detection and biometric based continuous authentication in high security mobile ad hoc networks. *IEEE Transactions on Wireless Communications, 8*(2), 806–815. doi:10.1109/TWC.2009.071036

Sim, T., Zhang, S., Janakiraman, R., & Kumar, S. (2007). Continuous verification using multimodal biometrics. *IEEE Transactions on Pattern Analysis and Machine Intelligence, 29*(4), 687–700. doi:10.1109/TPAMI.2007.1010

Yap, R. H. C., Sim, T., Kwang, G. X. Y., & Ramnath, R. (2008). Physical Access Protection using Continuous Authentication. *IEEE Conference on Technologies for Homeland Security*, Waltham, MA (pp. 510 – 512).

KEY TERMS AND DEFINITIONS

Biometric-Based Continuous Authentication: The use of biometric data to continuously monitor and identify individuals in a target environment.

Biometrics: Human physiological or behavioral characteristics that can be used recognize an individual and differentiate this individual from others in a reliable and sustained manner.

Continuous Authentication: A system that continuously monitors user behavior and uses this as basis to re-authenticate her periodically throughout a login session.

Session Hijacking: The ability for an attacker to take control illegally of an active session.

Transparency: The ability to capture and process CA data unobtrusively without active involvement or participation of the user.

Chapter 2
Performance Metrics and Models for Continuous Authentication Systems

Ahmed Awad E. Ahmed
University of Victoria, Canada

Issa Traoré
University of Victoria, Canada

ABSTRACT

Continuous Authentication (CA) systems represent a new class of security systems that are increasingly the focus of much attention in the research literature. CA departs from the traditional (static) authentication scheme by repeating several times the authentication process dynamically throughout the entire login session; the main objectives are to detect session hijacking and ensure session security. As the technology gains in maturity and becomes more diverse, it is essential to develop common and meaningful evaluation metrics that can be used to compare and contrast between existing and future schemes. So far, all the CA systems proposed in the literature were by default evaluated using the same accuracy metrics used for static authentication systems. As an alternative, we discuss in this chapter dynamic accuracy metrics that better capture the continuous nature of CA activity. Furthermore, we introduce and study diverse and more complex forms of the Time-To-Authenticate (TTA) metrics corresponding to the authentication delay. We study and illustrate empirically the proposed metrics and models using a combination of real and synthetic data samples.

DOI: 10.4018/978-1-61350-129-0.ch002

INTRODUCTION

User authentication is the process of verifying whether the identity of a user is genuine prior to granting him access to resources or services in a computer system. Traditionally, authentication is performed statically at the point of entry of the system (e.g., login). However, the main issue with this approach is that a successful authentication at the beginning of a session does not provide any remedy against the session being hijacked later by some malicious user.

One of the solutions proposed to address these shortcomings is *continuous authentication (CA)* (de Lima & Roisenberg, 2006; Calderon et al., 2006; Liu et al., 2007; Azzini & Marrara, 2008). CA consists of the process of positively verifying the identity of a user in a repeated manner throughout a computing session. Different technologies can be used to develop a CA system, and examples of these include a face recognition camera on a computer that can detect when a user has changed, the sequence of commands entered by a user in a computing session (Lane & Brodley, 1999), keystroke dynamics (Gunetti & Picardi, 2005; Ahmed and Traoré, 2008), mouse dynamics (Ahmed & Traoré, 2007), and gait (Gafurov & Snekkeness, 2009) etc.

To this date, most of the CA applications proposed in the literature have been evaluated using classical accuracy metrics inspired by signal detection theory (Swets & Pickett, 1992). The existing evaluation framework fails to capture important characteristics of CA systems including the dynamic nature of underlying continuous monitoring activities and the implication of successive alarms being potentially generated in a login session.

A common characteristic of CA applications that the existing evaluation framework fails to capture is the need to generate timely alarms in case of unusual behavior. Here, unusual behavior corresponds to any deviation of a computed profile from an expected one. Not only is the accurate detection of unusual behavior important, but so is the time interval between the triggering of this behavior to its detection. Although the significance of this time interval may vary according to the kind of monitoring application considered, in general the shorter it is the better. For instance, in computer intrusion monitoring, ideally one would expect the monitor to be able to detect intrusive activity before the end of such activity. So the *time-to-recognize* accurately the user must be shorter than the time required by the intruder to succeed in his or her task. In contrast, in network forensics analysis, some flexibility can be allowed regarding the length of the *time-to-recognize*; the primary concern in this case is the gathering of reliable evidence that may be used against perpetrators, possibly after the fact.

Furthermore CA systems may generate multiple alarms that actually are of unequal importance; in general, only the first alarm is significant (Fawcett and Provost, 1999). In principle, after the first alarm appropriate action is taken, such as terminating the fraudulent activity. Subsequent alarms, if any, do not contribute anything new to the state of knowledge.

In this chapter, we introduce a new evaluation framework for CA applications that addresses the above concerns. Specifically, we define new accuracy metrics that capture the dynamic nature of CA systems. We also introduce and analyze various metrics that capture the length of an individual authentication period. The length of a single authentication period can be captured in terms of either the time or the amount of data involved. We identify and study various monitoring scenarios, and for each scenario we provide a formal definition of corresponding length metrics.

The remainder of the chapter is structured around 5 sections as follows. In the second section, we discuss related work on CA evaluation. In the third section, we introduce an abstract CA model and corresponding parameters, and discuss possible performance metrics for CA. In the fourth section, we introduce dynamic accuracy metrics and provide a corresponding formal definition. In the fifth section, we identify different monitoring scenarios and define formally corresponding length metrics. Finally, in the sixth section, we make some concluding remarks.

RELATED WORK

Continuous authentication has been the focus of several proposals in the recent literature (Ikehara & Crosby, 2004; de Lima & Roisenberg, 2006; Calderon et al., 2006; Liu et al., 2007; Sim et al., 2007; Azzini & Marrara, 2008).

Ikehara and Crosby (2004) proposed a continuous identity authentication system (CIAS) that uses multimodal sensors to monitor and protect access to critical computer systems. The proposed system is intended for the protection of critical systems with a limited number of users (e.g., 1 to 3 users). The multimodal sensors consist of a set of passive sensors built into a computer mouse measuring the pressures applied to the mouse during clicking when performing a task of varying difficulty. According to Ikehara and Crosby, a pilot study involving six participants yielded 95% accuracy after two clicks when using discriminant analysis.

Sim *et al.* (2007) proposed a multimodal CA system that combines a digital camera-based facial recognition scheme with a mouse-based fingerprint recognition scheme. The system involves a feedback mechanism into the operating system that automatically locks up the computer by delaying processes or suspending them entirely. The mouse sensor is a modified computer mouse that incorporates an optical fingerprint scanner at the place where the user would position their thumb when using the mouse. The authors also proposed a holistic fusion technique using Hidden Markov Model (HMM) that integrates the face and fingerprint across modalities and time for CA. It was claimed that the proposed fusion scheme captures more suitably the characteristics of CA systems than traditional ones. Azzini and Marrara (2008)

proposed a multimodal biometric CA system that combines face and fingerprint recognitions using a fuzzy controller. After the initial authentication, the user identity is continuously checked on the sole basis of the facial recognition, until the computed score falls below a certain threshold, at which point fingerprint recognition is triggered.

CA MODEL AND METRICS

In this section, we introduce an abstract framework to characterize CA activity monitoring and outline a list of metrics that potentially may be used to assess CA systems.

Model

A CA system receives streams of data items from authentication data sources, processes those data items, and matches the results against stored profiles to make recognition decisions on a regular basis. The received data items consist of an alternation between *activity* and *silence periods*. A *silence period* is a time period when no data item is generated by the data source.

When studying the operation of a CA system, we are frequently concerned about events, which are points in time when specific authentication data items or information is generated either by the environment (e.g. data source) or by the system itself. Thus, we define an event as a pair *(d, t)*, where *t* is an instant in time and *d* is the generated information (e.g. data item, decision). What a data item means varies according to the CA data source. For instance, for the mouse dynamics data source, a data item (or an action or token) corresponds to a mouse movement; for the keyboard dynamics data source, it corresponds to a keystroke; and for the command strings monitoring, it corresponds to a command.

Given an event *e,* let *d(e)* and *t(e)* denote the corresponding information item and timestamp, respectively. We define an *activity period* as a triple $A=(e_1, e_2, C)$, where e_1 and e_2 are two events marking the start and end of the activity period, and C is the number of data items generated in this period, respectively. A *silence period* is a particular kind of activity period $A=(e_1, e_2, C)$, such that $t(e_1)<t(e_2)$ and $C=0$. Let Σ denote the set of all activity periods recorded by the CA system during an entire observation period.

Recognition decisions are made on a regular basis at specific points in time and result in the generation of what we call *decision events*. A *decision event* may correspond either to an *acceptance* (information item $d=yes$) or to a *rejection* (information item $d=no$). A rejection typically will lead to the occurrence of an alarm; so we will simply refer to a rejection event as an alarm. In contrast, acceptance events are passive events, which may simply be recorded or even be ignored.

CA activity monitoring is characterized by a sequence of monitoring intervals, which we refer to as *monitoring periods*. During a monitoring period, received data items are queued and then processed at the end of the period, resulting in a decision event. So each monitoring period is characterized by a unique decision event; for convenience, we will represent a monitoring period by its corresponding decision event.

CA activity monitoring is performed on a *login session* basis; monitoring starts with the user login and ends with the user logout. A regular login session is decomposed by the observer into a sequence of monitoring periods, which are virtual sessions. Formally, we represent a login session as a sequence of monitoring periods $s=\{e_1,...,e_n\}$, where each e_i is a corresponding decision event. Figure 1 illustrates an example of CA activity monitored over a login session. The login session involves 3 activity periods and 4 monitoring periods.

Monitoring periods can be time-based or count-based, according to whether their length is determined by the elapsed *time* or by the action (or token) *count*. Although time-based analysis may be convenient in many respects, the effectiveness of CA systems is often heavily dependent on the number of data items generated; a minimum amount of source data items must be collected for the monitor to be able to build accurate profiles. Moreover, action count may be considered as a convenient metric since it is an indicator of the presence or lack of activity. Arguably, for unusual behavior to happen, some activity must take place. Figure 1 shows an example of time-based monitoring; in this case, monitoring is performed over variable time intervals.

When monitoring user behavior through a CA, we are frequently concerned about intrusive or unusual behavior. In particular we are interested in the start and end of the intrusive behavior. We

Figure 1. CA activity monitored over a login session. Each vertical dashed line with a star on top represents the end of a monitoring period. Activity periods are represented by horizontal thick line segments. The login session involves 3 activity periods and 4 monitoring periods.

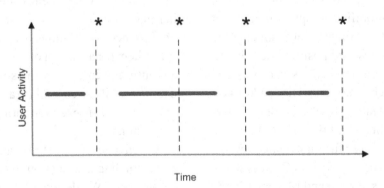

Figure 2. Event streams for continuous authentication

model *intrusive period* as a pair of source events (u_s, u_e), where u_s and u_e express the start and end of the intrusive activity, respectively, and $t(u_s) \leq t(u_e)$.

Figure 2 illustrates the monitoring activity carried out by a hypothetical CA system. The activity being monitored by the system is represented as an event stream consisting of a sequence of source data items x_i and a sequence of alarms a_j; intrusive behavior is represented as a pair (u_s, u_e).

Under the scenario depicted by Figure 2, alarm a_1 corresponds to a *false alarm*, while subsequent alarms occurring after the start of the unusual activity corresponds to true alarms also referred to as *hits*. In principle, later alarms such as a_3 and a_4 have less significance than a_2 which is the first alarm to occur after the start of the unusual behavior. A miss would correspond to a situation where no alarm is generated by the end of the observation period.

Performance Metrics

In order to assess or rank CA systems objectively, we need to identify suitable performance metrics. Based on the above CA model, possible metrics include the following:

- How long it takes to identify or recognize a user.
- How long it takes to establish that a legitimate identity has been hijacked by some malicious user.
- Accuracy of the recognition task in a dynamic context, including false alarm and false acceptance rates.
- Richness of the authentication data.

- Authentication data collection rate or speed.

The measure of how long it takes to recognize a user, which in our case is the *monitoring session length*, can be either a time measure or a measure of the amount of data involved. For the *time-based model* this corresponds to the *time-to-authenticate*, or TTA, while for the *count-based model* it corresponds to the amount of data required for identifying a user, also referred to as an *action count*. Time-based and count-based models are related and can be compared by specifying a richness value for the authentication data, which typically will take into account the rate at which input data is being received or processed. We refer to this latter metric as the *arrival rate*. Similar definitions, used in the literature for the TTA, include the "time-to-alarm", "the mean run-length of normal classifications" (i.e. the mean time between alarms) or as "a measure of the maximum time an impostor can escape detection" (Lane and Brodley, 2003).

ACCURACY METRICS

In this section, we provide formal definitions for the accuracy metrics outlined previously.

Let U denote the universe of users being monitored. We assume that each user is monitored over several login sessions. As indicated earlier, each login session is decomposed into monitoring periods, at the end of which authentication takes place. As also mentioned above, we represent a monitoring session by a corresponding decision event e, and a login session as a set of such events $s = \{e_1, ..., e_n\}$. Given a user $k \in U$, let S_k denote the set of all login sessions generated by k, and let S represent the set of all login sessions recorded during the entire observation period, $S = \bigcup_{k \in U} S_k$.

Under the null hypothesis that monitored behavior is normal, accuracy is traditionally measured using the following two different types of errors:

- **Type I (or α) errors:** the error of falsely rejecting the null hypothesis, also referred to as the false rejection rate (FRR).
- **Type II (or β) errors:** the error of falsely accepting the null hypothesis, also referred to as the false acceptance rate (FAR).

The main difference between static authentication and continuous authentication is that while verification is done only once for the former, the same process is repeated several times throughout the session for the latter. This impacts the way accuracy is computed. For static authentication, accuracy is computed per monitoring period-basis. A reference profile is computed for each user (i.e. *self*), and compared against all his or her remaining monitoring periods (not involved in the computation of the profile) and all the monitoring periods of other users (i.e. *nonself*). In this case, FAR stands for the probability that the CA system will output a matching decision event e while the monitored behavior is from nonself. FRR stands for the probability that the CA system will output a non-matching decision event e while the monitored behavior is from self. So, for static authentication, the FAR and FRR are calculated as the following conditional probabilities:

$$FAR = P(d(e) = yes \mid nonself)$$
$$FRR = P(d(e) = no \mid self)$$

Given users $i, j \in U$, let M_{ij} represent a numerical value of the matching decision between the reference profile of i and a monitoring period of j, such that

$$M_{ij} = \begin{cases} 1 & if\ matching \\ 0 & otherwise \end{cases}$$

FAR and FRR can be expressed more explicitly as follows:

$$FAR = \frac{\sum_{i,j \in U, i \neq j, e \in \bigcup_{s \in S_j} s} M_{ij}(e)}{\sum_{i,j \in U, i \neq j} count(\bigcup_{s \in S_j} s)} = \frac{\sum_{i,j \in U, i \neq j, e \in \bigcup_{s \in S_j} s} M_{ij}(e)}{\sum_{i,j \in U, i \neq j, s \in S_j} count(s)}$$

$$FRR = \frac{\sum_{i \in U, e \in \bigcup_{s \in S_i} s} (1 - M_{ii}(e))}{\sum_{i \in U} count(\bigcup_{s \in S_i} s)} = \frac{\sum_{i \in U, e \in \bigcup_{s \in S_i} s} (1 - M_{ii}(e))}{\sum_{i \in U, s \in S_i} count(s)}$$

A slightly different approach must be used for continuous authentication by computing accuracy per login session basis. As illustrated formally below, this slight difference in approach results in a significant difference in formulation and, as a consequence in accuracy rating. The computation of accuracy for CA systems depends on the selected decision policy. The decision policy can be restrictive or flexible, or somewhere in-between. For instance, a flexible policy may consist of relying only on the first event in deciding whether to flag a monitoring session as normal or intrusive. For instance, if the first event is normal the session will be considered as normal regardless of whether or not a subsequent event is reported as an intrusion. The underlying assumption in this case is that the events occurring in a monitoring session are close enough that if the user was considered initially as normal, there is no opportunity for the session to be hijacked during the rest of the monitoring session. In case where the first event is reported as an intrusion, by flagging the session as an intrusion, it is assumed that the machine will be locked, which means no subsequent event will occur in this particular session.

An example of restrictive policy consists of requiring all events to be normal for the session to be considered as normal. For instance, if the $n(n \geq 1)$ first events are normal while the $(n+1)^{th}$ event is reported as an intrusion, the entire session will be considered as intrusive.

Under such restrictive policy, to compute the dynamic false acceptance rate (DFAR), we compare the login sessions of *nonself* against the reference profile of *self*. The comparison is still done per monitoring period, but unlike in the static case, the match or non-match decision is made only after considering all the monitoring periods involved in the login session being checked. In the static case, such a decision is made independently from the other monitoring periods, whether they belong to the same login session or not.

The comparison of the reference profile of self against the monitoring periods involved in a login session of *nonself* is done incrementally by starting with the first monitoring period and going up. For a login session to be declared as a false acceptance, each incremental comparison must result in an acceptance. At the first rejection, the entire login session will be rejected, which corresponds to a correct rejection. Formally, the DFAR can be calculated as:

$$DFAR = P(\bigwedge_{e \in s, s \in S_{self}} (d(e) = yes) \mid nonself)$$

$$DFAR = \frac{\sum_{i,j \in U, i \neq j} \prod_{e \in s, s \in S_j} M_{ij}(e)}{\sum_{i,j \in U, i \neq j} count(S_j)}$$

Similarly, (under the above restrictive policy) to compute the dynamic false rejection rate (DFRR), we consider the entire login session. We compare the reference profile of self against each of the monitoring periods involved in one of his or her login sessions incrementally, starting by the first monitoring period in the sequence. We expect that each incremental verification result is an acceptance. So, at the first rejection, the entire login session will be flagged as a false rejection. Formally, the DFRR can be computed as:

$$DFRR = P(d(E) = no \mid self) = P(\bigvee_{e \in s, s \in S_{self}} (d(e) = no) \mid self)$$

$$DFRR = \frac{\sum_{i \in U} \min\left(\sum_{e \in s, s \in S_i} (1 - M_{ii}(e)), 1\right)}{\sum_{i \in U} count(S_i)}$$

Figure 3 compares between the static and dynamic accuracy metrics for mouse dynamics data for 5 users from the experiment and using the approach presented by Ahmed and Traoré (2007a). The figure shows the two ROC curves calculated for the same data using the static and dynamic metrics. To calculate the dynamic metrics, we assumed that the length of the login session follows a uniform distribution, ranging from 1 to 10 multiples of the monitoring period's length.

The dynamic ROC (Figure 3) curve follows the same shape as the static one; however, its values are 4 to 5 times higher than the static one. This significant difference indicates that it is harder to achieve lower DFAR and DFRR, and to tune the system for dynamic accuracy under the above restrictive policy.

SESSION LENGTH METRICS

In this section we present a number of mathematical models to compute the session length, which may have different impacts on the recognition process. The models presented can be organized

Figure 3. ROC curves for the mouse dynamics experiment calculated based on the static and dynamic accuracy metrics under restrictive policy

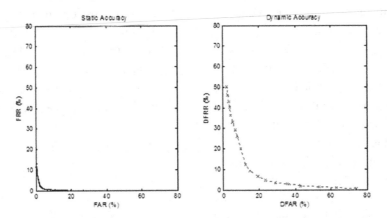

in two categories (time-based models and count-based models), depending on the main factor used to make the decision.

Time-Based Models

We consider four different categories of time-based models, described in the following.

Periodic Detection (Fixed Interval) (TB1)

In this model, the detection process is triggered periodically every fixed time interval τ. At the end of each interval, the data collected during this period will be processed. The detection period τ can be selected to ensure that the data processing module will always deal with recent authentication data. An obvious drawback of this model is that it does not take the amount of the collected data in consideration, making it possible to attempt to perform the recognition using an insufficient amount of data.

Figure 4 illustrates CA activity monitoring, based on periodic detection. The figure shows how the detection process is performed on three different activity periods with different durations. According to the detection criteria of this model, the process is performed on the data available every τ period of time. For the three activity periods shown in Figure 4, six decisions will be taken for the entire period.

Figure 4. CA activity monitoring based on the fixed time interval

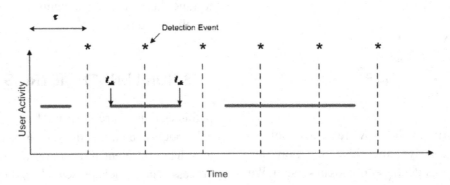

Since detection occurs at $t=n\tau$, in this model the mean time-to-alarm (TTA) can be calculated as:

$$TTA = \frac{\sum_{k \in \Sigma}\left(\left[(n_{ek} - n_{sk})\tau\right] + \left[n_{sk}\tau - t_{sk}\right]\right)}{\sum_{k \in \Sigma}(n_{ek} - n_{sk} + 1)},$$

where

$$n_{sk} = \left\lfloor \frac{t_{sk}}{\tau} \right\rfloor + 1$$

and

$$n_{ek} = \left\lfloor \frac{t_{ek}}{\tau} \right\rfloor + 1$$

This[1] will lead to:

$$TTA = \frac{\sum_{k \in \Sigma}(\tau n_{ek} - t_{sk})}{\sum_{k \in \Sigma}(n_{ek} - n_{sk} + 1)}$$

where Σ is the set of all activity periods, and given $k \in \Sigma$, t_{sk} and t_{ek} are the start and end time of activity period k, respectively, n_{sk} and n_{ek} are the first and last test numbers for activity period k respectively.

Fixed Upon Data Availability (TB2)

In this model the system will process the data only at the end of the monitoring period, which is determined when the silence time reaches a specific limit (τ_s). By silence, we mean a time period where the user generates no action. This model is suitable for systems where the whole session data is needed for making a decision. The decision criterion is simple; however, the model becomes less practical when the average activity period length is high. Figure 5 illustrates the model.

From Figure 5, we notice that the detection process is performed three times for the three activity periods. The TTA for a specific period is the sum of the activity period duration and the maximum silence time (τ_s). Hence the mean time-to-authenticate for this model can be calculated as:

$$TTA = \frac{\sum_{k \in \Sigma}(t_{ek} - t_{sk} + \tau_s)}{count(\Sigma)}$$

Maximum Activity Period Duration (TB3)

In this model, the detection process is performed every time the duration of a contiguous data sequence reaches a specific limit (τ_a).

The model ensures that the decision is done only when enough data is collected, assuming that the data collected in an activity period with τ_a duration is sufficient to make the decision. This

Figure 5. CA activity monitoring based on the silence time limit

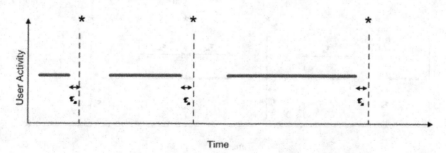

Figure 6. CA activity monitoring based on maximum activity period duration

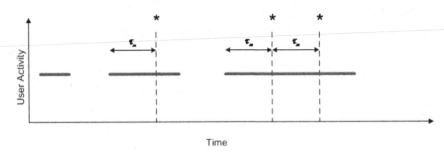

model will not work properly if the number of activity periods with a duration less than τ_a is high since all of the data collected in those sessions will not be used for detection. Figure 6 illustrates the maximum activity period duration model; we notice from the figure that the detection process will be performed once on the second activity period, and twice on the third activity period. The remaining data from the second and third activity periods, as well as the whole of the first period, will not be used.

In this model, the mean time-to-authenticate is always constant $TTA = \tau_a$.

Combined Fixed Upon Data Availability and Maximum Activity Period Duration Models (TB4)

This model combines the two detection criteria used in the two previous models. A detection process will be triggered when the activity period

duration reaches the limit τ_a or when a silence period of τ_s length is detected.

Figure 7 illustrates the combined model; we notice from the figure that six detection processes will be performed, covering all the data of the three activity periods. The mean time-to-authenticate for this model can be calculated as:

$$TTA = \frac{\sum_{k \in \Sigma} \left(t_{ek} - t_{sk} + \tau_w \right)}{\sum_{k \in \Sigma} \left(\left\lfloor \dfrac{t_{ek} - t_{sk}}{\tau_a} \right\rfloor + n \right)}$$

where

$$(\tau_w, n) = \begin{cases} (\tau_s, 1) & if \quad (t_{ek} - t_{sk}) - \tau_a \left\lfloor \dfrac{(t_{ek} - t_{sk})}{\tau_a} \right\rfloor > 0 \\[4mm] (0, 0) & if \quad (t_{ek} - t_{sk}) - \tau_a \left\lfloor \dfrac{(t_{ek} - t_{sk})}{\tau_a} \right\rfloor = 0 \end{cases}$$

Figure 7. CA activity monitoring based on the combination of models TB2 and TB3

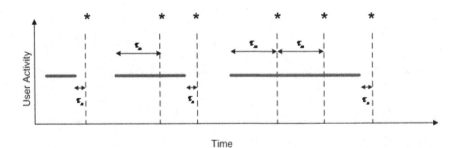

Count-Based Models

We consider three different categories of count-based models outlined in the following.

Fixed Count of Actions (CB1)

The count of actions is the single criterion used in this model. The detection process will be triggered every time the number of collected actions reaches a specific limit $C_{\max}$. This model does not consider any other parameters such as the silence time, making it less effective for systems with large silence periods (between activity periods).

Figure 8 illustrates the Fixed Count of Actions model. The figure shows the relation between the numbers of actions over time. The curve shows only the unprocessed actions; all processed actions will be dropped from the curve at detection time.

Note that for the first activity period, since the count of action is less than $C_{\max}$ the detection process was delayed in order to complete the remaining actions, which happened to be taken from the second activity period. The time needed to do so will also include the silence time between the two activity periods. For this model, the mean time-to-authenticate can be calculated as:

$$TTA = \frac{\sum_{k \in \Sigma} \left(\dfrac{C_k}{R_k} + \tau_w \right)}{\left[\sum_{k \in \Sigma} C_k \big/ C_{\max} \right]}$$

where

$$\tau_w = \begin{cases} \tau_{sk} & if \quad C_k - C_{\max} \left\lfloor C_k / C_{\max} \right\rfloor > 0 \\ 0 & if \quad C_k - C_{\max} \left\lfloor C_k / C_{\max} \right\rfloor = 0 \end{cases}$$

where R_k is the actions' arrival rate in actions per time unit for activity period k, C_k is the count of actions in activity period k, and τ_{sk} is the duration of the silence period following activity period k.

Fixed Count with Wait Time Restriction (CB2)

In addition to the count of actions, this model considers the silence time by setting a limit on the maximum wait time. This model avoids long wait periods by making decisions on the available data when the wait time reaches the limit τ_s.

Figure 9 illustrates such a process; from the figure, we notice that six detection processes will be performed covering all of the data of the three activity periods. Notice that decisions 1, 3, and 6 will be taken based on a low amount of data

Figure 8. CA activity monitoring based on fixed action count. The graph shows how the numbers of actions evolve over time. Detection takes place only when the number of actions reaches the specified limit.

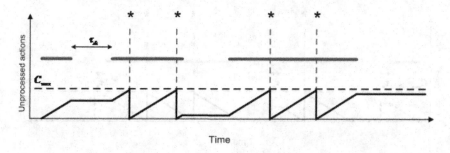

Figure 9. CA activity monitoring based on a fixed action count with restrictions on the wait time

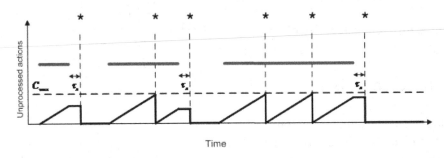

($<C_{max}$). The mean time-to-authenticate for this model can be calculated as:

$$TTA = \frac{\sum_{k \in \Sigma} \left(\frac{C_k}{R_k} + \tau_w \right)}{\sum_{k \in \Sigma} \left(\left\lfloor \frac{C_k}{C_{max}} \right\rfloor + n \right)}$$

where

$$(\tau_w, n) = \begin{cases} (\tau_s, 1) & if \quad C_k - C_{max} \left\lfloor C_k / C_{max} \right\rfloor > 0 \\ (0,0) & if \quad C_k - C_{max} \left\lfloor C_k / C_{max} \right\rfloor = 0 \end{cases}$$

Fixed Count with Wait Time to Drop (CB3)

In this model, the data will be processed only if the count of actions reaches the limit C_{max}. In ad-

dition to this, the model ensures the contingency of the data by not allowing large silence periods ($>\tau_s$) inside the data. The model will drop the data if the count does not reach C_{max} after a silence period of τ_s.

Figure 10 illustrates the model. The figure shows three detection events; note that the model dropped all of the data collected in the first activity period as well as the remaining data by the end of the second and third activity periods. The mean time-to-authenticate for this model can be calculated as:

$$TTA = \frac{\sum_{k \in \Sigma} \left(\left\lfloor \frac{C_k}{C_{max}} \right\rfloor \frac{C_{max}}{R_k} \right)}{\sum_{k \in \Sigma} \left\lfloor \frac{C_k}{C_{max}} \right\rfloor},$$

and as

Figure 10. CA activity monitoring based on fixed action count

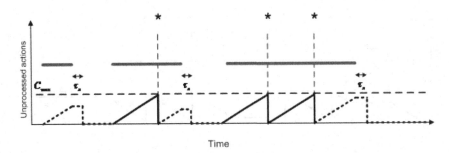

$$TTA = \frac{C_{max}}{R}$$

if the arrival rate is constant ($R_k = R$).

Empirical Study

In this section, we study the performance of the proposed mathematical models and highlight the differences between them, as well as the effect of each model's parameters on its performance. Our study is guided by a number of criteria necessary to describe and evaluate the performance of the models. The criteria were developed based on the general characteristics of specific detection

functionality and process. The following criteria are used for the evaluation:

1. *Mean time-to-authenticate (MTTA)*.
2. *The number of tests performed*: a test is performed on the collected data by the end of each monitoring session.
3. *Average processed data*: expressed in time format as the average of the activity periods for all monitoring sessions. Processed data is the data collected in each monitoring period.
4. *Percentage processed data*: represents the ratio between the sum of the processed active time periods over the sum of the active time for all sessions.

Figure 11. Evaluation metrics computed for the four time-based models. The tuning parameter is the monitoring session duration (x-axis) in minutes. The best value for τ_a can be calculated to satisfy the requirements of the adopted detection algorithm.

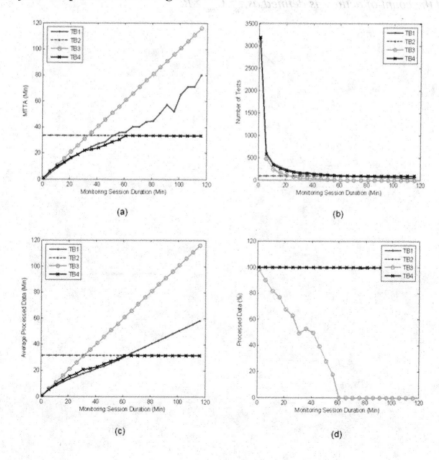

The sessions' start and ending times were prepared for this study in two data sets; the first set represents activity periods' durations and the second set represents the silence periods' durations. Both data sets were generated synthetically based on a uniform distribution with a sample minimum of 1 minute and a sample maximum of 60 minutes, representing the minimum and maximum activity/silence durations. For all of the models involving a silence period restriction (i.e. TB2, TB4, CB2, and CB3), we set τ_s=5 minutes.

Models were studied by computing the criteria mentioned above while varying key model parameters to demonstrate their effect on the calculated metrics. Figure 11 presents the four metrics for the time-based models.

Figure 11-a shows the MTTA for the four models when varying the monitoring session length from 1 to 120 minutes. We note from the figure that the combined model TB4 produces the lowest MTTA compared to the other time-based models.

Figure 11-b shows the number of tests performed for the four models. The curve follows the same shape for all of the models except TB2, which, because of its nature, will always be equal to the number of activity periods. This measurement helps in calculating the anticipated amount of computational load for the selected model. The aim is to lower this value to fit within the proposed system capability. From the curve, TB3 provides

Figure 12. Evaluation metrics computed for the three count-based models. The tuning parameter matches the one used in Figure 12 to allow comparing between all models. The relation between this tuning parameter and the count of actions is defined as $\tau_a = C_{max} \times R$.

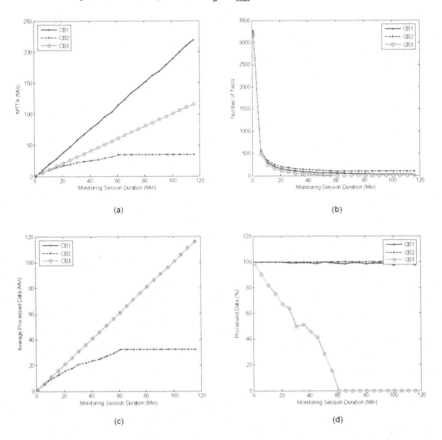

the lowest possible number of tests, while TB1 and TB4 produce similar results.

Figure 11-c shows the average processed data for the four models and this is related to the amount of data processed in each session. The aim is to increase this value as much as possible in order to increase the possibility for the adopted detection algorithm to make correct decisions. From the figure, we notice that TB2 and TB3 follow their corresponding MTTA curves. For the other two models — TB1 and TB4 — the former will produce better results when $\tau_a > 60$ and the latter will be better when $\tau_a < 60$.

Figure 11-d shows the percentage of the data processed in all sessions when selecting a specific monitoring session length τ_a. Notice that all of the models achieve 100% coverage for the data except TB3, which exhibits an increasing loss of the processed data and becomes useless when $\tau_a > 60$.

Similar to Figure 11, Figure 12 shows the four metrics computed for the count-based models. From the figure, we notice that for all values of τ_a the lowest MTTA is achieved by the CB2 model while the highest MTTA is achieved by CB1, and at the same time, CB2 yields the highest computation load requirement.

In terms of the amount of data processed (Figure 12-c), CB1 achieves higher value than CB2 for the price of the MTTA. Both models achieve 100% coverage for the collected data (Figure 12-d).

CB3 falls in between the other two models in terms of MTTA and is considered the best of the three models in terms of computation load requirement. However, using this model with large τ_a values leads to an increasing loss of the collected data according to Figure 12-d, which can contribute to the failure of the detection process.

CONCLUSION

We believe that as their performances improve, CA systems will play an important role in organiza-

tion security protection schemes; commercial CA applications have started coming on the market.

In this regard, we presented in this chapter new accuracy metrics that are more suitable for the evaluation of CA systems and defined and studied a number of session length-based models. We believe that the proposed evaluation framework will help system designers in choosing the proper model that will suit their requirements. It will also be useful in comparing and improving existing CA approaches and assist researchers and industry in developing better systems. Our future work will apply the proposed evaluation scheme to several sample CA systems proposed in the literature. Our goal in this case will be to compare and contrast the proposed systems and identify room for improvement.

REFERENCES

Ahmed, A. A. E., & Traoré, I. (2007). A new biometrics technology based on mouse dynamics. *IEEE Transactions on Dependable and Secure Computing, 4*(3), 165–179. doi:10.1109/TDSC.2007.70207

Ahmed, A. A. E., & Traoré, I. (2008). Employee surveillance based on free text detection of keystroke dynamics. In Gupta, M., & Sharman, R. (Eds.), *Handbook of research on social and organizational liabilities in information security* (pp. 47–63). Hershey, PA: Idea Group Publishing. doi:10.4018/978-1-60566-132-2.ch003

Azzini, A., & Marrara, S. (2008). Impostor users discovery using a multimodal biometric continuous authentication fuzzy system. In Lovrek, I. (Eds.), *KES 2008, Part II, LNAI 5178* (pp. 371–378). Berlin/Heidelberg, Germany: Springer-Verlag.

Calderon, T. G., Akhilesh, C., & Cheh, J. (2006). Modeling an intelligent continuous authentication system to protect financial information resources. *International Journal of Accounting Information Systems*, 7(2), 91–109. doi:10.1016/j.accinf.2005.10.003

de Lima e Silva Filho. S. R., & Roisenberg, M. (2006). Continuous authentication by keystroke dynamics using committee machines. In S. Mehotra, et al. (Eds.), *ISI 2006, LNCS 3975* (pp. 686-687). Berlin/Heidelberg, Germany: Springer-Verlag.

Fawcett, T., & Provost, F. (1999). Activity monitoring: Noticing interesting changes in behavior. *Proceedings of the Fifth International Conference on Knowledge Discovery and Data Mining* (pp. 53-62).

Gafurov, D., & Snekkeness, E. (2009). Gait recognition using wearable motion recording sensors. *Eurasip Journal on Advances in Signal Processing*, vol. 2009, Article ID 415817 (16 pages), Hindawi Publishing Corporation.

Guneti, D., & Picardi, C. (2005). Keystroke analysis of free text. *ACM Transactions on Information and System Security*, 8(3), 312–347. doi:10.1145/1085126.1085129

Lane, T., & Brodley, C. E. (1999). Temporal sequence learning and data reduction for anomaly detection. *ACM Transactions on Information and System Security*, 2(3), 295–331. doi:10.1145/322510.322526

Liu, J., Yu, F. R., Lung, C.-H., & Tang, H. (2007). *Optimal biometric-based continuous authentication in mobile ad hoc networks*. 3rd IEEE International Conference on Wireless and Mobile Computing, Networking and Communications (WiMob 2007).

Sim, T., Zhang, S., Janakiraman, R., & Kumar, S. (2007). Continuous verification using multimodal biometrics. *IEEE Transactions on Pattern Analysis and Machine Intelligence*, 29(4), 687–700. doi:10.1109/TPAMI.2007.1010

Swets, J. A., & Pickett, R. M. (1992). *Evaluation of diagnostic systems: Methods from signal detection theory*. New York, NY: Academic Press.

ADDITIONAL READING

Al solami, E., Boyd, C., Clark, A., & Khandoker, A. I. (2010). Continuous biometric authentication: can it be more practical?. *12th IEEE International Conference on High Performance Computing and Communications*, (pp. 1-3), Melbourne.

Bours, P., & Barghouthi, H. (2009). Continuous Authentication using Biometric Keystroke Dynamics. *The Norwegian Information Security Conference (NISK)* (12 pages)

Furnell, S. M., Dowland, P. S., & Singh, H. (2001). A preliminary investigation of user authentication using continuous keystroke analysis. *Proceedings of the IFIP 8th Annual Working Conference on Information Security Management & Small Systems Security*.

Ikehara, C. S., & Crosby, M. E. (2010). Physiological Measures Used for Identification of Cognitive States and Continuous Authentication. *ACM CHI 2010*, Atlanta, Georgia, USA. (4 pages)

Kurkovsky, S., & Syta, E. (2010). Approaches and Issues in Location-Aware Continuous Authentication. *13th IEEE International Conference on Computational Science and Engineering* (pp. 279-283)

Liu, J., Yu, F. R., Lung, C., & Tang, H. (2009). Optimal combined intrusion detection and biometric based continuous authentication in high security mobile ad hoc networks. *IEEE Transactions on Wireless Communications, 8*(2), 806–815. doi:10.1109/TWC.2009.071036

Yap, R. H. C., Sim, T., Kwang, G. X. Y., & Ramnath, R. (2008). Physical Access Protection using Continuous Authentication. *IEEE Conference on Technologies for Homeland Security*, Waltham, MA (pp. 510 – 512).

KEY TERMS AND DEFINITIONS

Biometric-Based Continuous Authentication: The use of biometric data to continuously monitor and identify individuals in a target environment.

Biometrics: Human physiological or behavioral characteristics that can be used recognize an individual and differentiate this individual from others in a reliable and sustained manner.

Continuous Authentication: A system that continuously monitors user behavior and uses this as basis to re-authenticate her periodically throughout a login session.

Session Hijacking: The ability for an attacker to take control illegally of an active session.

Transparency: The ability to capture and process CA data unobtrusively without active involvement or participation of the user.

ENDNOTE

[1]   Notation $\lfloor x \rfloor$ denote the floor of x.

Chapter 3
Continuous Authentication in Computers

Harini Jagadeesan
Virginia Tech, USA

Michael S. Hsiao
Virginia Tech, USA

ABSTRACT

In the Internet age, identity theft is a major security issue because contemporary authentication systems lack adequate mechanisms to detect and prevent masquerading. This chapter discusses the current authentication systems and identifies their limitations in combating masquerading attacks. Analysis of existing authentication systems reveals the factors to be considered and the steps necessary in building a good continuous authentication system. As an example, we present a continual, non-intrusive, fast and easily deployable user re-authentication system based on behavioral biometrics. It employs a novel heuristic based on keyboard and mouse attributes to decipher the behavioral pattern of each individual user on the system. In the re-authentication process, the current behavior of user is compared with stored "expected" behavior. If user behavior deviates from expected behavior beyond an allowed threshold, system logs the user out of the current session, thereby preventing imposters from misusing the system. Experimental results show that the proposed methodology improves the accuracy of application-based and application independent systems to 96.4% and 82.2% respectively. At the end of this chapter, the reader is expected to understand the dimensions involved in creating a computer based continuous authentication system and is able to frame a robust continual re-authentication system with a high degree of accuracy.

DOI: 10.4018/978-1-61350-129-0.ch003

INTRODUCTION

Security is a key concern in the internet age where an increasing number of transactions are made over an unsecured network and there is a greater chance for sensitive data to be misused. Authentication mechanisms usually form the first line of defense in an electronic system's security. They can be used for both initial authentication (verifying if a user is genuine) and re-authentication (continually verifying if the current user is the same as the logged-in user). Specifically, re-authentication or continuous authentication (CA) technologies are becoming more prevalent due to continued login into systems like laptops, netbooks, mobile devices, etc. For example, if an authenticated user temporarily leaves a system unattended without exiting the application or webpage completely, the session can still be in use. These sessions can be used by intruders to gain access to sensitive information. Also, if traditional authentication mechanisms are broken via stolen passwords, PINs, hardware keys, etc., the computer system currently has no way to distinguish the hacker from the authentic user. This, in turn, would compromise the entire system's security if the authentication mechanisms consist only of traditional authentication methods.

Authentication of a user is generally performed at the beginning of a user session and during subsequent logout-logins. Although sufficient for one-time validation, it is ineffective in preventing masquerade attacks. Unlike user authentication, which attempts to determine if the person trying to enter the system via a controlled setting (e.g., typing of a password) matches the expected behavior, we try to determine if the user's uncontrolled behavior matches the expected behavior. Thus, a user re-authentication system aims to continuously check if the *current-user* is the *logged-in user*. The *logged-in user* refers to the user whose initial login information authenticated the session. The *current user* refers to the person who is presently using the system. In general, we expect that the *current-user* and the *logged-in user* are the same.

However, imposters can intercept the system and become the *current user*. In such scenarios, the *current user* is not the same as *logged-in user* and should be identified. In computer system authentication, this scenario is known as *Masquerading*.

Identity thefts due to masquerading cannot be successfully prevented by traditional methods since the intruder has already broken the authentication system. Two major factors in masquerading effort are:

- **Accessibility to a user's session:** This is possible by stolen passwords, PINs, unsecure session exits, etc. and can be prevented by using a second (and possibly, third) layer of authentication which is accurate and has a high cost of cryptoanalysis. A search for such a layer of authentication points towards mechanisms that involve characteristics which are unique to a user. A user's biometric characteristics and to a certain extent, to her behavioral characteristics satisfy this requirement. For example, biometric characteristics like the iris print, finger print, DNA, etc. are unique and cannot be replicated easily. Similarly, a user's behavioral characteristics are very hard to imitate. Research shows that it is impossible for a person to demonstrate a set of behavioral characteristics that are different from her own. Such an exercise usually results in a mixed set of behavioral characteristics that borrows from both the original set and the new set. If a system is sensitive enough to identify the subtle differences in a user's behavior, it can easily identify the intruder despite masquerade attempts.
- **Time of access:** Gaining access to a user's session when it is in use by a genuine user (if the authentic user is away temporarily – without securely locking the system) is a common example for the time of access factor in masquerading efforts. As a secu-

rity measure against this possibility, it is necessary for the authentication system to ensure that at any point of logged-in time, the current user is the same as the logged in user. This need is satisfied by continuous authentication of the user which ensures that the logged-in user's profile matches the current user's profile. When done periodically, they help mitigate the time of access factor in masquerading.

So the second layer of authentication should include non-intrusive real-time or continuous authentication mechanisms that use physiological and behavioral systems. Physiological systems like fingerprint scanning, iris scanning, etc. are expensive, require special equipment and may be difficult to deploy in all places while behavioral systems are less expensive and are easy to deploy in nearly all places. Since we primarily deal with computers in this chapter, we have to choose behavioral characteristics based on the computer system and their specific attributes for data collection and analysis.

Computers (desktop, laptop, netbook) form a major group under electronic systems. They have specific characteristics (usage of standardized input systems like keyboard, mouse, etc.,) and specific requirements (continuous usage of the system by the user, large amount of processing and simultaneous execution of different applications, ability for the CA technologies to be application-independent, platform-independent, ability to support different hardware and software, etc.). Designing a re-authentication mechanism for computers needs to take into account its special requirements and characteristics. Also, computers are used in large numbers in different types of environments (from schools and homes to enterprises and laboratories). They are also used by millions of people of different ages, creeds, nationalities, etc. In order to create a re-authentication system that can be successfully implemented across such a wide group and in different environments, it is

necessary that the re-authentication mechanism be easily deployable, preferably with little to no extra hardware.

This chapter focuses on design and development of user re-authentication mechanisms for electronic systems, primarily computers. We discuss about the importance of CA in computer systems, characteristics of a good re-authentication system, design steps involved in building a robust and reliable re-authentication system, selection of the right attributes for the system, development of novel heuristics for use in the system, advantages and limitations of different heuristics and future work in this area. Specifically, heuristics that are used in artificial intelligence, system-modeling, etc. and that can be successfully modified for use in CA technologies to obtain a reliable system are explored.

Continuous Authentication: Why Is It Important?

Computers are widely used to access and process both sensitive and non-sensitive data. In most such cases, authentication mechanisms are used to identify and validate the user before she gets access to information. *Authentication* refers to the process of confirming the identity of a user for the purpose of granting access to specific information or to do a particular task. It can be done by a number of methods (the most popular ones are listed below). A detailed discussion of each of the authentication mechanisms is beyond the scope of this chapter and we will focus only on some of them:

- **Traditional authentication (involving passwords, PINs, etc.):** This is the most common authentication mechanism and is very easy to implement. However, this is also the most susceptible to being stolen or lost. This type of authentication is valid only as long as the password, PIN, etc. are known only to the authorized users.

- **Hardware authentication (involving smart cards, dongles, etc.):** This type of authentication depends on the usage of a particular hardware component for validation. However, it also depends on the condition that the hardware component be accessible only to authorized users.
- **Biometric authentication (involving biometric features like iris scanning, fingerprint scanning, etc.):** This type of authentication is most accurate amongst all known methods. It uses the biometric features of genuine users to create a database/set of valid users and matches them against the current user. The access is granted only if a match is present. Biometric attributes are unique to each user and stealing/losing these attributes is very difficult. Due to the high cost of implementation, it is not a viable option for a distributed, low-cost authentication system.
- **Behavioral authentication (involving some behavioral attributes of the user for identification):** This type of authentication uses behavioral attributes to build a database/set of valid users. Since they change over time as the behavior of the user changes, they require periodic data refreshment. The cost of implementation and distributed nature of the system depend on the behavioral attribute set chosen.

As we discussed in the introduction, *Masquerade attacks* can be caused either by illegal usage of one user's account information (password, dongles, etc.) by another user or by illegal access to a user's session when logged-in. In such cases, validation needs to be done during the session and in real-time. This prevents illegal access to sensitive information and hence plugs in security leaks. *Continuous authentication systems* use similar methods as static authentication systems but contain real time feedback loops. They continuously obtain validation information from the user and perform authentication based on it. If the validation fails, the user is logged out and required to be validated again by static validation methods. They are also known as *user re-authentication systems* since they are used to re-authenticate the user at periodic intervals. These intervals range between a few seconds to a few minutes for effective blockage of masquerade attacks.

CHARACTERISTICS OF A GOOD CONTINUOUS AUTHENTICATION SYSTEM

From above discussion, we see that continuous authentication adds an additional but essential layer of security over the static authentication mechanisms. They form a critical part in creating a highly secure system. They should be very reliable, hard-to-replicate, fast, non-intrusive and easily deployable. An ideal approach would be to use existing hardware (keyboard and mouse) for computers. Previous research on this field has shown that the keystrokes and mouse movements, when taken in adequate detail, can sufficiently identify one user from another. Further, they also satisfy other requirements of a good authentication parameter. They cannot be easily replicated by another user (unlike passwords/PINs), cannot be easily "stolen" from the original user (unlike hardware security modules) and cannot be extracted from the user knowingly or unknowingly.

We have already discussed that one possible solution to prevent masquerading is to use a non-intrusive and real time continuous authentication system with behavioral attributes. In order to perform successful re-authentication, the authentication system should have the following characteristics:

- **Continual:** Any user re-authentication system should be able to identify anomalies in user behavior by performing re-authentication periodically. This ensures the prevention of passive attacks on the system that would otherwise render it useless.

- **Non-intrusive:** Intrusive re-authentication mechanisms would interrupt the user repeatedly making the system unviable from the user's standpoint. For example - prompting for password or PIN periodically would be intrusive and result in a negative user experience for the user. The effort, time and cost of using such systems may be too high compared to the security advantages provided by it. So, the system must be non-intrusive and must perform re-authentication while providing a seamless, friendly experience. The data from keyboard and mouse can be collected as the user works with them. There is no necessity for the user to perform specific steps for re-authentication. Also, since this is a continuous process that happens in the background, the user can continue to perform her normal activities without any intrusions from the system. If the system identifies that the current user is not the logged-in user, it would immediately prevent the user from operating the system.

- **Behavioral:** The keyboard and mouse are the most commonly used input devices in a computer. They are continually used in every session and do not require special input devices for analysis. Further, extracting behavioral attributes from normal operations using keyboard and mouse have various inherent advantages such as cost-effectiveness, easy integration with existing system, fast deployment, uniqueness of each user, etc. So, the behavioral attributes from the keyboard and mouse are chosen to distinguish between users in our user re-authentication system.

- **Application-independent:** Every application that requires an input from the user has to use input devices. Keyboard and mouse are the most commonly used input devices

and hence the data generated by the keyboard and mouse is the same independent of applications or other software.

- **Hardware-independent:** Although a large variety of keyboards and mouse are available, the data collected from them are dependent only on the attributes of the keyboard and mouse usage of the user. Research shows that differences in hardware do not affect the re-authentication process substantially.

- **Fast:** The data from keyboard and mouse is already collected by the system for input to different applications. The re-authentication mechanism operates on the collected data thereby reducing the time taken for re-authentication process. It is important that this time be small in order to get a quick response in preventing an intruder masquerading as a genuine user.

BACKGROUND

The earliest work in real-time user authentication was done by Denning in 1985. She suggested the use of behavioral characteristics for distinguishing users in the system. This led to an interest in the usage of behavioral attributes for identification. In the past, keyboard attributes were studied in a number of experiments. Primitive studies using keyboard attributes found that human generated patterns can be used directly to model normal behavior of a user through the user's command line input as shown by Coull et al. (2003), Lane et al.(1999) and Lunt et al(1992), keystrokes and other related parameters as shown by Monrose et al.(1997) and Shavlik et al.(2001). In the last few years, Gaines, Lisowski, Press and Shapiro (1960), Umphress and Williams (1985), Garcia (1986), Leggett, Williams and Umphress (1988), Leggett and Williams (1988) and Young and Hammon (1989) have studied the use of keystroke characteristics in verifying identity of a person among a group of users sharing a common machine.

Keystroke digraph latency refers to the latency between pressing two consequent keys on the keyboard. For example, the time taken to press 'b' followed by 'i' in 'biometric' may be different for different users. Gaines et al. (1960) use such a concept for five specific combinations (viz., in, io, no, on, and ul) to obtain a zero false authentication ratio (FAR) and false rejection ratio (FRR). FAR is defined as incorrectly identifying the imposter as legitimate user and FRR as incorrectly identifying the legitimate user as an imposter. The experiments conducted by Umphress et al. (1985) and Leggett et al (1988) use the user's typing speed and ratio of valid digraph latencies to total latencies in the test string for authentication. These works highlighted the insufficiency in Gaines' proposition of using only five digraph latencies for user authentication and proved that their experiments using all digraphs involving lower-case letters gave better results. Joyce and Gupta (1990) extended Garcia's work by including PIN numbers along with a person's name. Monrose (1997) used modified k-nearest neighbor algorithm for authentication. The experiments by Hussain B (1989), Brown (1993), Obeidat (1997) and Bleha (2002) achieve good results using back propagation method for limited number of users. However, their results show a high FRR for larger databases. All the aforementioned related work in keyboard authentication use *controlled settings* (where the user is given a predetermined task – controlled by the system) to perform authentication. Our work is different in that we use general settings (where the user can perform any task – not controlled by the system) for authentication.

Mouse movements and other attributes were studied by various authors including Goecks et al. (1999), Pusara et al. (2004), Hashia (2004), Gamboa et al (2003),Weiss et a. (2007), Schulz et al(2006) and Ahmed et al (2007). Pusara (2004) creates a system consisting of a training

phase (includes collection of data, extraction of parameters and identification of user to the corresponding parameters) and a verification phase. It recursively checks if the registered parameters match with the collected parameters for the logged in user. This experiment was performed for a single application. Our work is different from Pusara's in that our work aims to design an *application independent* user re-authentication system that uses *both* keyboard and mouse. Our system is not constrained by the application usage and creates a generic model for all applications. Further, usage of both keyboard and mouse results in higher accuracy for the system.

Shavlik (2001) examined cursor movements and mouse dynamics in order to determine whether these attributes would be suitable for user re-authentication. They used supervised learning techniques to identify the current user. The results generated an FRR of 3.06% and FAR of 27.5%. Hashia describes the results of authentication and re-authentication using different sets of parameters. Although their authentication experiment produced good results, their re-authentication study did not prove to be effective. Hugo Gamboa et al(2003) used statistical pattern recognition techniques to develop a sequential classifier that determines user authenticity based on a predefined accuracy level. Weiss et al (2007) used the nearest neighbor algorithm for comparison with the pre-generated profile of every user.

Hocquet et al (2004) perform an exploratory study to analyze user re-authentication by using a game based on fast mouse movements and clicks. Ahmed and Traoré (2007) try to improve on the attributes given by Hocquet and used artificial neural networks to perform active authentication of users. Revett et al (2008) deal with active authentication using mouse attributes. Researchers at Pace University, NY performed a feasibility study by Weiss (2007) to determine if mouse authentication is a viable security method using modified Next Nearest Neighbor algorithm. Our work makes use of these independent heuristics and creates a modified heuristic that can successfully identify a user from the given behavioral data.

STEPS INVOLVED IN DESIGNING A CONTINUOUS AUTHENTICATION SYSTEM

A good CA system contains all the characteristics defined in the above section. Making use of previous research, the steps involved in designing a robust CA system has been formulated below:

1. **Choice of attributes:** This step decides the behavioral attributes to be collected for analysis to create a highly accurate system while reducing the processing time. They form the input variables to the continuous authentication system. They should be easily collectible and should be limited in number to aid easier and faster data collection.

2. **Choice of analysis methods:** This step decides the heuristics and analytical methods to be used in creating a continuous authentication system. The choice of analytical algorithms should be compatible with the attributes chosen. They should be able to get meaningful results from the collected data. They form the back bone of the continuous authentication system and should be fast enough to provide results within the expected time.

3. **Choice of system phases/states:** This step involves a continuous loop of data collection, analysis, results and expected behavior of the system based on the results. Since the continuous authentication system is a real-time system, it needs to complete each of the system phases/states within a short span. Also, the implementation details should be considered at this step – the choice of programming language, threads, functions, entry/exit points, status messages, memory requirements, CPU consumption, etc.

4. **System test and design reiteration:** This step consists of thorough testing of the system to verify functionality, ensure robustness and performance. This step also makes sure that system requirements like memory, expected runtime, etc. are met. Design reiteration adds improvements to the design by trial and error method where the number and mix of attributes are changed and heuristics are modified to improve the accuracy and robustness of the design.

The CA system design is explained with the help of a sample user re-authentication system for computers. This design uses certain behavioral attributes and heuristics and follows a design framework to create a robust system. The testing procedure, result analysis and future work are also explained with this design. Hence forth this design would be referred as *System under design (SUD)*. The SUD was created for a home user environment where it would be used by a small set of users with high accuracy. Also, the SUD was designed to be application independent (i.e.) the user can work on any application and the system would still be able to detect between genuine users and intruders. Comparisons between application based design and application independent design for the SUD are discussed later in the chapter.

Attribute Selection

Attributes refer to the behavioral characteristics chosen for analysis. They are observed and measured in a quantifiable manner. Since the SUD is designed specifically for computers and uses keyboard and mouse input devices, the attributes chosen for data collection should be compatible with the input devices. Keyboard and mouse attributes of the user can be differentiated into two major categories: base and derived. Attributes that can be directly measured from the keyboard or mouse are called base attributes. They include the keystroke time lengths, mouse movements, angles and slopes, etc. Attributes that require some computation by the re-authentication mechanism are called complex or derived attributes. They are usually generated from different combinations of simple attributes. Selection of specific simple and derived attributes is a major step in the design of re-authentication systems. It is important to choose the right set of attributes for a high success rate.

Base attributes refer to those attributes that are directly extracted from the raw data. For the SUD, we have chosen 62 base attributes (10 mouse attributes and 52 keyboard attributes). The mouse attributes include the general speed and acceleration of the mouse in all directions and the direction-based mouse speed. The former broadly classifies the users based on mouse movements while the latter couples the direction information with the speed to narrow down the choices. The keyboard attributes include the speed and speed/time values along with keystroke digraph latencies for fifty most frequently used alphabetical digraph combinations in English. These digraph combinations were determined through a preliminary study where ten articles in different topics were chosen from popular editorials and magazines and analysis done for the frequency of occurrence. For example, digraph latencies of keystrokes are generated from letter combinations of keystroke latencies. Their weightage varies by the usage of letter combinations. The letter combination 'at' is more common (and hence carries more weight) compared to 'ux'. Among the 728 combinations possible (26 letters and space – the 'space space' combination is not considered – 27*27 – 1 = 728), during the preliminary study, we also saw that the impact of the keystroke digraph latencies reduced dramatically beyond the top 50 pairs. Hence, the 50 most frequent pairs are chosen for analysis. It should be noted that as the attribute set size is increased, the analysis time and storage requirements also increase exponentially. A balance between these factors is aimed for. These attributes were chosen from a large pool

of attributes after exhibiting promising results in preliminary studies.

Derived attributes refer to those attributes that require some computation on the base attributes. For example, the ratio between mouse and keyboard operations is used in the SUD as one of the derived attributes. *Mouse-to-keyboard interaction ratio* refers to the total number of mouse events to the total number of keyboard events in an observation period. The system is designed to produce one event for every action in the mouse or keyboard. The mouse-to-keyboard interaction ratio is also computed from the raw data collected. For instance, a computer game based solely on mouse movements has a high mouse-to-keyboard ratio whereas a text editor has a very low mouse-to-keyboard ratio. *Interaction Quotient (IQ)* refers to the percentage of interaction using the mouse and/or keyboard to the total interaction possible in a period of time. A high IQ implies more interaction between the user and the system whereas a low IQ refers to sparse and sporadic interactions with the system. This is generally dependent on the application used and task performed. The interaction quotient is very high for a game (requires the users to continuously move the mouse or enter input into the keyboard) while it is very low for a news reader site (the user does not do any interaction other than move the mouse very sporadically over long periods of time). The interaction quotient (IQ) of the collected raw data is computed in tandem with other data. A mouse game that is fast paced has a high IQ and high mouse-to-keyboard ratio while a slow mouse game has a low IQ and a high mouse-to-keyboard ratio. Some example applications with varying IQ and mouse-to-keyboard ratios are specified in Table 1. However, the exact values of the IQ and the mouse-to-keyboard ratio are dependent on the keyboard and mouse behavior of a particular user. Preliminary studies show that the user behavior can cause marked deviations from the normal behavior based on the mouse-to-keyboard interaction ratio and the IQ of the application.

Table 1. IQ\mouse-to-keyboard interaction ratio example table

IQ\Mouse-to-Keyboard Ratio	Low	High
Low	News Website	Minesweeper
High	Text Editor	Combat Games

Although the base keyboard and mouse attributes are small in number, they can be used to create a large number of derived attributes. Some preliminary analysis into the selection of derived attributes and the right mix of base and derived attributes is necessary while building a continuous authentication system. Also, if the system being designed is application dependent, the attributes can be chosen accordingly. For example, if the application predominantly uses mouse movements, then more weightage should be given to mouse based derived attributes in the mix. Else, if the application is keyboard-intensive, more keyboard based derived attributes should be used. Care should be taken to ensure that the derived attributes added to the design actually improve the accuracy of the system. While designing the SUD, we found that certain attributes, when added to the attribute mix, did not show marked improvements in the accuracy of the system. These attributes were later removed from the attribute mix to keep the attribute set size small to facilitate easy data analysis and lesser memory usage.

Heuristics Selection

Heuristics selection depends on the number of attributes in the system and the type of attributes. Further, the selected heuristics should return results within the expected time. For a continuous authentication system, the data collection, analysis and result feedback happen in a real time loop. Since an intruder who knows the outlay of the computer system can cause a lot of damage within a small amount of time, it is essential that the authentication system identify the intruder as soon as possible. So each iteration of the feedback loop has to be completed within a very short span of time. This is not possible if the algorithms take a long time to arrive at the final result since the following iteration is dependent up on the results of the present iteration. This fact should be kept in mind when the heuristics for the continuous authentication system are designed.

The re-authentication mechanism chosen can employ different methods like statistical analysis, neural networks and other artificial intelligence algorithms. The system can also use a combination of algorithms to improve the overall accuracy of the system. The major requirement of such algorithms is that they be able to extract the information hidden in the given attributes and use that information to generate a unique profile for the genuine user. Although the uniqueness depends on the data set size, training time (time taken to build the profile) and the differences in the profiles used for training, the algorithm chosen should be able to give quick results with minimal training and data set size. It should successfully capture the behavioral patterns of the genuine user and use it to validate the current user's behavioral patterns.

When two or more algorithms are used for analysis, it is recommended to choose them to concentrate on extracting different information from the attribute set and easily discern the user from a larger set to improve the overall accuracy of the system. The design should also provide for the scenario where the two algorithms produce different results. For example, if algorithm A returns that the user is an intruder while algorithm B returns that the user is genuine, the design can either go with algorithm A or algorithm B or choose to repeat the exercise with another set of inputs from the user to finalize if the user is an intruder or a genuine user. This decision depends on the security requirement of the system. For a system with very high security requirements, the design can choose to denote the user to be an intruder if any of the algorithms return that result.

For systems with lower security requirements, it would be beneficial to repeat the observation with a different set of inputs from the same user and use that information to decide the final result.

For the SUD, we proposed an analysis engine that employs three heuristics based on statistic measures, neural networks and k-nearest neighbor algorithms. These heuristics were chosen based on their ability to extract different information from the user data. For example, the neural network heuristic can extract patterns in user behavior despite variances in the speed, acceleration and other attributes. The result from each of the heuristics is taken into account when the final decision is taken. The operation of these heuristics is independent of each other and the results of each heuristic with suitable weights are used for final result computation. Explaining all possible heuristics that can be used in designing a continuous authentication system is out of scope of this chapter. A short explanation of each of the heuristics used in SUD and their contribution to improving the system's overall accuracy is given below.

Statistical Analysis

Statistical Analysis involves the usage of average differences and Pearson product-moment correlation as shown by Vijaya kumar et al(2005). Correlation of two random variables is defined as the measure of similarity and possibility of prediction between the numbers. Simply, two random variables are correlated if knowing something about one variable gives some attribute of the other variable. The random variables can have positive or negative correlation. The main aim of correlation in this system is to capture the level of similarity of the test data with the trained data. Pearson's product-moment correlation coefficient is used in this analysis due to its applicability to the problem. It measures how widely spread the values in a data set is compared to the training data where p is the Pearson's product-moment correlation coefficient and no_attributes represents the number of attributes used in analysis. (Box 1)

One of the main reasons to choose this heuristic is that the percentage of similarity of the input sample with the user profiles in the database can be significant. This provides a simple yet effective way to identify the user without intensive computation. Average differences between the sample input and collected data are computed and the cumulative weight is calculated. Weights are assigned for the attributes based on their ability to differentiate between users. For example, typing speed has a higher weight compared to the digraph latency of one combination. Also, general mouse speed has a higher weight compared to the mouse speed in a particular direction. This heuristic identifies the user that has the highest cumulative weight and maximum correlation.

However, this method has certain limitations. Suppose there exists a user who moves the mouse at a slower speed on average. But, when she plays a

Box 1.

```
Obtain the input values for all the attributes
Do
        For every user u in the database
                P = Pearson_Correlation(u,p,no_attributes);
        End
        P    = Min(P);
         user
Until end of training session
Network ready for testing
```

game, she might move the mouse faster and hence not correspond to her usual behavior. In such a case, statistical analysis would match her better with a user who generally moves the mouse fast and hence identify the user incorrectly.

Feed Forward Network with Back Propagation Algorithm

This heuristic uses a feed forward neural network with back propagation method as shown by Kung et al (2004). Artificial neural networks refer to the set of algorithms modeled based on biological neural networks and uses similar strategies to achieve the results. The algorithm creates a set of neurons that are interconnected to each other and produce results based on these interconnections. The advantage of this system is that they can easily adapt to the changes in the input and output and vary their weights to produce good results. Given sufficient data, they can easily model any non-linear system. They are also very good at pattern recognition.

In Figure 1, the feed forward network is shown. The inputs are fed into the neurons in the input layer (I_j). Their weights are labeled W_{ij} and are initially assigned random values. Their activation values are denoted by A_{ij}. They specify the probability of activation of the corresponding neuron. The output of the input neuron layer is fed to the neurons in hidden layer (H_j). Their weights are labeled W_{hj} and are initially assigned random values as well. Their activation values are denoted by A_{hj}. The results from the hidden layer neurons act as inputs to the neuron in output layer. Since we need only one output from the system (if it is the user (denoted by a 1) or not (denoted by a 0)), only one output neuron is shown in the figure. The weights of the output neuron are denoted by W_{oj}.

The back propagation algorithm refers to the propagation of the calculated error from the back of the system (i.e., from the output layer) to the front of the system (i.e., from the input layer). Suppose the calculated output is O_1 while the expected output is O_{C1}. So, the error difference is $e_1 = O_{C1} - O_1$. This difference is fed back to the

Figure 1. A simple feed forward network

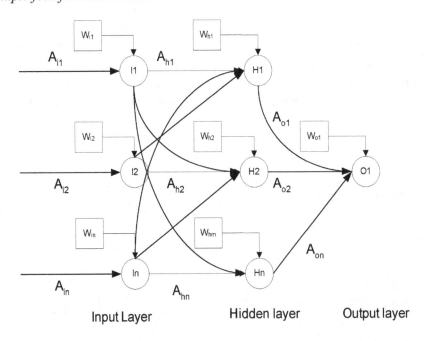

hidden layer where the weights are varied. This change in weight from W_{hj} to W_{hj1} is given by:

$$dw_{hij} = r * a_i * e_f$$

where r is the learning rate and a_i represents the activation of W_{hj}.

Since the system tries to find patterns based on the trained data, it follows supervised learning i.e. the system starts with a random set of weights for its neurons, obtains the inputs and calculates the outputs based on the weights and the inputs. The calculated output is compared with the expected output and the error is fed back to the network using back propagation algorithm. As a result, the weights of the neurons are suitably modified to make the calculated output to more closely match the expected output. This procedure is repeated for the given data set and is known as network training phase. At the end of the training phase, the system consists of optimized weights for the neurons that can more closely predict the actual function's outputs. The accuracy of the system depends on various factors such as stopping criterion, number and accuracy of samples, number of neurons in each layer, etc. The algorithm of a simple feed forward neural network with back propagation is given in Box 2. Where

$\Delta_H \rightarrow$ *the difference in sample output and calculated output is fed to the nodes in the hidden layer*

$\Delta_I \rightarrow$ *the difference in the hidden layer results are fed to the nodes in the input layer*

One of the reasons to use neural networks as a heuristic is to obtain the complex system denoted by behavioral attributes as inputs and the user as output. The neural network starts with random weights. The initialization data are given to the neural network and trained for a particular user. As the training data is given, neural network is continuously re-calibrated to predict the user correctly. When test data is fed to the system, it is given to all user networks and the closest match is chosen from them.

Our algorithm creates a neural network for every user. For IQ with only mouse movements, the neural network disables keyboard inputs and trains only with mouse attributes. Conversely, mouse attributes are disabled for only-keyboard input sessions as well. This ensures that the system can better train for given inputs. As a result, even when the user acts out of his normal behavior (for example, moving the mouse fast when playing a game), the neural network identifies the underlying similarities and matches the user to corresponding user profile. This is very useful in identifying users in corner cases. A Mersenne Twister has been used to generate the random numbers needed for initial weights for the neural network.

Box 2.

```
Initialize the network with neurons, neuron connections and random weights
Do
      For every sample t in training set
          Z = Network(t); feed forward network.
          Zt = Sample output from the data
          Find (Zt - Z), ΔH and ΔIUsing ΔH and ΔI, modify the weights of each
node in the network.
Until system classifies correctly or above stopping threshold
Network ready for testing
```

k-Nearest Neighbor(k-NN) Algorithm

The k-nearest neighbor algorithm identifies a sample to belong to a group among a collection of groups based on its proximity in a vector space to the members of the group. It is a typical example of instance-based learning or lazy learning where all samples are obtained and computation is done in the end unlike neural networks where calculation is done after each sample is fed to the network in the training phase. In training phase, samples are obtained and their classification is stored. In testing phase, the test sample's distance from all training samples are found and k-training samples closest to it are chosen. Their classification is studied and the test sample is assigned the class of majority of k-neighbors. As the number of k increases, the accuracy and complexity of the system increases. Usually k is small; it is chosen such that it is odd and not a divisor of total number of samples. (Box 3)

Consider a simple example of five vectors of set 1(denoted by filled circles) and five vectors of set 2(denoted by empty circles) in Figure 2. Here, we see that the point A is closest to set 1(filled circle cluster) and is hence classified as such. Point B is closest to set 2 (empty circle cluster) and is classified as such. However, point C has three points from set 1 and two points from set 2. Since number of filled points close to C is greater than number of empty points close to C, C is classified as set 1 as shown in Figure 3.

It treats the attribute set as dimensions and the sample set as set of points satisfying certain relationships such as rotation, translation, etc. In SUD, k-NN uses Euclidean distance, Chebyshev distance and Manhattan distance for analysis. Based on the most frequently occurring user in all the three distance calculations, the result is given. The user identified the maximum number of times in this set is chosen to be the result. A user's behavior averaged over a large period of time remains consistent. So, when we map the vectors on an n-dimensional space, we see that these points cluster together for each user.

Statistical analysis and k-NN algorithm cover the normal behavior of a user input while neural network covers excited/abnormal behavior of the user. All three heuristics are important in reaching a good accuracy. A pseudo code of the algorithm used is given in Box 4.

Box 3.

```
Obtain the input values for all the attributes
Do
        For every user u in the database
                D_euclidean = Euclidean_distance(u,p) where p is the test sample; .
        D_chebyshev = Chebyshev_distance(u,p)
        D_manhattan = Manhattan_distance(u,p);
        End
        E_user = k-Min(D_euclidean);
        C_user = k-Min(D_chebyshev);
        M_user = k-Min(D_manhattan) ; where k = Min(3,no_of_users);
        User = Max(E_user,C_user,M_user);
        return(User) ;
Until end of training session
Network ready for testing
```

Figure 2. Example showing k-NN algorithm usage

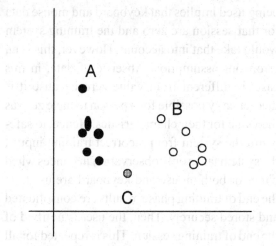

Figure 3. Example with sample C sorted using k-NN algorithm

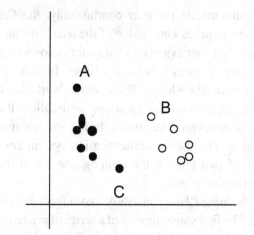

Box 4.

```
Initialize system
Do
        Add user u to database
           /*Training session begin*/
Do
              Get user data/session
              Train_system();
         Until profile==training_threshold
  /*Training session end*/
Until all users are added
/*Testing begins*/
Login user u
Do
Get user data/session
Test_system();
if correct_identification
        continue;
else
        flag++;
While flag<=threshold
if flag>threshold
        report security_breach
else
     continue_testing
end
```

System Phase Selection

To authenticate the user continuously, the CA system requires knowledge of the user's normal "expected" behavior (i.e.) the system knows how the user operates in normal settings. In order to gain such knowledge, the system should have a training session for each user and collect the user's behavioral attributes during the training session. The user re-authentication system consists of two phases: the training phase and the verification phase.

Training Phase consists of two stages of training. The first stage consists of a series of predetermined tasks which the user is required to perform. These tasks involve the usage of either or both the keyboard and mouse at both high and low levels of interaction with the system to get a cross-section of the user's behavior across various scenarios. Suitable behavioral attributes are extracted from the collected raw data for a period of 10 observation sessions. The system tries to correctly identify the user based on observed data and results are validated by the user's responses. Based on user inputs, the behavioral attribute profile of each user is modified suitably. This process is repeated for every user in the system. This results in a database of user profiles that detail the behavioral attributes of the users. The observation sessions can range from a minute to an hour or longer per session. The longer the session, more data is collected and a better-defined user profile is gotten. However, it must be noted that increasing the observation session time period would also increase the total training time per user. A period of two minutes has been used as the observation time period in our experiments. This phase is completed during user account setup in a computer. Once the user profile is created, system uses that profile to verify the user's genuineness during login sessions.

During the training session, the system takes only the instances (i.e. observation periods) when either or both the mouse and keyboard were used in order to maintain consistency. Using the data from the keyboard and mouse when they are not being used implies that keyboard and mouse data for that session are zero and the training system would take that into account. However, this is an erroneous assumption. Absence of data, in this case, is different from value zero because it is theoretically possible for a person to have zero as the value for their characteristics. Hence, to safeguard the system from incorrect training inputs, the system takes only observation instances when either or both mouse and keyboard are used. At the end of training phase, results are consolidated and stored securely. Then, the user is notified of the end of training session. This is repeated for all users of the system and their respective profiles are stored in the system. This marks the end of training phase of the system.

Once the training phase is completed for all users, the system enters the *Verification Phase*. In verification phase, the user logs in to system via a normal initial authentication. Then, she proceeds to perform different tasks on various applications. The system is application-independent and can collect information across applications. This ensures that user re-authentication is not limited to particular applications and the user is not constrained to use a particular application throughout usage session. For every observation session, the system collects both keyboard and mouse usage data from the user's actions.

The system consists of seven processes and five stages linked to one another as shown in Figure 4. The Recorder process records keyboard and mouse inputs of the user. This value is stored in Tester.txt and is passed to other processes. Profile collector and profile analyser processes create the profiles of each user. The profile system and profiler processes repeat this procedure for all users and the resultant profiles are given to the full system process. The software then performs re-authentication using Tester and Recorder processes. This is a continuous operation and is done until the software is exited.

Figure 4. High level diagram of processes and their interactions in analysis engine

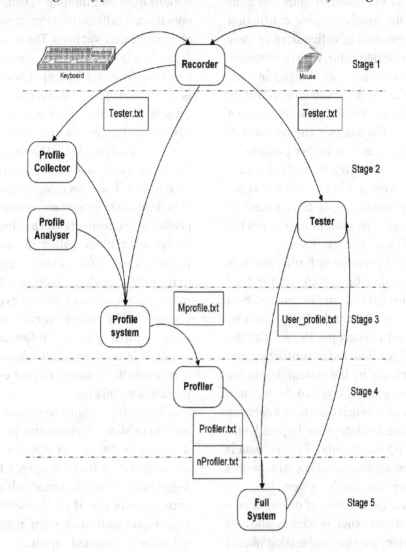

Stage 1: This stage consists of a key logger and mouse event logger in a Recorder and its life is controlled by the processes in stage 2. It consists of two threads, a Worker thread that collects data without interruptions and a Master thread that extracts useful information from the collected data. The output of Recorder process is stored in the tester.txt file.

Stage 2: This stage controls the Recorder and performs basic analysis of collected data. Here, all analysis functions are separate so as to enable cleaner integration with other analysis methods of future work. These processes are used throughout the observation period and are activated based on the period of observation and number of intervals per user.

Stage 3: This stage combines the processes of stage 2 into one system and creates a tangible output for each observation of the user. It creates Mprofile.txt for every observation period. The inner analysis engine applies the data collected in stage 2 to the heuristics and gets the results from each of them. The results are compared with each other. If all three heuristics return the same user, that user is sent as the result to outer environment system. If the heuristics give conflicting results (possible because of differences in their approach to the collected data), then their results are compared with the currently logged-in user. Even if one of the heuristics' result is the currently logged-in user, the analysis engine returns that heuristic's result as the analysis engine's result. Such an approach leads to a higher probability of false-positives (identifying wrongly that *current user* is same as *logged-in user* when it is not so) and very low probability of false-negatives (identifying wrongly that *current user* is not the same as *logged-in user* when it is so).

Stage 4: This stage performs further analysis on the data collected so far and creates the final profile for every user. It activates the processes in stage 3 once per user. The results from Mprofile.txt are analyzed and a master profile list of all the users is created. This is stored in profiler.txt and is used for comparison by the system during the testing phase. This process is called by the main process for every user so that each user's data can be obtained, analyzed and stored in the profiler.txt with application IQ information. Further, data is modified to suit the application of neural networks and k-Nearest neighbor for the system.

Stage 5: This stage consists of the main program that controls all other processes and ties up the initialization, training and testing phases together. It calls the process in stage 4 to perform

initialization and training. Then, during normal operation, it calls the tester process periodically to observe the user's actions. The results are analyzed using data from profiler.txt, nprofiler.txt and uprofile.txt. Based on the output, user authentication is performed. This is conducted periodically for continual re-authentication of the user without adversely affecting the user's operations.

In our framework, SUD consists of two blocks that interact with each other to correctly identify the current user. The outer *environment block* collects data from the keyboard and mouse event loggers, performs pre-analysis calculations and sends it to the inner block called the *analysis engine*. Keyboard and mouse event loggers are hooked to respective device drivers and securely record mouse and keyboard events in every observation session. At the end of observation session, data is overwritten with new information. Raw data is stored in encrypted form during analysis and is deleted after usage to protect user privacy and prevent data misuse.

The analysis engine runs recorded data across three heuristics with the stored profile and returns the most probable user match in database. The environment system compares the result with *logged-in user* and determines if user behavior is anomalous or not. If so, the behavior is flagged. Else, re-authentication starts again. If anomalous behavior is detected repeatedly and crosses an allowed threshold, then the user is asked to pass

Figure 5. Block diagram of process interaction in user re-authentication system

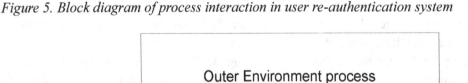
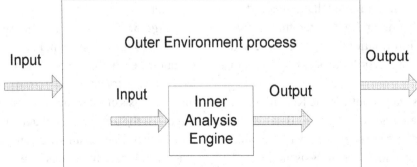

through authentication methods again. If authenticated in the next attempt, the system allows the user to resume normal operation and continues re-authentication procedures.

System Testing and Verification

Software testing and verification procedures form an integral part in a system development cycle. This stage ensures that system functionality at all levels (function, code block, classes, objects, threads, processes and system) is as expected. Since the CA system works in tandem with traditional authentication mechanism and runs in parallel with other applications in the computer system, integration testing should be done to ensure that the system works as expected in these scenarios. Also, stress tests and performance tests are conducted to ensure system robustness and performance. This step also makes sure that system requirements like memory, expected runtime, etc. are met. For a detailed discussion about system testing and verification concepts, please refer to additional resources given at end of chapter.

The SUD is implemented in C# and contains both threads and processes with GUI and console components. Further, the results between processes are stored in files. Hence efficient and correct file management is critical. All these aspects make testing and verification complex. The testing phase consists of exhaustive testing of the system using various coverage metrics like functional coverage, statement coverage, path coverage, etc. Among these metrics, we see that statement coverage and path coverage cover all other coverage metrics. Hence they are used as metrics for testing quality. Theoretically, both statement and path coverage should be 100% for a given code. The statement coverage is 100% and path coverage is 99.994%. The path coverage rose to 71.523% and to 99.994% by black box testing and then white box testing. A detailed discussion of the coverage types and procedures

to improve coverage metrics is beyond the scope of this chapter.

Software verification of SUD constituted using a specification system called Spec# from Microsoft research for the C# code. It consists of Spec# programming language, Spec# compiler and the Spec# static program verifier (described in detail by Barnett et al (2005)). Spec# is an extension of C#. It extends the type system to include non-null types and checked exceptions. It provides method contracts in the form of pre- and post-conditions as well as object invariants. Preconditions refer to conditions that must be true for a function to execute. Post conditions refer to conditions that must be true when control quits the function. Assertions refer to conditions that are true at a particular point in the function. Invariants refer to conditions that are true at any point of execution in the function. A simple example of C# code and its corresponding Spec# code with keywords of properties are given in Box 5.

The code in Box 5 consists of four properties that need to be verified statically. The keywords and properties are listed below:

- 'requires x !=null' – here, the variable x is verified for non-null condition.
- 'ensures' – this keyword denotes a post-condition (i.e.) a condition that has to hold after control quits the function.
- 'invariant' – this keyword denotes that the specified condition must hold true for every run of the loop – in this example, there are two 'invariant' properties that need to be verified.

The code to be verified is written in Spec# programming language with requisite non-null conditions, assertions, pre and post conditions, invariants and assumptions. This is fed to Spec# compiler that performs both static and dynamic checks and converts the code to bytecode. This is then given to the translator which converts it to a form with BoogiePL language and feeds it to the

Box 5.

```
C# code:
void activate(Neuron n)
{
     for (int j = 0; j < 62; j++)
     {
        n.Excitement += n.Preons[j].Pre.Output * n.Preons[j].Weight;
     }
     n.Output = 1 / (1 + ((-lambda * (n.Excitement + n.Bias))));
}
Spec# code:
void activate(Neuron n)
        requires n!=null;
        ensures n.Output!=0;
        {
        assume n.Preons!=null;

           for (int j = 0; j < 62; j++)
           invariant j>=0;
           invariant j<=62;
           {
               n.Excitement += n.Preons[j].Pre.Output * n.Preons[j].Weight;
           }
           n.Output = 1 / (1 + ((-lambda * (n.Excitement + n.Bias))));
        }
```

Boogie engine. It creates verification constraints and conditions and passes it on to the internal SMT solver (Z3 by default). The SMT solver solves the constraints and gives error list, if any. If there are no errors, it assumes that all conditions are satisfied (i.e) the system is correct by verification. Care is taken when choosing verification blocks. The verification block size should not be too complex or too big for the verifier for analysis.

Simple verification showed various loopholes in the program that can *possibly* affect the program operation. C# compiler, when it performs compilation and execution, assumes certain properties. The compiled program works well when these assumptions are true. However, the program can give unexpected results when they are false. The static verifier shows the possible loopholes and makes the programmer write better code with built-in assumption validation. Program code changes, as a result of verification, were incorporated into the design.

Experimental Results

Once the SUD was designed and created, two sets of experiments were conducted on groups of five users chosen randomly from a pool of 20 users. First set of experiments involved the development of an application based user re-authentication system. We conducted four different experiments in the first group. It involved the usage of either all or selective attributes. The training was also varied between general training (training session with two or more applications) and application-specific (training session in one application only).

In the second set of experiments, an application independent model was created from the behavioral attributes of users. The training session was general and the selection of attributes was based on the IQ and mouse-to-keyboard ratio. A high mouse-to-keyboard ratio implied more weight to mouse attributes whereas a low mouse-to-keyboard ratio implied more weight to the keyboard attributes during computation.

For both sets of experiments, each user group (2-user, 3-user and 4-user groups) was asked to train and test with normal operations. Thirty samples were taken from each user group (20 samples where the *current-user* is the *logged-in user* and 10 samples where the *current-user* is not the *logged-in user*). The results of first set of experiments are shown in Figures 6, 7, 8 and 9. Figure 6 shows the accuracy of the re-authentication for 4 applications. The training, however, is general and not targeted toward any specific application. Nearly 100% accuracy was obtained for Applications 1 and 4 as their tasks closely matched the tasks performed by the user in the training session. For Applications 2 and 3, we observed lesser accuracy and surmise that

it is because the user's behavior in applications 2 and 3 did not match that obtained during the "general training". To validate our hypothesis, we conducted application-specific training and tested the user behaviors in the applications again. Figure 7 shows the accuracy of our re-authentication system when the training matched the application under test. Here, we see that the accuracies improve very much as compared with Figure 6, as expected. Figures 8 and 9 report similar results where a selective attribute set is used for analysis.

The results of second set of experiments are tabulated in Table 2. All the values of Table 2 are expressed in terms of percentages and plotted, shown in Figure 10. The accuracy is expressed as the percentage of correct identification instances to total identification samples. Since the training did not target any specific application, and the testing also was not application-based, the accuracy would be slightly lower than the

Figure 6. Graph showing the accuracy of system vs. applications and number of users for application based testing with general training

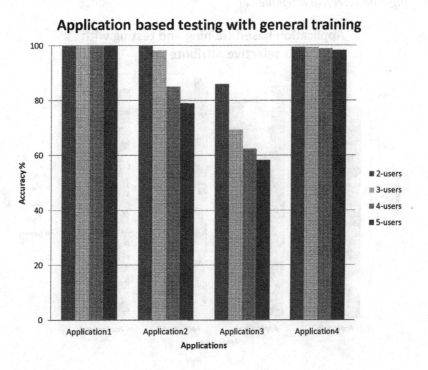

Figure 7. Graph showing the accuracy of system vs. applications and number of users for application based testing and training

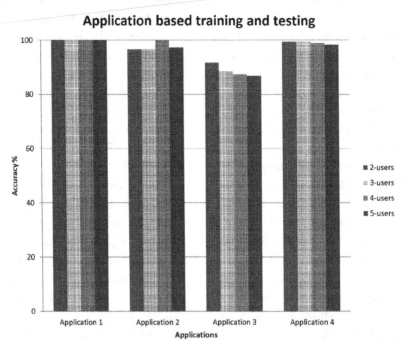

Figure 8. Graph showing accuracy of system vs. applications and number of users for application based training and testing with selective attribute set

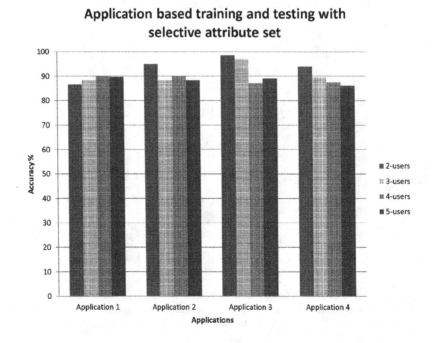

Figure 9. Graph showing ratios vs. percentages for application independent user re-authentication

Application independent User Re-authentication

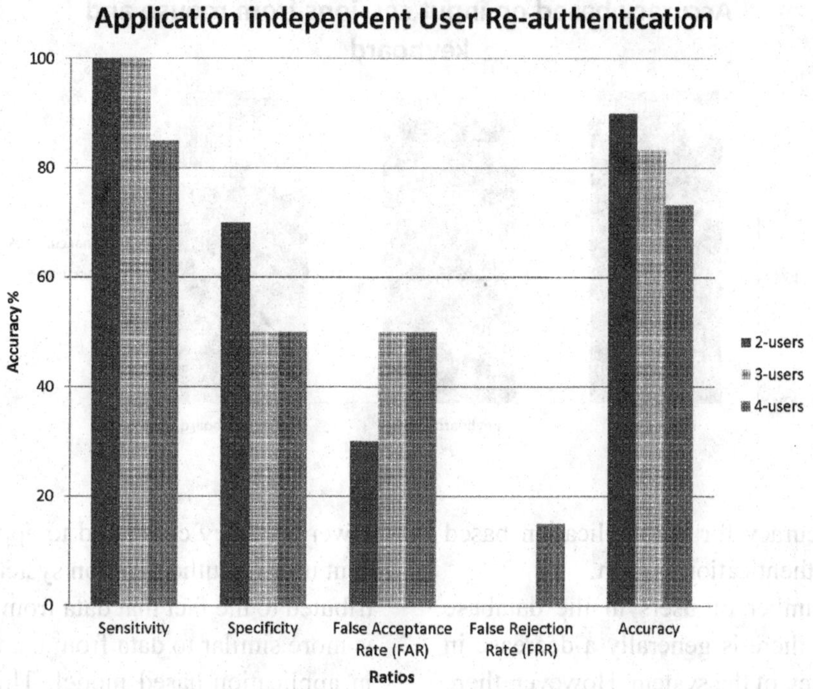

Table 2. Results of application independent user re-authentication system

Process and Function Name	Total Number of Paths	Number of Paths Covered by Black-Box Testing	Number of Paths Covered by White-Box Testing	Number of Paths Yet to be Covered
Recorder.exe	241	240	1	0
ProfileCollector.exe	118	112	6	0
Profile analyser.exe	1360	678	682	0
Tester.exe	1360	678	682	0
Profile system.exe	1848	1037	811	0
Profiler.exe	3841	241	3600	0
Fullsystem.exe	12657	12338	319	12
Total	**21425**	**15324**	**6089**	**12**

application-based counterpart. From above experimental results, we summarize the following:

- The average accuracy of application-based user re-authentication system is 96.4% with 0% FRR and 3.6% FAR for 2-, 3-, 4- and 5-user sets.

- The average accuracy of application-independent user re- authentication system is 82.22% for 2-, 3- and 4-user sets.

- The training session data plays a huge role in obtaining an accurate result: the closer the test session matches the training session, the better is the accuracy. We surmise that the above conclusion is the reason for

Figure 10. Graph showing accuracy vs. mouse and keyboard actions/session

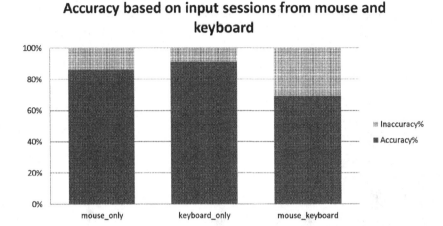

higher accuracy for the application based user re-authentication system.

- As the number of users in the database increases, there is generally a decrease in the accuracy of the system. However, there were cases where this trend was not true. So, a clear relation between the two variables in specified conditions is absent.

During the training phase, user is asked to perform normal operations on any application of her choice. The user can even shift between applications and use either or both keyboard and mouse in each session. During the testing phase, user is asked to perform regular operations. Her actions are not constrained to a particular application. On analysis, we see that the results are very good when the user's actions match that in training phase. For example, in training phase, if the user has predominantly used mouse-based actions, then the system can better identify the user when she performs only-mouse activities compared to mouse-and-keyboard or only-keyboard activities. This is true for other activities too. We see that the prediction accuracy is lowest when both mouse and keyboard are used as shown in Figure 8.

Although the application independent user re-authentication system is ideal, it has a slightly lower accuracy compared to application dependent user re-authentication system and this is attributed to the fact that data from the test session is more similar to data from the training session in application-based model. This is less likely the case for application-independent models. As a result, the system has a higher probability of incorrectly identifying the user. Experiments with larger user groups and larger sample size per user group may provide a more accurate view of these scenarios in the system.

CONCLUSION AND FUTURE WORK

Insider attacks are a huge but under-addressed problem in computer security. This work addresses identity thefts through masquerading, one of the major security concerns for insider attacks. Research in continuous authentication systems has generated a number of interesting results and observations. Behavioral authentication is particularly attractive in that it is easy to deploy and cost-effective. In particular, keyboard and mouse authentication methods are effective since they are commonly used (hence very cost-effective and easily deployable into the existing system), do not require extensive maintenance (unlike iris scanning, fingerprint scanning, etc.), cannot be easily hacked (unlike traditional methods like passwords, PINs, etc.), cannot be tampered with (unlike hardware authentication methods like smart cards, dongles, etc.) or easily forgotten/lost by the user. Their only drawback is that these systems should be periodically retrained to reflect the minute behavioral changes of the user. However, with continued usage of the system, this drawback can be alleviated by incorporating the training as part of the system. The proposed system can successfully identify imposters from authentic users based on their behavioral biometrics. On comparison with previous work, our system has a lower false rejection rate. This in turn increases the accuracy of the system. The user re-authentication system for application based design has an accuracy of 96.4% while user re-authentication system for application independent design has an accuracy of 82.2%. Our results show that we have been successful in enhancing the security of the system.

The accuracy results of the system are dependent on attributes and algorithms. Related to this, we aim to include more algorithms to our heuristic and incorporate physiological aspects of the user in our future work. This may lead to higher accuracy in user re-authentication since it can model the user in more detail. Further work in attributes can include research into other physiological attributes, behavioral attributes, etc. In case of behavioral aspects, systems that include other mouse attributes such as mouse click, mouse double click, mouse wheel movement and keyboard attributes that include numeric keys, special keys such as Enter, Ctrl, F1-F12, symbols, direction keys may be designed. This can lead to increased accuracy in identifying the user in a large user group. However, care should be taken when including these attributes to the system because a large attribute group can slow down the system's ability to quickly identify the user. Including one or more heuristics to improve the success rate

of the CA system enables it to be deployed on a larger scale. When adding more heuristics, it is necessary to ensure that the speed of feedback from the system is not reduced considerably. This is indispensible for the system's quick response to an intruder trying to use a genuine user's log-in session. Thus a trade-off between suitable attributes, data structures and heuristics is essential for the robustness of the system.

In short, a good re-authentication system for computers employs a small and selective set of attributes and an advanced heuristic that identifies the intruder from the genuine user in a short time span. From this chapter, we hope that the reader has gained a clear understanding of the basics of continuous authentication, steps involved in designing a continuous authentication mechanism using behavioral attributes for computers and has a snapshot of the previous and current research being done in this regard. Continuous authentication mechanisms, combined with traditional authentication systems, can provide adequately strong security to prevent masquerading and other security loopholes.

REFERENCES

Ahmed, A., & Traoré, I. (2007). A new biometric technology based on mouse dynamics. *IEEE Transactions on Dependable and Secure Computing, 4*(3), 165–179. doi:10.1109/TDSC.2007.70207

Araujo, L. C. F., Sucupira, L. H. R., Lizarraga, M. G., Ling, L. L., & Yabu-Uti, J. B. T. (2005). User authentication through typing biometric features. *IEEE Transactions on Signal Processing, 53*(2), 851–855. doi:10.1109/TSP.2004.839903

Barnett, M., Leino, R. M., & Schulte, W. (2005). The SPEC# programming system: An overview. *Construction and Analysis of Safe, Secure and Interoperable Smart devices (CASSIS) 2004* [Springer.]. *LNCS, 3362,* 49–69.

Beizer, B. (1995). *Black-box testing: Techniques for functional testing of software and systems.* New York, NY: Wiley.

Bleha, S. A., Knopp, J., & Obadiat, M. S. (2002). Performance of the perceptron algorithm for the classification of computer users. *Proceedings of the ACM/SIGAPP Symposium on Applied Computing.* New York, NY: ACM Press.

Brown, M., & Rogers, S. J. (1993). User identification via keystroke characteristics of typed names using neural networks. *International Journal of Man-Machine Studies, 39*(6), 999–1014. doi:10.1006/imms.1993.1092

Coull, S., Branch, J., Szymanski, B., & Breimer, E. (2003). Intrusion detection: A bioinformatics approach. *Proceedings of the Nineteenth Annual Computer Security Applications Conference,* (pp. 24-34). Las Vegas, NV.

De Oliveira, M. V. S., Kinto, E. A., Hernandez, E. D. M., & de Carvalho, T. C. M. (2005). User authentication based on human typing patterns with artificial neural networks and support vector machines. *XXV Congresso de Sociedade Brasileira de Computacao,* (pp. 484-493).

de Ru, W. G., & Eloff, J. H. P. (1997). Enhanced password authentication through fuzzy logic. *IEEE Expert, 12*(6), 38–45. doi:10.1109/64.642960

Denning, D. E., & Neumann, P. G. (1985). *Requirements and model for IDES - A real-time intrusion detection system. Technical report, Computer Science Laboratory.* Menlo Park, CA: SRI International.

Gaines, R., Lisowski, W., Press, S., & Shapiro, N. (1960). *Authentication by keystroke timing: Some preliminary results.* Rand Report R-256-NSF. Santa Monica, CA: Rand Corporation.

Gamboa, H., & Fred, A. (2003). An identity authentication system based on human computer interaction behavior. *Proceedings of 3rd International Conference on Pattern Recognition in Information Systems.*

Garcia, J. (1986). *Personal identification apparatus.* (Patent Number 4.6X.334). Washington, DC: US Patent and Trademark Office.

Goecks, J., & Shavlik, J. (1999). Automatically labeling Web pages based on normal user actions. *Procdings of the IJCAI Workshop on Machine Learning for Information Filtering.*

Hamdy, O., & Traoré, I. (2009). New physiological biometrics based on human cognitive factors. *Proceedings of the International Conference on Complex, Intelligent, and Software Intensive Systems (CISIS),* Fukoka, Japan, (pp. 910-917).

Hashia, S. (2004). *Authentication by mouse movements.* San Jose State University.

Hetzel, W. C. (1998). *The complete guide to software testing* (2nd ed.). Wellesley, MA: QED Information Sciences.

Hocquet, S., Ramel, J. Y., & Cardot, H. (2004). Users authentication by a study of human computer interaction. *Proc. Eighth Ann. (Doctoral) Meeting on Health, Science and Technology.*

Hussain, B., McLaren, R., & Bleha, S. (1989). An application of fuzzy algorithms in a computer access security system. *Pattern Recognition Letters, 9,* 39–43. doi:10.1016/0167-8655(89)90026-3

Jagadeesan, H., & Hsiao, M. (2009). A novel approach to design of user re-authentication systems. *Proceedings of the IEEE Conference on Biometrics: Theory, Applications and Systems,* (pp. 379-384).

Joyce, R., & Gupta, G. (1990). Identity authentication based on keystroke latencies. *Dependable Computing. Communications of the ACM, 33,* 168–176. doi:10.1145/75577.75582

Kung, S. Y., Mak, M. W., & Lin, S. H. (2004). *Biometric authentication, a machine learning approach* (pp. 1–20). Prentice Hall.

Lane, T., & Brodley, C. E. (1999). Temporal sequence learning and data reduction for anomaly detection. *ACM Transactions on Information and System Security, 2*(3), 295–331. doi:10.1145/322510.322526

Leggett, J., & Williams, G. (1988). Verifying identity via keyboard characteristics. *International Journal of Man-Machine Studies, 28*, 67–76. doi:10.1016/S0020-7373(88)80053-1

Leggett, J., Williams, G., & Umphress, D. (1988). Verification of user identity via keyboard characteristics. In Carey, J. M. (Ed.), *Human factors in management Information Systems*. Norwood, NJ: Ablex Publishing.

Looney, C. (1997). *Pattern recognition using neural networks – Theory and algorithms for engineers and scientists* (pp. 124–126). Oxford University Press.

Lunt, T. F., Tamaru, A., Gilham, F., Jagannathan, R., Neumann, P. G., & Javitz, H. S. … Garvey, T. D. (1992). *A real-time intrusion detection expert system IDES - Final report*. Technical Report SRI-CSL-92-05, SRI Computer Science Laboratory, SRI International.

Micheli-Tzanakou, E. (1999). *Supervised and unsupervised pattern recognition – Feature extraction and computational intelligence* (pp. 265–267). CRC Press.

Monrose, F., & Rubin, A. (1997). Authentication via keystroke dynamics. *Proceedings of the Fourth ACM Conference on Computer and Communications Security,* (pp. 48-56).

Nazar, A., Traoré, I., & Ahmed, A. A. E. (2008). Inverse biometrics for mouse dynamics. [IJPRAI]. *International Journal of Artificial Intelligence and Pattern Recognition, 22*(3), 461–495. doi:10.1142/S0218001408006363

Obaidat, M. S., & Sadoun, S. (1997). A simulation evaluation study of neural network techniques to computer user identification. *Information Sciences, 102*, 239–258. doi:10.1016/S0020-0255(97)00016-9

Pusara, M., & Brodley, C. (2004). User reauthentication via mouse movements. *Proceedings of the 2004 ACM Workshop on Visualization and Data Mining for Computer Security,* (pp. 1-8).

Raj, S. B. E., & Santhosh, A. T. (2009). A behavioral biometric approach based on standardized resolution in mouse dynamics. *International Journal of Computer Science and Network Security, 9*(4), 370–377.

Revett, K., Jahankhani, H., de Magalhães, S. T., & Santos, H. M. D. (2008). A survey of user authentication based on mouse dynamics. *Communications in Computer and Information Science, 12*(4), 210–219. doi:10.1007/978-3-540-69403-8_25

Revett, K., Magalhaes, P. S., & Santos, H. D. (2005). *Developing a keystroke dynamics based agent using rough sets*. The 2005 IEEE/WIC/ACM International Joint Conference on Web Intelligence and Intelligent Agent Technology Compiegne, (pp. 56–61).

Sang, Y., Shen, H., & Fan, P. (2004). *Novel imposters detection in keystroke dynamics using support vector machines* (pp. 666–669). Berlin/Heidelberg, Germany: Springer. ISSN 0302-9743

Schulz, D. A. (2006). *Mouse curve biometrics*. Biometric Consortium Conference, 2006 Biometrics Symposium, (pp. 1-6).

Shavlik, J., Shavlik, M., & Fahland, M. (2001). Evaluating software sensors for actively profiling Windows 2000 users. *Proceedings of the Fourth International Symposium on Recent Advances in Intrusion Detection.*

Shen, C., Cai, Z., Guan, X., Sha, H., & Du, H. (2009). feature analysis of mouse dynamics in identity authentication and monitoring. *Proc. of IEEE International Conference on Communications (ICC '09)* (pp. 1-5). Dresden, Germany.

Sung, K. S., & Cho, S. (2006). *GA SVM wrapper ensemble for keystroke dynamics authentication.* International Conference on Biometrics, (pp. 654–660). Hong Kong.

Tapiador, M., Sigenza, J. A., & Tcnica, E. (1999). Fuzzy keystroke biometrics on Web security. *IEEE AutoID '99 Proceedings Workshop on Automatic Identification Advanced Technologies,* (pp. 133–136).

Umphress, D., & Williams, G. (1985). Identity verification through keyboard characteristics. *International Journal of Man-Machine Studies, 23*(3), 263–273. doi:10.1016/S0020-7373(85)80036-5

Vijaya Kumar, B. V. K., Mahalanobis, A., & Juda, R. (2005). *Correlation pattern recognition.* Cambridge University Press. doi:10.1017/CBO9780511541087

Weiss, A., Ramapanicker, A., Shah, P., Noble, S., & Immohr, L. (2007). *Mouse movements biometric identification: A feasibility study.* Pace University. doi: 10.1.1.88.7902

Young, J. R., & Hammon, R. W. (1989). *Method and apparatus for verifying an individual's identity.* (Patent Number 4,805,222). Washington, DC: U.S. Patent and Trademark Office.

Section 2
Continuous Authentication Based on Physiological and Cognitive Biometrics

Chapter 4
Multimodal Biometric Hand–Off for Robust Unobtrusive Continuous Biometric Authentication

P. Daphne Tsatsoulis
Carnegie Mellon University, USA

Aaron Jaech
Carnegie Mellon University, USA

Robert Batie
Raytheon Company, USA

Marios Savvides
Carnegie Mellon University, USA

ABSTRACT

Conventional access control solutions rely on a single authentication to verify a user's identity but do nothing to ensure the authenticated user is indeed the same person using the system afterwards. Without continuous monitoring, unauthorized individuals have an opportunity to "hijack" or "tailgate" the original user's session. Continuous authentication attempts to remedy this security loophole. Biometrics is an attractive solution for continuous authentication as it is unobtrusive yet still highly accurate. This allows the authorized user to continue about his routine but quickly detects and blocks intruders. This chapter outlines the components of a multi-biometric based continuous authentication system. Our application employs a biometric hand-off strategy where in the first authentication step a strong biometric robustly identifies the user and then hands control to a less computationally intensive face recognition and tracking system that continuously monitors the presence of the user. Using multiple biometrics allows the system to benefit from the strengths of each modality. Since face verification accuracy degrades as more time elapses between the training stage and operation time, our proposed hand-off strategy permits continuous robust face verification with relatively simple and computationally efficient classifiers. We provide a detailed evaluation of verification performance using different pattern classification algorithms and show that the final multi-modal biometric hand-off scheme yields high verification performance.

DOI: 10.4018/978-1-61350-129-0.ch004

INTRODUCTION

The goal of continuous authentication is to prevent intruders from hijacking the user session of an authorized individual who may momentarily step away from his terminal. Access control has traditionally been achieved through means such as passwords and pass-cards. Passwords suffer from a variety of vulnerabilities including brute-force and dictionary based attacks. Pass-cards or other physical tokens used for authentication can be lost or stolen. Biometric systems identify a user based on characteristics such as face, iris or fingerprint which are tightly coupled with physical identity (Klosterman & Ganger, 2000). Biometrics can be continuously monitored which makes them an ideal solution for continuous authentication systems. This work focuses primarily on computer workstations, however, continuous authentication systems have been proposed for other environments. For example, Carillo (2003) outlines a design for continuous biometric authentication in airplane cockpits to prevent an unauthorized takeover of the aircraft.

The ideal continuous authentication system is fully transparent to the user who need not alter his routine to allow himself to be monitored continuously. Robust biometric modalities such as iris and fingerprint require cooperation from the user, usually in the form of touching some kind of biometric sensor or being at a fixed distance for suitable quality iris acquisition. These two modalities are not suitable for continuous and transparent monitoring. On the other hand, facial images can be used to identify an individual but not to the same degree of accuracy as iris and fingerprint especially when a longer interval has elapsed between testing and training.

A system that combines multiple biometrics benefits from the advantages of each modality. Typically, the stronger biometric will be used for the initial verification to establish the subject's identity. This modality can then hand control of the authentication system to another less intrusive biometric, such as facial modality, which begins to continuously take readings and has the ability to quickly train on the appearance of the authenticated user. This second biometric modality, although weaker when used as a standalone authentication solution, has an easier task to perform: it only needs to solve the following problem, "Is the user I see now the same as the one I just saw a moment ago?". It can incorporate temporal data from the recent past when making this decision. This strategy allows for continual and unobtrusive identity management.

During the last decade, new developments in hardware, such as the rapid increase in CPU clock speeds, the proliferation of multi-core CPUs and larger memory available in retail desktop machines, combined with computationally efficient face detection algorithms like the one developed by Viola and Jones (2004) have made it possible to design a real-time continuous authentication system that runs as a background process on a typical computer. Many laptops now ship with built-in web-cams convenient for the collection of application-relevant face image data, making them ideal mobile continuous authentication stations. This chapter gives an overview of a real continuous authentication system, which employs the aforementioned multi-biometric hand-off strategy. The application is light-weight in CPU and memory usage, so the typical user will not notice any reduction in performance while using the computer for his work as a result of our continuous system application running in the background. In our system, the initial static log-on uses a Daugman-style iris recognition approach (Daugman, 2004), followed by biometric hand-off to the face recognition component. We use the Viola-Jones face detection algorithm to detect faces, pre-process and crop them for different types of face recognition classifiers. Later in this chapter, we give a detailed background of the algorithms used in our application.

The verification accuracy of an authentication system designed in this manner can be experimentally tested. We collected video sequences from over sixty individuals while they were using their desktop and laptop computer stations under normal operation. This data was used to simulate the arrival of a malicious intruder at a workstation that had been trained on images from someone else. This allowed us to perform a series of evaluations using a variety of classifiers with different parameters. These results can be found in the result section of this chapter. We evaluated five different classifiers: Global Principal Component Analysis (GPCA) Individual Principal Component Analysis (IPCA), Fisher Linear Discriminant Analysis (FLDA), Minimum Average Correlation Filters (MACE) and Support Vector Machines (SVM). These tests establish the accuracy of our continuous authentication system. We compare the performance and computational workload of these methods. We selected the highest performing classifier for use in our system.

We conclude by showing that a relatively simple approach such as building an individual subspace to represent a person's current variation is computationally efficient and performs sufficiently well for unobtrusive continuous authentication. Other classifiers are also able to achieve high performance but at the cost of higher computational burden during training and testing.

BACKGROUND

Continuous Authentication

Continuous authentication performs three types of verification (Niinuma, Park & Jain, 2010). First, the users' identity is initially verified during the log-on. Then, the system monitors and verifies the continued presence of the user in front of the computer workstation and locks down if the user leaves or if an un-authorized user attempts to use the system. Finally, if the user returns after leaving, the system must re-authenticate the user. Each of these three decision points should be examined

individually. Some systems do not distinguish between these three decisions in their verification methods (Yap & Ramnath, 2008). We believe that a significant usability and security gain is possible by treating each of these cases individually.

Initial Log-On Authentication

The initial log-on authentication is the basis for all future authentications so a strong match is typically required. Additionally, there is no need for the initial log-on authentication process to be transparent to the user. Fingerprint and iris are appropriate biometric modalities for initial user authentication since both of these modalities are capable of matching with a high degree of confidence. Although these modalities require the user to cooperate to some degree (e.g. provide their finger, or place their eye at an acceptable distance for their iris to be acquired), they are less of an interruption at the beginning of the session. It is also less of an interruption to ask the user to re-authenticate if the sensor fails to acquire correctly or if the verification classifier gives a marginal verification score. For the same reason, it is acceptable for the initial verification process to take some amount of time and use the full computing power of the workstation.

We selected iris authentication as the initial secure log-on modality in our system. The details of iris recognition can be found in the background section of this chapter. Fingerprint recognition can also be used for initial log-on especially since many laptop computers ship with fingerprint sensors. When designing such a system, the user may prefer fingerprint over iris depending on the specifics of the application.

Continuous Authentication Module

The continuous authentication phase occupies the majority of the time that the user spends at the workstation. The greatest opportunity for intruders to access the workstation is when the authorized user has just left but not logged out. Malicious users can cause irreparable damage to a computer system with just a few seconds of access to the terminal, steal sensitive information, or install malware to compromise the system. A typical screen saver (triggered by prolonged idleness) will not protect the computer from these attacks. The system must verify frequently, possibly several times per second. The system is, in effect, repeatedly asking the same question, "Is the person who was using me a moment ago still here?" If the answer is 'no', the workstation is automatically locked. An incorrect answer to this question is disruptive to the user and if the false reject rate is too high the system will quickly become unusable. Hence, we need to be careful about how frequently the continuous verification step is performed. If the continuous verification is performed frequently enough, the probability at the time of the next verification that the authorized user has left will be very small. This knowledge allows the system to leverage the information obtained during the initial log-on authentication in order to learn the facial appearance of the user.

It is also important that this verification step be transparent to the user; there should be no notable differences in the behavior or usability of the workstation as a result of the continuous authentication. The application is expected to run as a background process on the same machine that services the user's other processes. Transparency encompasses keeping memory and CPU usage low as well as obtaining all biometric samples without any special cooperation or actions from the user. Although heavy use of computing resources allows for more accurate algorithms, if they monopolize the CPU the authorized user will experience decreased utility. Additionally, with today's multi-core CPUs, one core may be dedicated to continuous authentication without blocking the flow of execution of the user's other processes.

Suggested modalities for continuous authentication include face and keystroke analysis. Some

researchers have recommended using a mouse with an embedded fingerprint sensor (Kumar, Sim, Kanakiraman & Zhang, 2005) (Sung, Lim, Park, Lee & Li, 2004). Keystroke recognition and fingerprint mice cannot reliably provide continuous sensor input since the user may be using the workstation to read a document for an extended period of time without providing much in the way of keyboard or mouse input. These systems must come up with a way to handle this problem such as supplementing these modalities with a true continuous biometric or requiring the user to put his thumb to the mouse at pre-specified periodic intervals.

Additional methods have been proposed including the combination of soft-biometric indicators and color histogram measurements (Niinuma et al., 2010) of the whole image. We note that color histogram measurements are heavily influenced by the color of the subject's shirt and may be considerably less reliable in a professional environment where different users conform to a standardized uniform or dress code. Moreover, such histograms are vulnerable to changes in ambient illumination or severe background illumination changes, thus resulting in the undesirable event of locking-out the 'authorized' user from his workstation.

It may be desirable to augment the system with a feature that prevents authorized users from logging someone else in by authenticating himself and passing control to an unauthorized friend. This can be achieved without too much difficult by keeping a record of the users' biometric data from a previous session.

Re-Authentication

If the user turns away from the workstation for a brief period such as to read a document or leaves briefly to make a phone call we would like to quickly restore the user's access when he returns. We would also like to gracefully recover from errors in continuous verification. If the system mistakenly believes that the user has left when he is in fact still present he should be able to regain access without taking the time to acquire an iris image or fingerprint reading. If more time has passed since the user was last observed the system should be more stringent when it tries to re-authenticate. Eventually, the system will revert back to the initial log-on authentication procedure.

Face is the most suitable biometric modality for this part since it can instantly be collected the moment the user looks at the screen. Many laptops and some computer monitors now have built-in cameras which capture images of more than sufficient quality for our purposes.

This re-authentication step is more difficult than the continuous authentication step. Its performance is crucial to the total security of the system. While it is difficult to measure the accuracy of the continuous authentication step without hours of data recorded under real-world conditions, the re-authentication procedure is easily evaluated. In our review of the state-of-the art research literature, there is no work which analyzes the performance of this verification step. In this chapter, we present a careful analysis of re-authentication accuracy using face recognition. This is detailed in the Results section.

Keystroke Recognition

Keystroke recognition is a biometric modality which has been repeatedly proposed as well-suited for continuous authentication. The technique uses statistical features extracted from the pattern and timing of the user's keystrokes. These features are expected to be consistent over time. A positive authentication is achieved when the sample features closely match those of a training sample. High verification rates have been obtained by Villani et al. (2006) but only with large training samples. Once the training data has been collected a writing sample of about 200 characters is needed to extract statistically significant features for verification.

This modality is limited to systems where the keyboard is the main input device and more im-

portantly, the user needs to be typing at all times. As mentioned above, keystroke recognition is not a continuous biometric per se since it is only one form of input on the typical computer. An intruder could quite easily affect his malicious intentions without so much as touching the keyboard, using only the mouse for input. Keystroke recognition may accurately identify the author of an email or some other document but it cannot by applied to quickly re-authenticate the user after a brief absence.

Iris Recognition

In automated iris recognition systems, there are two predominant approaches that are used as a basis for all systems: that of Daugman (2004) and that of Wildes (1996). Both systems can be broken into four steps. First, image acquisition is performed which attempts to capture images of an eye of sufficient quality for processing. Current acquisition systems focus upon either improving the quality of the acquired images or on making acquisition less intrusive to the user. The "Iris on the Move" (Matey et al., 2006) system is aimed at making iris acquisition less intrusive. There are several groups working to improve the quality of images as a function of focus, occlusion, lighting and pixel count. However, these systems are also large and very costly, keeping them outside of the form-factor framework for continuous authentication.

Once an iris image has been acquired by the optical sensor, the system needs to segment the image in order to isolate the iris section of the eye region. There are numerous publications which discuss various techniques used to find the papillary and limbic boundaries which use edge detection and a Hough transform originally proposed by Wildes (1996). For example, Sung et al. (2004) present an additional step after the traditional method that locates the collarette boundary using histogram equalization and high-pass filtering. Camus and Wildes (2002) on the other hand, present an approach that does not depend on edge detection or the Hough transform. A lot of work has also been applied to the preprocessing of images and to dealing with off-angle images. Li (2006) uses rotation and scaling of an ellipse that is fitted to the pupil boundary to correct off-angle images. A more extensive discussion of the various approaches can be found in (Bowyer, Hollingsworth & Flynn, 2008).

The third step is texture analysis during which a representation of the iris is extracted and used for the last step: matching. In order to derive the features from a normalized iris image, Daugman in his work (2004) convolves the image with Gabor filters to get a localized spatial-frequency response array. He then creates a two-bit binary code representation from the filter response to represent every iris image as a series of encoded bits, called the iris code. The first bit, of each two bit pair, corresponds to the real part of the response, and the second bit to the imaginary part. For each part, if the coefficient is positive the bit is set to '1', otherwise it is set to '0'. Daugman then measures the similarity between these binary codes by using the normalized Hamming distance; the lower the Hamming distance, the more iris code bits that were identical and hence the stronger the match. Wildes applies the Laplacian of a Gaussian (LoG) filter to create a model and calculates the similarity by using normalized correlation (Yao, Li, Ye, Zhuang & Li, 2006). One of the more popular approaches used in place of Gabor filters, is the approach presented by Yao et al. (2006). They use modified log-Gabor filters since they more faithfully represent higher frequencies, which contain the majority of iris information. Various methods for feature extraction and matching are represented in the literature.

Face Detection

The training process for a face detector relies upon three main components. The first component, which is key to the success of the detector, is the quality and variation represented in the training data set used to train the system. For face detection, it is important that the set include faces with angular rotations, occlusions, variations in pose, illumination and expression. Not only is it important to include a large number of positive training faces, but it is also important to present the algorithm with an even larger number of negative samples, which are images that include no faces but include patterns that are similar to faces and might confuse the detector. The second important component is the selection of the type of feature extraction which will be fed into the classification module. Lastly, the actual pattern classification scheme must be selected.

One of the most common face detectors is the Viola-Jones face detector (Viola & Jones, 2004). Though other face detectors exist, such as the Schneiderman and Kanade (2000) detector, the Viola and Jones face detector is prevalent and accessible among the research community. Our system employs a specially trained implementation of this algorithm. The Viola-Jones face detector is composed of a cascade of simple weak classifiers that when combined make a strong face detection classifier.

The features used by Viola and Jones are local rectangular features. They were dubbed "Haar-like" for their resemblance to the 2D-Haar basis functions (Umbaugh, 2005). These features capture the presence of edges, texture and pixel intensity changes on a face. The reason why these features are attractive is the speed with which they can be computed using a computational trick called "integral image". With this method, the response of a "Haar-like" feature can be obtained in constant time regardless of the size, location and orientation of the feature.

To combine all these feature-based classifiers, Viola and Jones (2004) used AdaBoost (Freund & Schapire, 1995). Adaboost is an ensemble learning method that builds an accurate classifier by combining multiple weak classifiers. Initially, all of the training samples are weighted equally. In each iteration AdaBoost invokes a learning algorithm to find the simple classifier which minimizes the weighted classification error. The samples which were misclassified by the simple classifier are up-weighted so that in subsequent iterations the algorithm will select simple classifiers that address those errors. The final strong classifier is a linear combination of the weak classifiers where each classifier is weighted by its training error.

Lastly, Viola and Jones split the final strong classifier learned by AdaBoost into a sequence of smaller classifiers. This cascaded architecture greatly contributes to the ability of their detector to run in real time. This set up allows an early exit when it is determined that a given window in an image does not contain a face. Since most windows will not contain faces, this greatly speeds up the process by allowing the detector more time to focus on windows with possible faces.

SYSTEM ARCHITECTURE

We constructed a functional application which demonstrates the key features of a continuous authentication system. Our system uses an iris camera to grant initial access. It then hands off control to the continuous face verification module which is also used for re-authentication. The demo application was written in C++ for the Windows operating system.

We used IriTech's IriTerminal MD-300 product along with the IriTech SDK to grant initial access. The IriTerminal has the capability of encrypting and matching biometric data on the device. During recognition, the device quickly captures a series of images and automatically selects the best one for matching (see Figure 1). This device is also used for enrollment. We enroll both irises of each individual for ease of use.

Once access to the system has been granted, a USB web-cam mounted above the monitor is activated. We use a variant of the Viola-Jones face detection algorithm to detect the user's face. The

Figure 1. The IriTerminal MD-300 used for iris enrollment, acquisition and matching in our application

first eighty detected faces are cropped and used to train a detector which will be used later on. Using larger training sets can lead to better verification rates but this application is under strict memory constraints, which limits the amount of data it can store. Usually not all eighty faces are of the same value to the classifier but the cost of choosing which ones to use outweighs the expected benefit.

The face detector runs approximately 12 times per second to monitor the continued presence of the user. No other verification is performed here since it is assumed that the authorized user must leave before an impostor can take over the system. An adjustable parameter controls how much time must elapse without detecting a face before the system is judged vulnerable to attack. Once that point is reached, the system blocks access to the workstation until the user's identity is re-confirmed. If only a short amount of time passes before the user attempts to re-authenticate the system tries to verify the user's identity on the basis of eighty face images captured during the training stage. If more time has passed or the system cannot identify the user's face, the user must re-authenticate using the iris camera. Again, an adjustable parameter controls the length of this time period. The system works well in conjunction with a screen saver that is triggered by a period of inactivity (see Figure 2).

Figure 2. A user operating our demo application. For demonstration purposes, we display the image from the camera on the screen.

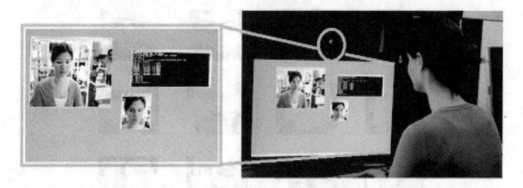

Our demo application does not attempt to implement certain security features that are necessary in production applications. Other authors describe how to encrypt communication between biometric sensors and the workstation (Kumar et al., 2005) and how to securely interface with the operating system to lock the computer when the absence of the authorized user is detected (Klosterman & Ganger, 2000).

SYSTEM EVALUATION

The re-authentication decision is crucial to a high performance continuous authentication system. In order to quantify the accuracy of the re-authentication system we conducted an experiment with five different classifiers on data similar to that which would be seen by a deployed system. The data allows us to compare the accuracy of the classifiers and select the best performing classifier for our system.

Experimental Sample Data Collection

Data for our study was collected from sixty-one volunteers. Each volunteer was seated at a desktop with a USB web-cam or a laptop with a built-in camera for about five minutes. The volunteers were instructed to briefly look into the camera and then copy a short document in a word processor to simulate normal computer usage. For part of each data collection the experimenter conversed with the volunteers to stimulate some expression variation. Data was collected in a workplace setting and in various other locations on campus. In some cases, when a table was not available, the volunteers held the laptop in their laps. These factors have implications for lighting, pose and other types of variation. For selected volunteers (about twenty-five in total) we were able to capture data at a second date which varied between one day to three weeks from the time of the initial capture (Figure 3).

Experimental Sample Data Pre-Processing

To localize the faces in the video frames, we used a variant of the Viola-Jones face detection algorithm. The detector was trained on images within thirty degrees of a full frontal pose. After detection, all of the cropped faces were scaled to 150 x 150 pixels for further processing.

Histogram equalization attempts to scale the pixel intensities such that there are an equal number of pixels at each intensity. This is the simplest way to correct for illumination variation. Other methods do more to correct for illumination but are much more computationally-intensive which

Figure 3. Selected cropped faces from 16 of the subjects in our study, corrected for illumination using histogram equalization

quickly becomes cumbersome in a continuous-authentication setting. We envision our system operating in a well-lit environment with little illumination variation in the time between training and re-authentication. As mentioned above, some of the data was collected in a well-lit office setting and others were recorded in a darker residential environment. In a normal operational setting we expect minimal lighting variation.

We extracted five hundred cropped faces from each of the volunteers. This study does not explicitly deal with the inability of the face detector to correctly detect every face. Frames without detected faces were discarded. Two individuals were dropped from the study because the face detector was unable to detect five hundred faces in their recordings, possibly due to bad illumination.

The five hundred cropped faces were divided into testing and training images. The first eighty crops were used for training. In our demo application, these would be the frames captured immediately after the user authenticates with the iris camera while the system is still highly confident as to the identity of the user. The training sets were created by combining 80 positive training images from the beginning of one individual's dataset, and 4 images each of 20 negative individuals' datasets, creating a balanced number of positive and negative training samples for the classifier. The remaining 38 individuals were used for testing.

It would be unfair to measure system performance without leaving a gap between the testing and training stage since the user is likely to maintain the same expression and pose for some time after the training period has ended. In particular, were there is no gap, the last training image would be highly similar to the first testing image. To address this issue we use only the last eighty crops for testing, giving the user enough time (at least a few minutes) to vary his posture and expression. The experimental data was analyzed with each of the following discrimination methods.

Global Principal Component Analysis

Global Principal Component Analysis (GPCA) for facial recognition was first introduced by Turk and Pentland in (1991). Their work outlines an unsupervised approach of representing faces with an eigenvector basis set called eigenfaces. The process begins with the acquisition of a training set and the calculation of a subspace that models the face variations. Later, when a test face image is presented for testing, it is projected into this face subspace and its classification is based upon its distance to other faces in this face subspace.

Let Γ be the set of all training images $\{\gamma_1, \gamma_2,\ldots,\gamma_n\}$, where each γ_i is a $d \times d$ training image in vector form. Allow the mean to be represented as μ. These eigenfaces are actually the eigenvectors of the covariance matrix $C = \dfrac{1}{n}\sum_{i=1}^{n}(\gamma_i - \mu)(\gamma_i - \mu)^T$ computed from the training image set.

However, because C is a $d^2 \times d^2$ matrix and typically of very low rank, it is computationally inefficient to determine its eigenvalues/eigenvectors directly from C. Instead, by using the Gram trick we are able to associate the eigenvalues of the Gram matrix ($C^T C$) to those of C as follows. Allow u to be the desired eigenvectors and λ the desired eigenvalues. Let $A=[(\gamma_1 - \mu), (\gamma_2 - \mu), (\gamma_3 - \mu),\ldots, (\gamma_n - \mu)]$, such that $C=AA^T$. From the equation $AA^T U=\lambda u$ and by setting $v=A^T u$, it can be determined that $A^T A v=\lambda v$. The eigenvalues of $A^T A$ (an $n \times n$ matrix) are also those of AA^T (a $d^2 \times d^2$ matrix). Thus, the eigenvectors of $A^T A$ are computationally more efficient to compute when the dimensionality of the data is much larger than the number of samples when $d \gg n$.

The desired eigenvectors can be related to the Gram matrix eigenvectors v by $u \cong Av$. Once these eigenvectors have been normalized to have unit energy, they can be used as a projection basis to calculate the projection coefficients, ω_k, of an image, γ. This is done by the following projection operation, $\omega_k = u_k^T(\gamma - \mu)$ for each eigenvector u_k.

The eigenvalues of the covariance matrix represent the variance captured in the direction of each eigenvector. In general, the first few eigenvectors to represent most of the variation in the data while the last set of eigenvectors is dominated by noise. In theory, the verification rate can be improved by dropping the last few eigenvectors. In our experiment we tried keeping different combinations of eigenvectors.

The same operation is used to find the projection coefficients of a testing image, and the vector $\omega^T=[\omega_1,\omega_2,\ldots,\omega_m]$ contains the weights that every eigenface contributes to an incoming test image. The classification of a test image can most easily be determined by the minimum Euclidean distance $\|\omega-\omega_i\|^2$ where ω_i describes the ith face class.

Though GPCA is not a classifier we included it in our analysis as a baseline. Since GPCA is optimal for data compression, dimensionality reduction for feature extraction and representation, it is often used as a pre-processing step for the classifiers that follow. We do not expect GPCA to give high accuracy rates for face verification.

Individual Principal Component Analysis

Individual Principal Component Analysis builds a PCA subspace for every class in the training set as done for PCA described above. Testing images are then projected onto each subspace from every person in the gallery set, and then reconstructed from each subspace. The reconstructed images from each subspace are then compared to the original input image, and the test image is classified based upon which subspace gave the lowest mean squared error between the original image and its reconstruction. This is also called distance to face space (DFFS) (Liu, Chen & Kumar, 2002). If a sample image belongs to a particular class, its reconstruction, which is based upon a linear combination of the eigenvector basis generated from the training images of the same class will be very similar to the original image. This yields a low mean squared error. It is often beneficial to use normalized correlation instead of mean

Figure 4. The test image, the reconstructed image and the error image of an individual in the genuine and imposter class

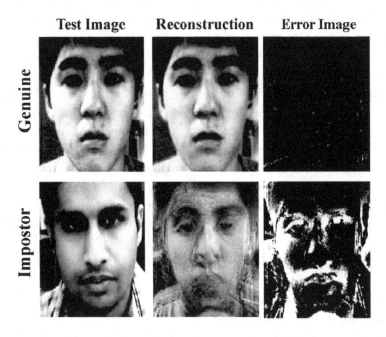

squared error since normalized correlation is less sensitive to global illumination intensity variation (Figure 4).

Fisher Linear Discriminant Analysis

Fisher Linear Discriminant Analysis (FLDA) for facial recognition was first introduced by Belhumeur, Hespanha, and Kreigman (1997). GPCA, discussed above, does not take into account the existence of multiple classes. Its projection vector maximizes the variance of the projected data. In FLDA, the projection vector maximizes the inter-cluster variance, while minimizing the intra-cluster variance. The projection method used in FLDA is based upon Fisher Linear Discriminant Analysis, a class specific method that tries to form the projection points more reliably for classification (Fisher, 1936). Images are initially projected onto a GPCA subspace to reduce the dimensionality of the data. Then these projected images are projected into the FLDA space creating "Fisherfaces."

Let μ_i represent the mean image of a class and N_i represent the number of samples in the class. The inter-class (between class) scatter matrix $\mathbf{S}_B$ and the intra-class (within class) scatter matrix $\mathbf{S}_W$ are defined below:

$$\mathbf{S}_B = \sum_{i=1}^{c} N_i (\mu_i - \mu)(\mu_i - \mu)^T$$

$$\mathbf{S}_W = \sum_{i=1}^{c} \sum_{k=1}^{N_i} (\mathbf{x}_k - \mu_i)(\mathbf{x}_k - \mu_i)^T$$

The goal of FLDA is to find projection matrix, $\mathbf{W}$, such that the ratio of the inter-class scatter matrix and the intra-class scatter matrix is maximized.

$$\mathbf{W}_{optimal} = \max_{\mathbf{W}} \frac{\left| \mathbf{W}^T \mathbf{S}_B \mathbf{W} \right|}{\left| \mathbf{W}^T \mathbf{S}_W \mathbf{W} \right|}$$

To generate an impostor class, for each test we randomly partitioned the subjects into a training set with twenty individuals and a testing set containing the remaining thirty-eight individuals. Four images were randomly selected from each of the individuals in the training set to comprise the imposter class images.

Support Vector Machines

Support Vector Machines (SVM) attempt to find a decision boundary solution vector that maximizes the margin between two classes (Boswer, Guyon & Vapnik, 1992). SVMs are strong, supervised learning algorithms, used extensively in binary classification. SVMs improve on LDA and neural networks by finding a hyperplane that maximizes the projected distance between the closest elements of separate classes.

Let us represent the training images as a collection of examples $\mathbf{x}_i$ with labels y_i, where $y_i=1$ if $\mathbf{x}_i$ is an element of class A, and $y_i=-1$ if it is an element of class B. $\mathbf{x} \in \mathbf{A}$ if and only if $y_j D(x_j) \geq 0$ where $D(x) > 0$ if $\mathbf{x} \in \mathbf{A}$. The linear discriminant function is:

$D(x) =^T x + b$

The functional margin is $M = \dfrac{2}{\|\mathbf{w}\|}$, thus by minimizing $\|\mathbf{w}\|$ we maximize the margin so our final optimization function is of the form $\min_{\mathbf{w}} \|\mathbf{w}\|^2$ such that $y_j D(x_j) \geq 0$.

The above discriminant function is linear and thus has difficulty solving non-linearly separable classification problems. SVMs overcome this limitation by projecting the data to a higher-dimensional feature space where the data is linearly separable. To do this optimization we utilize Kernel functions to compute the higher-dimensional inner-product without actually finding the higher-dimensional feature mapping for every sample $\mathbf{x}$. The above optimization is in what is typically referred to as the 'primal space' but we need to formulate a dual space formulation

where we can reconfigure the equation such that there are no single term higher-dimensional feature projection mappings. To maximize the margin in the dual space the above equation needs to be transformed by means of the Lagrangian. Details of this dual space optimization can be found on the further reading section.

For our evaluation, we utilized the popular implementation SVMlight by Joachims (1999). Images in the negative training set were selected in the same way as the impostor class was formed for FLDA, as described above. For our application since we care about small computational footprint of the classification scheme, we found that linear SVM (which obtains a single projection vector $\mathbf{w}$) worked sufficiently well, and more importantly could do classification using a single inner-product vector operation.

Correlation Filters

Correlation filters detect the presence of a known reference pattern in a noisy target signal. The simplest correlation filter is the matched filter which is the cross-correlation of the reference with the observed target. Matched filters are well known because of their ability to maximize the signal to noise ratio (Vijaya Kumar, Mahalanobis & Juday, 2005) in the detection plane. It is computationally efficient to perform this calculation in the frequency domain where the above process can be computed with three two-dimensional Fourier transform operations. First, we compute the 2-D FFT of the reference pattern image and perform an element-multiplication with the complex conjugate of the 2-D FFT of the input image. The correlation output plane is the 2-D inverse FFT of this element-wise product.

In our analysis we used the Minimum Average Correlation Energy (MACE) filter (Villani et al., 2006) which seeks to minimize the average correlation energy resulting from cross-correlations with the given training images while satisfying specific linear constraints to provide a specific value at the origin of the correlation plane for each training image. If **X** is a complex valued L x N matrix where each column contains the vectorized versions of the 2-D Fourier transforms of the N training images and **u** is an L-dimensional vector containing the desired correlation values for each training image then the MACE filter **h** must satisfy the constraint $\mathbf{X}^+\mathbf{h}=\mathbf{u}$. The filter selects **h** such that the correlation plane energy (expressed as $\mathbf{h}^+\mathbf{Dh}$) is minimized. The MACE filter can be expressed in closed form:

$$\mathbf{h}=\mathbf{D}^{-1}\mathbf{X}(\mathbf{X}^+\mathbf{D}^{-1}\mathbf{X})^{-1}\mathbf{u}$$

where **D** is a diagonal L^2 x L^2 matrix with the average power spectrum of the training images along its diagonal.

Conventionally, the constraint values for the training images are set to +1 for each of the positive training images. We followed this procedure in our experiment and empirically found that sampling the training set at 8 frame intervals yielded good performance. Additionally, from a computational point of view, this approach is attractive as it only requires computation of a single FFT based correlation output to perform the verification process. The filter output is scored by estimating the sharpness of the correlation peak. As shown in Figure 5, authentic test images will have sharp peaks while impostors should have no discernable peak. A common metric is the Peak-to-Sidelobe Ratio (PSR) which takes the mean and standard deviation of the area around the peak and is computed using the equation below. The area immediately around the peak is masked when calculating the mean and standard deviation.

$$PSR = \frac{peak - mean}{\sigma}$$

Correlation filters have several nice properties for pattern recognition. They are shift (i.e. translation) invariant so it is not necessary to perfectly align the reference pattern with the observed signal. They gracefully handle noise and occlusions.

Metrics

Sim et al. (2000) suggest that the standard method of evaluating biometric verification systems does not apply to continuous authentication. The authors suggest two alternative metrics: Time to Correct Rejection (TCR) which is the number of seconds elapsed before an impostor is denied access to the system and Usability which is the total fraction of the time that a legitimate user is granted access to the system.

Since a different system is used to deny access to the user once he leaves the workstation, the concept of usability as defined by Sim et al.

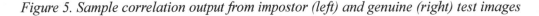

Figure 5. Sample correlation output from impostor (left) and genuine (right) test images

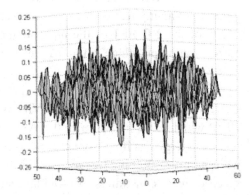
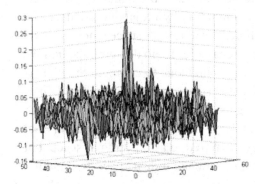

(2000) does not apply. In the experiment, we have the concept of a decision window which is the amount of time we allow ourselves to make a decision as to the identity of the user. Recognition rates tend to improve with longer decision windows but the usability declines if the user has to wait to get access. Time is measured in frames. We decided to cap the decision window at eighty frames for our experiments. However, the classifiers in our experiment operate on one image at a time. Therefore for every test authentication the classifier produces eighty scores. The method for combining these scores to reach a decision is described in the Results section.

RESULTS

The experimental data allowed us to measure the system with different parameters and uncover its strengths and limits under various configurations. A re-authentication system needs to accurately decide the identity of a test subject within a short time frame. The configuration which best satisfies that need should be selected for use in the application.

In our study there was significant performance degradation for classifiers trained on images collected on day one but tested on images from another day. These two sets of images were also collected in different lighting conditions and more importantly with different cameras and resolutions. All of these factors introduce variation that is not captured by the training set. The difficulty of performing authentication increases as time passes between training and testing. We present these results to illustrate the need of a biometric hand-off strategy. The ability to learn the user's appearance at the beginning of each log-on session allows continuous face verification to operate at accuracy levels that would not otherwise be possible in a real time system (Figure 6).

As shown in Figure 7, the verification rate taken at 10% false accept rate (FAR) for the MACE filter trained on data collected between one day and two weeks before testing is less than 50%. This is significantly worse performance than that achieved by using the proposed hand-off strategy as will be shown later on.

The eigenvalues of the covariance matrix represent the variance of the data captured by each eigenvector. In the case of faces, it is common for the first few eigenvectors to explain most of the

Figure 6. The cropped faces on the top row were collected more than twenty-four hours after the images from the bottom row under different lighting conditions

Figure 7. ROC curve for MACE and IPCA where the classifiers were trained on face data collected between one day to two weeks before testing

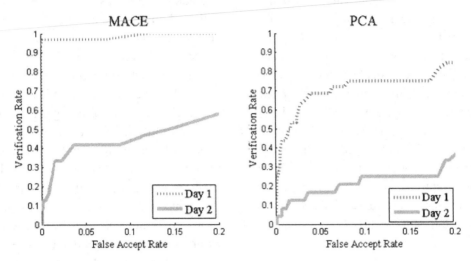

variation in the data while the last eigenvectors are dominated by noise. In theory, the verification rate might be improved by dropping the last few eigenvectors. We tried keeping eigenvectors cor-

responding to 90%, 95%, 99% and 100% of the variation in the data. The resulting ROC curves, shown in Figure 8, show that there was little difference between the four methods.

Figure 8. ROC curve showing verification rate versus false-accept rate for GPCA using different eigenvectors to capture a range of variation in the training data. Note that there is little difference between the four curves.

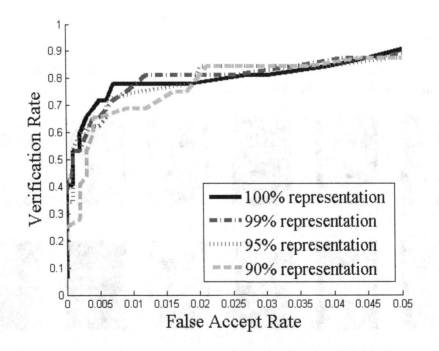

Each of the five classifiers, except SVMs, gives some kind of similarity score. Since each test consists of eighty frames we have eighty similarity scores. These scores must somehow be fused together and then thresholded to decide whether or not a given test matches the training data. There are a variety of ways to combine multiple classifier scores. Common methods are sum, min and median (Duin & Tax, 2000). A general method of combining the eighty scores is to produce a sorted list and sample it at regular intervals to determine the optimal sampling point. For instance, taking the first value from the list is equivalent to finding the minimum of the eighty values. Classifiers where outliers are more common will do better by taking values farther down the list. This way, an impostor who happens to closely match the testing data on just a few frames will still be rejected. The accuracy of the SVM classifier, in particular, benefited from this method. For IPCA, which produced fewer outliers, the opposite was true (Figure 9).

Although our demo system does not work this way, an alternative configuration is to immediately grant access to any user as soon as he returns to the workstation and then block access as soon as it has enough data to make an informed decision. In this case, it is desirable to come to a conclusion quickly. We evaluated performance degradation due to a smaller decision window. As shown in the Figure 10, longer decision windows allow for improved accuracy but the difference is not large.

The five classifiers that we tested were GPCA, IPCA, FLDA, MACE, and SVM. At 1% false-accept rate, all of the classifiers (GPCA excluded) had a verification rate in excess of 75%.

The MACE filter classifier gave the highest verification rate at all false-accept rates. As shown in Figure 11, it was the only classifier that performed well at a 0.1% FAR where its true verification rate was 97%. At this setting only one in a thousand intruders would be able to gain access to the system while the legitimate user would only be negatively impacted less than 3% of the time. Our sample size was not large enough to measure accuracy rate at false accept rates lower than 0.1%. This result illustrates the strength of the biometric hand-off strategy especially when contrasted with the data from Figure 7 which did not employ this strategy. IPCA is the most computationally efficient algorithm among the candidates as it only uses images from that one subject.

Figure 9. ROC curve of the SVM and IPCA classifier sampled at the min, 5th, 15th and 25th frames

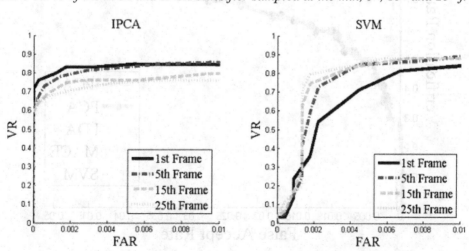

Figure 10. ROC curve for IPCA with different sized decision windows. Note that there is not a significant difference.

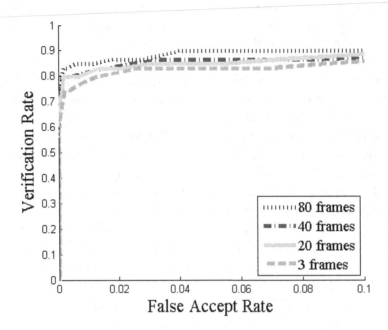

Figure 11. ROC curves from the five different classifiers used in our study

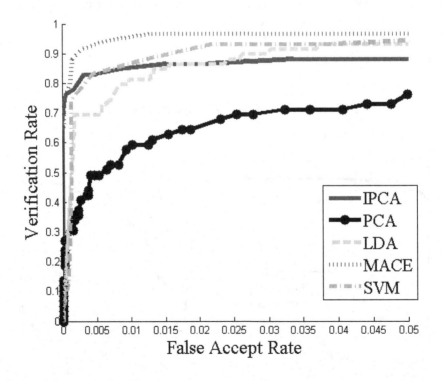

CONCLUSION

Continuous authentication solves a critical security loophole preventing intruders from hijacking or tailgating an authorized user's session. Our system combines multiple biometric modalities (iris and face) to unobtrusively and robustly protect sensitive data or other secure resources. Iris recognition is the first authentication biometric; it is quick, reliable and difficult to spoof. Face recognition is unobtrusive and is easily implemented in a continuous authentication system. In addition, facial images are easily captured from an off-the-shelf USB web-cam or built-in laptop camera. Our proposed biometric hand-off strategy combines the strengths of each modality to form a robust access control system that continually ensures the presence of a user at the terminal.

As our results show, matching performance degrades to less than half the accuracy when more than one day has expired since the training data collection. This is one reason why face recognition is normally such a challenging problem. In our system, the user is initially authenticated with iris, the face recognition component can retrain each time the user starts a new session thereby learning the current appearance of the user. This flexibility keeps the system secure to daily changes in appearance. This specific operating mode for continuous authentication achieved 97% verification rate with less than 3% false accepts using the MACE filter. The IPCA classifier gave 84% verification rate also with less than 3% false accepts. In addition, the IPCA classifier benefits from low computational and memory overhead. This allows the application to run as a background process on the same processor without interfering with the user's work. For these reasons, we expect IPCA to be a popular solution for continuous authentication applications.

ACKNOWLEDGMENT

We would like to extend our appreciation to Raytheon NCS (Dan Teijido and Jon Goding) and Raytheon IIS (Guy Swope and Charlie Li) for their collaborative effort to fund this research as well as the Raytheon Advanced Virtual Environment (RAVE) team for their innovative thinking. This research was also supported by CyLab at Carnegie Mellon under grants DAAD19-02-1-0389 and W911NF-09-1-0273 from the Army Research Office.

REFERENCES

Belhumeur, P. N., Hespanha, J. P., & Kreigman, D. J. (1997, July). Eigenfaces vs. Fisherfaces: Recognition using class specific linear projection. *IEEE Transactions on Pattern Analysis and Machine Intelligence*, *19*(7), 711–720. doi:10.1109/34.598228

Boswer, B. E., Guyon, I. M., & Vapnik, V. N. (1992). *A training algorithm for optimal margin classifiers*. 5th Annual Workshop on Computational Learning Theory (pp. 144-152).

Bowyer, K. W., Hollingsworth, K., & Flynn, P. J. (2008). Image understanding for iris biometrics: A survey. *Computer Vision and Understanding*, *110*, 281–307. doi:10.1016/j.cviu.2007.08.005

Camus, T. A., & Wildes, R. P. (2002). *Reliable and fast eye finding in close-up images*. In International Conference on Pattern Recognition (pp. 389-394).

Carrillo, C. (2003). *Continuous biometric authentication for authorized aircraft personnel: A proposed design*. Master's thesis, Naval Postgraduate School.

Daugman, J. (2004). How iris recognition works. *IEEE Transactions on Circuits and Systems for Video Technology*, *14*(1), 21–30. doi:10.1109/TCSVT.2003.818350

Duin, R. P. W., & Tax, D. M. J. (2000). Experiments with classifier combining rules. *Proc. First Workshop Multiple Classifier Systems,* (pp. 16-29).

Fisher, R. A. (1936). The use of multiple measures in taxonomic problems. *Annals of Eugenics, 7,* 179–188. doi:10.1111/j.1469-1809.1936. tb02137.x

Freund, Y., & Schapire, R. E. (1995). A decision-theoretic generalization of online learning and an application to boosting.

Joachims, T. (1999). Making largescale SVM learning practical. In Scholkopf, B., Burges, C. J. C., & Smola, A. J. (Eds.), *Advances in kernel methods- Support vector learning.* MIT Press.

Klosterman, A. J., & Ganger, G. R. (2000, May). *Secure continuous biometric-Enhanced authentication.* (CMU-CS-00-134).

Kumar, S., Sim, T., Kanakiraman, R., & Zhang, S. (2005). Using continuous biometric verification to protect interactive login sessions. *Proceedings of the 21st Annual Computer Security Applications Conference* (ACSAC 2005).

Li, X. (2006, January). Modeling intra-class variation for non-ideal iris recognition. *Springer International Conference on Biometrics, LNCS 3832* (pp. 419-427).

Liu, X., Chen, T., & Vijaya Kumar, B. V. K. (2002, May). *on modeling variations for face authentication.* In *the Proceedings of the International Conference on Automatic Face and Gesture Recognition 2002,* (pp. 369-374).

Matey, J. R., Naroditsky, O., Hanna, K., Kolczynski, R., LoIacono, D. J., & Mangru, S. (2006). Iris on the move: Acquisition of images for iris recognition in less constrained environments. *Proceedings of the IEEE, 94*(11), 1936–1946. doi:10.1109/JPROC.2006.884091

Niinuma, K., Park, U., & Jain, A. K. (2010, December). Soft biometric traits for continuous user authentication. *IEEE Transactions on Information Forensics and Security, 5*(4), 771–780. doi:10.1109/TIFS.2010.2075927

Savvides, M., & Vijaya Kumar, B. V. K. (2003). Efficient design of advanced correlation filters for robust distortion-tolerant face recognition. *Proceedings IEEE Conference on Advanced Video and Signal Based Surveillance* (pp. 45-52).

Schneiderman, H., & Kanade, T. (2000). *A statistical method for 3D object detection applied to faces and cars* (pp. 746–751). Proc. Of IEEE Computer Vision and Pattern Recognition.

Sim, T., Zhang, S., Janakiraman, R., & Kumar, S. (2007, April). Continuous verification using multimodal biometrics. *IEEE Transactions on Pattern Analysis and Machine Intelligence, 29*(4). doi:10.1109/TPAMI.2007.1010

Sung, H., Lim, J., Park, J., & Li, Y. (2004). *Iris recognition using collarette boundary localization.* In International Conference on Pattern Recognition (pp. 857-860).

Turk, M. A., & Pentland, A. P. (1991, June). Face recognition using eigenfaces. *Proceedings of IEEE International Conference on Computer Vision and Pattern Recognition,* (pp. 589-591).

Umbaugh, S. E. (2005). *Computer imaging: Digital image analysis and processing* (pp. 239–245). CRC Press.

Vijaya Kumar, B. V. K., Mahalanobis, A., & Juday, R. D. (2005). *Correlation pattern recognition.* Cambridge University Press. doi:10.1017/CBO9780511541087

Vijaya Kumar, B. V. K., Savvides, M., Venkataramani, K., & Xie, C. (2002). *Spatial frequency domain image processing for biometric recognition.* International Conference on Image Processing (vol. 1, pp. 53-56).

Villani, M., Tappert, C., Ngo, G., Simone, J., St. Fort, H., & Cha, S. (2006). *Keystroke biometric recognition studies on long-text input under ideal and application-oriented conditions*. Computer Vision and Pattern Recognition Workshop, (p. 39).

Viola, P., & Jones, M. (2004). Robust real-time face detection. *International Journal of Computer Vision, 57*(2), 137–154. doi:10.1023/B:VISI.0000013087.49260.fb

Wildes, R., Asmuth, J. C., Hanna, K. J., Hsu, S. C., & Kolczynski, R. J. Matey, J. R., & McBride, S. E. (1996 and 1998). *Automated, non-invasive iris recognition system and method*. (U.S. Patent No. 5,572,596 and 5.751,836).

Yao, P., Li, J., Ye, X., Zhuang, Z., & Li, B. (2006, August). *Iris recognition algorithm using modified log-gabor filters*. In International Conference on Pattern Recognition, (pp. 461-464).

Yap, R. H. C., & Ramnath, R. (2008). *Physical access protection using continuous authentication*. IEEE.

ADDITIONAL READING

Abe, S. (2005). *Support Vector Machines for Pattern Classification. Springer Science + Business Media*. LLC.

Bishop, C. M. (2006). *Pattern Recognition and Machine Learning. Springer Science + Business Media*. LLC.

Bradski, G., & Kaehler, A. (2008), *Learning Open CV: Computer Vision with the OpenCV Library*. Sebastopol, CA, U.S.A, O'Reilly Media, Inc.

Campadelli, P., Lanzarotti, R., & Lipori, G. (2005), Face localization in color images with complex background. *Proc. IEEE International Workshop on Computer Architecture for Machine Perception*, (pp. 243-248).

Chellapa, R., Wilson, C. L., & Sirohey, S. (1995, May). Human and machine recognition of faces: a survey. *Proceedings of the IEEE, 83*(5), 705–741. doi:10.1109/5.381842

Chen, T., Hsu, Y. J., Liu, X., & Whang, W. (2002, September). Principal component analysis and its variants for biometrics. [Rochesters, NY, USA.]. *Proceedings of the IEEE International Conference on Image Processing, 2002*, I-61–I-64.

Daugman, J. (2003). *The importance of being random: statistical principle of iris recognition* (pp. 279–291). Pattern Recogntion.

Duda, R. O., & Hart, P. E. (1973). *Pattern Classification and Scene Analysis*. Wiley and Sons.

Duda, R. O., Hart, P. E., & Stork, D. G. (2001). *Pattern Classification (2nd)*. U.S.A: John Wiley and Sons.

Grudin, M. A. (2000). On internal representation in face recognition systems. *Pattern Recognition, 33*(7), 1161–1177. doi:10.1016/S0031-3203(99)00104-1

He, Y., Cui, J., Tan, T., & Wang, Y. (2006), Key techniques and methods for imaging iris in focus, *International Conference on Pattern Recognition*, (pp. 557-561).

Herbrich, R. (2002). *Learning Kernel Classifiers: Theory and Algorithms*. Massachusetts Institute of Technology.

Hester, C., & Casasent, D. (1980, June). Multi-variant technique for multiclass pattern recognition. *Applied Optics, Vo., 19*(11), 1758–1761. doi:10.1364/AO.19.001758

Kim, T., & Kittler, J. (2005). Locally linear discriminant analysis for multimodally distributed classes for face recognition. *IEEE Transactions on Pattern Analysis and Machine Intelligence, 27*(3), 318–327. doi:10.1109/TPAMI.2005.58

Li, M., & Yuan, B. (2004), A novel statistical linear discriminant analysis for image matrix: two-dimensional Fisherfaces. *7th International Conference on Signal Processing, 2004. Proceedings. ICSP '04.*

Li, Y., Savvides, M., & Vijaya Kumar, B. V. K. (2006, May), Illumination tolerant face recognition using a novel face from sketch synthesis approach and advanced correlation filters. *Proceedings of IEEE International Conference on Acoustics, Speech and Signal Processing,* (pp. II-357 – II-360), Toulouse (France), IEEE.

Liu, C., Collin, C., Burton, A., & Chaurdhuri, A. (1999). Lighting direction affects recognition of untextured faces in photographic positive and negative. *Vision Research, 39,* 4003–4009. doi:10.1016/S0042-6989(99)00109-1

Masek, L. (2003) Recognition of human iris patterns for biometric identification. Master's Thesis, University of Western Australia.

Phillips, P. J., Flynn, P. J., & Scruggs, T. Bowyer, K.W., Change, J., Hoffman, K., Marques, J., Min, J. & Worek, W. (2005, June), Overview of the face recognition grand challenge. *Proceedings of IEEE International Conference on Computer Vision and Pattern Recognition,* 2005, (pp. I-947 – I-954), Sand Diego CA (USA), IEEE.

Ratha, N., & Connell, J. Bolle, R.N. & Chikkerur, S. (2006, August), Cancelable biometrics: a case study in fingerprings. *Proceedings of IEEE International Conference on Pattern Recognition, 2006.* Pp. IV-370 – IV-373, Hong Kong (China), IEEE.

Savvides, M., Vijaya Kumar, B. V. K., & Khosla, P. K. (2004), Illumination tolerant face recognition using advanced correlation filters trained from a single image. *Presented at the Biometrics Consortium,* Crystal City, VA (USA).

Thornton, Jason, Savvides, Marios and Vijaya Kumar, B.V.K., (2007, September), An evaluation of iris pattern representations, *Biometrics: Theory, Applications, and Systems.*

Webb, A. (2002). *Statistical Pattern Recognition (2nd).* West Sussex, England: John Wiley & Sons. doi:10.1002/0470854774

Yang, J., Zhang, D., Frangi, A. F., & Yang, J. (2004, January). Two-dimensional PCA: a new approach to appearance-based face recognition and recognition. *IEEE Transactions on Pattern Analysis and Machine Intelligence, 25*(Issue 1), 131–137. doi:10.1109/TPAMI.2004.1261097

Yang, M., Kriegman, D., & Ahuja, N. (2002, January). Detecting faces in images: a survey. *IEEE Transactions on Pattern Analysis and Machine Intelligence, 24*(1), 34–58. doi:10.1109/34.982883

Ye, J., Janardan, R., and Li, Q. (2004),. Two-dimensional linear discriminant analysis. *Neural Information Processing Systems 2004.*

KEY TERMS AND DEFINITIONS

Access Control: Systems that grants access to selected individuals and control to which parts of the system they have access.

Biometrics: Physical traits and behaviors that uniquely identify and individual.

Continuous Authentication: The constant monitoring and verification of an individual who is using a system.

Face Detection: Detecting and extracting facial images within larger images.

Face Recognition: The use of facial images to identify an individual.

Hand-Off Strategy: A biometric system in which a strong biometric identifies a user and transfers control to another modality for continuous monitoring.

Iris Recognition: The use of biometric iris data to identify an individual.

Chapter 5
Low Level Multispectral Palmprint Image Fusion for Large Scale Biometrics Authentication

Dakshina Ranjan Kisku
Asansol Engineering College, India

Phalguni Gupta
Indian Institute of Technology Kanpur, India

Jamuna Kanta Sing
Jadavpur University, India

Massimo Tistarelli
University of Sassari, Italy

C. Jinsong Hwang
Texas State University, USA

ABSTRACT

Continuous biometric authentication is a process where the installed biometric systems continuously monitor and authenticate the users. Biometric system could be an exciting application to log in to computers and in a network system. However, due to malfunctioning in high-security zones, it is necessary to prevent those loopholes that often occur in security zones. It has been seen that when a user is logged in to such systems by authenticating to the biometric system installed, he/she often takes short breaks. In the meantime some imposter may attack the network or access to the computer system until the real user is logged out. Therefore, it is necessary to monitor the log in process of the system or network by continuous authentication of users. To accomplish this work we propose in this chapter a continuous biometric authentication system using low level fusion of multispectral palm images where the fusion

DOI: 10.4018/978-1-61350-129-0.ch005

is performed using wavelet transformation and decomposition. Fusion of palmprint instances is performed by wavelet transform and decomposition. To capture the palm characteristics, a fused image is convolved with Gabor wavelet transform. The Gabor wavelet feature representation reflects very high dimensional space. To reduce the high dimensionality, ant colony optimization algorithm is applied to select relevant, distinctive, and reduced feature set from Gabor responses. Finally, the reduced set of features is trained with support vector machines and accomplishes user recognition tasks. For evaluation, CASIA multispectral palmprint database is used. The experimental results reveal that the system is found to be robust and encouraging while variations of classifiers are used. Also a comparative study of the proposed system with a well-known method is presented.

INTRODUCTION

Computer and network systems which are placed in high security zones often need user interaction and authentication even in the case of log in multiple times to the systems. Knowledge-based and token-based systems are mostly available authentication systems which use passwords, PIN and smart cards information. However, as we are well aware, passwords and PIN can be shared, stolen and lost. The users often prefer to use loosely built passwords. Since the complex passwords are found to be difficult to remember. In case of smart cards information can be stolen, shared or lost. The main disadvantage of using the computer or network system is that it can authenticate people only at the initial phase of log-in process and the user is not re-authenticated until logging out of the system. This can exploit critical security threats when the user goes out for a short time during logged-in session. To overcome this problem continuous authentication can be a reliable process through which any system can be almost secured from attacking of imposters. A large number of systems have been studied on continuous biometric authentications in (Monrose & Rubin, 2000; Altinok & Turk, 2003; Sim, et. al., 2007; Azzini, et. al., 2008; Azzini & Marrara, 2008; Kang & Ju, 2006; Carrillo, 2003; Klosterman & Ganger, 2000). These systems use one or more biometric traits (e.g., fingerprint or face) for continuous authentication of users. However, like other conventional biometric traits multispectral palm images can be used for continuous authentication while multispectral images are fused to obtain a common authentication perspective.

There exists a large number of computational approaches in intra-modal fusion (Wong, et. al., 2007; Ross, et. al., 2006) at different levels of human recognition. However, both mono-modal biometric and intra-modal biometric systems face some challenges, such as lack of accurate image registration methods, template matching with loss of complementary information, association of redundant adaptive parameters (Ross, et. al., 2006). These factors explain the poor performance of the system. Intra-modal biometric image fusion can remove some of the limitations of uni-biometric systems (Jain, et. al., 2007) because the uni-modal biometric system usually compensates the inherent limitations of the secondary sources. Intra-modal systems have the following advantages (Sun, et. al., 2008; Hao, et. al., 2007) over uni-modal biometric systems.

- Combining the evidence obtained in different form from the same or different sources using an effective fusion scheme can significantly improve the overall accuracy of the biometric system.
- Intra-modal biometric can address the problem of non-universality which often occurs in uni-modal system.

- Intra-modal systems can provide certain degree of flexibility.
- Availability of multiple sources of information can reduce the redundancy in unimodal system.

Biometric image fusion at sensor level/low level (Kisku, et. al., 2009) refers to a process that fuses multispectral biometric images captured by identical or different biometric sensors. This fusion performed at low level produces a fused image in spatially enhanced form which contains richer, intrinsic and complementary information. Biometric verification systems seek considerable amount of improvement in reliability and accuracy.

Automatic authentication of users by their biometric characteristics is playing a major role in security. A biometric system recognizes the identity of a person with certain physiological/behavioral characteristics, such as fingerprints, face, iris, speech, hand geometry, etc. Recent advancement of biometric systems based on palmprint can be found in (Zhang, 2004; Zhang, et. al., 2003; Kong & Zhang, 2004; Zhang, & Zhang, 2004; Kong, et. al., 2003). The palmprint recognition system has many advantages over other biometric systems with respect to reliability, low cost and user friendliness. Palmprint is one of the most reliable means in personal identification because of its stability, user friendliness, acceptability and uniqueness (Zhang, 2004).

Palmprint image consists of wrinkles and creases along with three principal lines, namely, heart line, head line and life line (Zhang, 2004). These lines vary little over time and wrinkles are much thinner than the principal lines and much more irregular. Creases are detailed textures, like the ridges in a fingerprint, found all over the palmprints. They can only be captured using high resolution cameras. With the low-resolution palmprint image, the principal lines and thick wrinkles can be used for recognition.

Variations in different palmprint images of an individual can be combined to produce a fused palm image. Images from different imaging sensors have been fused using various techniques discussed in the literatures (Kisku, et. al., 2009; Sun, et. al., 2008; Hao, et. al., 2007). The necessity for fusion techniques increased with the inception of new image acquisition devices. By fusing images, it is possible to discern the useful information from the input images. However, biometric fusion using multiple palm images (Sun, et. al., 2008; Hao, et. al., 2007) at low level is expected to produce more accurate results than the systems that integrate information at later stages, namely, feature level, score level, etc (Ross, et. al., 2006). This is because of the availability of more relevant and precise raw information. Apart from integrating the contributive features to other levels of fusion, an image fusion scheme of a higher abstraction suppresses inconsistencies, artifacts and noise in the fused images.

Another problem often occurring in biometric applications is the selection of an appropriate set of feature (Dash & Liu, 1997) at feature extraction level. Feature selection is the most important step which can affect the performance of recognition system. It is often necessary to select an optimal set of features that reflects the relevancy among the features.

Figure 1. Multi-spectral sensor

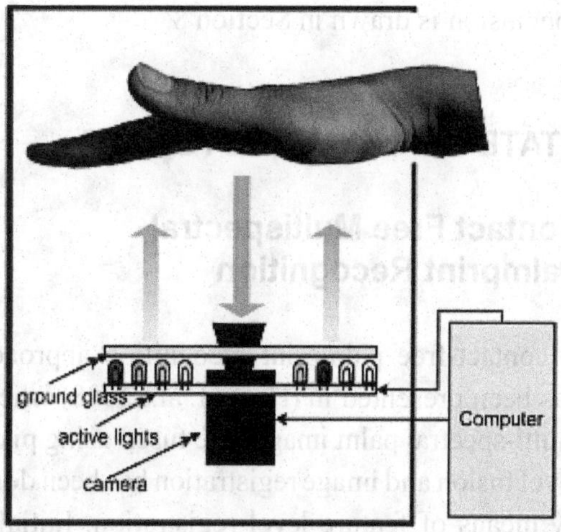

This chapter presents a novel palmprint verification method in which palm images are fused at low level by wavelet transform (Kisku et. al., 2009) and the fused palm is then represented by Gabor wavelet transform (Zhang et. al., 2003; Kong & Zhang, 2004; Zhang & Zhang, 2004) *to capture the palm characteristics in terms of neighborhood pixel intensity changes. Gabor palm responses contain high dimensionality features and due to this high dimensionality ant* colony optimization (ACO) (Dorigo, et. al., 2006) is applied to select the optimal set of distinct features. Finally, support vector machines (SVMs) (Burges, 1998) are used to train the reduced feature sets of different individuals and verify the identity. Proposed palmprint system is evaluated with CASIA palmprint database (Sun, et. al., 2008; Hao, et. al., 2007) and the results are also compared with other existing methods to measure the effectiveness and robustness of the system.

The chapter is organized as follows. Section 2 presents some preliminaries used for the proposed system. Section 3 briefly describes the proposed model and wavelet-based palm image fusion scheme. Gabor wavelet representation of fused palm image is discussed in the next section. Feature selection using ant colony optimization algorithm is presented in Section 5. Classification method is discussed in Section 6. Experimental results and a comparative study with a well known method are presented in the next section. Finally, conclusion is drawn in Section 8.

STATE-OF-THE-ART SYSTEMS

Contact Free Multispectral Palmprint Recognition

A contact-free palmprint recognition approach has been presented in (Hao, et. al., 2008) where multi-spectral palm images are fused using pixel level fusion and image registration has been done by means of feature level registration. Initially preprocessing operation is used to locate region of interest (ROI) from each palm image and then feature level registration method has been adopted to align ROIs from different spectral images. Finally fusion of these multi-spectral is performed by pixel level fusion method.

The proposed approach system has the following steps.

- First a sequence of multi-spectral hand images is obtained by illuminating the hand with multiple active lights as shown in Figure 1.
- In the next step some preprocessing operations are performed to obtain the coarse localization of ROI in palm image. The localization of ROI is shown in Figure 2.
- The localization results in each sequence of images are then further refined through feature level registration.
- Finally, fusion of refined images is done and verification is performed for performance evaluation.

Multispectral Palmprint Recognition Using Feature Band Selection

Feature band selection based multispectral palmprint recognition has been proposed in (Guo, et. al.,

Figure 2. Localization of palm image

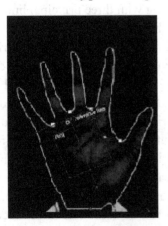

Figure 3. Hyperspectral palm cube

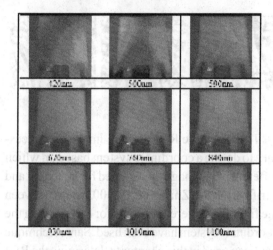

2010) where the statistical feature is extracted and compared for each single band. In the next level score level fusion is performed to determine the best combination from all candidates. The most discriminative information of palmprint images can be obtained from two special bands. ROI is determined from hyperspectral palm cube using local coordinate system. Some sample hyperspectral palm cubes are shown in Figure 3.

Whole-Hand Based Multispectral Palmprint Recognition

In this work (Rowe, et. al., 2007), multispectral palmprint recognition has been presented where multiple information related to hand are used. Hand shape, fingerprints and palmprint modalities are used for recognition. This system shows good recognition accuracy on a medium size database while fusion is performed with multiple fingers and fusion of finger and palm. The system has the following steps.

- In the first step, some preprocessing operations exploit on the whole hand. The whole-hand MSI data converts the raw Bayer data into a gray scale image using the average of Bayer pattern. Nest step in-

volves the operation which segments the image into foreground and background information to identify shape and region of a hand. Finally the points with maximum curvature are identified as fingertips. In Figure 4, segmentation of original palm image is shown and the Figure 5 shows fingertips localization.

- Skin feature extraction is performed in the next step where metacarpal skin feature is extracted from MSI data.

- Finally matching is done for performance evaluation.

- For palmprint matching preprocessing steps involve enhancing the palm image and binarizing the enhanced palm image. After that anchor points are detected from palm image using two major steps: (i)

Figure 4. Segmentation of an original palm image

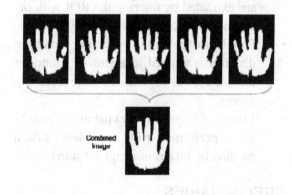

Figure 5. Fingertips localization

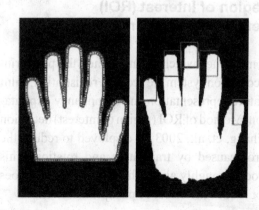

Figure 6. ROI region extraction

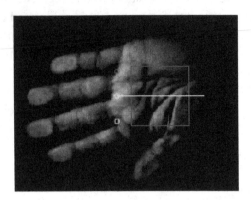

Figure 7. Ordinal feature extraction

first the alignment of hand images is performed. Later the origin of the coordinate system of anchor points is determined. (ii) ROI is extracted which lies on the horizontal line passing through the midpoint of each band image. Figure 6 shows ROI region extraction.

- After initial preprocessing, ordinal features are extracted by filtering the ROI with orthogonal line ordinal filter (see Figure 7).
- Finally for palmprint matching hamming distance is applied to a pair of palmprint feature vectors for obtaining the matching scores.
- Fusion of fingerprint and palmprint matchers is performed using score level fusion method by means of weighted sum rule.

PRELIMINARIES

Region of Interest (ROI) Detection from Palm Image

Some issues which often degrade the palmprint recognition system are accurate registration, palm feature representation and redundancy exploitation. Method of ROI (region of interest) detection (Zhang, et. al., 2003) is employed to reduce the error caused by translation and rotation. This process roughly aligns the palmprint and it does not reduce the effect of palmprint distortion.

To extract the ROI of palm image it is necessary to define a coordinate system based on which different palm images are aligned for matching and verification. In (Zhang, et. al., 2003) gaps between the fingers as reference points for determining the coordinate system have been used. Same technique has been used in this chapter to determine the ROI of the multispectral palm image. The following steps are followed to extract the central part of the palmprint image as ROI and further this ROI is used for multispectral fusion of palm images.

- Convert the multispectral palm image to a binary image. In order to do so, Gaussian smoothing has been used to enhance the image.
- Next step uses boundary tracking algorithm (Zhang, et. al., 2003) to obtain the boundaries of the gaps between the fingers. Since the ring and the middle fingers are not useful for processing, boundary of the gap between these two fingers is not extracted.
- By computing the tangent of the two gaps with any two points on these gaps, palmprint coordinate system is determined. The Y-axis is considered as the line joining these two points. To determine the origin of the coordinate system, midpoint of these two points are taken through which a line is passing and the line is perpendicular to the Y-axis.
- Finally, based on the palmprint coordinate system, central part of the palmprint image is extracted as ROI for feature extraction.

Figure 8 illustrates ROI palm image which is cropped from palmprint image. In practice, it has been seen that principal lines do not contribute adequately to high accuracy because of their similarity amongst different palms. Although wrinkles play an important role in palmprint authentication but accurately extracting them is still a difficult task. This problem motivates to apply texture analysis to palmprint authentication. In palmprint research, many texture based palmprint verification schemes (Zhang, et. al., 2003; Kong & Zhang, 2004; Zhang & Zhang, 2004; Kong, et. al., 2003) including Gabor filtering, wavelet, etc have been proposed.

Image Fusion Using Wavelet Decomposition

The image fusion extracts information from each source image and obtains the effective representation in the final fused image. The aim of image fusion technique is to process the fusing detailed information obtained from both source images.

By convention, multi-resolution images which are obtained from different sources are used for image fusion. Multi-resolution analysis of images provides useful information for several computer vision and image analysis applications. The multi-resolution image is used to represent the signals where decomposition is performed for obtaining finer detail. Multi-resolution image decomposition gives an approximation image and three other images viz., horizontal, vertical and diagonal images of coarse detail. The Multi-resolution techniques are mostly used for image fusion using wavelet transform and decomposition.

Prior to image fusion, wavelet transforms are determined from face and palmprint images. The wavelet transforms contain low-high bands, high-low bands and high-high bands of the face and palmprint images at different scales including the low-low bands of the images at coarse level. The low-low band has all the positive transform values and remaining bands have transform values which are fluctuating around zeros. Larger transform values in these bands respond to sharper brightness changes and thus respond to the changes of salient features in the image such as edges, lines, and boundaries. The proposed image fusion rule selects the larger absolute values of the two wavelet coefficients at each point. Therefore, a fused image is produced by performing an inverse wavelet transform based on integration of wavelet coefficients corresponding to the decomposed face and palmprint images.

More formally, wavelet transform decomposes an image recursively into several frequency levels and each level contains transform values. Let I be a gray-scale image, after wavelet decomposition the first level would be

$$I = I_{LL_1} + I_{LH_1} + I_{HL_1} + I_{HH_1} \qquad (1)$$

Figure 8. Detection of ROI and cropped palm image

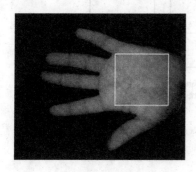

Generally, I_{LL_1} represents the base image which contains coarse detail of positive transform values and the other high frequency detail such as I_{LH_1}, I_{HL_1} and I_{HH_1} represent the vertical, horizontal and diagonal detail of transform values respectively and these details fluctuate transform values around zeros.

After n^{th} level decomposition of the base image in low frequency, the nth level would be the following:

$$I_{n-1} = I_{LL_n} + I_{LH_n} + I_{HL_n} + I_{HH_n} \qquad (2)$$

So the nth level decomposition consists of $3n+1$ sub-image sequences. These sub-image sequences are then fused by applying different wavelet fusion rules on the low and high frequency parts. Finally inverse wavelet transformation is performed to restore the fused image. For further illustration, the generic wavelet-based decomposition and image fusion approach is shown in Figure 9.

Gabor Wavelet Filters

Fundamentally, 2D Gabor filter (Zhang, et. al., 2003; Kong, & Zhang, 2004; Lee, 1996) can be defined as a linear filter whose impulse response function is the multiplication of harmonic function and Gaussian function in which Gaussian function is modulated by a complex sinusoid. Convolution theorem states that the Fourier transform of a Gabor filter's impulse response is the convolution of the Fourier transform of the harmonic function and the Fourier transform of the Gaussian function. Gabor function is a non-orthogonal wavelet and it can be specified by the frequency of the sinusoid $\omega = 2\pi f$ and the standard deviations of σ_x and σ_y.

The 2D Gabor wavelet Filter can be defined as

$$g(x, y : f, \theta) = \exp(-\frac{1}{2}(\frac{(m)^2}{\sigma_x^2} + \frac{(n)^2}{\sigma_y^2})\cos(2\pi f(m)))$$
$$m = x\sin\theta + y\cos\theta;$$
$$n = x\cos\theta - y\sin\theta;$$

$$(3)$$

where f is the frequency of the sinusoidal plane wave along the direction θ from the x-axis, σ_x and σ_y specify the Gaussian envelop along x-axis and along y-axis, respectively. This can be used to determine the bandwidth of the Gabor filter.

CASIA Multispectral Palm Database

The CASIA Multi-Spectral Palmprint database (Sun, et. al., 2008; Hao, et. al., 2007) contains 3,600 palm images which are acquired from 100 subjects. The palm images are captured by using multi-spectral sensors as shown in Figure 1 and in two different sessions for each hand and the images are set to 8 bit gray-level BMP files. In each session three different sets of images are captured and each set contains 6 palm images which are captured with 6 different electromagnetic spectrums. Between two sets, a certain degree of posture variations is allowed. All palm images are taken with uniformly distributed illumination and with uniform colored background.

Figure 9. Generic structure of wavelet based fusion approach

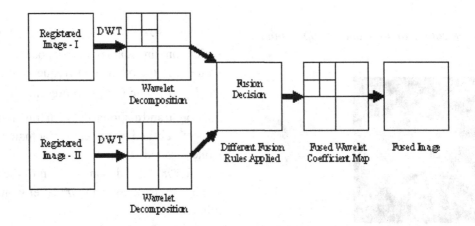

Multispectral Palm Image Fusion

The wavelet transform (Kisku, et. al., 2009) provides a multi-resolution decomposition of an image. In wavelet based palm image fusion, decomposition is done with high resolution palmprint images. Decomposition generates a set of low resolution images with wavelet coefficients for each level where the basis functions are generated from one single basis function known as the mother wavelet. The mother wavelet is shifted and scaled to obtain the basis functions. Then, it replaces a low resolution image with a multispectral (MS) band at the same spatial resolution level. Finally, a reverse wavelet transformation is performed to convert the decomposed and set to the original resolution level.

The operations of a wavelet fusion scheme are outlined in Figure 10. The input images are decomposed by a discrete wavelet transform and the wavelet coefficients are selected using a wavelet fusion rule (viz. 'maximum' rule) (Kisku, et. al., 2009) and an inverse discrete wavelet transform are performed to reconstruct the fused image. In this experiment Haar wavelet is used for extracting wavelet coefficients.

Gabor Responses of Fused Image

For the sake of experiment, 200 dpi gray scale fused palm image with the size of 40 × 40 has been used. Along with this, 40 spatial frequencies are used, with $f=\pi/2^i$, (I = 1,2,…,5) and $\theta=k\pi/8$, (k=1,2,…,8). For Gabor palm representation, fused palm image is convolved with the Gabor filter bank for capturing substantial amount of variations of palm images. Gabor filter bank with five frequencies and eight orientations are used for generation of 40 spatial frequencies and for Gabor palm extraction.

In order to compute the Gabor responses of a fused palm image, Gabor filter is convolved with the fused image. Let $f(x, y)$ be the intensity of the point (x, y) in a fused image, its convolution with Gabor filter $G(x, y: f, \theta)$ can be given as

$$GR(x,y: f,\theta)=f(x,y)\otimes G(x,y: f,\theta) \tag{4}$$

where $\otimes$ denotes the convolution operator. The response to each Gabor kernel representation is the complex function of real part and an imaginary part given as $\Re(GR(x,y: f,\theta))$ and $\Im(GR(x,y: f,\theta))$ respectively. The magnitude response is represented by

Figure 10. Framework for wavelet based palmprint image fusion technique (using 'Haar' wavelet)

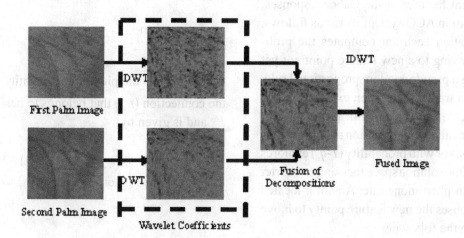

$$\|GR(x,y:f,\theta)\| = \sqrt{\Re^2(GR(x,y:f,\theta)) + \Im^2(GR(x,y:f,\theta))} \tag{5}$$

Here the magnitude responses are used as wavelet coefficient features. The variations in lighting conditions can be normalized by the output of the Gabor filter about each direction.

Feature Selection Using Ant Colony Optimization

One of the critical issues underlying instance-based learning is related to the improvement of features quality. Feature quality can be improved generally by two ways. One way is to select the relevant and distinct features, while another way is to assign weights to features. In this work, we follow the first approach and feature selection from high dimensional Gabor response space is accomplished with a swarm intelligence technique, namely, ant colony optimization (ACO) algorithm (Dorigo, et. al., 2006). The algorithm is inspired of ant's social behavior in their search for the shortest paths to food sources. In the proposed algorithm, classifier performance and the length of selected feature vector are adopted as heuristic information for ACO. So we can select the optimal feature subset without the prior knowledge of features.

Initially artificial ants are placed randomly on the coefficient features of the Gabor responses. The algorithm in ACO system works as follows. In each iteration each ant computes the probability of moving to a new feature point not yet visited using a pseudo-random proportional rule. This rule is a trade-off between exploration and exploitation. An ant either with probability q_0 exploits the available information about previous good solutions or with probability $(1-q_0)$ explores new areas of the solution space focusing on shorter distance with pheromone rate. An ant k located at node i chooses the new feature point j to move according to the following

$$j = \begin{cases} \arg \max_{l \in N_i^k}\{P_{il} H_{il}^\beta\} & \text{if } q \leq q_0 \\ S & \text{otherwise} \end{cases} \tag{6}$$

where P_{ij} is the pheromone trail on connection between feature point i and j, H_{ij} is the problem dependent heuristic, N_i^k is the set of remaining feature points yet to be visited by the ant k located at node I, β is a parameter that determines the relative importance of pheromone versus heuristic, q is a random variable distributed in [0, 1], q_0 is a parameter, $0 \leq q_0 \leq 1$ and S is a random variable selected according to the following probabilistic rule.

$$S = \begin{cases} \dfrac{P_{ij} H_{ij}^\beta}{\sum_{l \in N_i^k} P_{il} H_{il}^\beta} & \text{if } j \in N_i^k \\ 0 & \text{otherwise} \end{cases} \tag{7}$$

After all artificial ants have completed their tours, only the ant that finds the global best tour (so far best tour obtained from the beginning of the algorithm's execution) reinforces the pheromone trails on the distance belonging to its tour. The amount of deposited pheromone is inversely proportional to the length of the global best tour. This is called *global pheromone update* and is given by:

$$P_{ij} = (1-\sigma)P_{ij} + \sigma \Delta p_{ij}^{bs} \tag{8}$$

where ΔP_{ij}^{bs} is the pheromone quantity added to the connection (i, j) that belongs to best solution L^{bs} and is given by:

$$\Delta p_{ij}^{bs} = \begin{cases} 1 / L^{bs} & \text{if } (i, j) \text{ belongs to the best tour} \\ 0 & \text{otherwise} \end{cases} \tag{9}$$

where σ is the trail evaporation such that $(1-\sigma)$ represents the pheromone persistence. This parameter is used to avoid unlimited accumulation of pheromone trails and allows the algorithm to forget previously selected bad choices.

Updating of the global pheromone increases the probability for other ants to use the shorter distance having greater amount of pheromone trail and in turn increases the probability to build better solution. The pheromone evaporation mechanism is applied on only the edges that have been used by an ant. Every time an ant uses a distance, it decreases the pheromone intensity on this distance. This is called *local pheromone update* and is given by:

$$P_{ij}=(1-\gamma)P_{ij}+\gamma P_0 \qquad (10)$$

where γ is another pheromone evaporation parameter and P_0 is the initial pheromone value. Updating of the local pheromone encourages the exploration of new areas of the search space by reducing the importance of the visited edges while updating of the global pheromone encourages the exploitation of previously good solution by giving extra weight to the distance of global best solutions.

For classification, a subset of important features is selected. Suppose G is the original feature set of n features representing Gabor palm responses and S is the reduced set of features of m dimensions, (where $m < n$). In the process of searching a subset of features from Gabor responses, each ant randomly chooses a feature subset of m features. First the best k subsets ($k <$ number of ants) are used to update the pheromone trial and influence the feature subsets in the next iteration. In the subsequent iterations, each ant starts with $m - p$ features that are randomly chosen from the previously selected *k-best* subsets where p is an integer that ranges between 1 and $m - 1$. In this way, the features that constitute the best k subsets have more chance to be present in the subsets of the next iteration. However, it is still possible for

each ant to consider other features as well. For a given ant j, those features are the ones that achieve the best compromise between pheromone trails and local importance with respect to S_j where S_j is the subset that consists of the features already selected by ant j.

Classification Using Support Vector Machines

After applying ant colony optimization, a subset of features is obtained which achieves the best compromise between pheromone trails and local importance. For decision making, Support Vector Machines (SVMs) (Burges, 1998) are used. SVM is a statistical learning technique based on the principle of structural risk minimization. The aim is to minimize the upper bound on expected or actual risk which is defined as

$$R(\alpha) = \int \frac{1}{2}\left|z - f(x,\alpha)\right| dP(x,z) \qquad (11)$$

where α is a set of parameters which can be used to define a trained machine and z is a class label associated with a training sample x, $f(x, \alpha)$ is a function which can be used to map training sample to class labels and $P(x, z)$ is the unknown probability distribution associating a class label with each training sample. Let l denote the number of training samples and choose some η such that $0 \leq \eta \leq 1$. On expected risks with the probability $1 - \eta$, the following bound holds

$$R(\alpha) \leq R_{emp}(\alpha) + \sqrt{\frac{h(\log(2l / h) + 1) - \log(\eta / 4)}{l}} \qquad (12)$$

where h is a non-negative integer called Vapnik Charvonenkis (VC) dimension [14] and is a measure of the complexity of the given decision function. The term in R.H.S. is known as VC bound. Risk can be minimized by minimizing the empirical risk as well as VC dimension.

To separate a given training sample, an optimal hyperplane is chosen from a set of hyperplane. This optimal hyperplane minimizes the VC confidence that provides best generalization capabilities. The optimal hyperplane is used to minimize the sum of the distances to the closest positive and negative training samples. This sum is known as the *margin* of the separating hyperplane. It can be shown that the optimal hyperplane $w \cdot x + b = 0$ is obtained by minimizing $||w||^2$ subject to a set of constraints which is a quadratic optimization problem.

It is inspired to apply this for non-separable and non-linear case. The separability problem can be solved by adding a term to the expression subject to minimization. It is the sum of the deviations of the non-separable training samples from the boundary of the margin. To control the cost of misclassification, the sum is weighted. The problem of non-linear decision boundaries is solved by mapping the training samples to a high-dimensional feature space using kernel functions. In this high-dimensional space, the decision boundary is linear. For the proposed system, two kernel functions are used, namely, linear and radial basis functions (RBFs) defined as

$$K(x_i, x_j) = x_i \bullet x_j \tag{13}$$

$$K(x_i, x_j) = e^{-\gamma ||x_i - x_j||^2} \tag{14}$$

where x_i and x_j denote two training samples and γ is the user-controlling parameter in case of Radial Basis Function (RBF).

In addition to SVMs with kernel functions, the following classification rule is implemented as baseline for experiment.

$$d_C(x, \omega_k) = \frac{|x^T \omega_k|}{|x| |\omega_k|} \tag{15}$$

The normalized correlation (NC) measure is used as classification rule specified in Equation (15) and a claimed identity is accepted if the normalized correlation measure $d_C(x, \omega_k)$ exceeds a pre-specified threshold τ_{Ck}.

The pre-specified threshold is determined from Receiver Operating Characteristic (ROC) curves computed on an independent evaluation set which is compared with the training set. These curves are produced by generating false accept (FA) and false reject (FR) rates separately and each computed percentile denotes pre-specified threshold. Initially, these percentiles are computed by comparing training set with the evaluation set and finally these pre-specified thresholds are used for acceptance and rejection of candidates using normalized correlation measures.

Experimental Results

To conduct the experiments with the CASIA Multi-Spectral Palm Database, a unified framework is built with a simple protocol. In order to construct a protocol for experiment, the entire multi-spectral palm database is divided into three disjoint sets of palm images. First set contains training set of 1985 palm images while evaluation set contains 966 palm images and query set contains 649 palm images. The training set is used to build client models. The evaluation set is used to obtain the client and imposter scores for verification thresholds and the query set of palm images is used to obtain the verification rates.

Table 1 shows the verification performance of the proposed multi-spectral palm image fusion on CASIA database with two different classifiers, namely, normalized correlation and SVM. Further SVM classifier is used with two kernel functions viz. linear and RBF. Kernel parameter for RBF function is set to 0.015. On the other hand, linear kernel and normalized correlation are used without using kernel functions. Prior to Gabor wavelet coefficients extraction from a fused palm image, normalization of fused palm image is done with histogram equalization. Image enhancement using histogram equalization makes the intensity distribution uniform. This can compensate or suppress the noise level to a certain level with the most relevant data. This is a large amount of wavelet coefficients extracted from palm image. Ant Colony Optimization system is applied to obtain reduced set of transformed coefficients which reflect rich and distinctive features. SVM is then used for authentication of query palm samples by using evaluation set of palm images. Using evaluation set, Equal Error Rates (EER) and Total Errors (TE) are determined and further these error rates are used to compute the false accept (FA), false reject (FR) and total error (TE) rates for query set. Normalized correlation (NC) is found to be sensitive to coefficients. However, SVM classifier with linear and RBF kernels are found to be robust to wavelet coefficients as well as reduced set of features. When normalized correlation (NC) is used as classifier, false accept, false reject and total error rates obtained by using EER of evaluation set are 4.51%, 6.27% and 10.78% respectively. On the other hand, these error rates are found to be 3.09%, 5.11% and 8.2% respectively when SVM classifier is used with linear kernel function. Use of linear function with SVM classifier reduces total error by 2.58%. Best performance is achieved with RBF kernel function and it is found to reduce the total error to 4.53% and 1.95% when the performance of RBF

kernel is compared with normalized correlation and linear kernel function respectively. Thus

- SVM can be efficient one while it is applied to reduced set of features and even there exists little noise in the fused palm image.
- The combination of Gabor wavelet features and Ant Colony Optimization is found to be useful to extract the most relevant and distinctive coefficients.
- Wavelet decomposition is used to fuse multi-spectral palm print images to a fused one in which the initial raw characteristics are present with intensity distortions and illumination noises. However, these noises are minimized when Ant Colony Optimization system and SVM classifier are used.
- Classification through SVM with RBF kernel is found to be better than the classification through SVM with linear function and normalized correlation.

CONTINUOUS AUTHENTICATION FRAMEWORK

The proposed multispectral palm image fusion method can be used as a continuous biometric system that can provide meaningful authentication of users at any time when it requires. Multi-spectral palm images are obtained by illuminating the hand with multiple active lights. Therefore, it is necessary to place the multi-spectral sensor where a user can place his/her hand in front of active lights and

Table 1. Verification performance determined on the CASIA multi-spectral palm database

Classifier	Kernel Function	Kernel Parameter	Evaluation Set		Query Set		
			EER	TE	FA	FR	TE
NC	--------	--------	6.19%	12.38%	4.51%	6.27%	10.78%
SVM	Linear	--------	5.02%	10.04%	3.09%	5.11%	8.2%
	RBF	$\gamma = 0.015$	3.97%	7.94%	2.21%	4.04%	6.25%

a camera is used to capture the multispectral palm images. Further, these multiple illuminated palm images are fused for authentication. The proposed system will be important for high-security zones (border control) as well as low-security zones (home computing environment). Since it has been proved that single modality is not found to be very efficient while evidence not observed in static as well as continuous biometrics authentication. Therefore, multiple evidences are only way to improve the authentication performance in continuous authentication environment.

There exists a sharp difference (Sim, et. al., 2007) between conventional biometrics authentication and continuous biometrics authentication. Conventional authentication system authenticates people one-time prior to enter into some secured environment to access resources. It may be login to a computer system or it may be access to some resources kept in a secured environment. On the other hand, continuous authentication requires people to be authenticated every time whenever he or she tries to enter into the secured environment or access to a computer system. A framework for the proposed continuous authentication using multispectral palmprint image fusion has been shown in Figure 11.

A multispectral palmprint image capture device is placed beside a computer system into which the user will login and access the resources. Before login to the system user needs to place his palmprint on the multispectral palmprint device which then captures palmprint image under blue, green, red and near-Infrared illuminations. Finally the multispectral palmprint system authenticates the legitimate user. It is necessary to observe that whenever the user need to access the system the previous authentication records must be discounted and the current authentication record must be active till the user logoff to the system.

CONCLUSION

In this chapter, an efficient palmprint authentication system which is based on fusion of multi-spectral palm images has been presented for continuous authentication. It uses wavelet decomposition for palm image fusion, Gabor wavelets for coefficients extraction and Ant Colony Optimization system for selection of prominent features of optimized set. For authentication, SVM is used to classify query samples against training samples. Multi-spectral palm images are fused at low level by wavelet transform and decomposition where fused palm image is further represented by Gabor wavelet transform to capture the minimal intra-class diversity of the same instances and maximized the inter-class differences between the different subjects in terms of neighborhood pixel intensity changes. Gabor palm responses contain high dimensionality features and due to this high dimensionality, ant colony optimization (ACO) algorithm is applied to choose a set of distinct features. Finally two different classifiers are used, namely, normalized correlation and SVM with linear and RBF kernels. To measure the efficacy and robustness of the proposed system, CASIA multi-spectral palm database is used and the results are found to be encouraging.

Figure 11. Framework for multispectral palmprint fusion based continuous authentication (Guo, et. al., 2010)

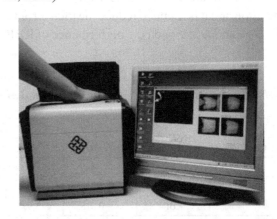

REFERENCES

Altinok, A., & Turk, M. (2003). Temporal integration for continuous multimodal biometrics. *Proc. Workshop on Multimodal User Authentication,* (pp. 131–137).

Azzini, A., & Marrara, S. (2008). Impostor users discovery using a multimodal biometric continuous authentication fuzzy system. *Lecture Notes In Artificial Intelligence, 5178,* 371–378.

Azzini, A., Marrara, S., Sassi, R., & Scotti, F. (2008). A fuzzy approach to multimodal biometric continuous authentication. *Fuzzy Optimization and Decision Making, 7,* 243–256. doi:10.1007/s10700-008-9034-1

Burges, C. J. C. (1998). A tutorial on support vector machines for pattern recognition. *Data Mining and Knowledge Discovery, 2*(2), 121–167. doi:10.1023/A:1009715923555

Carrillo, C. (2003). *Continuous biometric authentication for authorized aircraft personnel: A proposed design.* Master's thesis, Naval Postgraduate School.

Dash, M., & Liu, H. (1997). Feature selection for classification. *Intelligent Data Analysis, 1,* 131–156. doi:10.1016/S1088-467X(97)00008-5

Dorigo, M., Gambardella, L. M., Birattari, M., Martinoli, A., Poli, R., & Stützle, T. (2006). *Ant colony optimization and swarm intelligence.* 5th International Workshop ANTS, LNCS 4150, Springer Verlag.

Guo, Z., Zhang, L., & Zhang, D. (2010). *Feature band selection for multispectral palmprint recognition.* International Conference on Pattern Recognition (pp. 1–4).

Hao, Y., Sun, Z., & Tan, T. (2007). Comparative studies on multispectral palm image fusion for biometrics. *Asian Conference on Computer Vision, 2,* (pp. 12–21).

Hao, Y., Sun, Z., Tan, T., & Ren, C. (2008). *Multi spectral palm image fusion for accurate contact free palmprint recognition.* 15th International Conference on Image Processing, (pp. 281–284).

Jain, A. K., Flynn, P., & Ross, A. (2007). *Handbook of biometrics.* Springer-Verlag.

Kang, H.-B., & Ju, M.-H. (2006). Multi-modal feature integration for secure authentication. *Proc. International Conference on Intelligent Computing* (pp. 1191–1200).

Kisku, D. R., Sing, J. K., Tistarelli, M., & Gupta, P. (2009). *Multisensor biometric evidence fusion for person authentication using wavelet decomposition and monotonic-decreasing graph.* 7th IEEE International Conference on Advances in Pattern Recognition, (pp. 205—208).

Klosterman, A., & Ganger, G. (2000). *Secure continuous biometric-enhanced authentication.* Technical Report CMU-CS-00-134, Carnegie Mellon University.

Kong, A., & Zhang, D. (2004). *Competitive coding scheme for palmprint verification.* International Conference on Pattern Recognition, 1, (pp. 520 – 523).

Kong, W. K., Zhang, D., & Li, W. (2003). Palmprint feature extraction using 2-D Gabor filters. *Pattern Recognition, 36,* 2339–2347. doi:10.1016/S0031-3203(03)00121-3

Lee, T. S. (1996). Image representation using 2D Gabor wavelets. *IEEE Transactions on Pattern Analysis and Machine Intelligence, 18,* 959–971. doi:10.1109/34.541406

Monrose, F., & Rubin, A. D. (2000). Keystroke dynamics as biometrics for authentication. *Future Generation Computer Systems, 16,* 351–359. doi:10.1016/S0167-739X(99)00059-X

Ross, A. K., Nandakumar, K., & Jain, A. K. (2006). *Handbook of multibiometrics.* Springer Verlag.

Rowe, R. K., Uludag, U., Demirkus, M., Parthasaradhi, S., & Jain, A. (2007). A multispectral whole-hand biometric authentication system. IEEE Biometrics Symposium (pp. 1 – 6).

Sim, T., Zhang, S., Janakiraman, R., & Kumar, S. (2007). Continuous verification using multimodal biometrics. *IEEE Transactions on Pattern Analysis and Machine Intelligence*, *29*(4), 687–700. doi:10.1109/TPAMI.2007.1010

Sun, Y. H. Z., Tan, T., & Ren, C. (2008). *Multispectral palm image fusion for accurate contact-free palmprint recognition*. IEEE International Conference on Image Processing, (pp. 281-284).

Wong, Y. W., Seng, K. P., Ang, L.-M., Khor, W. Y., & Liau, F. (2007). *Audio-visual recognition system with intra-modal fusion*. International Conference on Computational Intelligence and Security, (pp. 609 – 613)

Zhang, D. (2004). *Palmprint authentication*. Kluwer Academic Publishers.

Zhang, D., Kong, W. K., You, J., & Wong, M. (2003). On-ine palmprint identification. *IEEE Transactions on Pattern Analysis and Machine Intelligence*, *25*, 1041–1050. doi:10.1109/TPAMI.2003.1227981

Zhang, L., & Zhang, D. (2004). Characterization of palmprints by wavelet signatures via directional context modeling. *IEEE Transactions on SMC-B*, *34*, 1335–1347.

Chapter 6
Cognitive Biometrics:
A Novel Approach to Continuous Person Authentication

Kenneth Revett
British University in Egypt, Egypt

ABSTRACT

Cognitive biometrics is a new authentication scheme that utilises the cognitive, emotional, and conative state of an individual as the basis of user authentication and/or identification. These states of mind (and their derivatives) are extracted by recording various biosignals such as the EEG, ECG, and electrodermal response (EDR) of the individual in response to the presentation of the authentication stimulus. Stimuli are selected which elicit characteristic changes within the acquired biosignal(s) that represent unique responses from the individual. These characteristic changes are processed using a variety of machine learning algorithms, resulting in a unique signature that identifies or authenticates the individual. This approach can be applied in both static mode (single point of authentication), or in continuous mode, either alone, or in a multi-modal approach. The data suggest that the classification accuracy can reach 100% in many scenarios, providing support for the efficacy of this new approach to both static and continuous biometrics.

INTRODUCTION

Cognitive biometrics is a novel approach to user authentication and/or identification that utilises the response(s) of nervous tissue. The approach relies on the presentation of one or more stimuli, and the subsequent response(s) are acquired and used for authentication – a typical stimulus-response paradigm. The stimulus could be the presentation of a familiar photograph, song, or a Rorschach ink blot, either singly or in various combinations.

DOI: 10.4018/978-1-61350-129-0.ch006

This feature alone clearly distinguishes cognitive biometrics from traditional physiological biometrics, which relies on acquiring a fixed input-output relationship (i.e. a fingerprint).

The approach deployed by cognitive biometrics is to extract a unique signature from the user – but one based not on a constant physiological trait such as their iris or retina – but rather on the cognitive, affective, and conative state of the individual – either alone or more typically in various combinations. The motivation for this approach is to provide a more intuitive, potentially more robust and user-friendly authentication protocol that is also cost effective for both static and continuous authentication requirements. In addition, the cognitive approach can be combined with physiological approaches such as keystroke/mouse dynamics for example, augmenting the feature space and providing a truly multi-modal approach. Moreover, the authentication modality (visual, auditory, olfactory, or any combination) can provide a significant range of possible inputs that can be deployed for authentication purposes. For instance, a user can be authenticated while playing a game for a short interval as opposed to entering their user ID and password. Likewise, in a continuous authentication scheme, users can periodically be monitored, with or without their knowledge – simply by examining their responses to particular sets of stimuli at any point in time. The stimulus presented to the user is typically in video and/or auditory format – which can be provided by any standard mobile phone, notebook, or desktop computing device. What is required is the production of the stimulus and a way to record the response – this can be accomplished through a software only mechanism in some cases, or typically through a biosignal collection device (as discussed in detail in later sections). In addition, this approach may be considered to be less offensive to the user community relative to iris or retinal scanners – user acceptability and obtrusiveness is a critical design issue when developing a biometric.

Cognitive biometrics must in a sense compete against more traditional forms of biometrics, such as anatomical and even more recently, behavioural (physiological) approaches. Anatomical biometrics, such as fingerprint or iris scans have been deployed for over several decades, yielding very low classification errors (on the order 10^9). Typically, anatomical biometrics is deployed in a static fashion, providing a single access protection protocol. The continued deployment of a retinal scan for instance may be perceived as too invasive. The issues of usability, user perception, cost, and convenience are probably the limiting factors to their widespread distribution. Behavioural and physiological biometrics have provided a lightweight alternative in terms of the required hardware and user perception/convenience issues. Signature verification, gait analysis and keystroke dynamics provide a very acceptable mechanism for extracting authenticity information from an individual that is steeped in a long standing tradition (e.g., signature verification). In terms of deployment, keystroke dynamics could be deployed in both a static and continuous fashion, acquiring samples from the user during their interaction with a word processor, would be a very natural approach. The issue with respect to the widespread deployment of behavioural biometrics is probably based on the perception that the approach is not 'high-tech' enough. In part, it is human nature to believe that if something is going to work, it must be constructed from 'solid' materials – 'medicine must taste bad to be good' mentality. Research has demonstrated that the approach is sound, producing classification accuracies (sometimes reported as the equal error rates) approaching 95+% in many cases (Revett, 2009a, Revett 2009b, Nixon & Carter, 2004, Jain et al., 2002). The potential difficulty with behavioural biometrics is the inability of humans to perform repetitive motoric tasks in a reliable fashion. Our signatures are never the same: our typing cadence can vary based on mood or the input device type (e.g. laptop versus a desktop keyboard) (see Revett, 2008) for a comprehensive survey of this approach).

Cognitive biometrics has the daunting task of providing evidence to the relevant community at large that it is a viable alternative to anatomical (and behavioural biometrics). It must be demonstrated that it provides robust classification accuracies (exceeding 95%), without expensive and costly hardware, and must be readily accepted by the user community. In addition, the approach must be deployable in both a static and continuous fashion for maximal utility. The balance of this chapter will provide the reader with evidence supporting all of these claims – that the cognitive approach to user authentication is a viable approach.

COGNITIVE BIOMETRICS

Cognitive biometrics is a new type of biometric paradigm that utilises the responses of the individual to particular sensory stimuli as the basis of the authentication process. Note that cognitive biometrics is completely distinct from behavioural biometrics. The primary difference is behavioural biometrics such as keystroke dynamics, signature, and gait rely on the precise reproduction of motoric activities – which are only peripherally related (or potentially modulated at best) to cognitive state. Furthermore, the purpose of cognitive biometrics is to utilise an individual's response to a given stimulus (or set of stimuli) – which will invoke a response (typically non motoric). It is the response of the person in relation to the applied stimulus that forms the basis of the authentication task. How a person responds to a stimulus is very complex: typically there is a genetic basis, modulated by our experiential history which can significantly shape our behaviour.

Cognition

It is assumed that genetic variability is large – and experiential backgrounds are extremely varied – their combination will provide a very large number of possible states that can be used as a means of person authentication. Behaviour can be considered as a complex interaction between cognition, affect, and conation. Cognition involves conscious activity and forms the basis of our intellectual capacities – such as reasoning, memory, and inferential abilities. Affect is a term used to reflect the emotional state of an individual – the mood. Conation refers to drives, desires, and motivations for action. In very basic terms, all three aspects of behaviour entail the deployment of the central nervous system – and to some extent the peripheral nervous system. For example, viewing a familiar photograph generally will elicit memories of the associated context, with concomitant changes in the affective state of the individual. The responses generated by this stimulus presentation are not fixed though – the response will be modulated by past (and more recent) experience, the current state of the individual, and the context in which the stimulus was presented. One would therefore not expect that *all* of the responses to the stimulus will be identical across multiple presentations. The task in this scenario is to identify and hence extract salient features that persist across multiple stimulus presentations. Certainly, the photograph is not expected to elicit the same response from another individual – the question is how will the responses differ? If we keep the stimulus presentation scenario constant, then the differences in the response – if they indeed are different – must be related to either the current state and/or their experiential histories. Whether these two aspects actually need to be resolved is an open question. It is difficult to control for the current state of an individual – this depends on their cognitive, affective, and conative feature set at the moment of authentication. For now, this issue will remain an open question – to be discussed somewhat more thoroughly in a later section. The question now at hand is how do we measure the differential responses from individuals? That is, how do we obtain the response of an individual to a particular stimulus? In the approaches described here, the responses are acquired through biosignal measurements. The biosginals that have proposed and utilised in biometrics include the electroencephalogram (EEG), the electrocardiogram (ECG), and the electrodermal response (EDR). They are recordable from the body surface and provide information in real-time about the cognitive, emotional, and conative state of an individual. The central task of the cognitive biometrics approach is to deduce the relationship between the recorded biosignals and the brain states from whence they were generated.

Users could be asked to respond verbally to the stimulus – which could be recorded and analysed. The analysis could occur on several levels – at the speech recognition level and/or at the semantic level. Clearly speech recognition is a mature science, with a fairly high level of classification accuracy (typically 80%). Analysing the data at the semantic level is slightly more complicated – but again there is a large literature on natural language processing that could be invoked for this process. If we decide not to utilise natural language responses, what features do we have available to us? The question really boils down to the cardinality of the feature space available to us when we observe a particular stimulus? Not to be undone by the notion of qualia – we seek to engage various physiological changes that are both consciously and subconsciously produced when presented with a response invoking stimulus. The stimulus could be a game, a song, a puzzle, a photograph as simple examples. The question is does these stimuli produce changes that are recordable at the physiological level – and if so, what faculties do these changes involve.

Returning back to our cognitive triumvirate, we have cognition, affect, and conation available to us. How can we ascertain the states of these

aspects of behaviour without utilising natural language? Cognition is a very broad term encompassing a bewildering array of activities such as memory capacities, planning strategies, reasoning capacities, etc. This array of features is simply too large to examine exhaustively in real-time, so we must limit the search space (unlike behavioural biometrics!). Further, the authentication process is generally performed as a solitary event – so the features must be acquired without human intervention. Further still, we now know that the mind is responsible for cognition, and that the mind is actually in the head – so that is the place to start searching for features. One automated method for extracting information about brain states is by recording the electroencephalogram (EEG). The EEG is a real-time recording of the electrical potentials that are produced as a result of the firing of concurrently active and spatially organised neurons. In order to record the EEG, electrodes must be placed on the scalp surface, and the resulting electrical potentials are measured and stored on a computer system for automated analysis. The question becomes how is the EEG related to cognition – that is what does the EEG tell us about brain function – the main question driving the field of cognitive electrophysiology. More details on the deployment of EEG in the context of biometrics will be presented later in the case studies section. At the moment, it should be noted that the EEG is a common tool that is used to acquire information about cognition within certain constrained contexts.

Affect

Can we gather information concerning the affective state of an individual under the constraints of a real-time biometric facility? Again, we must rely on the deployment of an automated mechanism that can acquire features and store them for subsequent analysis (both on-line and off-line if required). There are several proposed mechanisms for extracting physiological information regarding the affective/emotional state of an individual, of which this chapter will focus on two: the electro-cardiogram (ECG) and the epidermal response (EDR). The basic premise behind this approach is that changes in emotional state produce physiological changes that yield measurable changes in either cardiovascular function or skin conductance properties. Please note that no assumption is made here about the mechanism of emotion production. All that is assumed is that there is a correlation between an emotional state(s) and a recordable signal from one or both of these devices (EEG/EDR). The feature space of emotional state is potentially large – depending on the taxonomy one chooses to utilise. In some instances, a basic set of affective states are assumed and all other emotions are derivable from this base set. Emotions tend to be manifest in a more stereotyped fashion in contrast to the electrophysiological activity of the brain. Also note that the time scale for emotion is highly variable – they can last for seconds (a fear response) to years (love). The stimulus that is presented to the individual should elicit an acute emotional response. We do not want to permanently alter the individual's affective state – otherwise this may alter subsequent authentication attempts at the very least! The fundamental question is how affective states manifest themselves in terms of alterations in cardiovascular physiology and skin conductance properties? This important question will be addressed empirically in the case studies section.

Conation

The conative state of an individual is probably the most difficult to acquire – as the notion of drive and motivation is typically of variable duration and a more 'cerebral' attribute. The research into this aspect of human behaviour is rather limited – virtually non-existent in the biometrics literature. The difficulty amounts to identifying how changes in conative states maps onto physiologically measurable changes. The psychology literature presents

several possible approaches to addressing drive and motivation – which may result from peripheral stimulation through emotional state alterations, producing measurable physiological changes. For instance, the fight-or-flight response, which results in the immediate sense of fear, will most certainly enhance the level of arousal, which in turn may yield an immediate effect on the conative state of the individual. Clearly, there will be changes associated with heart rate, respiration, and skin conductance which could be measured quite accurately. The issue with respect to biometrics is creating the stimulus necessary to produce a given conative response that is robust in terms of the reliability and the individuality of the states produced. The fight-or-flight scenario is possibly too limiting a stimulus, yielding a reproducible and potentially very stereotypical response. What are sought are stimuli which yield more subtle changes that may transcend reflexive responses. These stimuli may reveal subtle changes that reflect the genetic make-up and experiential history. One could envision a goal seeking task, such as solving a puzzle that would tend to focus and elicit a particular conative state. In the context of biometrics, one would like to produce a stimulus-response result that is unique as possible. Integration of conative states and emotional states may provide a more robust and richer set of states that could enhance the individuality of the response. This is an open and interesting area for further research, and will be discussed at a later time.

Thus far, the groundwork for a working definition of cognitive biometrics has been presented – with an emphasis on the nature of the source of measurable features and the available technology to record the responses. Essentially, a rational basis for designating the input-output relationships has been proposed. The inputs must be carefully designed to elicit a response that is measurable using typical recording methodologies such as the EEG and ECG. One should note that almost by definition, cognitive biometrics relaxes the constraint that the input-output function is one-to-one. Unlike fingerprints or iris scans, the stimulus presented during a cognitive approach does not have to be unique – any number of photographs may elicit the same response. Likewise, the same photograph may elicit different responses at different times. This relaxation of the input-output response is clearly not typical in the biometrics domain – though it may help to overcome some of the inherent difficulties associated with biometrics generally. The focus in most biometric research programmes has been to extract a unique and specific feature from an individual that is invariant over time – which is then utilised for the discrimination task inherent to biometric authentication. This is why fingerprints and iris scanners (the mainstay of physiological biometrics) are popular – they are based on the general understanding that these features are absolutely unique. In terms of behavioural biometrics – the issue of reproducibility and constancy is central to the success of the authentication mechanism. There is an explicit understanding that we cannot reproduce our signature exactly every time. The principle reason for this requirement is the lack of a robust feature space – the number of degrees of freedom is small relative to the inherent variance in the population. To compensate, thresholds for acceptance and rejection are narrowly construed, resulting in the typical FAR/FRR trade off. That is, when computing the equal error rate (EER), which is computed by plotting FAR against FRR, for a parametised stringency variable, one invariably finds that when FAR is reduced, FRR increases and vice versa. The approach adopted in typical biometrics assumes the classification task (imposter versus legitimate owner) is linearly separable, and as Minsky and Pappert have pointed out, simple linear discrimination methods do not work in all cases. The robust and feature rich approach engendered by cognitive biometrics may provide a way out of this dilemma. This will have to await empirical support before any final conclusions can be drawn.

Another principal advantage of cognitive biometrics relative to physiological approaches is the ability to integrate the authentication scheme on a continuous basis. Most physiological approaches present themselves at the entry port to an information portal, and once the authentication process has been accepted, the user is not subject to any further checks. This approach can lend itself to hi-jacking, where a machine can be accessed after the authentication process has completed. The incorporation of a continuous biometric is designed to thwart hi-jacking, because the user is being periodically authenticated while they are engaged in the usage of the information portal. Cognitive biometrics would actually benefit from such an approach, as there are more opportunities to sample the user, under a variety of circumstances. For instance, navigating through the file system, internet activities, word processing, and other applications provide the opportunity to evaluate the individual in a variety of scenarios that invoke particular cognitive skills, along with the induction of a variety of emotional states. Even notions of goal directed behaviour may become manifest when a person is searching on the internet etc. The ability to spoof such a system would be made more difficult, as clearly liveliness in required, to start with. Further, the large array of features that would be sampled, across several domains, would make this system extremely difficult to spoof. Over time, a profile of the user is developed along several dimensions – their cognitive and emotional states, theirs motivations – would be gradually developed, forming a mini-life story of the user. Whether someone else could replicate this feature – alone or in combination with other types of biometrics (e.g. behavioural) is highly unlikely.

In the next section, a variety of case studies is presented which highlight some of the relevant biometric approaches that have been published that fall within the purview of cognitive biometrics (though possibly unwittingly by the authors!). This is followed by a future trends and a conclusion section. Lastly, a further reading section is provided that will highlight some of the relevant literature in the field for those interested in pursuing this matter further.

CASE STUDIES

The sample of case studies presented in this work reflect the use of a biosignal based approach, whereby the inner mental (cognitive) and emotional states of an individual can be recorded in a more or less automated fashion. This approach utilises biological based signals such as the electrocardiogram (ECG), the electroencephalogram (EEG), and the electrodermal response (EDR) as the inputs to an authentication system, which are recorded using standard equipment in a non-invasive fashion. Each of these biosignals presents a wealth of information that can be extracted quite easily using a single recording system, such as the Vilistus system (www.vilistus.com), which provides up to 8 channels for recording a combination of EEG, ECG, or EDR, using wireless technology for data transport to a server for authentication purposes.

These biosignals are generated by the heart, brain, and the autonomic nervous system respectively – which are treated essentially as portals which provide real-time information regarding the on-going dynamics of the nervous system (both central and peripheral). This approach to user authentication is fairly recent – and the bulk of the research in this domain has focused on determining which features provide the maximal discriminatory capability. The bulk of the work published in the literature has thus far focused on discovering unique feature sets that maximise the resulting classification accuracy. The inputs are treated more or less as a time series – with various signal processing techniques applied to maximise the cardinality of the feature sets. The results are quite impressive – with classification accuracies up to 100% for small cohorts. This

work really has laid the groundwork – and has called upon – the signal processing technology which is well established in other domains. The next stage in the evolution of cognitive biometrics is to incorporate the biological aspects of behaviour that are manifest in these biosignals. For instance, there is a considerable literature on the heritability of aspects of the relevant biosignals – which indicates that on first principle, there is uniqueness contained with these signals that is independent of the phenotypic expression. This issue needs to be explored more thoroughly – as it may indicate that the results obtained from small cohorts may extrapolate to the population at large – clearly a requirement for any serious biometric implementation. Further, the stimulus-response paradigm should be made central to the authentication scheme – in order to explore the thresholds required for obtaining satisfactory results. These are issues to keep in mind when reading through the case studies. These topics will be addressed at the end of the case studies section, where the focus will be on the future of cognitive biometrics. Let's begin by exploring some examples of ECG based biometrics.

THE ELECTROCARDIOGRAM AS A BIOMETRIC

The use of the ECG as a biometric was first proposed by Forsen in 1977, a prescient paper that also discussed the deployment of EEG as a biometric tool (Forsen, 1977). The ECG records the electrical activity generated by the beating heart – generating a characteristic waveform which is depicted in Figure 1. This technology has a long and venerable history, beginning officially in 1887 (Waller, 1887). The heart utilizes electrical activity to activate the muscles required to pump blood through the circulatory system. By placing voltage sensitive recording electrodes at particular regions around the heart – the electrical activity of the heart can be detected. The signals generated by the heart beat forms a regular pattern (see Figure 1) that is maintained by homeostatic control (via the autonomic nervous system). This signal was utilized by Forsten in an attempt to determine the individuality of the ECG. He was the first researcher to address issues relating to the uniqueness of the ECG across individuals, in the context of biometrics.

In Forsten's approach, the recording of the ECG was accomplished in a very non-invasive fashion – he utilized two electrodes that were attached to the index fingers without the use of a ground lead or electrode paste. Data was collected from subjects at three sessions of 30-40 seconds each. The data was filtered with a 3 KHz cut-off frequency and the data was digitized for subsequent analysis (for more details consult [6]). Several features were extracted for subsequent classification purposes. A total of 10 features were utilized: five time intervals and five amplitude differences. The time points correspond to the 5 major deflection points in the signal (labelled P, Q, R, S, & T). The amplitude measurements were extracted using the same five time point fiduciaries, with the addition of a 6th halfway between S and T deflection points. These features were utilized to produce a reference vector for the individual. When the same user requests authentication, several heart beats are recorded (takes only a few seconds), and the average of the authentication request trials is compared with the reference vector. The results of this approach, based on Type

Figure 1. A typical ECG pattern for a single heart beat, with indications of the principle fiduciary marks

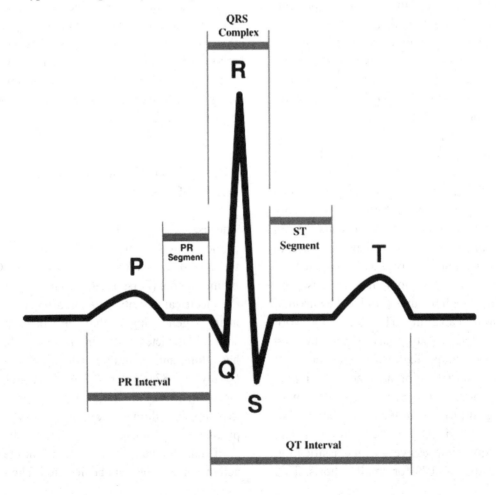

I and Type II errors, were extremely encouraging, yielding values of 1.2% and 1.1% respectively. This is a phenomenal result – considering the small number of features collected within a short time interval.

In work published by Israel and colleagues examined whether variations in anxiety level affect the classification accuracy (person verification) when deploying the ECG as the biometric modality (Israel et al., 2005). Further, the results from this study indicate that electrode placement does not alter the classification accuracy. In this study, data was collected from 29 subjects (males and females) between the ages of 22 and 48. Each subject took part in seven different experiments (each lasting approximately two minutes), which were designed to alter the subject's level of anxiety. During the experiments, the subjects ECG was recorded, and the ECG was averaged over each experiment. In addition, the affect of electrode placement was examined by utilising the data from specific electrodes individually and comparing the classification results across electrodes. A set of 15 features were extracted from the ECG data – corresponding to various fiducials, which were then normalised when used for subsequent classification purposes (see the reference for details on the selected fiducials used in this study). The authors deployed linear discriminant analysis with majority voting to perform the classification task. The authors first examined the classification accuracy based on lead placement, to determine the effect this yielded on the overall classification accuracy. The results from this study cohort yielded 100% correctly classified individuals (the baseline case). In addition, the authors examined whether the anxiety level could alter the classification accuracy. Test scenarios were employed that would produce either a low or high level of anxiety. Subjects would be enrolled under both types of scenarios, and then would be authenticated on the same scenarios. This provides a four way comparison – enrolled on high and tested on high and low and vice versa (a within and between

testing paradigm). The classification accuracy was reduced slightly – from 100% to approximately 97.5% on average for the variable anxiety conditions. The authors conclude that their approach, using normalised features are robust to changes in anxiety level based on their data. This is a very interesting and promising result – which needs to be examined across a wider range of affective/emotional states. Further, the extent to which the subjects actually had their anxiety levels altered during the experiments needs to be quantified before final conclusions can be drawn.

Typically, ECG based experiments aimed at user verification deploy the use of fiduciary marks – such as the time between successive R-peaks, in order to acquire a frame of reference. Wang and colleagues examined the deployment of a non-fiducial mark approach, deploying the autocorrelation (AR) and smoothed using the discrete cosine transform (DCT) (Wang et al., 2008). The authors deployed data from normal healthy subjects selected from two public databases (PTB and MIT-BIH). After suitable pre-processing, the authors extracted a set of 15 temporal features that were based on fiducial detection approaches, which were normalised to minimise the effects of alterations in heart rate (tachycardia and bradycardia). The authors deployed a nearest neighbour classifier on PCA and LDA (linear discriminant analysis) processed data. In addition, the authors extracted features that were obtained in a fiduciary independent fashion, using autoregression (AR), and discrete wavelet transform (DCT). The classification is based on the significant coefficients that were extracted using the DCT. The authors compare the classification results from both approaches (fiduciary and non-fiduciary) on both datasets (PTB and MIT_BIH to evaluate their classification accuracy. With the fiduciary approach, the classification accuracy was similar across approaches (PCA v LDA), but the overall classification accuracy was lower for the PTB database (93% versus 95%). In contrast, the non-fiduciary based approached yielded higher accuracy levels for the PTB database (95% versus 90% On average) for the MIT-BIH dataset. The exact classification accuracy was DCT parameter dependent, with results approaching 100% classification for both datasets (although the parameter (time lag and number of DCT coefficients) values were different for the two best cases). This study presents a novel method for feature extraction approach that is independent of landmark location for the most part – though at least the R-peak must be identified – but this is typically a simple task as it occurs only once during a heartbeat and is the largest peak.

The issue of stability over time was investigated by Wubbeler and colleagues in a study published in 2007 (Wubbeler et al., 2007). This study utilised ECG data from healthy subjects obtained from the PTB data repository (Physikalisch-Technische Bundesanstalt). The authors selected 234 ECG recordings from 74 Caucasian subjects (40 male and 34 female) ranging in age from 19 to 86 years (mean age of 45.5 years). Each ECG recording was 10 seconds long, and multiple recording from each subject were utilised, with an average of 500 days between recordings (16.6 months). The ECG recordings were derived using a three lead system fixed at the extremities according to the Einthoven's triangular scheme. The verification process was implemented by selecting two disjoint sets of samples, selecting 1 sample from each subject to form the reference vector and randomly selecting other samples from each subject for testing purposes. The matching algorithm did not utilise a fiducial or feature based representation because the authors felt the short duration did not provide a large enough sample to acquire meaningful statistics on fiducials. Instead, the authors chose to perform template matching on a representative sample from each subject. They used a standard nearest neighbour approach to assess similarity between the query sample and the target dataset. Briefly, the authors extracted a 100 ms interval centered on the R-peak, which they state is typically invariant to changes in heart

rate. The results obtained recorded type I and type II errors, and computed the detection error trade-off (DET) curve of the verification process. The equal error rate (EER) obtained from this study was 2.8%, and the FMR was 0.2% when FNMR was set at 10%, and the FMR was 2.5% when FNMR was set at 3%. These results are quite impressive considering the large age range of the subjects, the small amount of data (10 second samples), and the large time distance between multiple samples (over 16 months between sample collection points).

Silva and colleagues investigated whether a minimal set of electrodes (a single lead, V_2) could be utilised for user verification (Silva et al., 2007). The study utilised 25 subjects (male and female), with an average age of 23.4 +/- 2.5 years. Each subject was asked to performance a variety of cognitive tests during a 30 minute period, during which their ECG was recorded. The tasks included the Wisconsin intelligence test, a memory test and a discovery test [for more details consult X- Silva et al]. The ECGs collected during the task phase was analysed off-line, where all heartbeats from each individual were aligned along their R peaks. The mean for groups of 10 heartbeats (R-R peaks) was acquired and labeled with the individual's identity for subsequent processing and verification purposes (i.e. the enrollment data). The latency and amplitude for each of the *P-QRS-T* peaks were extracted, along with a sub-sampling of the waveform itself, providing a feature representation space of *53* features. For the classification protocol, a k-NN approach was deployed using randomly selected feature vectors from the database. When performing the classification, success rates approaching 100% were achieved when the classification method employed multiple instances from each subject in the database. The result is important as it indicates that a reduced number of leads can still achieve an accurate classification result. The deployment of an unobtrusive data collection mechanism is very important with respect to user acceptance – a single lead is much easier to deploy than a large cumbersome 12-lead apparatus that is used clinically.

A similar result was obtained by a study conducted by Mehta and Lingayat, whom compared QRS detection in a single lead and 12-lead ECG configuration (Mehta & Lingayat, 2007). In this study, the authors utilized the CSE data repository as the data source, and compared the accuracy of QRS detection of a single and 12-lead setup. The authors deployed the same machine learning approach (support vector machines - libSVM), which yielded very similar results (sensitivity of 99.70% and 99.93% for the single and 12-lead configuration respectively. These results are consistent with the Silva study and provide further evidence of the significant sensitivity and positive predictive value of this approach.

A study published by Biel and colleagues provide further evidence that a single lead provides virtually the same classification accuracy as a 12-lead system (Biel et al., 2001). This work utilized a set of 20 subjects (aged 20 to 55 years of age), with their ECG recorded 4 to 6 sessions over a six week period. A set of 30 features were utilized in the classification task, for which they deployed the SIMCA model, which utilised principle component analysis to detect similarities between test objects and classes. The classification accuracy was very high, yielding 95% in both training and testing sets. The authors conclude that a single lead system is as effective with respect to classification accuracy of individuals as the standard clinical 12-lead system, and therefore there must be substantial redundancy in the data collected from multiple leads. Unfortunately, the authors did not systematically examine their feature space (containing 30 fiduciary marks) to obtain a measure of the information content of each feature.

As an extreme case of electrode austerity, Chan and colleagues reduced the ECG input into a pair of electrodes (buttons really) that are held between the thumb and forefinger (Chan et al., 2008). ECG using this electrode system was collected from 50 subjects (45 were males, 6 females) ranging in age from 18 to 40. The subjects participated in three data-collecting sessions, each lasting 90 seconds, with a minimum of 1 day between recording sessions. The PQRST complexes were automatically detected using a multiplication of backward differences algorithm, and aligned temporally using cross-correlation measurements. The initial component of the data was used for enrollment, and the balance used for authentication (i.e. the first session was used for enrollment data). Classification was based on statistical methods, such as the percent residual difference, correlation coefficient, and a wavelet distance measure. The overall classification accuracies were approximately 89% - and as high as 95% when misclassification results were incorporated back into the data pool. Although these results are not as impressive as other approaches - the technology is very simple – and one could envision incorporating the Ag-AgCl 'button' electrodes into a hand held device such as a mobile phone or a standard PC keyboard.

A series of studies have been published focusing on the role of heritability with respect to a variety of physiological and behavioural traits. In a study published by Dalageorgou and colleagues, it was discovered that there is a significant genetic basis of the QT interval, a common fiducial that is correlated with the duration of cardiac repolarization (Dalageorgou et al., 2007). More specifically, the QT interval is significantly influenced by the heart rate, and hence there have been several proposals to normalize the QT interval as a function of heart rate, which is termed the QTc. It is the QTc that has been shown to have a significant genetic component, with heritability estimates of over 70% in some measurement studies. These types of studies typically deploy monozygotic and dizygotic twins, with fairly large sample populations (several hundred to several thousand in most cases), whereby results significant for monozygotic twins versus dizygotic reflect differences in genetic makeup as opposed to environmental influences. A larger study of

6,148 Sardinians has supported the observation of a genetic influence on the QTc interval, along with a wide range of cardiovascular (mean blood pressure, systolic and diastolic pressure) and personality traits (Pilia et al., 2006). These studies highlight the role of heritability of various aspects of the cardiovascular system which would clearly have an impact of the ECG. It may be prudent for the biometrics community to become informed on these types of studies, as they may provide a rational basis for feature selection. If certain features have a significant genetic component, then one would presume a level of uniqueness for a given trait, relative to a feature without heritability. As information becomes available, it should be incorporated into the feature selection process.

Lastly, there are a growing number of published studies that examine the effect of emotion on cardiorespiratory physiology (Cacioppo et al., 2000, McCraty et al., 1995, Rainville et al., 2006,). The effect of positive (recalling fond memories) or negative (anger/frustration) emotions, induced using the freeze-frame method on heart rate variability was investigated in (McCraty et al., 1995). The authors investigated the effect of polarized emotions on heart rate variability (the RR interval), and found that each emotion induced subtle and unique changes in the power spectral density of the RR peaks. These alterations in HRV were consistent across subjects and were easily recorded using a standard 12-lead ECG setup. An issue reflecting the practicality of this approach is associated with the induction of a specific emotional trait, which required subjects to undergo training in the freeze-frame method. It could be argued that similar changes in emotional state could be obtained using other approaches. The principle point to consider from this study is that there is a clear relationship between certain emotional states and ECG recordable signals. A study by Rainville and colleagues has produced similar results, demonstrating a significant effect on HRV as a function of a variety of emotional states (Rainville et al., 2006). In this study, four

basic emotions (fear, anger, sadness and happiness) were investigated to determine if they induced variations in cardiac function, detectable using a standard 3 lead ECG montage. The study involved recording the ECG during recall and experiential reliving of one or two potent emotional autobiographical episodes and a neutral episode from a cohort of 43 healthy subjects. The authors place this study within the framework of peripheral nervous system activation – principally the sympathetic and parasympathetic systems, with the later yielding effects that are partially couple to the respiratory system. The emotional state then exerts its effect through co-activation of the cardiorespiratory system. The causal chain here appears to be initiated by changes in the respiratory system, whereby changes in intra-abdominal pressure during changes in inhalation, which in turn through activation of baroreceptors, causes a change in the heart rate. The alteration in heart rate is not simply a function of the change in respiratory volume changes – there are subtle (and potentially non-linear) changes that result within the high frequency domains of the HRV. The authors examined a set of features relating to measures of the heart rate, respiratory period and respiratory amplitude, as well as indices of variability in both the heart rate and respiration. To reduce the dimensionality of the feature set, the authors deployed a PCA approach. When comparing emotions against a neutral emotional state, the results indicated that, a stepwise discriminant analysis using PCA factors led to a classification rate of over 65% for the four emotions individually, and upwards of 83% for pair-wise discrimination. These results are quite promising, expanding the set of emotions from previous studies.

The studies presented thus far are only a small sample of what has been published in the literature. The results from these studies indicate that the classification accuracies are very close to 100% in most cases, when considering the deployment of ECG alone for person verification. The sample sizes are typically small though – and most studies do not report enough statistical data regarding the typical biometric quality measures such as the FMR at a particular FNMR. These quality measures are extremely important in terms of evaluating the true classification rate of the system. The ease of use for ECG has been significantly improved, relative to a standard clinical approach using a full 12-lead data collection system. The deployment of a standard Ag-AgCl electrode in the form of a finger held button provides probably the maximal ease of use, which could be incorporated into a mobile handset, a mouse, or on a standard PC keyboard. The data acquisition time of 10s is sufficient in many cases to acquire a decent EER. It typically takes approximately 10 seconds to enter a login ID and password, so this time frame is quite suitable. The stability of the verification process appears quite robust – both in terms of temporal variations and emotional state (at the moment, the anxiety level has been examined). Stability over time is a necessary feature of a biometric, though in the case of C2 level security, most systems require changing one's password at regular intervals (typically 2-4 weeks). The long term stability needs to be examined more thoroughly – especially in lieu of any medical conditions that might occur which could alter the ECG – but again, this effect could be minimised by requiring users to re-enrol periodically. The effect of the emotional state of the user thus far has been to try and eliminate any effects they might have on variations in the ECG signal. Thus far, only anxiety levels (low and high) have been considered. This type of study should be examined more thoroughly, looking at a range of emotions to determine how they affect the ECG. One of the primary goals of the cognitive biometrics approach is not to try to eliminate the effects of emotional and/or cognitive states, but to try to invoke a particular state. This approach may obviate the need (if it is even possible) to control for variations in the state of the individual, and may also highlight additional aspects of the effect of cognitive/emotional states on human physiology (reflected in measurements of the ECG, EEG, and EDR). This will be discussed in more detail at a later section.

THE ELECTROENCEPHALOGRAM AS A BIOMETRIC

The EEG is a recording of electrical potentials generated by the collective activity of neuronal generators, obtained by placing voltage sensitive electrodes on the scalp surface (see Figure 2). That is, brain activity produces an electrical signal that can be recorded by placing voltage sensitive electrodes on the surface of the scalp (see Figure 3). What is required for the signal to be recorded at the scalp is a collection of neurons firing synchronously, and oriented towards the surface of the head. These conditions are met by collections of cortical pyramidal neurons that have the proper orientation and fire synchronously. Provided these conditions are met, a stereotyped signal is recorded from each electrode positioned over the entire surface of the scalp. As suggested by Figure 2, a tremendous amount of data is generated during an EEG recording. Typically, in a clinical application (i.e. the diagnosis of epilepsy), anywhere from 18-256 electrodes are positioned on the scalp, each providing a time series sampled at 0.5-1.0 KHz., with typical recording times of 10s of minutes or more, result in the production of hundreds of megabytes of data. The feature space of EEG data is very large - both from the fact that data is acquired in a parallel fashion (across multiple electrodes) - but also because the brain is a very complex dynamical system. The firing of neurons, which is an electrical process, generates recordable signals that form a background, upon which is superimposed the activities of specific collections of neurons that respond according to the engagement of a variety of cognitive tasks, such as reading, mental imagery, vocalization, etc. For clinical applications such as the diagnosis of epilepsy, the appearance of spikes and spindles, indicative of epilepsy, are readily apparent to the

Figure 2. Sample of cognitive states and the associated EEG waveform recorded from a normal adult male. Note the scales - the X-axis is time and the Y-axis is potential (measured in µV). (Source: www. arstechnica.com)

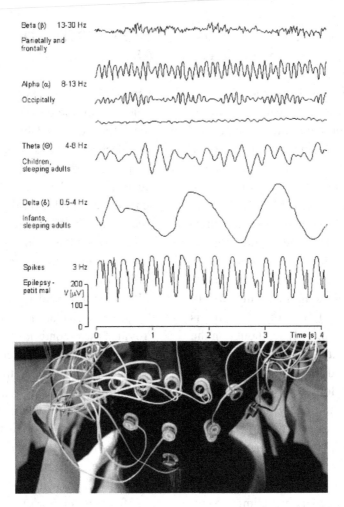

unaided eye. When deploying EEG as a biometrics application, the situation changes dramatically.

The EEG as a biometric (either for identification or more typically user verification) entails several constraints: the number of electrodes should be kept to a minimum (typically 1-4 electrodes) in order to facilitate quick recording setups, the recording time is kept to a minimum (typically 1 minute or so), and the features being examined are not readily apparent to the unaided eye. Instead of visual inspection, a series of signal processing and machine learning techniques are applied to pre-processed data. The principal ap-

proaches that have been deployed relies on the spectral analysis whereby the raw EEG data is processed, examining the power level at various frequency bands. There are five principle frequency bands, labelled delta, theta, alpha, beta, and gamma, which have characteristic frequencies within the 0-3, 2-7, 8-12, 13-20, and 20+ Hz frequency ranges respectively. These frequency bands have been associated with a variety of cognitive states of arousal. Figure 2 presents a set of examples of how states of arousal produce EEG spectra with characteristics frequencies and amplitudes. A spectral analysis approach examines

Figure 3. A typical clinical grade EEG setup, highlighting the positioning of the electrodes on the scalp, which are embedded in a skullcap (Source: www.lsa.umuch.edu)

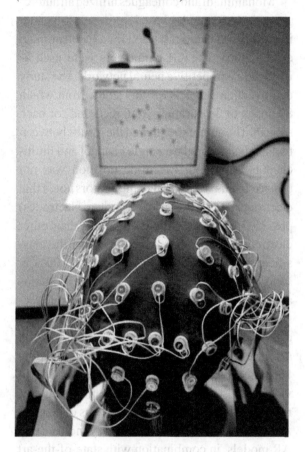

the power spectrum at these various frequency bands - and can be used for person authentication. The other major approach utilises the event related potentials (ERP), which are derived from raw EEG data (see Figure 4 for an example). ERPs are acquired by presenting a stimulus repeatedly, and performing an averaging over the data. For instance, when a person is engaged in a visual processing task, specific regions of the brain become active. It is assumed that these brain regions subserve the cognitive task at hand. If the stimulus elicits a specific response, it will be embedded in the on-going brain dynamics and may not be noticeable. If an average over several trials is presented to the subject, the on-going

background activity will tend to cancel out, leaving only that activity which is time locked to the stimulus. The result is a waveform, which is characterised by peaks which occur with a particular polarity (positive or negative), latency (in milliseconds), and spatial location (see Figure 3 for electrode placement). For instance, one can identify 5 ERPs in Figure 4, which are labelled accordingly (spatial location – the electrode position, is not presented). There are a variety of ERPs that have been identified - the prototypical one being termed a P300, first reported by Sutton in 1965 is presented in Figure 4 (see Sutton et al., 1965).

An ERP is identified by its latency, polarity, and spatial location. For instance, the 'P' in P300 reflects a positive deflection and the '300' reflects the delay in milliseconds after stimulus presentation. The location is a more difficult task - which requires significant modelling approaches. The location is not typically required for use in the current context - though this is a significant task in neuroimaging. The overall shape of the ERP waveform: the amplitude of the peaks and their latencies will typically vary across individuals.

Figure 4. An example of an ERP waveform, demonstrating a range of ERPS. Note that positive polarity is downward and the large P300 ERP component on the far right. (source: www. en.wikibbooks.org)

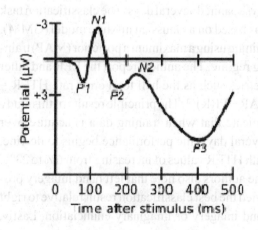

119

One must also consider that there are a variety of ERPs - which can be elicited within a single authentication scheme. It is this depth of the feature space that can be exploited for authentication purposes. In addition, when ERPs are combined with standard EEG signal analysis, the feature space becomes very large and has the potential to produce a very unique and characteristic profile for a given user. Exploiting such features enables EEG based biosignals to qualify as a biometric, the success of which can only be demonstrated at present empirically. How EEG and ERPs can be used for person identity verification is presented in what follows through a series of case studies.

Marcel and Millan published an early study on the deployment of EEG for person authentication (Marcel & Millan, 2007). In this study, nine subjects were employed, with their EEG recorded using a 32 electrode skull cap. The subjects were asked to perform a set of cognitive tasks, such as imagining self-paced hand movements (right and left), along with generating words that begin with the same letter. The samples were acquired at 4 minute intervals, with repetitions on the same day (10-15 minutes break in between), over a series of four days. The data was pre-processed to reduce noise, using a surface Laplacian operator in order to localise the signals to their spatial sources on the scalp. The authors investigated the stability of the EEG in terms of its ability to provide adequate classification errors when the training and testing days spanned several days. The classification task was based on a Gaussian mixture model (GMM), training using a maximum a posterior (MAP) training regime. The authors report the EER and other metrics such as the half total error rate HTER = (FAR + FRR)/2. The principle results of this study indicate that when training data is acquire over several days, the performance begins to decline, with HTER values of increasing from 6% to 23%. The authors also note that left hand imagery provided the best classification result relative to right hand imagery or imaginary enunciation. Lastly, the authors note that this approach needs to be validated with a larger subject cohort to determine how robust the results are.

Mohammadi and colleagues utilized an autoregressive (AR) model based approach to person identification using raw EEG data (Mohammadi et al., 2006). The AR parameters were used as inputs to a competitive neural network. The study deployed ten subjects for this study, from which 8 epochs of 3s duration were recorded for each subject. The authors compared the results between two analysis models: a single channel and multi-channel paradigm. Electrode position was not utilised in this work, though the authors noted that electrodes placed posteriorly (parietal electrodes) provided better classification scores than other electrodes. The authors concluded that the classification accuracy, which approached 100% in some instances, suggested that the EEG contains a genetic component, which is the principle reason for the very high identification rates. Typical classification rates were on the order of 95% on average, with some single channel results yielding 100% accuracy. The multi-channel approach provided consistently higher classification accuracy, reaching 100% in many combinations of channel AR vectors. The results of this study indicate that AR models, in combination with state-of-the-art neural network classifiers can be quite effective in utilising EEG data for person verification. The principle drawback of this work is the significant computational expense of calculating many AR coefficients – prohibiting this approach from deployment in a real-time authentication scheme.

In a paper by Palaniappan, a two stage identification process deploying EEG technology was introduced (Palaniappan & Krishman, 2004). In this work, a small cohort (five subjects were asked to engage in a variety of mental arithmetic operations (such as multiplying two-digit numbers), while their EEG was recorded. The electrodes were cap mounted (six were employed, excluding two reference electrodes), The data was sampled at 250 Hz, and digitised to 12 bits for subsequent off-line analysis. The subjects were asked to perform five mental tasks and their EEG was recorded for 10 seconds during task performance (please consult the reference for details on task performance). A set of features were extracted from the recording, which were used for subsequent subject verification. The data was pre-processed, which typically involves filtering to remove line noise and motion artefacts (i.e. eye-blinks and related muscular activity which can inject noise – but expected to be minimal over a 10s interval). The data was partitioned into 0.5s blocks, which provides data for model developing and testing (using a cross-validation approach). A series of features were extracted, which included the autoregressive coefficients, channels spectra powers, inter-hemispheric asymmetry, and non-linear complexity measures. In order to reduce the dimensionality of the feature set, PCA was applied, which reduced the feature set to 11 components. The data was partitioned into test and training sets and a two-stage threshold system was deployed, in order to de-couple the co-dependence of FAR and FRR. In the first step, the distances between training sets and testing sets were determined, producing two disjoints sets consisting of purported authentic and imposter samples. Those samples that were classified as imposters were used in the second authentication stage, and a second threshold was applied to reduce the FRR rate. The author then calculated the FRR and FAR, and found the results to be 0% for both measures in this study. This result is very promising, utilising a short amount of data (10s), but the subject cohort was relatively small. The approach further used a spectral approach in a paradigm that is typically ERP related – cognitive tasks typically are used for ERP elicitation.

Paranjape and colleagues examined the effectiveness of the electroencephalogram (EEG) as a biometric identification of individual subjects in a pool of 40 normal subjects (Paranjape et al., 2001). The EEG's second order statistics are computed using autoregressive models of various orders. The coefficients in these models were then evaluated for their biometric potential. Discriminant functions applied to the model coefficients were used to examine the degree to which the subjects in the data pool can be identified. The results indicate that the EEG has significant biometric potential. In this data pool, 100% of subjects are correctly classified when all data is used, and over 80% when the functions are computed from half the data and then applied to the remaining.

Current research has provided evidence that we generate recordable and reproducible signals that can be captured using EEG technology when we think of something, such as a password. In an interesting paper entitled "Pass-thoughts, authenticating with our minds," the notion that we may be able to authenticate by simply thinking of our password has been proposed (Thorpe et al., 2005). The authors of Pass-thoughts indicate that the signals recorded using EEG under the context of mental authentication were reliable and required little training by the subjects. The idea behind pass-thoughts is the utilisation of the Brain Computer Interface (BCI) approach, which is by now a well developed field of applied research, initially developed for assistive technology applications. BCI systems may utilise ERPs such as the P300 as an input device, which is mapped onto a set of commands the computer subsequently executes (Palaniappan, 2007). The subject has to produce the required input (i.e. a P300), in response to a particular stimulus, at the right time. There is a lot of interest in the BCI field, and one expects that cutting edge research in this domain might provide some very interesting approaches to this type of cognitive biometrics. There is a significant amount of work suggesting that imagined motor activities can produce a reliable 'brain signature' that has been used for successful authentication purposes – the question addressed by pass-thoughts is how far can the imagined mental activity be expanded – this is indeed an interesting area to explore.

As with the ECG, there is a significant literature on the heritability of the EEG. Several studies have reported links between EEG profiles and behavioural and cognitive traits (Hansell et al., 2001, Lalor et al., 2005). More generally, researchers have been investigating the heritability of brain function assessed by the EEG (e.g. Hicks et al., 2007). In order to evaluate the contributions of genetics versus environmental contributions to individual differences in CNS activities (measurable via EEG), large cohorts of twins have been employed. In a study by van Beijsterveldt and colleagues, the EEG of 16 year old twin pairs (91 MZ and 122 DZ) was obtained and analysed to determine the level of heritability of spectral power for the four principle frequency bands (delta, theta, alpha, and beta) (van Beijsterveldt et al., 1996). The measurements were acquired while the subjects were at rest, with eyes closed. To account for sex differences, the EEG was recorded in female and male same-sex twins and in opposite-sex twins. The results indicated a significant level of heritability for all frequency bands (76%, 89%, 89%, and 86% respectively). In addition, these results were independent of electrode position. The principal conclusion from this study is that brain rhythms are the most heritable characteristic in humans. The authors of this study remark that their results in terms of heritability are higher than other published studies – but this may be due to the age of the subjects (all were 16), whereas other studies tend to deploy subjects from a wide age range. The issue of variations in the EEG as a function of age needs to be assessed and accounted for in a biometric that relies on certain properties of the EEG.

In a study involving 309 twins (142 monozygotic and 167 dizygotic twins), it was found that the heritability was over 75% for the delta and theta bands (Smit et al., 2005). The study involved subjects from two age cohorts (the younger with a mean age of 26.2 years) and an older cohort, with a mean age of 49.4 years (though not all participants were twins – but all were family members). The study examined the heritability across the entire frequency spectrum, in terms of potential age related differences between the two age group cohorts. In addition, the study examined the stability of the EEG over time, with multiple recordings (retesting) after an average interval of 674 days (range: 354 – 1322 days). Recording were produced using a 19-electrode (excluding dual reference leads), while the subjects were resting and eyes closed. With respect to a possible heritability factor across the frequency bands, the younger cohort tended to have higher heritability measures (using Falconer's measure) across all frequency bands (approximately a 10% increase), independent of electrode position. It was also noted that the delta and theta band power was higher in the younger cohort. Likewise, the alpha and beta bands tended to yield slightly higher heritability factors in the older cohort. The authors also noted that the alpha and theta bands produced the consistently highest level of heritability (0.91 and 0.89 respectively). The heritability may reflect the anatomical structure of the calvarium, such as its thickness, which would affect the conductive properties of the brain and have an impact on the EEG. The authors also state that certain rhythmic generators, such as the septum for hippocampal slow wave activity (3-4Hz) or thalamocortical generators may be heritable. These observations might explain the systemic level of heritability that has been reported to occur when measuring the power spectrum across a wide range of frequency bands. The evidence is clear that there is a significant genetic component in the EEG, which may provide a rational basis for exploiting individual differences which are easily recordable. The concept of a genetic component that is associated with phenotypic behavior has been the subject of investigation into the search for endophenotypes.

An endophenotype is essentially a heritable bio-marker, which is associated with a disease/illness (Gottesman & Shields, 1972). In addition, an endophenotype is state-independent, which means it is omnipresent. A number of endophenotypes have been discovered since this concept was first enunciated in the 1960s. The search for factors that interpose between genes and overt phenotypic expression, easily discoverable through some form of biochemical test or other measuring approach (e.g. ECG or EEG) has enhanced the model details used in description of various psychophysiological manifestations such as schizophrenia and alcoholism. In the current context, alterations in phenotype recordable using standard EEG technology have been reported. Changes in sensory motor gazing, where subjects have difficulty filtering out multiple sensory inputs have been recorded in patients diagnosed with schizophrenia (Braff and freedman, 2002). Pulse pair inhibition deployed via presentation of a startling stimuli typically elicit an unconditioned response in the subject. If a weaker prestimulus is given prior to the startling stimulus, the response to the startling stimulus is significantly reduced (Gottesman, 2003). It is well known that in certain psychological diseases the reduction to the startling reflex is diminished. It should be noted that pulse pair inhibition changes are not strictly associated with schizophrenia – a number of conditions such as compulsive obsessive disorders, and Huntington's disease, amongst others have been reported. Another example of a purported endophenotype is associated with the P50 suppression which is typically measured by providing two auditory stimuli presented @ 500 ms intervals. Each auditory stimulus elicits an auditory evoked potential (a type of ERP), it is normal for the response to the second stimulus to be typically reduced in amplitude. In certain disorders, not exclusive to schizophrenia, subjects demonstrate P50 suppression, where the response to the second stimulus presentation is not reduced. Studies have indicated that there is a genetic link, and further that family members whom are not probands display a similar change in P50 suppression (Myles-Worsley, 2007). Abnormalities in electrophysiological measures of stimulus-evoked brain activity (including the P3 event-related potential (ERP) and its associated delta and theta time-frequency (TF) components),

and intrinsic, resting state brain activity (including EEG in the beta frequency band) have each been associated with biological vulnerability to a variety of externalizing (EXT) spectrum disorders, such as substance use disorders, conduct disorder, and antisocial behaviour (Gilmore et al., 2010). Other candidate endophenotypes recordable using standard EEG equipment include eye tracking movement variations, smooth pursuit, and working memory function (Lenzenwenger et al, 2007). The endophenotype literature is growing significantly, and the list of cognitive and sensory-motor functions which present recordable electrophysiological changes are growing likewise.

These results are promising - the deployment of native EEG and ERPs for user authentication have provided very high levels of accuracy - approaching more traditional physiological based approaches such as fingerprint based systems. The typical approach deployed in the case studies focused solely on the deployment of EEG for user authentication has focused in my opinion on standard signal processing approaches. The basic trend is to extract the EEG signal, extract as many features as possible, then reduce the number to more meaningful one using standard machine learning approaches such as PCA or rough sets, and then apply classifiers to map the feature space onto individuals. This approach has been quite successful for studies deploying small cohorts, but it yet remains to see how well this basic approach applies to the population at large – a requirement for any successful biometric. It is this author's belief that we should incorporate features within the EEG that have the potential for uniqueness instead of trying to acquire every possible feature. This is where the concept of the endophenotype is potentially very useful in this domain. The literature on endophenotype – and more generally, electrophysiological phenotypes may provide a rational basis for selecting features from the EEG, which will have a much better than chance of being person specific – at least person category specific. In order to take advantage of this approach, particular types of stimuli need to be provided – such as that used in P50 suppression experiments. With the proper stimulus, we may be able to extract information from the EEG that is more informative regarding the individual's phenotype. This approach may provide a more rational basis for user discrimination – and is really what makes the *cognitive biometrics* approach so different from behavioural or anatomical biometrics. In the next section, we present a summary of another biosignal based authentication scheme - utilising the response of the autonomic nervous system - the galvanic skin response (more formally termed the electrodermal response).

THE ELECTRODERMAL RESPONSE AS A BIOMETRIC

The electrodermal response (EDR) can be measured quite easily using the same technology deployed in EEG and ECG, providing a unified signal acquisition system. A typical EDR signal is presented in Figure 5, which displays a 60-second recording from a single subject. The EDR can be described as being either tonic or phasic. Tonic EDR reflects the basal or background level of skin conductance – and is termed the skin conductance level (SCL). The SCL is considered to be unique to an individual, which provides a useful measure of individuality. Phasic skin conductance changes

depending on the presence of a particular stimulus. These changes are typically referred to as the Skin Conductance Responses (SCR). A typical SCR may last for 10-20 seconds, and occur in response to a variety of stimuli – such as sounds, smells, and visual stimulation. Typically, the response rises from a baseline level and returns back to baseline – this is termed the galvanic skin response (GSR). What is characteristic about individuals is the frequency of GSRs, which occur about 2-3 times per minute under spontaneous non-stimulating conditions. One can also discuss the concept of event-related GSRs (which are referred to as ERGs in this work), which can be induced analogously to ERPs. The parameters that are used to quantify ERGs are the latency, amplitude, the rise time, and the half- recovery time (see Figure 5 for a typical GSR recording). The latency is the time between stimulus onset and the start of the response – some use the peak value as the end-point though. The amplitude of the GSR is the difference between the tonic skin conductance level and the maximal response during the evoked response. The rise-time is the time between the start of the response and the peak of the response. Lastly, the half-recovery time is the time between the peak and half recovery to tonic conductance levels. These values can be measured quite accurately – but what is the biological basis of these features of the GSR?

Figure 5. A sample of the EDR measured over a 60 second period using standard Ag-AgCl electrodes placed on the palmar surface (Taken from http://en.wikipedia.org/wiki/Galvanic_skin_response)

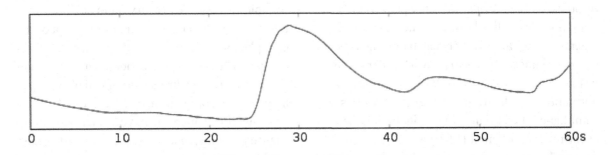

Essentially, the EDR measures the electrical resistance between two points. The resistance of the skin will change due to the emotional state of the subject, which is controlled by the autonomic (sympathetic and parasympathetic, as well as the enteric nervous system) nervous system. The autonomic system in turn controls the activity of sweat glands which are embedded in the middle layer of the skin. The prevailing model for the EDR is based on Edelberg's sweat circuit model (Edelberg, 1971). The model treats sweat glands as variable resistors, whose capacitance changes when the sweat glands become filled with fluid. The amplitude of the response is proportional to the amount of sweat that fills the glands and the number of ducts that are filled. Changes in skin conductance are controlled through activation of the sympathetic nervous system, which in this case utilises acetylcholine as the neurotransmitter. There are three descending control mechanisms for regulatory control of the SGR: pre-motor cortex through the pyramidal tract, the hypothalamus and limbic system, and the reticular formation.

The GSR is a readily measurable phenomemon – but one would like to know the stability of GSR. In an effort to ascertain the stability of the GSR response over time, Docter and Friedman recorded the GSR periodically over a 1 week period, followed by a follow up measurement 30 days later (Docter & Friedman, 1965). The study involved a set of 23 male university students, during term time. The study design also provided data on the stability of the GSR recording over 24 hour intervals. The results yielded significant correlations between measures obtained 24 hr apart, as well as a significant correlation between the median weekly rates of spontaneous GSR emission taken 30 days apart. Comparison of emission rates on comparable recording days 30 days apart failed to manifest a significant relationship. Present data support earlier studies of 24-hr spontaneous GSR stability. In spite of the failure to find significant relationships between emission rates

on comparable days of the two recording periods, the authors conclude that the significant relationship between median weekly rates of emission, taken 30 days apart, indicates that spontaneous GSR is an intra-individual characteristic which remains relatively stable, even over extended periods of time.

The stability and heritability of the EDR has been studied in a large cohort of monozygotic and dizygotic twins (Crider et al., 2004). The study utilised 345 twin pairs and 3 unpaired twins without participating co-twins, yielding a total of 693 subjects. The mean age of the subjects was 47.8 years, the bulk of which were Caucasians (92.2%). All participants underwent an identical testing sequence consisting of an initial rest period, a habituation procedure, a digit transformation task, and a final rest period. Participants were initially instructed to assume a comfortable position but to remain alert and refrain from movement. Following a 4-min rest period, a series of 1000-Hz tones was presented binaurally via audio tape at varying intervals of 30, 45, or 60 s. Tone duration was 1.0 s, with rise and fall times of 25 ms and amplitude of 80 dB at the earpiece. The tones continued for 10 trials and thereafter for a maximum of 18 trials or until a habituation criterion was reached. The latent phenotype accounted for 83% of the variance in resting SCR lability (95% CI 77–86%), 59% of the variance in trials to specific SCR habituation (95% CI 52–64%), and 61% of the variance in task SCR lability (95% CI 55–66%). In terms of heritability, the results of this study indicate that approximately 50% of the variance between individuals can be accounted for by a single latent phenotype (across all tests).

The deployment of GSR has provided useful information in terms of subjects with various cognitive impairments. In particular, these studies have deployed GSR as a means of segregating subjects into categories which are demarcated by level of cognitive impairment. In one study, the deployment of GSR was used to subcategorise a group of 20 schizophrenic patients into subcategories – responsive and non-responsive, based on the utilisation of the event related GSR (ERG) paradigm (Lopes-Machado et al., 2002). Granted, schizophrenia may be an extreme feature in person classification, but there are numerous studies which in which GSR has been employed to investigate patients with various degrees of attention deficit, sensory motor activity, and studies involving information processing (Bellak, 1994, Mirsky et al., 1995). That most of these studies deploy patients with cognitive deficits may serve only to indicate a tendency within subgroups within the scientific community. Whether these results extrapolate to the population at large is clearly an interesting research topic that needs addressing.

CONTINUOUS MODE AUTHENTICATION

The deployment of a biometric in a continuous mode has been proposed as a method to obviate the problem of hi-jacking – acquiring access to trusted and secured data by replacing the legitimate user. If a person leaves their workstation unattended, another individual can gain access to the same privileged data through direct physical access at the workstation. To avoid such scenarios, the workstation will have an inactivity timeout mechanism which causes the user to re-authenticate in order to re-gain access control. This process can be quite tedious and may enhance false rejection rates. This scenario is typical in businesses such as stock exchanges, where stock brokers must move around the office to view various information devices such as tickertapes etc. This exposes their workstation, and any information breech may be very costly indeed. In such a scenario, the inactivity timeout mechanism must be very short, necessitating multiple authentications during the course of a normal business day. Failure to re-authenticate can be very costly under these scenarios, so the system must be fast and reliable.

This is an extreme scenario, and one that is probably not well suited for a cognitive biometrics approach. Yet, the potential to perform continuous biometrics is applicable in many other domains that may not be so mission critical (Kwang et al., 2009, Flior & Kowalski, 2010). A useful mechanism for continuous biometrics is that based on keystroke dynamics. In keystroke dynamics, the user's typing patterns are utilised. The patterns are based on timing between successive keystrokes, and the amount of time a key is depressed. A pattern is produced that is acquired from a specific user, and this pattern is stored in a template (the biometric identification record) and is used for subsequent authentication purposes, where the current typing sample is examined over the same feature set and compared with the BIR for that ID. The suitability of this approach is that typing is a fundamental activity when a person interacts with a computer system. The user can be monitored even without their knowledge by collecting typing feature data while they are using the workstation. The utility of this approach is of course based on the classification accuracy obtained. Typical values for EER are on the order of a few percent – depending on the value of FAR one selects for measurement. How would a cognitive approach serve as a method of continuous authentication?

Simply put, the recording mechanism, whether it be a GSR, ECG, or EEG based approach would remain attached to the subject or at least made physically accessible from the workstation. Considering the desire for mobility, it would probably be best for the recording mechanism to be located on the workstation. If the authentication mechanism was integrated into the mouse as an example, the user will be in frequent contact with the device. During this period of interaction with the authentication medium, the appropriate biosignals would be acquired and utilised for authentication purposes. The deployment of EDR based recording electrodes, or blood pulse volume (BPV) electrodes integrated into a mouse would be a very suitable approach. This approach must provide comparable results in terms of EER values that other approaches provide. This is an empirical question – but the results indicate very low (near 0% EER), clearly comparable to a keystroke dynamics based approach. It must be mentioned that the results for EDR are obtained through more traditional methods of acquiring data from the skin surface – the electrode is not integrated into the mouse for instance. This is an area that we are currently investigating.

The ethical issue of collecting authentication data needs to be addressed when continuous monitoring is deployed. If users are told their credentials will be monitored covertly, this makes continuous authentication an easier task. Both behavioural and cognitive biometrics provide a natural mechanism for this approach – as it acquires data that is generated during the normal usage of the workstation. No special activity – such as providing a fingerprint is required, which may disturb the concentration of the user periodically, resulting in reduced productivity. The cognitive approach provides a range of activities that can be examined during the authentication process – which may increase the reliability of this approach towards continuous biometrics. An application may not require a significant amount of typing – instead interacting with the application via the mouse may be more suitable. One could deploy mouse stroke dynamics, but the reliability of this approach is not sufficient in many applications (see Revett, 2008 for details). The integration of the recording electrode into the mouse provides a natural approach in this scenario. Clearly, a multi-modal approach combining keystroke dynamics and a cognitive approach could provide for the widest range of opportunities to collect data from the user in a non-intrusive fashion.

FUTURE RESEARCH DIRECTIONS

Cognitive biometrics is a relatively new approach to biometrics – which relies on subtle differences in human behaviour. As discussed here, the approach relies on a cognitive approach to person discrimination, with its foundations in neurophysiology. The approach is implemented as stimulus-response paradigm, which in turn has its foundations in psychology. Behaviour has three basic dimensions – cognitive, affective, and conative. The cognitive facets of human behaviour include memory capacity, attention, mathematical, linguistic abilities etc. The affective state reflects the emotional of an individual – with associated valences. The conative component reflects desires, drives, and the ambition a person has at some point in time. The cognitive biometrics approach attempts to find a rational basis for each of these aspects of cognition in an attempt to produce a stimulus-response relationship that highlights differences between individuals along these dimensions. The fact that a genetic basis has been discovered for a particular response – such as the amplitude of the P300, may indicate that we should attempt to develop stimuli that are designed to highlight this feature. The literature is filled with a large number of examples of the notion of endophenotypes – recordable biomarkers of physiological tendencies which are heritable. Studies from twin studies have highlighted the genetic basis for many aspects of our neurophysiological responses – which should be utilised in our authentication protocols. For example, the power spectrum in the EEG is highly heritable, and certainly would serve as a feature that should be included in an EEG based authentication scheme. But the stimulus provided during this scheme should attempt to extract from the subject those features which have inherent individuality as much as possible. This is in contrast to the current techniques, which tend to extract as much information as possible, extract as many features as possible, then reduce the feature set, and apply this reduced feature set to a standard machine learning based classifier. Although this approach has been effective, it seems that this approach could be refined. If one deployed a considered SR approach, which could elicit multi-faceted aspects of behaviour – not just along a single dimension, then one may be able to extract a smaller but more appropriate feature set. In addition to reducing the processing overhead, this feature set may be more inherently stable, as it records actual physiological responses to particular stimuli. The issue here is that the data needs to be recorded at the appropriate time during the acquisition phase. The authentication process may entail several stimuli – auditory and visual stimuli in various formats may be presented. The responses provided by the user must be mapped temporally to the right time frames relative to the stimulus components, rather than simply recording for 30 seconds, and extracting a set of AR coefficients.

As discussed previously, there are three major venues for acquiring information in the cognitive approach – these are the EEG, ECG, and EDR. The EEG is utilised for extracting information regarding the cognitive state, ECG and EDR for the affective/emotional state. At this moment, there is very little information/data that suggests how one can effectively elicit the conative state of an individual. The literature suggests that each of these recording modalities is capable of recording a feature that has a significant level of heritability. The deployment of ECG alone, without regards to the emotional state of an individual provides very high classification accuracies – albeit on small cohorts. The utilisation of EDR has not really transcended the lie detector phase (in the related context of biometrics) – but clearly the notion of event related GSRs opens up exciting possibilities. The deployment of these biosignals as a means for authentication forms the practical basis for implementing cognitive biometrics.

There are several issues that need to be addressed if this approach is to become a viable technology. First, the issue of signal acquisition must be addressed. This is a technological issue - and the focus is on user acceptance. A typical EEG based device is depicted in Figure 3 - which is comprised of a collection of electrodes that must make direct physical contact with the scalp surface. Since the EEG records the electrical potential (relative to a reference point), it must make physical contact with the energy source (i.e. the surface of the skull). In addition, the impedance must be within certain limits (less than 5 KOhms) to enhance the SNR, necessitating the use of conductive gels. This combination makes the use of typical clinical grade EEG systems unrealistic - as the time required to fit the device, the application of sticky conductive gels makes it very unsuitable from a user acceptance perspective. There are alternative technologies - that utilise what is termed 'dry' electrodes. These do not require the use of conductive gels - and are quicker to apply and less cumbersome to the subject. Typically, these systems are implemented in some form of a helmet - which is placed on the head - and the electrodes make contact with the scalp directly. In addition, the number of electrodes is kept to a minimum - typically 4-12 are required. Further, the electrodes are attached to a small footprint device, which transmits the signals to a receiver (a personal computer) wirelessly - using blue tooth technology. It is certainly technologically possible to fit the EEG electrodes and related hardware into a cap like device - which can easily be applied to the head.

Further, all of the biosignals discussed in this chapter are obtainable through a single device - the electrodes used for EEG data acquisition can also be deployed for ECG and EDR recording simultaneously. The issue of electrode placement can be a cause for concern. The EEG electrodes can only be placed on the scalp - at locations specific to the type of data one wishes to acquire. With respect to electrode placement for ECG acquisition - there is also an option to place the electrodes on the chest or forearms. Forearm placement may be convenient for the subject - but may present difficulties if the subject must perform a physical task during the authentication process (e.g. typing). In this scenario, the electrodes would have to be placed on the chest - but note that in a typical non-clinical ECG application, three electrodes are sufficient (as opposed to the 12-lead version). Electrode placement for EDR can be positioned more or less anywhere convenient - and the signal is not affected by muscular activity to the same extent as ECG/EEG signals.

Since the biosginals can be acquired from a single physical platform, it is natural to employ a multi-modal cognitive biometrics approach, which would significantly extend the feature space. This augmented feature space would clearly provide a robust signature for person authentication - and identification. One could envision utilising one biosignal to substantiate the other - that is presenting our self via EEG and then verifying that against an ECG and/or GSR recording. In addition, biosignals could be used in a larger system that deploys a behavioural biometric such as keystroke dynamics or signature in conjunction with a cognitive approach. This would certainly provide a more comprehensive and lightweight approach to user authentication and identification which is acceptable by the user community - a requirement for any biometric system.

Lastly, the cognitive biometrics approach provides an ideal platform for operating either in static or continuous modes. In continuous mode, the person will have their details monitored typically at particular intervals, so as not to burden the system with feature extraction and classification overhead. One question that arises in this regard is what sort of schedule should be deployed for implementing the re-authentication? Should the re-authentication occur at synchronous time intervals, should it be associated with changes in task context, should it occur when there are periods of inactivity? These are decisions that need to be made for any continuous biometric approach. With regards to cognitive biometrics, it may be most suitable to invoke the biometric when a particular task switch has occurred. For instance, when switching to the internet, a variety of images and sounds may be presented to the user, which would engender certain cognitive and emotional states. If the user is playing a game, then clearly there will be a significant amount of cognitive expenditure, and probably significant alterations in their mood. The contention would be that for a multi-modal approach that deploys cognitive biometrics, the invocation of the later would be based on task context – context switching. If a user then switched to a word processing or email based application – the deployment of a keystroke dynamics based approach could be included in addition to a cognitive approach. These decisions would be left to the implementer, but clearly the addition of cognitive biometrics provides an extremely valuable added dimension to a continuous biometric (either singly or in a multi-modal approach).

CONCLUSION

Cognitive biometrics provides a novel approach to user authentication that is particularly suitable for a continuous mode of application. The evidence from twin studies indicate that all biosignals deployed in biometrics as discussed here have a significant heritability component, reaching upwards of 80% for certain characteristic such as spectral power in the EEG. This is a very encouraging fact – which provides a rational basis for the selection of features for use in an authentication system. One should at least start by selecting features from biosignals that are expected to be unique across individuals. It is further proposed that a multi-modal approach – within the biosignal domain, would provide enhanced levels of individuality – forming a concept equivalent to the endophenotypes. The likelihood that two individuals will produce the same EEG, ECG, and EDR in response to a given stimulus is quite remote. In addition, the multi-modal approach could be extended to include various types of behavioural biometrics, particularly keystroke dynamics.

Cognitive biometrics is particularly suited to a continuous authentication approach – as it can acquire data whilst a user is engaged in a variety of activities. For instance, visual and audio information serve well as stimuli that are expected to elicit a cognitive response from an individual. Users typically engage in a variety of activities – such as surfing the internet – which is essentially graphical, using a word processor, performing calculations in spreadsheets, and in some cases, even listening to music! Each of these activities could be used as the stimulus for authentication. As with any authentication system, a reference sample of user under a particular stimulus-response regime is required, stored and utilised for subsequent authentication. If a variety of stimuli types are to be used for authentication, then a reference sample would have to be acquired for each modality. This is typically not an issue, as the user would enrol with the various types of stimuli the system would wish to authenticate under. Unlike behavioural biometrics though, the stimulus doesn't have to be unique. In the case of keystroke dynamics, the user typically enrols by entering their user ID and password a set number of times, from which their user profile is generated and used for subsequent authentication purposes. With cognitive biometrics, classes of stimuli can be used for generating the user profile and in the actual authentication challenge as well. This process obviates the notion of cancellable biometrics - as the same stimulus need never be presented twice. Instead, if a stimulus has a particular emotional semantic, then there is generally an infinite number of such instances that can be presented. Shoulder surfing and the like therefore become obsolete in this framework.

Lastly, the issue of technological feasibility should be clarified. There is a well defined interplay between demand and supply. Typically, many people consider EEG as a complex, machine and knowledge intensive enterprise, which requires expensive and cumbersome equipment. Quite the contrary, the trend is for portable, lightweight, and inexpensive equipment that can be managed by the individual to monitor and take control of their own state of health. Systems for remote monitoring and eHealth are creating demands for such devices and the relevant industries are responding to these demands. In connection with this trend, mobile technology is expanding rapidly, with mobiles approaching the computation power of PCs of 10 years ago. These trends are providing devices that can fit in your pocket, are wireless, and can utilise software installed as a mobile app! The technology as it currently stands is sufficient to allow the deployment of the required equipment that would make the cognitive biometrics approach feasible. The need for biometrics is pervasive – and many governments and NGOs are very interested in any technology that will enhance security of physical and digital assets. It is up to the biometrics community to demonstrate that this technology is feasible, and that there is a demand for such technology.

REFERENCES

Bellak, L. (1994). The schizophrenic syndrome and attention deficit disorder: Thesis, antithesis, and synthesis? *American Psychologist, 49*, 25-29.

Biel, L., Petterson, O., & Stork, D. (2001). ECG analysis: A new approach in human identification. *IEE Transactions on Instrumentation and Measurement, 50*(3), 808–812. doi:10.1109/19.930458

Braff, D. L., & Freedman, R. (2002). Endophenotypes in studies of the genetics of schizophrenia. In Davis, K. L., Charney, D. S., Coyle, I. T., & Nemeroff, C. (Eds.), *Neuropharmacology: The fifth generation of progress* (pp. 703–716). Philadelphia, PA: Lippincott Williams, & Wilkins.

Cacioppo, J. T., Bernsten, G. G., Larsen, J. T., Poehlmann, K. M., & Ito, T. A. (2000). The pyschophysiology of emotion. In Lewis, M., & Haviland-Jones, J. M. (Eds.), *The handbook of emotion* (2nd ed., pp. 173–191). New York, NY: Guilford Press.

Chan, A. D. C., Hamdy, M. M., Badre, A., & Badee, V. (2008). Wavelet distance measure for person identification using electrocardiograms. *IEEE Transactions on Instrumentation and Measurement, 57*(2), 248–253. doi:10.1109/TIM.2007.909996

Crider, A., Kremen, W. S., Xian, H., Jacobson, K. C., Waterman, B., & Eisen, S. A. (2004). Stability, consistency, and heritability of electrodermal response lability in middle-aged male twins. *Psychophysiology, 41*(4), 501–509. doi:10.1111/j.1469-8986.2004.00189.x

Dalageorgou, C., Ge, D., Jamshidi, Y., Nolte, I. M., Riese, H., & Savelieva, I. (2007). Heritability of QT interval: How much is explained by genes for resting heart rate? *Journal of Cardiovascular Electrophysiology, 19*(4), 386–391. doi:10.1111/j.1540-8167.2007.01030.x

Docter, R. F., & Friedman, L. F. (1965). Thirty-day stability of spontaneous galvanic skin responses in man. *Psychophysiology, 2*(4), 311–315. doi:10.1111/j.1469-8986.1966.tb02659.x

Edelberg, R. (1971). Electrical properties of skin. In Elden, H. R. (Ed.), *A treatise of the skin (Vol. 1*, pp. 519–551). New York, NY: Wiley.

Flior, E., & Kowalski, K. (2010). *Continuous biometric user authentication in online examinations*. Seventh International Conference on Information Technology: New Generations (ITING), Las Vegas Nevada, USA, 12-14 April, 2010, 2010, (pp. 488-492).

Forsen, G., Nelson, M., & Staron, R. (1977). Personal attributes authentication techniques. In Griffin, A. F. B. (Ed.), *RADC report RADC-TR-77-1033*.

Gilmore, C. S., Malone, S. M., & Iacono, W. G. (2010). Brain electrophysiological endophenotypes for externalizing psychopathology: A multivariate approach. *Behavior Genetics, 40*(2), 186–200. doi:10.1007/s10519-010-9343-3

Gottesman, H., & Shields, J. (1972). *Schizophrenia and genetics: A twin study vantage point*. New York, NY: Academic Press.

Gottesmann, I. I. (2003). The endophenotype concept in psychiatry: Etymology and strategic intentions. *The American Journal of Psychiatry, 160*(4), 636–645. doi:10.1176/appi.ajp.160.4.636

Hansell, N. K., Wright, M. J., Geffen, G. M., Geffen, L. B., Smith, G. A., & Martin, N. G. (2001). Genetic influences on ERP slow wave measures of working memory. *Behavior Genetics, 31*(6), 603–614. doi:10.1023/A:1013301629521

Israel, S., Irvine, J., Cheng, A., Wiederhold, M., & Wiederhold, B. (2005). ECG to identify individuals. *Pattern Recognition, 38*(1), 133–142. doi:10.1016/j.patcog.2004.05.014

Jain, A., Griess, F., & Connell, S. (2002). Online signature verification. *Pattern Recognition, 35*, 2963–2972..doi:10.1016/S0031-3203(01)00240-0

Kwang, G., Yap, R. H. C., Sim, T., & Ramnath, R. (2009). An usability study of continuous biometrics authentication. *ICB 2009. LNCS, 5558*, 828–837.

Lalor, E. C., Kelly, S. P., Finucane, C., Burke, E., Smith, R., Reilly, R. B., & McDarby, G. (2005). Steady-state VEP-based brain-computer interface control in an immersive 3D gaming environment. *EURASIP Journal on Applied Signal Processing, 19*, 3156–3164. doi:10.1155/ASP.2005.3156

Lenzenwenger, M. F., Mclachlan, G., & Rubin, D. B. (2007). Resolving the latent structure of schizophrenia endophenotypes using expectation-maximization-based finite mixture modeling. *Journal of Abnormal Psychology, 116*(1), 116–129.

Lopes Machado, E. Z., de Souza Crippa, J. A., Cecdio Hcdlak, J. E., Quimarcies, F. S., & Zuardi, A. W. (2003). Electrodermically nonresponsive schizophrenia patients make more errors in the stroop color word test, indicating selective attention deficit. *Schizophrenia Bulletin, 28*(3), 459–466.

Marcel, S., & Millan, J. R. (2007). Person authentication using brainwaves (EEG) and maximum a posterior model adaptation. *IEEE Transactions on Pattern Analysis and Machine Intelligence, 29*(4), 743–752. doi:10.1109/TPAMI.2007.1012

McCraty, R., Atkinson, M., Tiller, W. A., Rein, G., & Watkins, A. D. (1995). The effects of emotions on short-term power spectrum analysis of heart rate variability. *The American Journal of Cardiology, 76*, 1089–1093. doi:10.1016/S0002-9149(99)80309-9

Mehta, S. S., & Lingayat, N. S. (2007). Comparative study of QRS detection in single lead and 12-lead ECG based on entropy and combined entropy criteria using support vector machine. *Journal of Theoretical and Applied Information Technology, 3*, 8–18.

Mirsky, A. F., Yardley, S. L., Jones, B. P., Walsh, D., & Kendler, K. S. (1995). Analysis of the attention deficit in schizophrenia: A study of patients and their relatives in Ireland. *Journal of Psychiatric Research, 29*, 23–42. doi:10.1016/0022-3956(94)00041-O

Mohammadi, G., Shousttari, P., Ardekani, B. M., & Shamsolhani, M. B. (2006). Person identification by using AR model for EEG signals. *Proceedings of WASET, 11*, 281–285.

Myles-Worsley, M. (2007). P50 sensory gating in multiplex schizophrenia families from a Pacific Island isolate. *The American Journal of Psychiatry, 159*, 2007–2012. doi:10.1176/appi.ajp.159.12.2007

Nixon, M. S., & Carter, J. N. (2004). On gait as a biometric: Progress and prospects. In *Proc. EUSIPCO 2004*, Sept, Vienna, (pp. 1401-1404).

Palaniappan, R. (2005). Multiple mental thought parametric classification: A new approach for individual identification. *International Journal of Signal Processing, 2*(1), 222–225.

Palaniappan, R., & Mandic, D. P. (2007). Biometrics from brain electrical activity: A machine learning approach. *IEEE Transactions on Pattern Analysis and Machine Intelligence, 29*(4), 738–742. doi:10.1109/TPAMI.2007.1013

Paranjape, R. B., Mahovsky, J., Benedicenti, L., & Kolesapos, Z. (2001). *The electroencephalogram as a biometric*. Canadian Conference on Electrical and Computer Engineering, (pp. 1363–1366).

Pilia, G., Chen, W.-M., Scuteri, A., Orrúm, M., Albaim, G., & Dei, M. (2006). Heritability of cardiovascular and personality traits in 6,148 Sardinians. *PLOS Genetics, 2*(8), 1207–1223. doi:10.1371/journal.pgen.0020132

Rainville, P., Bechara, A., Naqvim, N., & Damasiom, A. R. (2006). Basic emotions are associated with distinct patterns of cardiorespiratory activity. *International Journal of Psychophysiology, 16*, 5–18. doi:10.1016/j.ijpsycho.2005.10.024

Revett, K. (2008). *Behavioral biometrics: A remote access approach. (2008)*. Colchester, UK: Wiley & Sons.

Revett, K. (2009). A bioinformatics based approach to user authentication via keystroke dynamics. *International Journal of Control, Automation, and Systems, 7*(1), 7-15. ISSN: 1598-6446

Revett, K. (2009). Behavioral biometrics: A biosignal based approach. In Wang, L., & Geng, X. (Eds.), *Behavioral biometrics for human identification: Intelligent applications*. Hershey, PA: IGI Global Publishers. doi:10.4018/978-1-60566-725-6.ch005

Silva, H., Gamboa, H., & Fred, A. (2007). Applicability of lead V2 ECG measurements in biometrics. *Proceedings of Med-e-Tel 2007*, Luxembourg, April 2007.

Smit, D. J. A., Posthuma, D., Boomsma, D. I., & De Gues, E. J. C. (2005). Heritability of background EEG across the power spectrum. *Psychophysiology*, *42*, 691–697. doi:10.1111/j.1469-8986.2005.00352.x

Sutton, S., Braren, M., Zubin, J., & John, E. R. (1965). Evoked-potentials correlates of stimulus uncertainty. *Science*, *150*, 1187–1188. doi:10.1126/science.150.3700.1187

Thorpe, J., van Oorschot, P. C., & Somayaji, A. (2005). Pass-thoughts: Authenticating with our minds. *Proceedings of the 2005 Workshop on New Security Paradigms*, (pp. 45-56).

Van Beijsterveldt, C. E. M., Molenaar, P. C. M., de Geus, E. J. C., & Boomsma, D. I. (1996). Heritability of human brain functioning as assessed by electroencephalography. *American Journal of Human Genetics*, *58*, 562–573.

Waller, A. D. (1887). A demonstration on man of electromotive changes accompanying the heart's beat. *The Journal of Physiology*, *8*, 229–234.

Wang, Y., Agrafioti, F., Hatzinakos, D., & Plataniotis, K. M. (2008). Analysis of human electrocardiogram for biometric recognition. *EURASIP Journal on Advances in Signal Processing*, *2008*, 1–11. doi:10.1155/2008/148658

Wübbler, G., Stavridis, M., Kreiseler, D., Bousseljot, R.-D., & Elster, C. (2007). Verification of humans using the electrocardiogram. *Pattern Recognition Letters*, *28*, 1172–1175. doi:10.1016/j.patrec.2007.01.014

ADDITIONAL READING

Behavioral Biometrics

Ahmed, A. A. E., & Traoré, I. A new biometrics technology based on mouse dynamics. Technical Report ECE-03-5, Department of Electrical and Computer Engineering, University of Victoria, British Columbia, Canada, 2003.

Behavioral Biometrics for Human Identification. (2009). *Intelligent Applications, Edited By: Liang Wang, University of Melbourne, Australia; Xin Geng, Southeast University, China, IGI Global Publishers*. Penn., USA: Intelligent Applications, Behavioral Biometrics for Human Identification.

Brown, M., & Rogers, S. J. (1993). User identification via keystroke characteristics of typed names using neural networks. *International Journal of Man-Machine Studies*, *39*, 999–1014. doi:10.1006/imms.1993.1092

Doddington, G. R., Przybocki, M. A., Martin, F. A., & Reynolds, R. A. (2000). The NIST speaker recognition evaluation-overview, methodology, systems, results, perspective. *Pattern Recognition*, *36*(2), 383–396.

Foster, J.P., Nixon, M.S., & Prugell-Bennet., Gait recognition by symmetry analysis. AVBPA'01, pp. 272–277, 2002.

Furui, S. (1981b). Comparison of speaker recognition methods using statistical features and dynamic features. *IEEE Transactions on Acoustics, Speech, and Signal Processing*, *29*(3), 342–350. doi:10.1109/TASSP.1981.1163605

Gafurov, D., Helkala, K., & Sondrol, T. (2006). Biometric gait authentication using accelerometer sensor. *Journal of Computers*, *1*(7), 51–59. doi:10.4304/jcp.1.7.51-59

Hayashi, K., Okamoto, E., & Mambo, M. (1997). *Proposal of user identification scheme using mouse, ICICIS'97, Information and Communication Security, LNCS 1334* (pp. 144–148). Springer-Verlag.

Leggett, J., Williams, G., Usnick, M., & Longnecker, M. (1991). Dynamic identity verification via keystroke characteristics. *International Journal of Man-Machine Studies*, *35*, 859–870. doi:10.1016/S0020-7373(05)80165-8

Magalhães, S. T., Revett, K., & Santos, H. M. D. Password secured sites – stepping forward with keystroke dynamics. International Conference on Next Generation Web Services Practices (NWeSP '05), Seoul, Korea, August 22–26, 2005, pp. 293–298, 2005.

Mermelstein, P. (1976). Distance measures for speech recognition, psychological and instrumental. In Chen, C. H. (Ed.), *Pattern Recognition and Artificial Intelligence* (pp. 374–388). New York, NY, USA: Academic.

Monrose, F., & Rubin, A. D. Authentication via keystroke dynamics. Proceedings of the Fourth ACM Conference on Computer and Communication Security, pp. 48–56, Zurich, Switzerland, 1997.

Revett, K. On the use of multiple sequence alignment for user authentication via keystroke dynamics. International Conference on Global eSecurity 2007 (ICGeS), pp. 112–120, University of East London, April 16–18, 2007

Electroencephalography

Davidson, R. J., Jackson, D. C., & Larson, C. L. (2000). Human electroencephalography. In Cacioppo, J. T., Tassinary, L. G., & Bernston, G. G. (Eds.), *Handbook of Psychophysiology* (pp. 27–56). Cambridge: Cambridge University Press.

Hicks, B.M., Bernat, E., Malone, S.M., Iacono, W.G., Patrick, C.J., Krueger, R.F., & McGue, M., Genes mediate the association between P3 amplitude and externalizing disorders, psychophysiology 44(1), pp. 98-105, 2007.

Nunez, P. L., & Srinivasan, R. (1981). Electric fields of the brain: The neurophysics of EEG. *Oxford University Press*. ISBN.

Palaniappan, R. Identifying individuals using mental task based brain computer interface, in *Proceedings of IEEE*, ICISIP '05 Proceedings of the 2005 3rd International Conference on Intelligent Sensing and Information Processing, pp. 239–242, 2005

Poulos, M., Rangoussi, M., Alexandris, N., & Evangelou, A. (2001). On the use of EEG features towards person identification via neural networks. *Medical Informatics and the Internet in Medicine*, *26*(1), 35–48. doi:10.1080/14639230010015843

Ravi, K. V. R. Palaniappan, R., A Minimal Channel Set for Individual Identification with EEG Biometric Using Genetic Algorithm, International Conference on Computational Intelligence and Multimedia Application, Singapore, 13-15 December, 2007, pp. 328, 332.

Electrocardiogram

Guennoun, M., Abbad, N., Talom, J., Rahman, S. M. M., & Khatib, K. Continuous authentication by electrocardiogram data, IEEE International Conference on Science and Technology for Humanity (TIC-STH), Toronto, Canada, 40-42, 2009.

Kyoso, M., & Uchiyama, A. Development of an ECG identification system, in *Proceedings of the 23rd Annual International IEEE Conference on Engineering in Medicine and Biology Society*, pp. 3721–3723, Istanbul, Turkey, 2001

Russell, M. W., Law, I., Sholinksy, P., & Fabsitz, R. R. (1998). Heritability of ECG Measurements in Adult Male Twins. *Journal of Electrocardiology*, *30*(Suppl), 64–68. doi:10.1016/S0022-0736(98)80034-4

Electrodermal Response

Balloun, K. D., & Holmes, D. S. (1979). Effects of Repeated Examinations on the Ability to Detect Guilt With a Polygraphic Examination: A Laboratory Experiment With a Real Crime. *The Journal of Applied Psychology*, *64*, 316–322. doi:10.1037/0021-9010.64.3.316

Cacioppo, J. T., Berntson, G. G., Larsen, J. T., Poehlmann, K. M., & Ito, T. A. (2000). The psychophysiology of emotion. In Lewis, M., & Haviland-Jones, J. M. (Eds.), *Handbook of Emotions* (pp. 173–191). New York: The Guilford Press.

Mandryk, R.L. & Atkins, M.S., A fuzzy physiological approach for continuously modeling emotion during interaction with play technologies, International Journal of Human Computer Interactions 65 92007), 329-347.

Venables, P. H., & Christie, M. J. (1980). Electrodermal activity. In Martin, I., & Venables, P. H. (Eds.), *Techniques in Psychophysiology* (pp. 2–67). New York: John Wiley.

Cognitive Biometrics

Boehner, K., Depaula, R., Dourish, P., & Sengers, P., How emotion is made and measured, International Journal Human-Computer Studies 65 92007) 275-291.

International Journal of Cognitive Biometrics. Inderscience Publishers, ISSN: (www.inderscience.com/ijcb)

Khalifa, W., & Revett, K. (in press) A Survey of Techniques Used in Human Identification Based on Cognitive Biometrics: the Electroencephalogram, The 10th International Conference on Information, ICI'2010, Gamasa, Egypt, 4-6 December, 2010

Palaniappan, R., & Revett, K. (in press). Thought Based PIN Generation Using Single Channel EEG Biometric. *International Journal of Cognitive Biometrics.*

Revett, K., Deravi, F., & Sirlantzis, K. On the Role of Biosignals for User Authentication: The Foundations of Cognitive Biometrics, 2010 International Conference on emerging Security technologies: EST 2010 - ROBOSEC 2010 - LAB-RS 2010, 6-7 September, 2010, University of Kent, Canterbury, UK.

Revett, K., & Magalhães, S. T. *Cognitive Biometrics: Challenges for the Future*, 6th International Conference on Global Security, Safety, and Sustainability (ICGS3), Braga, Portugal, 1-3 September, 2010, pp. 79-86, ISBN: 3-642-15716-5, Springer-Verlag, Heidelberg, Germany.

Tantawi, M., & Revett, K. (in press) On the Use of the Electrocardiogram for Biometric Authentication, The 10th International Conference on Information, ICI'2010, Gamasa, Egypt, 4-6 December, 2010.

Anatomical Biometrics

Handbook of Biometrics (Ed.). (2010). *Anil K. Jain, Patrick Flynn, and Arun A. Ross* (1st ed.). Springer.

Jain, A. K., Bolle, R., & Pankanti, S. (2003). Introduction to biometrics. In Jain, A., Bolle, R., & Pankanti, S. (Eds.), *Biometrics. Personal Identification in Networked Society* (pp. 1–41). Kluwer Academic Publishers.

KEY TERMS AND DEFINITIONS

Biometrics: The scientific approach to user identification and or user authentication.

Continuous Biometrics: A mode of authentication that takes repeated authentication samples from the subject in order to ensure that the user of the secured device has not changed since the last authentication stage.

Electroencephalogram: The recording of the electrical activity of the brain through the placement of voltage sensitive electrodes on the surface of the scalp.

Electrocardiogram: The recording of the electrical activity of the heart, recorded by placing voltage sensitive electrodes over the surface of the chest cavity.

Electrodermal Response: The recording of the changes in the electrical conductivity of the skin by the placement of voltage sensitive electrodes on the skin surface – typically on the fingers or wrist.

Endophenotype: A property of an organism that relates its phenotype to its genotype – it is a set of one or more features that are heritable and measurable and are indicative, with a high probability that the possessor of the endophenotype will display a particular variant of a given trait that is endemic to a population.

Event Related GSR: A protocol that examines how changes in the GSR are related to the presentation of a specific stimulus.

Galvanic Skin Response (GSR): A recording of the change in the conductive properties of the skin measured using voltage sensitive electrodes placed on the skin surface.

Multi-Modal Biometrics: An approach to biometrics that deploys multiple types of responses of the subject to a given stimulus.

Chapter 7
Sitting Postures and Electrocardiograms:
A Method for Continuous and Non-Disruptive Driver Authentication

Andreas Riener
Johannes Kepler University Linz, Austria

ABSTRACT

Travelling by car is the preferred method of everyday transportation by most of the people in the world. Individuals from different age groups (at least exceeding the minimum age limit of 16 or 18 years) and health condition (meeting safe mental and physiological requirements) are traveling by car more often and increasingly by themselves.

With a rising number of assistance systems and increasing complexity of information to be presented, drivers demand the automatic operation of driver assistance systems. One of the main interaction mediums between a driver and a car is the driver seat. Given that the seat is occupied all the time while driving, it can be a possible solution for unobtrusive recording of personal characteristics to be used for continuous driver authentication. In this work we focus on a discussion of design and implementation issues for authenticating a driver based on his/her sitting profile and/or contactless collected electrocardiogram data using in-seat electrodes.

This approach is novel in terms of "participation" – the driver has neither to operate something nor to attach a device. Furthermore he/she must not be aware of the continuous collection of his/her personal profile at all.

DOI: 10.4018/978-1-61350-129-0.ch007

INTRODUCTION

Identification and verification of drivers is a topic that is increasingly attracting attention for several reasons and for different fields of application in the transportation domain. It can be used for safety systems continuously monitoring the health condition and alertness of a driver (for example a biological state observation system checking if the driver is tired or drunken). With the emergence of car sharing vendors offering different account types for rental, a problem to be solved is the rate of insurance due for the driven route. The insurance rate should not only be bound to the car and calculated on a yearly basis, but should be linked to the driver and his/her personal skills. The amount payable by a driver can be dynamically calculated based on the driven kilometers and on his/her style of driving. Driven distance can be obtained from the CAN-bus of a car or calculated from available GPS data, and the profile of a driver can be formed from sensors continuously monitoring the emotional state of a driver and/or the on-board diagnostic functions of a vehicle. An important requirement for this system is that it has to be effective in operation all the time and can also be able to authenticate a driver as he/she might use different cars.

An example showing that the topic of authentication is relevant is given by the recent developments of (Yubico, 2010). Their "YubiKey" is a USB-key for secure, easy and affordable access to different applications which also includes an authentication service. Yubico suggests using the YubiKey as a stronger and better alternative to smart cards. Automobile manufacturer have tried smart cards as method for driver authentication in the past; unfortunately, their replacement is very expensive and, more important, cards are prone to hacking – the car domain is nowadays looking for improved, universal applicable solutions.

Identity Authentication

Long-established methods of human authentication are relying on "something you have" (tokens, access cards, identity document/passport, keys, etc.) or "something you know" (secret knowledge: passwords, pass phrases; non-secret: user ID, mother's maiden name, favorite color, birthday of the cat, etc.). Widely used methods, even in combined settings such as user ID or access card + password, are not sufficient for identity authentication – if an object used for identification was acquired or the required knowledge was attained, it can be relatively easy to forge an identity (IBIA, 2010; Revett, 2008). With advances in technology enabling precise measurement of human characteristics along with the availability of greater computational power to transfer measurements into representations that can be compared in real-time, biometrical identification as an effective and convenient way for verifying the identity of a person emerged. "Biometrics" comprises automated methods for recognizing a person based on physiological or behavioral characteristics (based on "what one is" or "how one behaves").

Driver Authentication

The transportation domain is one of the most complex sectors involving user interaction. An important interaction involves the authentication of drivers aimed at verifying if they are authorized to access a vehicle or service, or to transport sensitive goods (IBIA, 2010). Drivers who pick up rental or shared cars will be biometrically screened to authenticate their identities, ensure that they are holding a valid driving license and are also allowed to drive the type of taken car (by checking their driving license categories) (Riener and Ferscha, 2008). Furthermore, authentication techniques can also be used in the future to verify that truck drivers are not exceeding time limits on working hours, for calculating tax or personal insurance rates, and even for improving driving comfort.

A few biometric identification methods are applied in cars that are available today. However, most of them are based on physical attributes requiring active engagement by the involved person, e.g. by pressing sensors located in the car door handles, using fingerprint readers inside the car (Philips et al., 2000) (p. 60), or looking into iris scan systems.

Other physical attributes that can be more or less conveniently collected in a car (and converted into mathematical representations for later comparison) include faces, hand geometry, retinal patterns, thermal imaging (of face or wrist), vein patterns, voice patterns, and deoxyribonucleic acid (DNA). Recently, an exploratory work has been done to establish whether physical characteristics such as the fingernail bed, earlobes (Choras, 2009; Hurley et al., 2008; Ramesh & Rao, 2009) or body odor (Korotkaya, 2003; Rashed & Santos, 2010) can be used for electronic identity authentication (Bhattacharyya et al., 2009; Olden, 2009) (p. 24).

Behavioral attributes: Mathematical representations of an individual can be assigned to the physical traits mentioned above as well as to implicitly detectable behavioral traits. Traditionally the signature dynamics (writing speed, angle of the pen, applied pressure, etc.) of handwriting are used as a representative to describe behavioral traits. Others are keystroke dynamics or movement dynamics when walking (gait recognition). These techniques however are not suitable for in-car detection, especially while driving.

Nevertheless, behavioral traits must not be fully omitted in the car domain – after conducting long-lasting driving studies, we have discovered that a combination of dynamically captured pressure images from the driver seat and wirelessly collected electrocardiograms (ECG's) from the driver is a promising approach to continuously authenticate a driver operating a car in an inattentive, unobtrusive, and convenient way. The proposed system combining several implicit gathering techniques will allow activity recognition while driving.

Outline

In this chapter we elaborate authentication based on static/dynamic evaluation of pressure images from car seat and backrest together with contactless collected ECG signals. We start with individual traffic as a motivation for automatic and continuous driver authentication, and conclude this section with a definition of terms such as identification and authentication as used throughout this work. Subsequent to that we describe the individual building blocks of the proposed system including identified problems. In the section after that the single components are merged to a continuous driver authentication system and results of previous studies are indicated and elaborately discussed. The last two sections give an outlook to possible future research directions and finally conclude the chapter.

Background

Recently, a steadily *increasing volume of traffic* (most likely caused by a decreasing number of carpools due to more flexible work schedules, longer journeys to the place of work, and the desire of people for a more mobile lifestyle) has become evident – according to the U.S. Census Bureau 2000 report (Reschovsky, 2004), 88 percent of workers use a car to commute.

A second point to mention is that the *average travel time per route increased* to 25.5 minutes in 2000 from 21.7 minutes in 1990 with more than 5 percent spending between 60 and 89 minutes per direction in their cars; for nearly 3 percent of workers it takes more than 90 minutes to go to work every day. As expected, the trend for longer traveling times will not stagnate in the near future.

Thirdly, average vehicle occupancy rate (AVO), another measure useful to determine the mobility of persons in a specific area, has recently shown a *declining average number of persons per vehicle.* (The vehicle occupancy rate represents the average number of persons per vehicle, including the driver.) According to (Rimsley, 2003), the average number of persons/vehicle in Greater Lafayette decreased to 1.11 persons per vehicle in 2003, after 1.24 persons/vehicle in 1980. A similar study done in the Phoenix Metropolitan area (Maricopa Association of Governments, 2006) reported that the average occupancy rate has dropped from 1.34 (1992) to 1.23 (2006). A study presented by (Shafie et al., 2008) indicated average vehicle occupancy between 1.54 and 1.61 persons/vehicle. Latest data published by the (U.S. Department of Transportation, 2009) stated an AVO of 1.59 persons per car for the U.S.

The conclusion to be drawn from these studies is the majority of workers use their car to reach their place of work, car drivers commute mostly alone and for continually longer traveling times a day. Individuals are solely responsible for operating not only the car but additionally for supervising all of its information and assistance systems, substantiating the necessity of attention-free authentication techniques.

The demand for rising personal mobility and individual traffic, together with information and communication technology present in cars at reasonable costs, have meanwhile led to a new generation of smart networked vehicles. In car-to-car (C2C) or car-to-infrastructure (C2I) networks, information about traditional system states like vehicle status, road occupancy or weather conditions is not only exchanged but more personal data of the driver is communicated to adopt individuality.

Individuality in Vehicle Operation

To achieve the goal of personal data exchange on one side and to avoid misuse on the other side, the spread of information between cars and infrastructure calls for continuous identification or authentication of the driver while operating a vehicle. Classical approaches, even if claiming to operate noninvasively, have to be withdrawn as vehicle drivers are often highly saturated in their regular task of steering; therefore, it is out of question that they can provide PIN codes, passwords, or pull their finger over a fingerprint reader to authenticate themselves. Fully automatic and at the same time safe solutions are required to fulfill the operational needs in cars – the car seat or contactless operating ECG devices as media for implicit data collection come into play (Figure 1).

Figure 1. A passive operating driver authentication system with several examples of personalized vehicular services

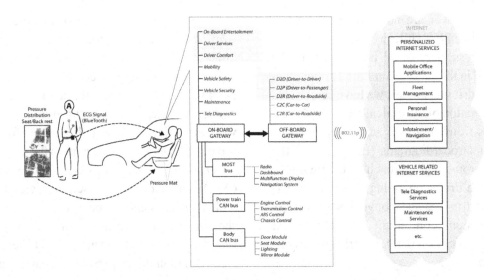

The application of biometric based implicit authentication of an individual will provide a new class of vehicular services such as personalization (once a driver is seated, he/she will be automatically identified while the vehicle will adjust seat position, AC, radio, mirrors, etc.) and safety functions (only authorized drivers are permitted to start the engine or drive the car while this privilege will be denied to others; posture pattern based identification, as an example for biometrics, is thought to be an effective method for car-theft protection).

Before discussing specific applications, it is also essential to critically examine possible limitations of such systems. Suppose, for instance, that the driver of a car gets injured or incapacitated to drive and someone else is asked to drive him/her to a hospital – can there be any chance for a driver to use his/her vehicle by skipping the authorization process, allowing the helping person to operate the vehicle in a "rescue mode" without a personalized profile (Riener, 2010) (p. 246)?

DEFINITION OF TERMS: IDENTIFICATION VS. AUTHENTICATION

Biometric identification refers to identifying a person based on his/her physiological or behavioral characteristics and biometric identifiers. Identification and authentication (also verification) are significantly different terms: Identification in a biometric system answers the question "who a specific person is" (this is a 1:N relationship, comparing the currently acquired pattern against biometric profiles from a database), whereas authentication attempts to answer the question "is this person A?" after the user claims to be A (Woodward et al., 2003) (p. 2). It has to be noted that the second case (authentication) is much more complex than identification; nevertheless, it can be solved in the designated automotive domain.

Authentication may be defined as "providing the right person with the right privileges the right access at the right time". In general, in the security community three types of authentication methods ("proof of identity") are distinguished (Woodward et al., 2003) (p. 6), (Liu, 2001) (p. 27):

- **Physical** or "something you have", e.g. an access card, smart card, token, or key,
- **Mental**, cerebration or "something you know", for instance a password, PIN-code, or piece of personal information (the birthday date of one's mother or the name of one's dog),
- **Personal** or "something you are", which is a biometric characteristic dividable into an active (explicit) type, such as the interpretation of retina/iris, voice, face, or finger print, and a passive (implicit) type, comprising for instance sitting posture pattern or ECG signal evaluation.

Physical or mental systems have the disadvantage that they are not based on any inherited attributes of a person; from this point of view it should be clear that the remaining class (personal) is the most secure verification option – because it cannot be lost, stolen or borrowed (such as keys). Furthermore, it cannot be forgotten or guessed by an imposter (as for example a password), and forging of a biometric characteristic is in general very complex. Nevertheless, biometrical characteristics exhibit adverse properties legitimating its universal application, such as

- Some characteristics are dependent on the age or the gender of a person,
- Individuals lacking a specific characteristic may be excluded from the possibility of authentication,
- Correct authentication is always bound to probability levels. To rate the quality of a biometric system two metrics, False Accept Rate (FAR) and False Reject Rate

(FRR), are widely used. Both methods focus on the system's ability to allow limited entry to authorized users. FAR and FRR are interdependent and can vary significantly (Liu, 2001) (p. 32), thus both measures should always be given together, e.g. plotted one against the other.

Continuous and implicitly operating authentication methods based on biometric features can prevent the driver from additional cognitive load and distraction; that is particularly important for situations where the person is continuously highly challenged (for example during a city trip at rush hour). Another advantage of the proposed system can be seen in the fact that once a driver is authenticated using the pressure sensing system in the seat it can be assumed that the person remains the same unless the continuous data flow from the mat system tears off – only in this situation, the complex authentication process needs to be repeated.

Building Blocks for Continuous Driver Authentication

Sensor systems for continuously measuring signals from a person (a driver) must not be obtrusive or annoying as potential consequences can be caused by distraction or overlooked information. Considering this issue, we follow a fully implicit and attention-free approach to acquire the "state" of the driver using only the car seat.

According to a former review of sensors suitable for fulfilling this task, we selected a combination of ECG sensors and force-sensitive (pressure) sensor arrays as novel approach for implicit identification. As outlined in Figure 2, GPS data is gathered additionally for synchronization issues (GPS time) and for location estimation reasons (validation).

Permanent Seat Pressure Image Detection

The behavior of an individual in dynamic environments is dependent on numerous dimensions including context and time. (Bobick, 1997) divides the expression "behavior" into the three sub terms

Figure 2. Driver identification from continuously collected ECG and pressure sensor data. GPS position data is collected to relate sensor data to specific segments of the driven route (validity checking); the GPS time field is used as external basis for data synchronization.

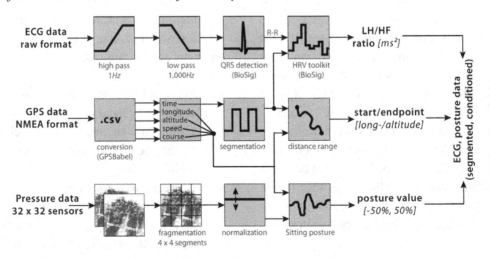

(1) movements (these are the basic behaviors and they have no linkage to situational context or temporal structure), (2) activities (these are short sequences of movements combined with some temporal structure), and (3) actions (these are recognized from activities, and interpreted within the larger contexts of participants and environments).

Latest approaches to solve these issues are more user-centered. For example, analysis of a driver's body postures in real time (Cheng et al., 2005; Oliver & Pentland, 2000; Trivedi et al., 2007; Veeraraghavan et al., 2005). Unfortunately, most of the solutions presented to date are image or video based (tracking of roads, pedestrians/obstacles, and the driver) operating on a combination of color and thermal pictures and markers for pose estimation and are therefore subject to the known problems of image/video detection and processing. The utilization of sitting posture patterns to recognize a car driver's identity is a promising method operating totally implicit. Force-sensitive array mats are used for feature acquisition (Figure 3); acquired data is then analyzed and post-processed using novel algorithms. The sensors are (1) capable of being integrated into almost any type of seat (the mats are highly flexible and have a thickness of just above 1mm) and (2) not reliant on the attention of a person using the system. Finally, they are

(3) requiring no active cooperation of the user, and are (4) continuously in operation while the person is seated.

The Seat as Medium for Collecting Pressure Data

The car seat is, in general, covered by the driver all the time while steering a car; it is therefore an optimal medium for collecting driver data in a fully unobtrusive and implicit way.

The application of continuous driver authentication is not limited to the car seat. Preliminary findings encourage an adaptation of the posture pattern acquisition system to operate in other domains like office, industry or at home. Pressure sensor mats have been used to detect sitting postures in a regular chair (Tessendorf et al., 2009), evaluate a driver's behavior (Riener & Ferscha, 2007) (Figure 4) or a person's stress level (Arnrich et al., 2010), as smart system for measuring health-related signals of airplane passengers (Schumm et al., 2010; Setz et al., 2010), and as a measure for comfort (De Looze et al., 2003) and physical wellness (Prado et al., 2002).

Figure 3. Continuous tracking of sitting postures for one person (seating only). The first line shows the pressure distributions as recorded, the second line indicates pressure images with applied zero pressure filter to identify differences between two consecutive readings. (Remark: Data analysis is done on raw data; images are only used for visual inspection.)

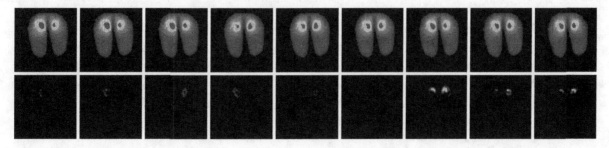

Figure 4. Dynamically collected pressure distributions from backrest (upper row) and seating (lower line) of a car seat. Pressure images show a person in different sitting postures/driving situations (from left to right): Driving normal (sitting upright), accelerating (increased pressure in clavicle region), braking (high pressure at thighs), driving a left curve, and switching gears.

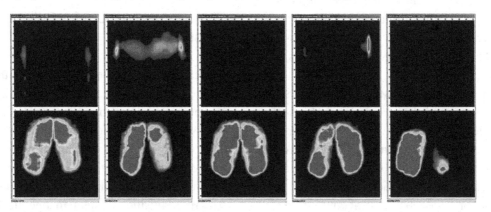

Requirements of the Sensing System

A force-sensitive array system has at least to fulfill the following requirements to be usable for continuous driver authentication: (1) The area of common seats in a car is about 50 x 50cm², thus the size of the utilized pressure sensing system should be similar; the mat itself should be flexible and thin so that it is easy deployable in a car; (2) the system should be able to reliably collect data from any person possibly driving that car, e.g. persons ranging in age from 18 up to 80 years and weighing between ~50 and more than 130 kg; (3) the hardware interface should provide precise measurements at a high update rate (e.g. at least one measurement per second), and (4) data acquisition should be accurate (i.e. large number of sensors per mat, low inter-sensor distance, high sensing range and resolution).

System Selection and Setup

Two systems matching our requirements have been reviewed. We used a "FSA Dual High Resolution System" from (Vista Medical Ltd., 2010) (32 x 32 piezoresistive sensors = 1,024 sensing points)

for preparatory studies, and a "X3 Pressure Mapping System PX100:48.48.02" (48 x 48 capacitive coupled sensors = 2,304 sensing points) from (XSENSOR Technology Corporation, 2010) for later productive application. Both systems employed for dynamic pressure distribution analysis allow the loads to be recorded on thin, flexible sensor mats. Each sensor covers a pressure range 0 to 26.67kPa (0-200mmHg), the mats are sized 430 x 430mm² (FSA) and 610 x 610mm² (X3). Initial studies have shown that even the smaller mat is virtually sufficient large for data acquisition; only exceptionally thick, heavy persons can exceed the sensing area (but, as indicated below, in not a single of our cases the pressure range). Both systems offer maximum sampling rates equal to (or higher than) 10Hz, while typical used refresh rates were in the order of magnitude of 1Hz (connection errors sometimes lead to an additional slight delay).

- **Calibration:** Prior to its initial use a calibration of the sensing system was required. The purpose is to compensate for any inevitable constructional heterogeneity of individual sensors. During the calibration process each sensor is matched with a determined weight factor in order to later obtain homogenous, similar pressure values. Repeated calibration would be required every four to ten weeks, depending on the frequency of use.

- **Maximum measurable weight:** The pressure range 0 to 26.67kPa (200mmHg, 26,664N/m^2), detectable with both (FSA, X3) acquisition systems, seems to be high enough for posture detection in seats; this is true in the case of "normal" sitting (i.e. homogeneous pressure distribution), but may lead to problems in specific areas like around the pelvic bones (see "Problems" below). The analysis of a large number of posture patterns has shown that only about 35% of the sensing elements on the seat mat are covered when a driver is seated. This directly translates into a maximum weight of a person to be reliably measured of 180kg (35% of the maximum weight to be applied to the entire mat in case of uniform distribution). A loose forecast of the weight of a person can be computed from the accumulated force applied to all 1,024 (2,304) sensors; nevertheless, the exact weight of a particular test subject cannot be determined using this technique. The main reasons for that are unbalanced load sharing as well as dead space between the sensor elements.

Problems

The use of these pressure sensor arrays is, nevertheless, not always unproblematic. During our recent work with this type of interface placed in a driver seat, we identified several problems but also potentials for improvement. The most influential are:

- **Mat artifacts:** White noise in everyday life caused by different clothes worn by drivers' (season-specific, e.g. beach wear, jeans, ski-overall, etc.), trouser buttons or objects in the back-pockets (cell phone, small bunch of keys, wallet, coins) pressing on the mat, or even a changing weight of a person over time affect the results.

- **Fixation:** To further avoid faulty measurements and to increase system accuracy it is absolutely important to retain the sensor array mats to the car seat (if not integrated in the seat cushion). Problems were experienced in preliminary tests where the mats were only fixed on the seat with fabric tape: The quality of the test database was deteriorated by changes in the position of the mats, caused by the large number of seated persons in the data collection phase.

- **Unbalanced forces**: In some body regions, particularly around the pelvic bones, pressure forces much higher than on average occurs. These forces may exceed the maximum capable sensor value (26,664N/m^2), resulting in a distortion of results. This problem is virtually unpredictable because it is not only dependent on a person's weight, but also on the shape of the back (e.g. pointed pelvic bone).

- **Gender discrimination:** As described by (Luo, 1995; Phenice, 1969) the pelvic bone distance is a suitable metric for accurate differentiation between female and male persons. Due to the low number of only 32 sensors per dimension used in the first experiment series (FSA sensory system) this distinction cannot be made reliably. Data evaluation revealed a mean distance between the two pelvic bones over all 34 test subjects of $\bar{x} = 13.12$ and a median of $\tilde{x} = 12$ sensors. More importantly, data analysis showed that there are only a few feasible distance-values (in the range 12 ± 3 sensors), fostering the request for sensor mats with a higher resolution. Repeated tests with the more precise X3 sensory system

(48 by 48 pressure sensors) are promising, however still in progress.

Continuous ECG Measurement

Measurement and processing of ECG signals has been known for nearly 150 years – longer than for any other complex sensing technique. For a stable measurement of pulse rate, heart rate variability, and other biorhythm related parameters, devices normally demand a placement of the electrodes on the human body, i.e. three conductively coupled electrodes attached to the skin and providing direct resistive contact. The ECG records electrical potentials on the body (the visualized gradient of the curve is generally known as electrocardiogram). For normal cases the process of cardiac stimulus generates patterns as shown in Figure 5. The time interval between two heart beats can be calculated by observing the time between two consecutive R peaks using a QRS detector. This R-R interval is known as the inter-beat time and is used for the measurement of the heart rate. Some issues may have to be considered before employing electrocardiography in vehicular applications:

- **Infeasibility:** It is not surprising that the application of such a device is unfeasible in a twenty-four-seven operating authenti-

cation system due to lack of user friendliness and inconvenience (e.g. carrying the device, attaching electrodes, using a conductive gel, stowage of cables, changing batteries).

- **Interference factors:** Opposed to the technically mature ECG devices there are, according to (Mendes, 2009), several factors that can interfere with such an ECG recording:
  - Hairiness can make recording difficult when using adhesive disposable sensors (possible solutions: shaving, adjustment of sensor positions, usage of non-adhesive electrodes),
  - Person's skin characteristics (electrodes might slip on oily or sweat skin),
  - Changes in temperature during the course of the measurement (heating, stress) can make recordings unusable.
- **Drawbacks of emotion recognition:** Facial expression and the voice (e.g. pitch) are signals often used as input channels for human-computer interaction; however, they are not feasible for autonomic person authentication as information conveyed through these channels can be deceiving as they can be faked by the person. (For ex-

Figure 5. Electrocardiogram of a healthy person (driver) recorded wirelessly using a "Heartman" ECG device

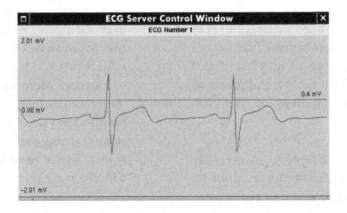

ample, actors can show certain emotions in films or in the theater. Although emotions appear to be realistic, their truthfulness is debatable.) The other problem with relying on such signals is the setup needed for data acquisition. Such setups rely on sensors like cameras or microphones which are, particularly in the car, constrained by factors like placement and environment conditions (e.g. lighting, background noise), see (Riener, 2010) (p. 93f.). For these reasons, we recently focused our research on the use of bio signals derived from ECG, and conveying affective states to which a person has less influence on (Benovoy et al., 2008).

The Seat as Medium for Collecting ECG Data

(Aleksandrowicz & Leonhardt, 2007; Curio & Mueller, 2007) have independently developed ECG measurement systems operating on capacitive coupled electrodes (cECG). These systems record ECG signals through the clothes, without a direct skin contact. cECG measurements would be therefore insusceptible to interference from skin characteristics and, as skin irritation often evoked by the contact gel between skin and the electrodes can be avoided, it is also expected that these devices will increase user acceptance. Most of the other interference factors and restrictions mentioned before, in particular unfeasibility, will not occur.

Given the strong electrical activity of the heart (Mendes, 2009), a clear ECG signal should be in most cases obtainable with cECG devices. Moreover, cECG devices can immediately start recording once a driver is seated without wiring and distraction during the measurement. Although the measurement is, compared to that from the conventional conductive ECG devices, more sensitive to moving artifacts and is strongly dependent on the subject's clothing, it is supposed suitable

for convenient heart rate detection and real-time evaluation in mobile fields of application.

(Schumm et al., 2010) have successfully shown its utilization for physiological monitoring of persons in airplane seats. Following their setting, a similar application in the vehicle seat, with two electrodes embedded into the backrest and the reference electrode integrated into the seating, should provide good results. It can operate fully autonomously and attention-free and thus can be one of the missing building blocks for implicit and continuously operating biometric sensing systems.

System Selection and Setup

In the research conducted in the scope of this work, a common body-mounted ECG device (type HeartMan 301, HeartBalance AG) was used (and not a measurement system with capacitive coupled electrodes similar to the one described above).

The choice for a wired in favor of a contactless operating device was made based on the criteria (1) higher accuracy; (2) more stable signal; and (3) increased resolution as well as the fact that potential restrictions for everyday use, like inconvenience, etc., are negligible in a prototype.

The HeartMan device as representative of wired ECG's was chosen based on the success criteria for ECG data analysis (sampling rate, signal-noise ratio, and data formats available for recording) introduced by (Clifford et al., 2006) (pp. 30-50). The HeartMan appliance is small-sized, lightweight, operates reliably, records up to 24 hours with one battery pack, and delivers highly precise data. Datasets are either transmitted wirelessly and in real time via a Bluetooth communication interface or stored in European Data Format (EDF) on the integrated SmartMedia memory card (space for up to 24 hours of data).

Results of the previous experiments highlighted some problems. Subsequently they are named together with potential improvement solutions.

- **Attribute combinations:** The quality of any biometric identification system can be improved when combining more than one technique. This knowledge has already been applied by adding the ECG signal to the posture pattern recognition system. Adding further measurement categories, such as for instance galvanic skin response (GSR), skin moisture, etc., for collecting person-related data is expected to further enhance the identification system performance.

- **Noise in ECG signals:** When carrying out experiments indoor (e.g. driving simulator studies), it has to be regarded that ECG signals might be influenced by noise from mains or power-lines (50-60Hz). Noise can in particular interfere with ECG data logged at low sampling rates; in such a case appropriate filters have to be applied to clean data from ripple voltage. This issue can be disregarded when using ECG devices in vehicular applications.

- **Sampling frequency:** Sample rate used for recording has to be chosen in order to suit the desired application. For accurate heart rate variability and R-R interval measurements a sampling rate of at least 500Hz is highly recommended; unfortunately, this suggestion cannot be fulfilled using HeartMan devices as they offer a maximum sampling rate of only 200Hz.

- **Data format and storage:** ECG devices either provide the facility to store data internally or by using an external device (e.g. a PC). Device selection, in terms of storage capacity, is dependent on (1) sampling rate; (2) projected recording time for an experiment; and (3) data format used to store ECG data (e.g. EDF/EDF+, WFDB, HL7, and ecgML (Clifford et al., 2006) (p. 36)). Problems with storage capacity shortage are not an issue when using HeartMan devices, as they offer both real time data transmission to a host computer using a Bluetooth communication interface and recording of up to 24 hours of data on the internal memory card.

GPS Data

A GPS receiver (type ATR062x3, ANTARIS 4 GPS chipset (u-blox, 2010); this receiver is optimized for automotive and mobile terminal applications) was carried in the test car and used to gather a vehicle's exact geo-location.

GPS position data was logged in the National Marine Electronics Association (NMEA) 1083 format at a rate of one hertz. GPS data was then converted from the NMEA format to a simplified comma separated values (CSV) file format using (GPSBabel, 2010) (an open source toolkit for the conversion between multiple GPS device formats). Transformed data consisted of a car's position data (latitude, longitude, speed, and course) and a time stamp. This information was later used for visual inspection of the driven route. The GPS time field was consulted as external synchronization basis for the different sensing systems. It has to be noted here, that due to factors like driving speed variation, changed road/traffic conditions, emerging and disappearing jams, etc., an exact synchronization of routes driven by the test participants based on driving time or GPS position only is not possible (we used route segmentation, as indicated in Figure 2, for dataset comparisons).

Environmental and On-Board Sensors

Modeling the interactions among a driver and the vehicle has to address two major aspects of complexity. First, on the driver side, it has to reflect the complex cognitive task of controlling the vehicle (which is determined by the four sub-processes (1) perception; (2) analysis; (3) decision; and (4) expression). Second, on the vehicle side and apart from biometric identification/authentication technologies, sensor values captured from acceleration or brake pedals, vehicles on board diagnostics (OBD) interface, the steering wheel, etc. should provide substantial added value towards personalized in-car applications (in particular, if possible to associate "sensor states" with driver behavior). (Erzin et al., 2006) conducted driving experiments utilizing the behavior of a driver (derived from speed variants and pedal pressures). They found out that the "vehicle context" allows verification and, in succession, reaction to the driver's physical or mental condition (alert, sleepy, drunk) to a certain degree.

Modeling the driver-vehicle interaction loop is a difficult task, as it may be influenced by reaction time discrepancies between vehicle and driver. Recording, instrumentation, and processing of vehicle-related data (=input) as well as actuator control (=output) by far excels the human perception-analysis-decision-expression process. This may cause steering mistakes due to unnecessary operation delays. This problem is not new – there are some solutions available to counteract this reaction-time issue: Driver Assistance Systems (DAS) have emerged, aiming to improve (power steering) or compensate (ABS breaking) driver performance, but potentially elevating cognitive load at the same time. In addition, on-board entertainment systems can lead to an overload of the visual or auditory channels of perception having a negative impact on reaction time. Last, but not at least vital parameters like fatigue, stress, attention, etc. crucially affect driver performance. All these essential aspects have been taken into consideration in the design phase of our feature-rich driver emotional state recognition system including identification and authentication components. The test bed used for studying continuous driver authentication while driving includes video data, accelerometers at all 4 axes of the vehicle, ECG data plus related measures (heart rate variability (HRV), standard deviation of all normal R-R intervals (SDNN)), pressure data, driving speed, as well as GPS information.

CONTINUOUS DRIVER AUTHENTICATION IN VEHICLES

Services that demand unambiguous, unmistakable, and continuous identification and/or authentication of drivers have recently attracted reasonable research interest. (DeLoney, 2008; Koenig, 2004) reported that most efforts have been directed to identification techniques based on face or pose recognition (using still or moving images) or acoustic analysis.

An overview of the characteristics of appropriate biometric identification technologies for vehicular use is presented in Table 1; a description of biometric security technologies in more detail is given for example in the underlying research study published in (Liu, 2001). It is assumed that all the explicit identification techniques used to date can be replaced by implicit identification methods. Sitting postures, the ECG, and also a person's voice are qualified biometrics for providing implicit acquisition.

For employing personalization from biometrics (appropriate for the vehicular domain), the identification demand can be divided into two main categories:

- **Personalized settings**, such as seat and mirror adjustments, radio station presets, calibration of the running gear, chassis set-up, horsepower regulations, etc., where the adaptation to predefined settings requires an identification once at the time of boarding,
- **Personalized services,** such as a car insurance rate, road pricing, cause-based CO_2 taxation, etc., demands for continuous authentication of the driver while seated and/or operating the car.

Implicitly acquired biometrics, combined with additional sensors and processing capacity, can allow for new advanced fields of vehicular applications such as (1) automatic allowance/disallow-

Table 1. Comparison of biometrics (extension based on Liu's work (Liu, 2001))

		Fingerprint	Hand Geometry	Retina	Iris	Face	Signature	Voice	Sitting Posture	ECG
Characteristic	**Ease of Use**	high	high	low	medium	medium	high	high	high	high
	Error Incidence	dryness, dirt, age	hand injury, age	glasses	poor lighting	light, age glasses, hair	changing signatures	noise, colds, weather	age, weight	clothes, vibrations
	Accuracy	high	high	very high	very high	high	high	high	medium	high
	Cost	*)	*)	*)	*)	*)	*)	*)	*)	*)
	User Acceptance	medium	medium	medium	medium	medium	very high	high	very high	very high
	Required Level of Security	high	medium	high	very high	medium	medium	medium	medium	high
	Long-Term Stability	high	medium	high	high	medium	medium	medium	medium	low to medium
	Implicit Acquisition	no	no	no	no	no	no	yes	yes	yes

*) The large number of factors involved makes a simple cost comparison impractical.

ance of vehicle operation (e.g. by determining if the person sitting in the driver seat is authorized to steer the vehicle) or (2) increased safety functions (promoting safe driving by monitoring a driver's behavior to determine for example if the driver is sleepy or drunk and to prohibit further operation of the vehicle if a certain threshold is exceeded).

Recommendation: Authentication from Body Behavior and ECG

We propose an automatic driver authentication system based on personal characteristics or "something the driver is…" (Woodward et al., 2003) (p. 6), (Liu, 2001) (p. 27). The two characteristics body behavior and driver ECG are passive representatives of biometrics, thus assumed not to influence the driver in his/her regular task of steering a vehicle. Examples of application for the first type include (1) the analysis of movement trajectories of torso, limbs, and the head; (2) intentional gestures, e.g., with an arm or hand; and (3) the shift of a person's weight over the time,

identifiable via pressure sensors in a chair/seat. A recorded ECG can be analyzed and interpreted in numerous ways, e.g. (1) dynamic developing of the signal from heartbeat to heartbeat; (2) progress of the R-peak value; (3) R-R interval; (4) power spectrum of the ECG signal; (5) HRV analysis (derived unit of measurement), etc.

The building blocks for the research presented in this article are (1) static body postures; (2) dynamic body postures recorded/analyzed while driving; and (3) ECG signals (in particular the derived unit HRV) evaluated in real time. Each of these subcomponents can be used fully autonomic (as the paragraphs on initial experiments below shows). Furthermore, there is evidence that a combination of several aspects may improve the overall (authentication) accuracy (Liu, 2001). This approach is feasible and can be noted from Table 1 – it relates the usability of sitting postures or ECG signals as biometric identification techniques for in-car usage to other known methods, such as retina or iris scan, face recognition, fingerprint, signature, etc.

Both sitting posture acquisition from a sensor matrix attached to the seat and contactless ECG recording convince by the key point that data gathering can be, opposed to most other biometric methods, completed fully implicit. But not only the possibility for implicit acquisition qualifies the use of sitting postures and ECG's for continuous driver authentication – other criteria like ease of application or a high expected user acceptance (both types of sensors are integrated into the seat cushion and are whether visible nor noticeable by the driver) furthermore promotes their application.

The continuity of measurement is also guaranteed all the time as the driver has to be seated while steering the car, providing pressure to the force sensors and electrical signals of the heart to the ECG measurement system.

Static Sitting Posture Evaluation

For data acquisition in our first prototype (Figure 6) we used force sensor arrays (FSA) connected via USB to a standard notebook computer. The system setup is universal, thus can be used in any type of car (e.g. utility-driven car, sports car with body-contoured seats, family van, comfort station wagon, etc.) and for arbitrary style of sitting or driving. Recently, we used the same setting in office chairs for authentication in a porter's lodge. We suppose that a combination of different features received from static sitting postures

are unique, thus allowing driver (or in general person) authentication. For further verification, experiments have to be conducted in different types of cars, respectively seats, and with a large number of subjects.

Test Execution

To assess the quality and accuracy of the prototype, a database with pressure patterns from 34 volunteers has been created. All recordings have been processed in a comfort station wagon (type Audi A6) with pressure mats attached to both, seat and backrest. For initial evaluations, the Euclidian distance metric – a well-researched approach in the field of pattern recognition – was used to match a person's current sitting posture against earlier stored patterns. The experiment was conducted in two stages, (1) recording of the training set, and (2) system evaluation with a testing set.

- **Training set:** In the first phase, data samples were captured and the test subject features were extracted and stored in a relational database. For that, consecutive readings of sensor data alternating between seat and backrest mat, were written as raw-data into the database. Pressure data was completed by a timestamp and personal data (age, gender, size, weight). The duration for recording of one person was less

Figure 6. Dynamic pressure distribution acquired from different types of car seats: comfort station wagon, sports car, and race car (from left to right)

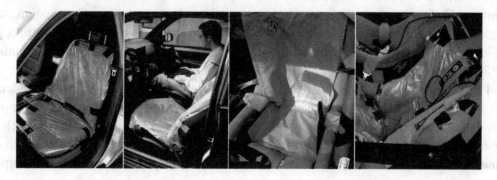

than 5 minutes, including introduction and briefing.

- **Testing set:** Samples of any acquired person have been compared in the "live system" to all stored datasets to detect the best matching dataset (that with most similar pressure dissemination).

To eliminate the impact of sudden movements during data acquisition on the driver seat, the median of each of the 1,024 pressure sensor values over a series of measurements was calculated. Initial tests confirmed that using five measurements is sufficient to create a stable matrix of pressure values. To ensure data integrity (Hamming distance), for each test participant four independent datasets were captured and stored.

Features

Feature vectors for a person were calculated using a weighted combination of several parameters extracted from the sitting posture matrix, and referred to as the personal sitting profile. The following features were utilized for evaluations regarding person identification from static sitting posture patterns.

- **Weight:** A weight approximation for the driving person was calculated as the sum of all pressure values on the seat mat (therefore, sensors were calibrated before to exhibit similar pressure distribution). The total weight cannot be exactly estimated from the charged sensors as already mentioned before.
- **High pressure area:** This attribute considers only high pressure values exceeding 90% of the maximum pressure.
- **Mid to high pressure area:** This parameter is similar to the "High pressure area", but calculated from sensor values exceeding 10% of the normalized pressure minimum.

- **Pelvic bones area:** This factor is more sophisticated, determined by the location as well as the distance of the thighs on the seat mat. It is relatively simple to identify the pelvic bones on the mat because they are responsible for two areas of very high pressure. The Euclidian distance between the midpoints (x and y coordinates) of left and right pelvic bone was calculated and used as fourth parameter for feature vector calculation. Using the pelvic bone area benefits from the following stability characteristics;
  - *Durability:* The feature is permanent as distance between the pelvic bones does not change if people gain weight or wear different clothes (in contrast, size/shape of the area indicating pelvic bone region does).
  - *Gender dependency:* It is established that pelvic bones of males and females are different (Phenice, 1969) and the feasibility of discrimination has been shown, e.g. by (Giles, 1970; Stewart, 1954).

Biometric Characteristics: Experiments and Results

Permanency: This characteristic specifies the potential of a feature to always stay the same. Sitting postures of a person, however, do not stay constant as persons wear, dependent on the season, different clothes (thick jacket in winter, beach wear in summer). Furthermore, objects like wallet, cell phone, bunch of keys, coins, etc. in the back-pockets as well as trouser buttons providing additional force to the sensor elements which adversely affect the measurements.

An experiment to investigate the susceptibility to "noise" (with different artifacts in the pockets) provided the following results (Table 2). All sitting posture variants[1] of a subject with objects (artifacts) in the back-pocket are compared to each other and to the underlying normal posture. The confusion matrix shows the distinction of postures with different artifacts in percent. The base quantity for differences in postures was defined as the maximum difference of any two regular sitting postures in the database of 34 subjects and set to 100% (independently for seat and back). As no artifacts have been applied on the backrest mat (i.e. placed on a person's back), there was no significant change in the backrest postures detected. On the seat, however, the maximum difference for pressure patterns between one subject in normal posture and the same person with applied artifacts in the back-pockets is, with 58.9%, high. Reliable person identification would therefore be not possible when using the actual feature vector calculation, particularly when compared to the maximum difference of any two

persons which is 100%. Statistical analysis (Table 3) of the artifact-afflicted datasets is very similar to that of the normal datasets.

Uniqueness: For determining the accuracy and uniqueness of pressure patterns, this feature has been evaluated for two test subjects (Figure 7) with a large number of recordings. Candidates were seated in the car again, and larger series of consecutive readings were processed. For each of the trials, gathered postures were compared to all stored patterns in the database. Deviations were calculated and saved in a separate database table. Table 4 shows the results for the feature weight only (weights are normalized, i.e. factorized with the predetermined reference weight). The mean-value gives a relative precise estimation of a person's actual weight, but the deviation is rather large.

Table 2. Confusion matrix of normal postures compared to postures with applied artifacts for the seat (maximum differences in percent compared to database of regular postures)

-	N	KL	KR	CL	CR	DL	DR	DRKL
N	-	29.4	39.8	50.0	46.5	55.6	52.7	58.9
KL		-	38.3	42.6	43.0	48.4	49.9	51.0
KR			-	33.8	33.5	49.0	36.0	47.7
CL				-	34.0	37.0	37.6	45.4
CR					-	36.9	28.8	39.5
DL						-	41.8	34.3
DR							-	31.5
DRKL								-

Table 3. Statistical analysis of the feature "permanency"

Data Sets	Database	Min x_{min}	Max x_{max}	Mean $\overline{x}$	Median $\tilde{x}$	Std. Dev. σ	(P_{25})	(P_{75})
Seat mat (normalized)								
34	Normal	24.78	100.00*	54.79	52.93	12.39	46.45	62.08
8	Artifacts	28.82	58.55	41.89	40.79	8.13	35.59	48.75
Backrest mat (normalized)								
34	Normal	15.16	100.00*	41.10	38.43	12.00	32.21	45.56
8	Artifacts	11.61	28.27	20.02	19.47	4.16	17.37	2.45
* Maximum difference of any two normal datasets has been set to 100%								

Figure 7. Two persons (both male, similar age and figure) sitting upright in a stopped car (right after boarding). Already the visual inspection of pressure images allows for clear differentiation.

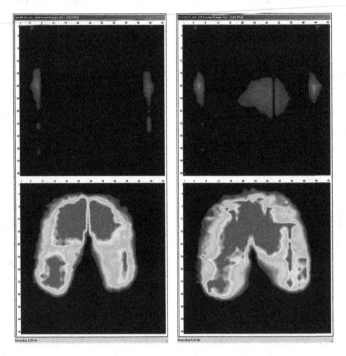

Table 4. Measurement accuracy for 2 subjects (parameter weight only)

Data Sets	Actual Weight	Min x_{min}	Max x_{max}	Mean $\overline{x}$	Median $\tilde{x}$	Std. Dev. σ	(P_{25})	(P_{90})
105	75.5	58.797	83.667	75.251	75.682	6.192	67.223	82.246
31	80.0	69.433	90.381	81.925	83.779	5.937	70.571	88.295

For the entire feature vector a rank was calculated and assigned in the order of minimal differences. For example rank 1 reads as least deviation between the current feature vector and the feature vector in the database currently checked against, thus represents the best match; rank 34, in a database with 34 datasets, is the largest difference or worst match.

Dataset matching for the drivers with 31 independent readings resulted in ranks 1 to 6. In worst case, that occurs in only 3.33%, the matching between measurements against all 34 postures in the database results in place 6. This stands for rather high stability of the sitting posture of that person. On the other hand, however, it can be seen that an exact match (= rank 1) is obtained in less than 25%, which, of course, is poor. The results for the 2nd test read divergent. An exact match is given here in 48.08%, but the remaining 51.92% are distributed to nearly all ranks (86.54% of readings are assigned to ranks 1-10, the absolute worst case, occurring in less than 1 percent, is an assignment to rank 30). From the results of these two tests it is not possible to draw generally acceptable conclusions (additional studies, using the more precise X3 mat system, are currently in progress).

Conclusion

Motivated by an ample emergence of in-car services going beyond the usual automatic customization of vehicle functions or services (which all are reliant on unambiguous, unmistakable, and continuous driver authentication), we have developed a driver identification method based on the biometrics of sitting.

Our approach is based on implicitly inspected sitting postures acquired from pressure sensor mats on the driver seat and backrest. Posture recognition does not suffer, opposed to vision detection techniques, from environmental conditions like brightness or weather; moreover, the measuring system itself is invisibly integrated into the vehicle seat and the unobtrusive disposition avoids driver distraction.

Experimental results showed that posture patterns are in some respect a feature suitable for describing an individual, and thus, applicable for identifying or authorizing a person in a vehicle seat. With the investigated method of feature vector calculation and its comparison against the "training set", at least persons usually sharing a car should be clearly differentiable.

The current accuracy of the prototype necessitates improvements: On-line analysis of a driver and a training data base containing 34 datasets resulted in authentication rates of 22.33% for one individual and 31 trials and 48.08% for the second test with another person and 105 readings. Conducted experiments showed further that the achieved authentication rate was prone to changed sitting postures for an individual (e.g. due to artifacts) to a stronger degree than initially expected.

Dynamic Sitting Posture Evaluation

Intelligent driver assistance can relieve the driver from manipulative and cognitive issues by e.g. adaptively controlling the vehicle before activities from the driver actually take place. The aim of the initial experiment was to prove the hypothesis of a visually detected phenomenon. Video analysis of dynamic sitting postures and steering behavior revealed that a driver has low or moderate ambition to compensate centripetal force in low speed driving while in high speed cornering situations the readiness to compensate lateral forces is high. If this behavior can be substantiated in real driving situations, it can be utilized to enhance intelligent driver assistance systems (e.g. to avoid over- and under-steering). The next step toward automatic driver authentication would be the investigation of driver's dynamic developing postures.

As an extension to the previously described static posture acquisition system, we deployed the system of 32 by 32 sensors per array in a dynamic environment. To increase system stability and to improve the quality of the measurements we added supplementary sensors. The parameters vehicle speed, steering angle, body posture, GPS position, vehicle acceleration forces, and driver's ECG were recorded. Video cameras were used for visual inspection and verification of obtained results. Vehicle-specific data were gathered via the vehicles On-Board Diagnostics (OBD) interface.

Experimental Setting

In common road traffic we can distinguish between a number of different types of turns, e.g. right-angled streets or crossings, freeway entrance and exit ramps, U-turns, banked corners or "regular" curves. In the first of a series of experiments reported here, we were focused on driving situations while cornering left or right (curves with different radii) in a closed environment. The field study was conducted in a driving safety center on a specified race course with a length of about 1,150 meters.

Reference weight: As the expected correlation body posture – cruising speed is dependent on the driver's weight (centrifugal force) it is also necessary to obtain a coarse estimation of the weight of the seated driver. Therefore, we initially applied a reference weight to it: A person with a given weight (74.80kg) was seated and 100 consecutive readings from the 32x32 sensor matrix were recorded. The mean value of the accumulated pressure has been set as reference factor for further weight estimations.

$$\overline{pressure} = \frac{1}{100}\sum_{j=1}^{100}\sum_{i=1}^{1024}sensor_i$$

$$factor_{pressure} = \frac{weight_{real}}{\overline{pressure}} = \frac{74.80kg}{176.589} = 0.4235$$

Data Processing

Data from different sensors was recorded and preprocessed (filtered and time-aligned using the GPS time field) to meet the requirements of the statistical analysis tool set. Table 5 presents five datasets out of the entire data table of 3,786 rows.

Accelerometer data: The utilized type of accelerometer (InertiaCube, (Intersense, 2010)) provides data at a high update rate of 180Hz. The car itself acts as a reference coordinate system, consequently all accelerometer readings had to be aligned to the vehicle coordinate system (x-coordinate is in vehicles direction of motion, y is oriented in the right angle of x, z face upwards). Although accelerometers were placed around each axis of the vehicle, for the present evaluation only the one accelerometer mounted near-by the front, left wheel was used.

Normalized accelerator data is, after time-synchronization, smoothed with a ramp function taking the current value and the previous 8 sensor values into account. (Remark: Using a Gaussian bell-shaped function instead may improve the results.)

Pressure mats: FSA11, FSA12, FSA13,... FSA44 indicate the aggregated pressure regions from the sensor matrix. Each value stands for the sum of 64 sensor values in a specific region. (To give an estimate for the "direction of leaning", the evaluation based on a single-sensor will be impossible.) As the pressure sensors are intended to reason about "leaning postures", we defined "leaning left" as a deviation from the initial symmetric pressure distribution (indicating an up-right sitting position of the driver) to the left. Analogously, "leaning right" is a deviation of the sitting pressure distribution towards right.

Vehicle speed, time, GPS: Vehicle specific parameters have been obtained from the OBD interface, the remaining attributes were provided by the GPS receiver. The GPS time field was used as external basis for data synchronization.

Results

Results for some of the experiments are presented in the subsequent Figures 9, 10. The plots contain three variables: vehicle lateral acceleration force (acc_y) in the range [−20, 40] m/s², vehicle speed (v) in the range [0, 125] km/h and driver's sitting

Table 5. Tabular specification of incorporated features

Time ms	FSA11 kPa	FSA12 kPa	...	FSA44 kPa	Accelerometer1			v km/h	GPS φ GRD	GPS λ GRD
					x	y	z			
540,687	5.444	19.144	...	0.000	-2.195	7.427	-3.456	118.648	1,519.736	4,812.780
540,890	5.420	19.026	...	0.004	-1.698	9.657	-0.201	119.528	1,519.739	4,812.781
541,109	10.086	24.365	...	0.004	-1.466	8.422	0.101	120.477	1,519.472	4,812.782
541,640	12.104	28.130	...	0.020	-0.368	8.729	3.824	122.778	1,519.778	4,812.786
541,828	12.081	28.277	...	0.000	-3.925	8.606	-3.213	123.593	1,519.751	4,812.786
...	...	...	...	...	...	...	...	...	...	...

posture (as "direction of leaning" to the left or right side) (pr_{right_norm}) in the range [−50, 50].

Figure 8 shows a clipping of 11 minutes of one experiment considering only sections driven at low speed (below the driver-dependent break-even speed v_{BE}). The weight-dependent value for the current driver was calculated at 75km/h. (The Euclidean distance between acceleration force and normalized mat pressure is smallest at this

speed; evaluation for speed values between 0 and 120 km/h in steps of 1 km/h).

It has to be noted that the relation between leaning behavior and driving speed also depends on the geometry of the curve – a lower speed at a tight turn can probably produce the same result as high-speed driving in a wider turn or in a banked curve. As task for future improvement, the break-even speed v_{BE} has to be actualized dynamically

Figure 8. Incoherence of vehicle lateral acceleration force and driver's sitting posture while cruising at low speed (below person dependent break-even speed; here: 75km/h)

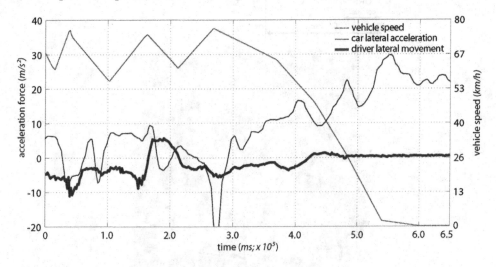

Figure 9. Dynamic sitting postures for high speed driving above a person-dependent break even speed (here: 75km/h) indicates a close relation to vehicle lateral acceleration force (shown as thin blue line)

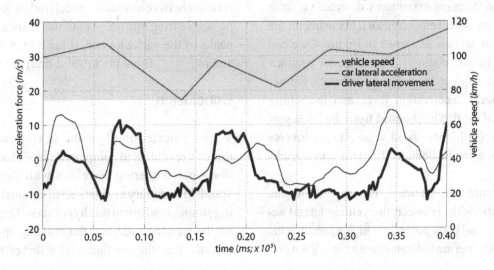

Figure 10. Electrocardiogram of a healthy person (left); 3-lead mobile ECG device type "Heartman 301" attached to a person (test driver)

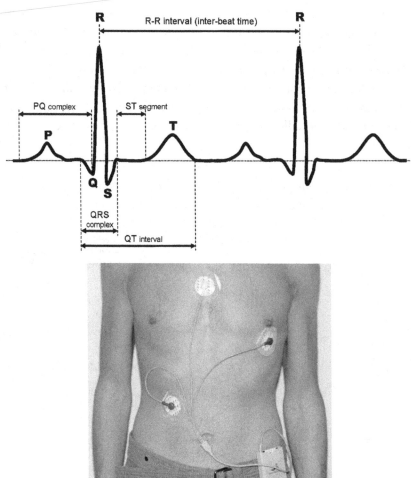

(according to curve parameters, detected i.e. from the steering wheel angle sensor). Focusing on the low-speed section as shown in Figure 8 we can identify no correlation (at least not for sections driven at a speed around zero) between the vehicle lateral acceleration force and the sitting posture of the driver obtained from the force sensor array (in higher speed segments, an inverse correlation can be deduced from the curve gradients).

In contrast to Figure 8, Figure 9 shows the interrelationship between the vehicle lateral acceleration and body postures in high-speed driving section. Cornering indicates here a significant correlation between vehicles acceleration force and persons sitting attitude – both the shapes and the peaks of the variables acc_y (blue thin, solid line) and $pr_{right—norm}$ (blue thick, solid line) are similar.

Conclusion

We investigated the hypothesis emphasizing a driver's readiness to compensate lateral acceleration when cornering correlates with the driving speed. Preliminary evaluations of conducted driving studies confirmed this hypothesis: Depending on the steering ratio and the cruising speed, we identify that the readiness of a driver to compensate lateral forces exhibits counterintuitive characteristics. Low speed cornering is attempted with moderate readiness to compensate centripetal force (Figure 8), while high speed cornering leads to an increased readiness to compensate lateral forces (Figure 9). This preliminary result motivates to extend the setting towards continuous driver authentication based on a driver's dynamic developing posture gradient.

ECG Analysis for Arousal State Detection

In order to improve driver authentication we added another feature (ECG evaluation) to the sitting posture acquisition system. Unfortunately, the gradient of the electrocardiogram is not a person-specific feature suitable for unique identification; moreover, it is highly susceptible to factors like stress, tiredness, sickness, age, manual work, etc. Electrocardiograms are typically used by medical doctors for early diagnosis of heart disease or for identifying the cause of a heart attack after it occurred.

It is also well known that bio signals are related to the autonomic nervous system (ANS), which controls, amongst others, cardiac muscles. Cardiovascular activity is, according to (Mendes, 2009), one of the most widely used noninvasive methods for measuring ANS activity in emotion research, and electrocardiography (ECG) is one of the most common ways of measurement. Despite the fact that sensors exist for the acquisition of bio signals, the usage of data from such signals for emotion recognition is neither an easy nor a direct task. In relation to other approaches there are no established "golden rules" for the usage of bio signals.

For normal cardiac activity, a balance is maintained between the sympathetic and the parasympathetic activities. (The sympathetic system is responsible to prepare the body for a stressful condition; the parasympathetic is responsible to put the body in a calmer state.)

The assumption of the research, followed in the initial experiments, was twofold:

- **Divergence in the arousal state:** Differing affective state values for a person identified during a trip (testing set) in comparison to the training set represents some kind of abnormality and should be immediately forwarded to the driver to avoid danger situations.

- **Person-dependent sympathetic/parasympathetic activity:** Hypothesizing that persons respond with different emotional states for one and the same fixed experimental setting (i.e. driven route), the different behavior, measureable, for instance, as developing over time and/or by applying statistical methods, may be helpful to support or improve driver authentication.

Experimental Setting

In order to study the relationship between a driver's arousal state and a driven route, we conducted initial experiments measuring ECG/GPS pairs, and calculating representations for the two branches of the ANS, the sympathetic (high arousal) and the parasympathetic (low arousal) system. Tests were processed on a specific route and at a fixed daytime on weekdays only to avoid environmental influence, e.g. on traffic jams, as good as possible. A total of 22 trips with more than 500 kilometers driven were logged and analyzed for a single identical person. Based on this data a "personal emotional profile" (for the route and a specific daytime) can be compiled (="training set"), indicating the state of that person for each position on the track.

Signal processing: The ECG signal was preprocessed with a high-pass filter of 1 Hz followed by a low-pass filter of 1,000 Hz (see Figure 2). In order to calculate the R-R interval series, we first must detect the R peaks throughout the entire ECG signal. For that we used a QRS complex detector provided by the Matlab "BioSig" toolkit according to recommendations given by (Nygårds & Sörnmo, 1983). The detector returns the fiducial points of R peaks, which then were used to perform HRV analysis (i.e. calculate LF/HF ratios as an index for autonomic balance).

Generally, the time between consecutive heartbeats, the so-called "inter-beat time" (Figure 10), is irregular (unless the heart is paced by an artificial electrical source such as a pacemaker or due to medical conditions). A widely-used method to measure this irregularity is heart rate variability (HRV). HRV is a promising tool for applications involving medical diagnoses and stress detection. (Blobel et al., 2008; Kim et al., 2008) have reported that HRV statistics is qualified for mental stress estimation. This can be applied to vehicular applications as well, as the estimation of emotional state can gain additional benefit in automation.

Calculation of HRV relies on the analysis of the series of R-R interval differences in the time or frequency domain. Measures of time domain include, for instance, root mean square of differences of consecutive R-R intervals. Frequency domain analysis represents deviations with respect to frequency. For that, several frequency bands, like the very low frequency (VLF) (<0.04Hz), low frequency (LF) (0.04-0.15Hz), and high frequency (HF) (0.15-0.40Hz), should be analyzed independently. VLF measure was indicated as being unreliable for short time intervals; the LF/HF ratio is, however, an indicator for autonomic balance. High values are thought to indicate the dominance of sympathetic activity with vagal modulation and low values indicate dominance of parasympathetic activity.

Typically, HRV analysis is done for time windows of 5 minutes or for longer periods like 24 hours (there is no standard mentioned for an ideal time window frame (Clifford et al., 2006) (p.71-83)) and can provide good indication for arousal (but not valence!).

GPS data was converted from the NMEA format to a simplified comma separated values (CSV) file format using (GPSBabel, 2010). Transformed data consisted of the car latitude and longitude, speed, course, and a time stamp. Due to factors like driving speed, road conditions, and traffic congestions the time needed to travel a route varied every day; therefore, an exact synchronization of data based on GPS time was not possible. In order to overcome the synchronization problem, reference routes for the morning and the evening trips were defined. In addition, a time window for segmenting and analyzing the data had to be chosen. We experimented with several time window sizes ranging from 1 to 5 minutes. The least time window we can use, that provided us with the best resolution, was 60 seconds (since a journey lasted between 20 to 30 minutes, a large time frame was not able to provide us with variations of LF/HF ratios over distance). With a time window of 1 minute the lowest frequency that can be resolved is $1/60=0.016Hz$ which is below the lower limit of the LF region. The highest frequency that can be resolved is calculated by applying the Nyquist constraint of $N/2T >= 0.4$, where N is the number of beats and T is the time in seconds (Nygårds & Sörnmo, 1983)(p. 79). Applying this formula leads to a lower limit of $N=48 beats$. (As our subject is a healthy adult with an average of 75 beats per minute (bpm), and since we are interested in analyzing the LF and HF bands this time window choice was appropriate).

Discussion: After collecting and processing the datasets, the aggregated LF/HF ratios were visualized along the routes. Figure 11 shows the autonomic balance in relation to the distance to destination (outbound direction only). Higher values are thought to exhibit higher levels of arousal (implied by increased sympathetic activity), lower values are opt to demonstrate lower levels of arousal (as a result of the dominance of parasympathetic activity).

In the following we try to give reasons, based on road characteristics noted throughout the ex-

Figure 11. Distance ranges and aggregated LF/HF ratios of the driver for two weeks. Highest ratio (gray area) occurs in jammed road sections.

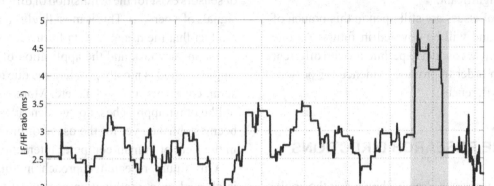

periment, that might be likely to exhibit the observed measurements; indeed, we have no means to proof the reasons behind the phenomenon in the data. Looking on Figure 11, the most interesting road segment is that from kilometer 17 to 18.6 (gray area). The state of arousal, varying between 4.2 and 4.8m/s², is here much higher than in any other region of the gradient. The reason for this is probably the incipient traffic congestion (dense traffic, but vehicles are still moving) on the borders of the city. Driving on workdays at around 7.30AM, a traffic jam (standstill) will appear every day between the kilometers 18.5 and 20. The final segment (low to very-low LF/HF ratio) is driven at walking-speed on the parking lot at the destination, with only very little traffic at that time.

One particular issue to cope with is the sensitivity of HRV to parameters like age, gender, activity, medications, and health (Clifford et al., 2006) – it is ambiguous how to differentiate appropriately, e.g. whether a high LF/HF ratio is caused by an increased mental load (attention on the road) or the raised activity of vehicle steering (braking and accelerating, changing gears, steering).

Conclusion

It is undoubted that the cognitive workload of a car driver is increasingly demanded by modern driver assistance systems. The consequence is a possible threat, mainly caused by distraction from driving due to information overload. In this study we have investigated the proof-of-possibility for the application of heart rate variability (HRV) analysis for representing the driver's affective state in terms of autonomic arousal levels in a noninvasive and a non-distractive way. The post-experiment interview revealed that the subject was not feeling stressed during the experiment, which indicates that LF/HF ratios can be used as an indicator for subconscious stress. Differences in the "personal affective profile" of a driver (curve as indicated in Figure 11) can be used for proactive notifications on possible danger situations (data evaluation has shown, for instance, higher levels of arousal at times of higher volume of traffic) and may also be helpful to improve driver authentication systems, e.g. by analyzing root-mean-square deviation.

It has to be stated once more that we cannot back our observed phenomenon in relation to the road characteristics with a proof; nevertheless, the stated observations are only remarks on what we think is significant.

A lot of issues are still open in this branch of research and will be covered in future. As one focus, we will conduct experiments with different drivers in order to provide evidence for person-related differences.

FUTURE RESEARCH DIRECTIONS

Previous work has already shown that the application of data from bio sensors can be assumed promising; however, contrary to their potential, applications are uncommon today (although a lot of sensors exist for the acquisition of different bio signals of a person). This is most likely caused by the fact that the usage of data from such signals is not an easy task and the application of only a single method is mostly problematic due to measurement errors, noisy data, etc. Moreover, and unlike other approaches, no "golden rules" have been established yet for the usage of bio signals in the field of human-computer interaction.

Our future research approach in this field is aligned on a combination of several sensory channels. For that, we plan to integrate other bio sensors to improve overall data set quality. Table

Table 6. Sensory channels usable for bio signal detection (adapted from (Aly, 2009))

Response System	Technique	Description	Analysis Technique
Central nervous system (CNS)	Electroencephalogram	electrical activity of the brain	time and frequency domain analysis
	Functional magnetic resonance imaging	a form of magnetic resonance imaging of the brain that registers blood flow to functioning areas of the brain	higher blood flow indicates increased brain activity; image analysis techniques
	Positron emission tomography	provides a 3D image of the functional processes in the body by using a radioactive positron emitter	Regions with greater activity in the brain is assumed to have the highest amount of radioactivity; image analysis techniques
Autonomic nervous system (ANS) through electro dermal activity measures	Skin conductance	A small current is passed through the skin and the resistance is measured	time and frequency domain analysis of skin conductance level, skin potential response, skin conductance response, and skin potential level
	Skin potential	skin resistance is measured by unipolar placement of sensors	
ANS through cardiovascular measures	Electrocardiogram (ECG)	Measurement of the electric signal variations of the heart	Heart rate (HR); Heart rate variability (HRV) analysis
	Respiration	measurement of the rate and depth of breaths during inspiration and expiration	time domain analysis
	Impedance cardiography	estimation of blood flow changes in the heart	cardiac output (CO); stroke volume
	Blood pressure	measurement of the pressure on the vessel walls during cardiac cycle	time domain analysis of systolic blood pressure and diastolic blood pressure
ANS through other measures	Pupillary responses	measurement of pupil diameter variation	time domain analysis of size variations and other statistical tools
	Skin temperature	measurement of temperature variation in different skin areas	Time domain analysis
	Skin blood flow	measurement of the volume of blood flowing in skin areas	non-oscillary duration index

6 indicates an overview of the most widely used noninvasive techniques for bio signal acquisition. Any combination of channels from this table can be used for system improvement and extension in future systems and applications. Furthermore, we will put effort in improving the computational models, e.g. for emotion representation and interpretation.

CONCLUSION

The authentication of persons and/or the recognition of activities in the highly dynamic automotive environment based on an evaluation of sitting postures and ECG signals can offer great potential on one hand, however, is subject to several issues on the other. For instance, sudden movements can cause erroneous data collection, resulting in an increased False Accept Rate and/or False Reject Rate, finally leading to an unexpected system behavior. Calculating extended features from the posture patterns, using improved evaluation techniques (such as those established for face recognition in still or moving images), or establishing improved computational models for emotion representation can help to enhance the reliability and stability of the system. Further improvements should be achieved when integrating other biometric measures, such as incorporating the skin conductance of the driver measured with a galvanic skin response (GSR) sensor embedded into the steering wheel or gear shift. Biometric based implicit information processing depending on individual characteristics can enable a new class of vehicular services, such as a safety function that authorizes a person automatically when seated. Only permitted persons would be then allowed to start or drive the car. Posture pattern based identification can furthermore be conceived as an effective car-theft protection system.

On the other hand, notable limitations have to be considered. Suppose that the driver of a car gets injured or incapacitated and someone else is asked to drive him/her to a hospital – would there be any chance to override the authorization process, allowing the helping person to use the vehicle without granted permission (e.g. in a "rescue mode")? Besides these application related issues, the measurement/data acquisition process faces some problems. Sudden movements, as noted above, can cause invalid posture patterns as well as noisy ECG signals. Powerful and effective data cleaning techniques needs to be developed to get this problem under control – as both sensor channels are affected at the same time this is still an open issue maybe requiring the integration of other unaffected sensory channels for compensation.

REFERENCES

Aleksandrowicz, A., & Leonhardt, S. (2007). Wireless and non-contact ECG measurement system – The Aachen SmartChair. *Acta Polytechnica. Journal of Advanced Engineering, 47*(4–5), 68–71.

Aly, M. A. M. (2009). *A framework for integrating drivers' affective states in GISs using biosignals in a vehicle.* Master thesis, International School of Informatics, Johannes Kepler University Linz, Hagenberg.

Arnrich, B., Setz, C., La Marca, R., Tröster, G., & Ehlert, U. (2010). What does your chair know about your stress level? *IEEE Transactions on Information Technology in Biomedicine, 14*(2), 207–214. doi:10.1109/TITB.2009.2035498

Benovoy, M., Cooperstock, J. R., & Deitcher, J. (2008). Biosignals analysis and its application in a performance setting – Towards the development of an emotional-imaging generator. *Biosignals, 1*, 253–258.

Bhattacharyya, D., Ranjan, R., Alisherov, A., & Choi, M. (2009). Biometric authentication: A review. *International Journal of u-and e-Service. Science and Technology, 2*(3), 13–28.

Blobel, P., Zvanmi, L., & Aka, B. (2008). Estimation of mental stress levels based on heart rate variability and stress factor in mobile settings. In *CeHR E-Health Conference Proceedings 2007: Combining Health Telematics, Telemedicine, Biomedical Engineering and Bioinformatics to the Edge*. Akademische Verlagsgesellschaft.

Bobick, A. F. (1997). Movement, activity and action: The role of knowledge in the perception of motion. *Philosophical Transactions of the Royal Society B. Biological Sciences, 352*(1358), 1257–1265. doi:10.1098/rstb.1997.0108

Cheng, S. Y., Park, S., & Trivedi, M. M. (2005). Multiperspective thermal IR and video arrays for 3D body tracking and driver activity analysis. In *Proceedings of the 2005 IEEE Computer Society Conference on Computer Vision and Pattern Recognition (CVPR'05)*, (p. 3), Washington, DC: IEEE Computer Society.

Choras, M. (2009). Ear biometrics. In Zi Li, S. (Ed.), *Encyclopedia of biometrics* (pp. 233–241). doi:10.1007/978-0-387-73003-5_173

Clifford, G. D., Azuaje, F., & McSharry, P. (2006). *Advanced methods and tools for ECG data analysis*. Norwood, MA: Artech House, Inc.

Curio, G., & Mueller, K. R. (2007). *Contactless ECG system for emergencies. Press release*. Berlin: Charity, Berlin and Fraunhofer Institute FIRST.

De Looze, M., Kuijt-Evers, L., & Van Dieen, J. (2003). Sitting comfort and discomfort and the relationships with objective measures. *Ergonomics, 46*(10), 985–997. doi:10.1080/0014013031000121977

DeLoney, C. (2008). *Person identification and gender recognition from footstep sound using modulation analysis*. (Technical Report TR 2008-17), University of Maryland. Retrieved December 28, 2010, from http://drum.lib.umd.edu/bitstream/1903/8379/3/DeLoney.pdf

Erzin, E., Yemez, Y., Tekalp, A. M., Ercil, A., Erdogan, H., & Abut, H. (2006). Multimodal person recognition for human-vehicle interaction. *IEEE MultiMedia, 13*(2), 18–31. doi:10.1109/MMUL.2006.37

Giles, E. (1970). Discriminant function sexing of the human skeleton. In Stewart, T. D. (Ed.), *Personal identification in mass disasters* (pp. 99–109). Washington, D.C.: Smithsonian Institution.

GPSBabel. (2010). *Convert, upload, download data from GPS and map programs*. Retrieved December 28, 2010, from http://www.gpsbabel.org/

Hurley, D., Arbab-Zavar, B., & Nixon, M. (2008). The ear as a biometric. In S. Zi Li (Ed.), *Handbook of biometrics*, (pp. 131–150). Springer Science+Business Media.

IBIA. (2010). *International Biometrics & Identification Association* (IBIA). Retrieved December 28, 2010, from http://www.ibia.org/

Intersense. (2010). *Precision motion tracking solutions – InertiaCube*. Retrieved December 28, 2010, from http://www.intersense.com/categories/18/

Kim, D., Seo, Y., Kim, S.-H., & Jung, S. (2008). Short term analysis of long term patterns of heart rate variability in subjects under mental stress. In *Proceedings of the 2008 International Conference on BioMedical Engineering and Informatics (BMEI 2008)*, (vol. 2, pp. 487–491). Washington, DC: IEEE Computer Society.

Koenig, P. (2004). Personal identification method and apparatus using acoustic resonance analysis of body parts. *Acoustical Society of America Journal, 116*(3), 1328–1328. doi:10.1121/1.1809922

Korotkaya, Z. (2003). Biometric person authentication: Odor. In *Advanced topics in information processing: Biometric person authentication* (p. 16). Department of Information Technology, Laboratory of Applied Mathematics, Lappeenranta University of Technology.

Liu, Y.-C. (2001). Comparative study of the effects of auditory, visual and multimodality displays on drivers performance in advanced traveller Information Systems. *Ergonomics*, *44*(18), 425–442. doi:10.1080/00140130010011369

Luo, Y.-C. (1995). Sex determination from the pubis by discriminant function analysis. [Forensic Anthropology Around the World.]. *Forensic Science International*, *74*(1–2), 89–98. doi:10.1016/0379-0738(95)01739-6

Maricopa Association of Governments. (2006). *Vehicle occupancy study*. Technical report. Retrieved December 28, 2010, from http://www.mag.maricopa.gov

Mendes, W. B. (2009). Assessing the autonomic nervous system. In Harmon-Jones, E., & Beer, J. (Eds.), *Methods in social neuroscience* (pp. 118–147). Guilford Press.

Nygårds, M., & Sörnmo, L. (1983). Delineation of the QRS complex using the envelope of the ECG. *Medical & Biological Engineering & Computing*, *21*(5), 538–547. doi:10.1007/BF02442378

Olden, M. (2009). *Biometric authentication and authorisation infrastructures*. Phd Thesis, University of Regensburg, Germany. Retrieved December 28, 2010, from http://epub.uni-regensburg.de/12680/

Oliver, N., & Pentland, A. (2000). Graphical models for driver behavior recognition in a Smartcar. In *Proceedings of the IEEE Intelligent Vehicles Symposium*, (pp. 7–12).

Phenice, W. T. (1969). A newly developed visual method of sexing the Os Pubis. *American Journal of Physical Anthropology*, *30*, 297–302. doi:10.1002/ajpa.1330300214

Philips, P. J., Martin, A., Wilson, C. L., & Przybocki, M. (2000). An introduction to evaluating biometric systems. *IEEE Computer*, 56–63. National Institute of Technology.

Prado, M., Reina-Tosina, J., & Roa, L. (2002). Distributed intelligent architecture for falling detection and physical activity analysis in the elderly, (vol. 3, pp. 1910–1911).

Ramesh, K., & Rao, K. (2009). Pattern extraction methods for ear biometrics - A survey. In *2009 NaBIC World Congress on Nature Biologically Inspired Computing, 2009* (pp.1657–1660).

Rashed, A., & Santos, H. (2010). Odour user interface for authentication: possibility and acceptance: Case study. *Proceedings of the International MultiConference of Engineers and Computer Scientists (IMECS 2010)*, March 17-19, Hong Kong, I:4. ISBN: 978-988-17012-8-2

Reschovsky, C. (2004). *Journey to work: 2000*. (Technical Report C2KBR-33), U.S. Department of Commerce, Economics and Statistics Administration, U.S. Census Bureau.

Revett, K. (2008). *Multimodal biometric systems*. John Wiley & Sons, Ltd.

Riener, A. (2010). *Sensor-actuator supported implicit interaction in driver assistance systems*, 1st ed. Wiesbaden, Germany: Vieweg+Teubner Research. ISBN: 978-3-8348-0963-6

Riener, A., & Ferscha, A. (2007). Driver activity recognition from sitting postures. In T. Paul-Stueve (Ed.), *Workshop on Automotive User Interfaces and Interactive Applications (AUIIA'07),* September 2–5, 2008, (p. 9). Weimar, Germany: Verlag der Bauhaus-Universität Weimar. ISBN: 978-3-486-58496-7

Riener, A., & Ferscha, A. (2008). Supporting implicit human-to-vehicle interaction: Driver identification from sitting postures. In *Proceedings of the 1st International Symposium on Vehicular Computing Systems (ISVCS 2008)*, July 22-24, 2008, Trinity College Dublin, Ireland. ACM Digital Library.

Rimsley, B. G. (2003). *Vehicle occupancy survey: US 52, Harrison, SR 26, US 231. Survey, Tippecanoe County, 20 North Third Street, Lafayette, Indiana 47901*. Retrieved December 28, 2010, from http://www.tippecanoe.in.gov

Schmidt, A. (2000). Implicit human computer interaction through context. *Personal and Ubiquitous Computing, 4*(2), 191–199. doi:10.1007/BF01324126

Schumm, J., Setz, C., Bächlin, M., Bächler, M., Arnrich, B., & Tröster, G. (2010). Unobtrusive physiological monitoring in an airplane seat. *Personal and Ubiquitous Computing. Special Issue on Pervasive Technologies for Assistive Environments, 14*, 541–550.

Setz, C., Arnrich, B., Schumm, J., La Marca, R., Tröster, G., & Ehlert, U. (2010). Discriminating stress from cognitive load using a wearable EDA device. *IEEE Transactions on Information Technology in Biomedicine, 14*(2), 410–417. doi:10.1109/TITB.2009.2036164

Shafie, S. A. M., Vien, L. L., & Sadullah, A. F. M. (2008). *Vehicle occupancy in malaysia according to land use and trip purpose*. In EASTS International Symposium on Sustainable Transportation incorporating Malaysian Universities Transport Research Forum Conference 2008 (MUTRFC08), (p. 8).

Stewart, T. D. (1954). Sex determination of the skeleton by guess and by measurement. *American Journal of Physical Anthropology, 12*, 385–392. doi:10.1002/ajpa.1330120312

Tessendorf, B., Arnrich, B., Schumm, J., Setz, C., & Troster, G. (2009). *Unsupervised monitoring of sitting behavior*. In Annual International Conference of the IEEE Engineering in Medicine and Biology Society (EMBC 2009), (pp. 6197–6200). IEEE.

Trivedi, M. M., Gandhi, T., & McCall, J. (2007). Looking-in and looking-out of a vehicle: Computer-vision-based enhanced vehicle safety. *IEEE Transactions on Intelligent Transportation Systems, 8*(1), 108–120. Retrieved December 28, 2010, from http://escholarship.org/uc/item/2g6313r2

u-blox. (2010). *Automotive GPS chips and chipsets*. Retrieved December 28, 2010, from http://www.u-blox.com/en/gps-chips/automotive-gps-chips.html

U.S. Department of Transportation. (2009). *2009 National household travel survey: Report, Federal Highway Administration*. Retrieved December 28, 2010, from http://nhts.ornl.gov/publications.shtml

Veeraraghavan, H., Atev, S., Bird, N., Schrater, P., & Papanikolopoulos, N. (2005). Driver activity monitoring through supervised and unsupervised learning. In *Proceedings of the 2005 IEEE Intelligent Transportation Systems*, (pp. 580–585).

Vista Medical Ltd. (2010). *Pressure mapping, pressure imaging and pressure sensing*. Retrieved December 28, 2010, from http://www.pressure-mapping.com/

Woodward, J. D., Horn, C., Gatune, J., & Thomas, A. (2003). *Biometrics – A look at facial recognition. Documented Briefing 396, RAND Public Safety and Justice*. RAND.

XSENSOR Technology Corporation. (2010). Pressure imaging systems for sleep, patient safety and automotive testing. Retrieved December 28, 2010, from http://www.xsensor.com/

Yubico. (2010). *The Yubikey*. Retrieved December 28, 2010, from http://www.yubico.com/yubikey

ADDITIONAL READING

Cheng and Trivedi. (2006). Cheng, S. Y. and Trivedi, M. M. (2006). Turn-Intent Analysis Using Body Pose for Intelligent Driver Assistance. *IEEE Pervasive Computing / IEEE Computer Society [and] IEEE Communications Society*, 5(4), 28–37. doi:10.1109/MPRV.2006.88

Coroama., et al. 2004Coroama, V., Bohn, J., and Mattern, F. (2004). Living in a Smart Environment – Implications for the Coming Ubiquitous Information Society. In *Proceedings of the International Conference on Systems, Man and Cybernetics 2004 (IEEE SMC 2004)*, volume 6, pages 5633–5638, The Hague, The Netherlands.

Coroama and Höckl. 2004Coroama, V. and Höckl, N. (2004). Pervasive Insurance Markets and their Consequences. First International Workshop on Sustainable Pervasive Computing at Pervasive 2004, Vienna, Austria.

Healey and Picard. 2000Healey, J. and Picard, R. (2000). Smartcar: detecting driver stress. In *Proceedings of the 15th International Conference on Pattern Recognition*, volume 4, pages 218–221.

McCall and Trivedi. (2007). McCall, J. and Trivedi, M. (2007). Driver Behavior and Situation Aware Brake Assistance for Intelligent Vehicles. *Proceedings of the IEEE*, 95(2), 374–387. doi:10.1109/JPROC.2006.888388

Moeslund, 1999Moeslund, T. (1999). Computer vision-based human motion capture – a survey.

Moeslund and Granum. (2001). Moeslund, T. B. and Granum, E. (2001). A Survey of Computer Vision-Based Human Motion Capture. [CVIU]. *Computer Vision and Image Understanding*, 81(3), 231–268. doi:10.1006/cviu.2000.0897

Oliver and Pentland. (2000). bOliver, N. and Pentland, A. P. (2000b). Driver behavior recognition and prediction in a SmartCar. In *Proceedings of SPIE Aerosense-Enhanced and Synthetic Vision*, 4023, 280–290.

Phenice, 1969Phenice, W. T. (1969). A newly developed visual method of sexing the Os Pubis. *American Journal of Physical Anthropology*, 30:297–302.

Picard., et al. 2001Picard, R. W., Vyzas, E., and Healey, J. (2001). Toward machine emotional intelligence: Analysis of affective physiological state. Technical report no. 536, MIT Media Laboratory, Perceptual Computing, 20 Ames Street, Cambridge, MA 02139, USA.

Schmidt, 2000Schmidt, A. (2000). Implicit human computer interaction through context. *Personal and Ubiquitous Computing*, 4(2):191–199.

Trivedi, (2004). Trivedi, M. M., Cheng, S. Y., Childers, E. M. C., and Krotosky, S. J. (2004). Occupant Posture Analysis with Stereo and Thermal Infrared Video: Algorithms and Experimental Evaluation. *IEEE Transactions on Vehicular Technology. Special Issue on In-Vehicle Vision Systems*, 53(6), 1698–1712.

KEY TERMS AND DEFINITIONS

Autonomic Nervous System (ANS): A part of a human's peripheral nervous system that controls visceral functions. It is classically divided into the two subsystems parasympathetic (body at rest, state of "calm") and sympathetic (high arousal, "power", active state) nervous system.

Biometrics: Method for uniquely recognizing humans based upon one or more physical or behavioral traits. Biometric characteristics can be divided into an active (explicit) type (e.g. interpretation of retina, voice, or finger print) and a passive (implicit) type, comprising for instance sitting posture pattern or ECG signal evaluation.

Electrocardiography (ECG): Records (and interprets) cardiac electrical potentials of the heart over time. Recording is normally done using skin electrodes connected to an electrocardiographic device. ECG is the best way to measure and diagnose abnormalities in the rhythm of the heart, such as HRV.

Explicit Interaction: This is a type of interaction where the user is in an active and attentive role. Explicit interaction demand active cooperation of the user, which can, in case of cognitive overload, result in unwanted behavior as delivered information or alerts tend to fail to raise the required attention.

Heart Rate Variability (HRV): Is a measure to detect inter-beat time (R-R) irregularities in an ECG. The HRV measure can be used to estimate mental stress (arousal state). Irregularity is the normal condition; a constant R-R time predominates only for artificial pacemaker and in medical conditions.

Implicit Interaction: "Implicit (human computer) interaction is an action, performed by the user that is not primarily aimed to interact with a (computerized) system but which such a system understands as input" (Schmidt, 2000).

NMEA (or NMEA 0183): A specification for communication between electronic devices like GPS defined by the National Marine Electronics Association. NMEA uses a simple, serial ASCII protocol for data communication.

Personal Sitting Profile: A sitting posture pattern is in some respects a feature of an individual, applicable for identifying or authorizing that person in a seat. The calculation of one's profile is based on a weighted combination of several individual parameters extracted from the sitting posture image of that person. Preliminary results have shown that the identification from a sitting posture is not as universal as, for instance, the retina of the eye or the genetic fingerprint.

Pressure Sensing: The utilization of sitting posture patterns to recognize a person's identity is a novel, implicit method compared to other state-of-the-art identification methods. Force-sensitive array mats are used for feature acquisition. These mats satisfies as they are (1) easily integrable into almost any type of seat (sensor arrays are thin and highly flexible), (2) not reliant on the attention of a person/requires no active cooperation of a "user", and (3) continuously in operation while the person is seated.

ENDNOTE

[1] Abbreviations: N...Normal posture, KL...Bunch of keys, left back-pocket, KR...Bunch of keys, right back-pocket, CL...Cell phone, left back-pocket, CR...Cell phone, right back-pocket, DL...Digital camera (Canon IXUS 500), left back-pocket, DR...Digital camera, right back-pocket, DRKL...Digital camera, right back-pocket and bunch of keys, left back-pocket

Section 3
Continuous Authentication
Using Behavioural Biometrics

Chapter 8
Towards Continuous Authentication Based on Gait Using Wearable Motion Recording Sensors

Mohammad Omar Derawi
Gjøvik University College, Norway

Davrondzhon Gafurov
Gjøvik University College, Norway

Patrick Bours
Gjøvik University College, Norway

ABSTRACT

Nearly all systems conduct some kind of user authentication before granting access to the objects or services. Moreover, humans pass through authentication steps more than once in their everyday activity, e.g. for entering a house you have to possess the correct key to open the door, to use a computer you need to know its password, etc. These authentications are one-time or static which means once the user's identity is verified the authentication lasts forever. However, some high security systems require ensuring the correct identity of the user throughout the full session. This then requires verification of user identity continuously or periodically. One of the important requirements for continuous authentication is that the method should be unobtrusive and convenient in usage. If this is not satisfied the users are not going to accept continuous authentication. Therefore not all authentication methods can be suitable for continuous authentication even if they provide higher security.

In this chapter we present continuous authentication using gait biometric. Gait is a person's manner of walking and gait recognition refers to the identification and verification of an individual based on gait. This chapter discusses advantages and disadvantages of gait biometrics in the context of continuous authentication. Furthermore, we present a framework for continuous authentication using gait biometrics. The proposed framework extends on traditional static (one-time) user authentication. The framework can also be applied to other biometric modalities with small modifications.

DOI: 10.4018/978-1-61350-129-0.ch008

INTRODUCTION

A particular way or manner of moving on foot is a definition for gait (Farlex). Every person has his or her own way of walking. From early medical studies it appears that there are twenty-four different components to human gait, and that if all the measurements are considered, gait is unique (BenAbdelkader, et al., 2001). This has made gait recognition an interesting topic to be used for identifying individuals by the manner in which they walk. Figure 1 illustrates the complex biological process of the musculo-skeletal system, which can be divided into several types of sub events of human-gait. The instances that are shown in this figure are used to extract parameters for being used as an identification system of each individual.

The analysis of biometric gait recognition has been studied for a longer period of time (Larsen, et al., 2008; Nixon, et al., 2002; Nixon, et al., 2005; Niyogi & Adelson, 1994; Wang, et al., 2003) for the use in identification, surveillance and forensic systems and is becoming important, since it can provide more reliable and efficient means of identity verification.

Today, computer systems demand authentication in case of using the system. Typically, the authentication is performed at login time either with a password, token, biometric characteristic and/or a combination of these. Performing the last mentioned might give further guarantee that the claimed user logging in is the authorized user instead of a burglar. However, once the user has been granted access; most systems assume that the user is continuously legitimated into the system.

In critical or high security environments, it should be ensured that the user must be the legitimated throughout usage. Therefore, user authentication needs to be performed in a continuous way within the time the system is actively being used. Furthermore, authentication needs to be "*attractive*" for the user. This means that in the authentication process the users do not need to do anything special, like for example periodically entering a password. Continuous authentication using biometrics can fit these needs. Thus, one of the important requirements in continuous authentication is unobtrusiveness, since this can be monitored in a non-intrusive way. The Wearable Sensor (WS) based method can be a very good candidate to fulfill this requirement, compared to current knowledge-based mechanisms.

This chapter is structured as follows: Section 'Background' gives the state of the art overview of gait recognition and activity recognition. Section 'Evaluation of a Biometric System' introduces the definition of static and continuous authentication. The next section introduces the biometric

Figure 1. Division of the gait cycle into five stance phase periods and two swing phase periods (Adapted from (Sminchisescu, et al., 2004))

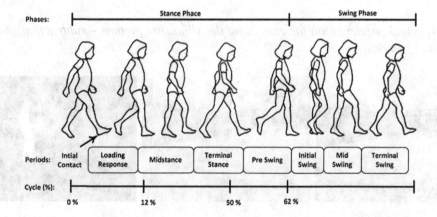

continuous authentication (CA) system using gait recognition. This is the major contribution in this chapter and discusses CA using gait. The last section concludes the paper and gives a description on how wearable gait recognition can be improved by proposing new ideas for future work.

BACKGROUND / STATE OF THE ART

This section is divided into 2 subsections. First subsection describes the motion-based (gait biometrics) identity verification. Second subsection introduces activity recognition.

Gait Recognition

From how the walking data is collected, gait recognition can be categorized in three approaches (Gafurov, 2009):

- Video Sensor Based (VS);
- Floor Sensor based (FS);
- Wearable Sensor based (WS).

We will give a short description on all three approaches, but we will mainly focus on the WS-based approach. We will illustrate how nicely this WS-based approach meets the requirements of continuous authentication which were specified in the previous section.

Video Sensor Based

In the VS-based approach, the system will typically consist of several video cameras with suitable optics for acquiring the gait data. Using techniques such as thresholding which converts images into simply black and white; pixel counting to count the number of light or dark pixels; and background segmentation, which performs a simple background subtraction could be some of the possible ways to identify a person. Figure 2 shows an example of the VS-based approach with processed background segmentation.

Scientist have during the last decade until currently been working on analyzing the movements of criminals caught on CCTV and compare them with those of a suspect (TimesOnline). Back in December 2004, there was a case where a perpetrator robbed a bank in Denmark (Larsen, et al., 2008). During the robbery, two surveillance cameras were recording the crime scene. One camera was placed at the entrance recording the robber in frontal view (walking in, standing and walking inside the bank during the robbery, and leaving the bank). The other camera was placed inside the bank recording the cashier's desk. The court used the gait-analysis tool to find the perpetrator of the robbery. Almost at the same time in late December 2004, there was a murder crime scene in the United Kingdom. A podiatrist told the supreme court jury that there were matches between the person captured on video and known

Figure 2. Background segmentation for extracting the silhouette picture – subtraction (Adapted from (Horprasert, et al., 1999))

videos of the murderer (CanadaNews). In a third case, around mid-April 2008, a burglar was caught because of his bow-legged walk (BBC-News). Even though that the burglars face was hidden, it was still possible to identify the burglar. In most cases in a robbery, usually the perpetrator wears a mask and gloves to hide his body characteristics such as face and hands so that no face or fingerprints can be shown or found at the crime scene. If cameras are available that recorded the gait of the burglar, then maybe enough information is present to link a person to the crime.

Floor Sensor Based

In the FS-based approach the sensors are placed on or in the floor where gait data is measured when people walk across. In the FS-based approach the force to the ground by human walking is measured. This is also known as the GRF (Ground Reaction Force). In a research from the University of Southampton, such a floor sensor

for gait recognition was prototyped as illustrated in Figure 3.

Wearable-Sensor Based

Apart from the MV-based and FS-based gait recognition, the WS-based gait approach is the most recent. This approach is based on attaching or wearing motion recording sensors on the body of the person in different places; on the waist, pockets, shoes and so forth, see Figure 4.

The WS-based approach can serve several purposes due to retrieving numerous types of data. Different types of sensors can for example be accelerometers (measuring acceleration), gyro sensors (measuring rotation), force sensor (measuring force of walking), etc. Most literature so far used accelerometer based gait recognition. Thus, these accelerometers are becoming an important tool into our every-day. Most of the modern mobile smart phones nowadays use built-in accelerometers to detect when the device is rotated. The data from the accelerometers is used

Figure 3. Gait collection by floor sensors. a) shows footsteps recognized; b) shows the time spent at each location in a; c) shows footstep profiles for heel and toe strikes (x and f(x) indicate the heal/toe locations and footfalls forces, respectively); d) is a picture of a prototype floor sensor carpet (Adapted from (Middleton, et al., 2005))

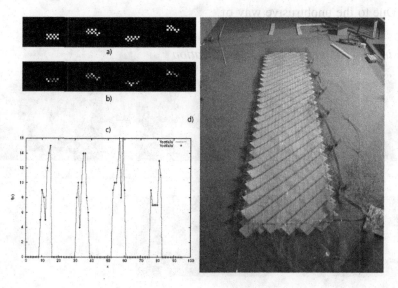

Figure 4. Sensor attached at various locations (Adapted from (Gafurov, 2008))

to display the information on the screen in either horizontal or vertical format. Moreover, the device can further detect when it is being lifted to the ear so that phone calls can be answered automatically. Feature extraction from gait signals is important for the efficiency of gait recognition. For a general gait analysis the signal processing flow is shown in Figure 5.

A WS-based gait recognition application can improve authentication in electronic devices. One of the advantages of WS-based gait recognition and the main argument towards CA is its unobtrusiveness. An example would be to integrate the Motion Recording Sensor (MRS) in clothing (e.g. footwear) or personal electronics of the user.

Whenever a user walks, the MRS can record motion and the recorded motion can be used for identity verification purposes unobtrusively in the background. Due to the unobtrusive way of collecting data it can be applied for continuous verification of the identity in mobile phones. This means that for each step a user takes, the identity of the user will be re-verified to ensure that the user has not changed. In addition, MRS are cheap and many recent personal electronic devices (e.g. mobile phone) are already equipped with such sensors.

Experiments

To the best of our knowledge, no public database has been created for accelerometer based gait recognition. However, researchers have made their own experiments and databases. Table 1 summarizes experiments performed in research with the type of activity performed, environment and the number of subjects.

Figure 5. Processing flow of method for gait verification

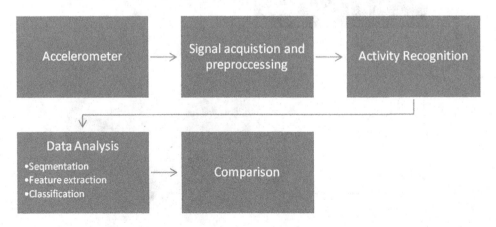

Table 1. Experiments summary

Study	Walking activities	# Subjects
(Henriksen, et al., 2004)	normal	20
(Bächlin, et al., 2009; Mantyjarvi, et al., 2005)	normal	36
(Gafurov, 2008)	normal	21,30,50,100
(Sprager & Zazula, 2009)	normal, fast, slow	6
(Rong, et al., 2005; Rong, et al., 2007)	normal	21,35
(Bächlin, et al., 2009)	treadmill (normal, fast, slow)	5
(Hynes, et al., 2009)	free normal, free resting	5
(Holien, 2008)	normal, fast, slow, circle	60

All of the mentioned experiments above except (Hynes, et al., 2009) are controlled experiments. A controlled experiment is defined as taking place under fixed laboratory settings and differs significantly from a real world scenario. People usually carry their mobile phones in their pockets or hold them while the phone is continuously moving and rotating in different directions. In the fixed, controlled settings the phone is usually attached to one particular location on the body at all times.

As can be seen further in Table 1, the amount of volunteers differs greatly. Many of the experiments had a low number of volunteers. Obviously this means that the recognition performances (viewed later in this chapter) are not directly comparable since the numbers of volunteers are dissimilar.

Finally, very few studies have researched gait-recognition with different behavioral settings. A study (Holien, 2008) has shown that the gait-signal of one person slightly changes from one day to another.

Data Acquisition

Accelerometer data can be derived from several types of sensors; from a dedicated accelerometer, a GPS device, a mobile phone etc. An accelerometer measures acceleration in three directions, being the x-direction (up-down), the y-direction (forward-backward) and the z-direction (sideways).

Table 2 gives an overview of the placement of sensors and sensor models that have been used in literature.

Accelerometers (whether they are built into cell phones or are dedicated devices) usually output different sample-rates per time unit. Most accelerometers have a low sample-rate/frequency while few have a high frequency rate. Moreover, some devices today contain multiple sensors, such as a gyroscope, magnetic-field etc.

Preprocessing

Preprocessing has been performed differently in literature. (Holien, 2008) and (Gafurov, 2008) applied the *linear time interpolation* on the three axis data (x,y,z) retrieved from the sensor to obtain an observation every X seconds since time intervals between two observation points were not always equal.

Measured acceleration signals are sometimes low-frequency components. The signals that are being outputted are easily affected by experiment environmental noise, such as electronic noise in the equipment, high frequency noise etc. which will obscure/reduce the clarity of the acceleration data. However, the accelerometer does not always measure gravitational acceleration; it might also measure the acceleration of light oscillation brought by the body of the human. This results in another weakness from the sensor that is acceleration data will be outputted with some noise. (Holien, 2008) and (Gafurov, 2008) removed this type of noise by using a *weighted moving average* filter which is fast and easy to implement, whereas (Mostayed, et al., 2008) and

Table 2. Data acquisition summary

Study	Acquisition From	Device
(Sazonov, et al., 2005)	shoe	MEMS accelerometer
(Iso & Yamazaki, 2006)	breast/hip	cell phone accelerometer
(Mostayed, et al., 2008)	whole body weight	force plate
(Gafurov, 2008)	ankle/pocket/arm/hip	3D accelerometer (MRS)
(Rong, et al., 2005; Rong, et al., 2007)	waist	3D accelerometer (analog)
(Annadhorai, et al., 2008)	leg	wireless accelerometer (Tmote Sky)
(Hynes, et al., 2009)	pockets	phone handset
(C.-Y. Lee & Lee)	waist	3D accelerometer (ADXL05, analog)
(Ailisto, et al., 2005)	waist	3D accelerometer (ADXL202JQ, analog)
(Mantyjarvi, et al., 2005)	waist	3D accelerometer (ADXL202JQ, analog)
(Sprager & Zazula, 2009)	hip	cell phone accelerometer
(Bächlin, et al., 2009)	ankle	MEMS accelerometer
(Henriksen, et al., 2004)	elastic belt on body	3D accelerometer
(Derawi, et al., 2010)	hip	3D accelerometer (MRS)
(Holien, 2008)	hip	3D accelerometer (MRS)

(Rong, et al., 2007) de-noised the signals with a Daubechies wavelet (wavelet transform). They meant that this transform showed satisfying results in noise suppression from previous experiments, preserving edges and would be helpful for the gait segmentation.

Since different accelerometers output different unit values, (Holien, 2008) and (Gafurov, 2008) had to convert their values into practical unit values (e.g. g-forces) by using properties of the sensor they derived the data from.

In the last preprocessing step, (Holien, 2008) and (Gafurov, 2008) calculated the resultant vector (also known as the vector magnitude) by applying the following formula,

$$r_t = \sqrt{x_t^2 + y_t^2 + z_t^2}, \ t = 1...,N$$

where r_t, x_t, y_t and z_t are the magnitudes of resulting, vertical, horizontal and lateral acceleration at time t, respectively and N is the number of recorded observations in the signal. However, for example (Sprager & Zazula, 2009) did not use any

combined vector, but instead kept the vector as is so they had a 3-component vectors of samples stored in a matrix A

$$A=[xyz]$$

where x, y and z represents vectors of acquired samples for each spatial direction.

Data Analysis

Identifying users from gait patterns using accelerometers is based on the assumption that the gait acceleration profile ("reference template") is unique to some extent for each and every person. First, a feature vector that represents the characteristics of the gait of the person to authenticate is computed and stored as the reference template. A similar feature vector is computed during the authentication process and compared to the reference template. Acceptance of the user is based on the distance between the new feature vector and the reference template.

The accelerometer data can be analyzed in two domains: the time domain or the frequency domain. In the time domain, the three acceleration signals (x,y,z) change over time (t), whereas in the frequency domain each frequency band over a range of frequencies is used. A given function or a given signal can be converted between the time and the frequency domain with a pair of mathematical operators called a transformation.

Segmentation (Data Analysis)

Gait segmentation is the process of identifying "boundaries" in the gait signal(s). Gait segmentation is an important sub-problem and can be performed in various ways. Gait signals obtained from an individual are composed of periodic segments called gait cycles. These cycles physically correspond to two consecutive steps of the individual. A gait cycle begins when one foot touches the ground and ends when that same foot touches the ground again as shown in Figure 1 and the acceleration data is illustrated in Figure 6.

The end of one gait cycle is the beginning of the next. To split the signal into gait cycles, a determination of the gait cycle period is needed. This can be determined by either using the x, y and z data separately or a combination of the data of two or three directions.

Table 3 summarizes three segmentation approaches that have been applied so far.

Feature Extraction in the Time Domain (Data Analysis)

The time domain is a term used to describe that the analysis of signals is done with respect to time, as mentioned earlier. The average cycle method was one of the first methods applied in gait biometrics within the time domain and also the most applied. The average cycle method is a simple approach that averages all cycles extracted. However, other extraction approaches have also been developed. Table 4 shows these extractions that have been developed until recently.

Feature Extraction in the Frequency Domain (Data Analysis)

Extracting features in the frequency domain is a bit different than in the time domain, since other (mathematical) approaches have to be applied. The best known approach is the Fourier transform, which is a mathematical operation that transforms a signal from the time domain to the frequency domain, and vice versa. Table 5 shows an overview of other applied methods.

Figure 6. One gait cycle: begins when one foot touches the ground and ends when that same foot touches the ground again

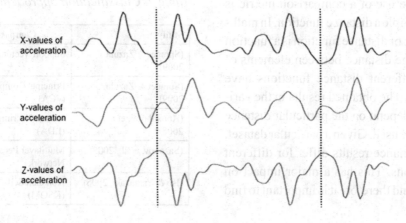

Table 3. Segmentation approaches

Study	Approach
(Ailisto, et al., 2005; Manty-jarvi, et al., 2005)	Cycle Detection Algorithm (1 step extraction)
(Gafurov, 2008; Holien, 2008)	Cycle Detection Algorithm (2 step extraction)
(Annadhorai, et al., 2008)	Period of a periodic gait cycle

Table 4. Time Domain feature approaches

Study	Approach
(Derawi, et al., 2010)	Matrix with cycles
(Ailisto, et al., 2005)	Average cycle detection
(Mantyjarvi, et al., 2005)	N-bin normalized histogram
(Sprager & Zazula, 2009)	Cumulants of different orders

Table 5. Frequency domain feature approaches

Study	Approach
(Rong, et al., 2007)	Discrete Fourier Transform (DFT)
(Bächlin, et al., 2009)	Fast Fourier Transform (FFT)
(Ibrahim, et al., 2008)	Discrete Cosine Transform (DCT)
(Mostayed, et al., 2008)	Discrete Wavelet Transform (DWT)
(Iso & Yamazaki, 2006)	Wavelet Packet Decomposition

Comparison Functions (Data Analysis)

Usually when two feature vectors are compared to each other the use of a comparison metric is applied, for example a distance function. In mathematics, a metric or distance function is a function which defines the distance between elements of a set. Many different distance functions have been developed. The obtained results in the various researches depend on the particular distance functions that are used. Given a particular dataset, then the performance results differ for different distance functions. This has a major impact on authentication and therefore it is important to find or create an adequate distance function. Table 6 shows which comparison metrics are used.

Classification (Data Analysis)

Another well-studied area that is used within gait recognition is the (un)-supervised learning approaches. Supervised learning is a machine learning approach of extracting a function from supervised training data, in which each sample has a pair of input objects and a desired output value. Within wearable gait recognition, the training data consist of pairs of input objects that are extracted from the accelerometer signals. The output of the function can be a continuous value, called regression, or can predict a class label of the input (feature vector), called classification. An overview is shown in Table 7.

From an authentication point of view in data analysis and as mentioned earlier, the purpose is to create a reference template that represents the subject. Accelerometer based gait recognition has been

Table 6. Comparison approaches

Study	Approach
(Ailisto, et al., 2005)	Cross-correlation
(Gafurov, 2008)	Absolute (Manhattan) distance
(Holien, 2008)	Euclidean distance
(Derawi, et al., 2010)	Dynamic Time Warping (DTW)

Table 7. Classification approaches

Study	Comparison Metric
(Sprager & Zazula, 2009)	Support Vector Machine (SVM)
(Sprager & Zazula, 2009)	Principal Component Analysis (PCA)
(Annadhorai, et al., 2008)	Linear Discriminant Analysis (LDA)
(Sazonov, et al., 2005)	Multilayer Perceptrons – Neural Network
(Iso & Yamazaki, 2006)	Kohonen Self-Organizing Map (KSOM)

explored since 2005, resulting in data analysis methods like the Average Cycle Method (ACM). The ACM became popular because of its simplicity as a feature extraction method for template creation. Many different features were used for creation of templates and comparison, such as correlation, cumulants, histogram similarity, ACM, FFT coefficients, and other regular features. It is difficult to estimate whether some of these techniques are in general practical for any given data from different devices, since the experiments performed and analyses applied varied to a larger extent.

Comparing Gait Performances

Unlike VS-based gait biometric, no public dataset on WS-based gait is available. This makes performance comparison more difficult because each result is based on a private data set. Therefore, no direct comparison can be considered in this section, but we will still give an overview of all reported performance results.

Table 8 shows a short summary of current WS-based gait recognition studies from 2004 to 2010. The last column, #TP, represents the number of test-persons.

Table 8. Performances of current wearable sensor-based gait recognitions

Study	EER	Recognition	#TP
(Bours & Shrestha, 2010)	1.68%	-	60
(Derawi, et al., 2010)	5.7%	-	60
(Gafurov, et al., 2010)	1.6%	-	30
(Gafurov & Bours, 2010)	7.5%	81.4	100
(Holien, 2008)	5.9%	-	60
(Morris, 2004)	-	97.4%	10
(Huang, et al., 2007)	-	96.93%	9
(Ailisto, et al., 2005)	6.4%	-	36
(Mantyjarvi, et al., 2005)	7%, 19%	-	36
(Rong, et al., 2007)	5.6%	-	21
(Vildjiounaite, et al., 2006)	13.7%	-	31

Activity Recognition

Wearable sensors have been shown to be adequate for activity recognition. This recognition is a required step towards continuous authentication in WS-based gait authentication using sensors in mobile devices. These devices come prepared with sensors such as accelerometers, gyro-scopes, Global Positioning Systems (GPS), etc., which can gather information about the actions of a user. For example, a phone might observe that a user is walking normally in a non-stressed environment, or it might make decisions regarding whether incoming phone calls should be answered or denied.

Figure 7 illustrates an excerpt of which activities can be recognized from the gait signal data.

Several applications for recognizing activities from sensor data have been implemented in a broad range of fields such as health care (Dong-Oh, et al., 2006), fitness (Choudhury, et al., 2008; Lester, et al., 2006), and security (Kale, et al., 2002). Different types of sensors have been applied, e.g., accelerometer data for recognizing physical activities (Kamiar Aminian & Najafi, 2004; Lester, et al., 2006; Merryn Mathie, et al., 2004) and both mobile phone usage data (Far-rahi & Gatica-Perez, 2008) and GPS data (Krumm & Horvitz, 2006; Liao, et al., 2007) for human mobility analysis.

Detecting primitive everyday activities, such as walking, running, biking, sitting and laying have in laboratory settings been analyzed by several researchers (K. Aminian, et al., 1999; Foerster & Fahrenberg, 2000; Foerster, et al., 1999; Frank, et al., 2010; Lester, et al., 2006; M. Mathie, et al., 2003; Ng, et al., 2003; Subramanya, et al., 2006). In all these studies data is collected using accelerometers built into wearable sensing devices. Most research has shown recognition accuracy above 85% on large, complex data sets using standard linear signal processing methods and a lot of signal statistics computations executed. Furthermore, "high weighted" feature extractions approaches were used to decide whether these features would

Figure 7. Different activities

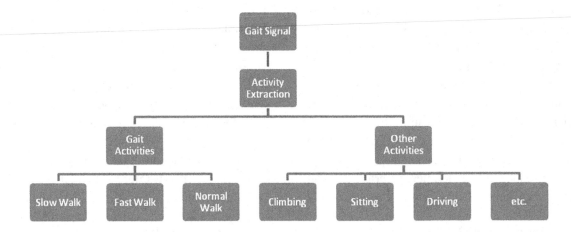

be useful for classification. Whilst these methodologies work fine, they need a lot of computing power. This will benefit applications suited for real-time detection of activities on low-powered devices, such as mobile phones. The applicability of the results which were presented in the studies mentioned above to out-of-lab monitoring is vague. In the study of (Foerster, et al., 1999) the recognition performance decreased from 95.8% to 66.7% as the experiment was shifted from inside to outside the laboratory. Furthermore, recognition of dissimilar activities involving dynamic motion has not yet been studied in detail. In some studies data has been composed outside the laboratory. The subjects placed accelerometers on their sternum, wrist, thigh, and lower leg. The same activities, i.e. sitting, standing, laying, and talking were recognized with an overall accuracy of 66.7%. In (Bao & Intille, 2004) five biaxial accelerometers attached to hip, wrist, arm, ankle, and thigh were used to recognize twenty everyday patterns. From 82 to 160 min of data was collected and a decision tree classifier was used for classification. The range of the recognition accuracies varied from 41% to 97% for different patterns.

Other research groups have studied activity recognition as fraction of context awareness research (Bao & Intille, 2004; Korpipää, et al., 2003;

S.-W. Lee & Mase, 2002). Context sensing and use of context information is a significant part of the ubiquitous computing scenario (Coutaz, et al., 2005; Streitz & Nixon, 2005). The purpose of context sensing is to provide a computing device (e.g., cellular phone, or a device integrated into clothes) with some "senses", with which it becomes attentive of its environment. With these "senses", the computing device is then able to observe and measure its surroundings and it will then become aware of its own context. The context describes the condition or status of the user or the device. Different devices can use the context information in special ways, e.g. for offering relevant services and information, for adapting its user interface, for annotating a digital diary (e.g. energy expenditure), etc. Location and time belong to the set of the most important contexts and the use of these contexts has been researched widely. However, to recognize the physical activities of a person, a sensor-based approach is required.

A very interesting research paper (Pärkkä, et al., 2006) studied the automatic classification of physical activities. The paper described how automatic classification of everyday activities can be used for promotion of health-enhancing physical activities and a healthier life-living. The application could therefore be used for an "activity diary" program that would explain to the user which activities were performed during the day and what the daily cumulative durations of each activity were. When the user is given this information, the user can draw his own conclusions and further adjust his behavior accordingly. This model is known as the behavioral feedback model. This model is being effectively used in for example weight management programs. Alternatively the activity diary information can be utilized by context-aware services and devices that propose adapted information or adapt their user interface (UI) based on the user's activity type.

The latest and most successful algorithm has been implemented in real time on a mobile phone by (Frank, et al., 2010) who proposed an alternative approach for representing time series data that significantly has lowered the memory and computational complexity. The memory and computational savings are crucial, given that for many applications, activity recognition would have to run in real time as a small component of a larger system on a low-powered mobile device. The study used accelerometer data; intuitively, the acceleration recorded by the mobile phone attaching this to the hips and legs. The techniques from nonlinear time series analysis (Kantz & Schreiber, 2008) was adopted to extract features from the time series. These features were used as inputs to an off-the-shelf classifier. The approach improves classification performance, while at the same time it extracts fewer features from the time series data.

EVALUATION OF A BIOMETRIC SYSTEM

Static Authentication

As can be seen in Figure 8, the user initially presents its biometric modality (e.g. gait) to the sensor equipment (e.g. an accelerometer sensor in a mobile phone), which captures it as raw biometric data

(e.g. a discrete time signal). After preprocessing this raw biometric data, features will be extracted from the data. In case of gait biometrics, these features would typically be periodic cycles. The extracted features can then be used for comparison against corresponding features stored in a database, based on the claimed identity of the user. The result of the comparison is called the similarity score, S where a low value of S indicates little similarity, while a high value indicates high similarity. The last step is to compare the similarity score S to a predefined system threshold T, and output a decision based on both values. In case the similarity score is above the threshold (S>T) then the user is accepted as genuine, while a similarity score below the threshold (S<T) indicates an impostor who is rejected by the system.

Obviously the biometric features of the user must initially be stored in the database before any comparison of a new biometric input can take place. This is done during the enrollment phase of a biometric system. During the enrollment phase also raw biometric data is captured from the biometric modality, after which it is processed and features are extracted. The extracted data is now stored in a database and linked to the identity of the user who enrolled. The stored data in the database is referred to as the (reference) template of the user. In case of gait biometrics it is very well possible that the raw biometric data is captured multiple times and these multiple samples are combined to make a single template. This is a well known technique in behavioral biometrics.

The calculation of the False Match Rate (FMR) and False Non-Match Rate (FNMR) is done in the following way. Suppose we have collected N data samples from each of M participants, then we can calculate similarity scores between two samples, either being from one person or from two different persons. A similarity score between two samples from the same person is called a genuine score, while an impostor score is the similarity score between two samples from different persons. Given our setting, we can have

Figure 8. A traditional verification process (one-time static)

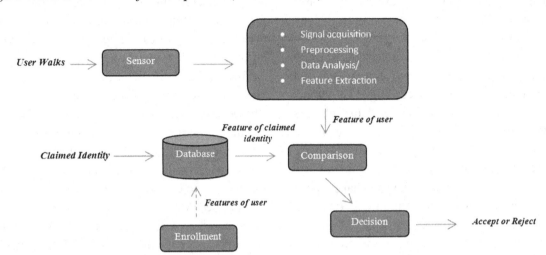

N*M data samples from which we can calculate the total number of $N_{Gen} = M*N*(N-1)/2$ different genuine scores and $N_{Imp} = M*N*(M-1)*N/2$. Given these sets of genuine and impostor scores we can calculate FMR and FNMR for any given threshold T as follows:

$$FMR(T) = \frac{\text{number of imposter scores} \leq T}{N_{Imp}}$$

$$FNMR(T) = \frac{\text{number of genuine scores} > T}{N_{Gen}}$$

Given various values of the threshold we can create a Decision Error Tradeoff (DET) curve which shows the relation between FMR and FMNR for various threshold values T. From this, we can find the point where FNMR equals FMR, or in other words the Equal Error Rate (EER). This rate is very common used value which is being used to compare different systems against each other, and it roughly gives an idea of how well a system performs.

Continuous Authentication

In a continuous authentication system we can no longer evaluate the performance of the system in terms of FMR and FNMR. In a static authentication system, the question is if a claimed identity is genuine or not. In a continuous authentication system the question is if the identity of the current user is still the same as the identity of the user that logged on the system. In particular, in continuous authentication the most important issue is not *if* an impostor is rejected by the system, but *how fast* he will be rejected. In a static biometric system, the lowest EER indicates the best performance. Similarly in a continuous authentication system, the best performance is indicated by the fastest rejection of impostors. A desirable property of a continuous authentication system might furthermore be that genuine users will never be rejected by the system, although this might not be realistic. In case a genuine user gets rejected, then this should obviously take much longer time in comparison to rejection of impostors.

In a continuous authentication system we also have to create a reference template for each user, which will be used for comparison against newly inputted raw biometric data. However, the resulting similarity score S will not directly lead to the rejection or acceptance of a user. First of all, as the user is already using the system, he/she is accepted by default, so in case of continuous authentication, we only have to consider the rejection of a user. Consider the situation where the genuine user is providing new biometric data to the system that is rather dissimilar to the stored reference template. This is a common situation in behavioral biometrics as biometric data is never exactly the same when it is presented to the sensor. This low similarity should not immediately result in a rejection of the user by the system, but merely in a lowered trust of the genuineness of this user. Similarly, if the similarity score S is high, indicating a high similarity between the reference template and the new biometric data, then the trust in the genuineness of the current user increases. This implies that the level of trust that the system has in the genuineness of the user fluctuates. In case of a genuine user, the level of trust will in

general stay high, while for an impostor the level ideally should drop as fast as possible. There will be a system threshold such that a trust level below the threshold will result in a lock out of the current user and a fall back to a static authentication procedure (which can but need not be a biometric system). In terms of performance of a continuous authentication system, we can then say that the faster impostors are detected (and locked out) the better the system performs.

Figure 9 represents the foundation of a CA system using gait on how to verify an identity of the user continuously. The main distinction between static and continuous gait verification is that for continuous gait verification the *data analysis*, *evaluation* and *authorization* are no longer one-time static happening. They are now elements of a continuous procedure.

Figure 9. Continuous authentication using gait

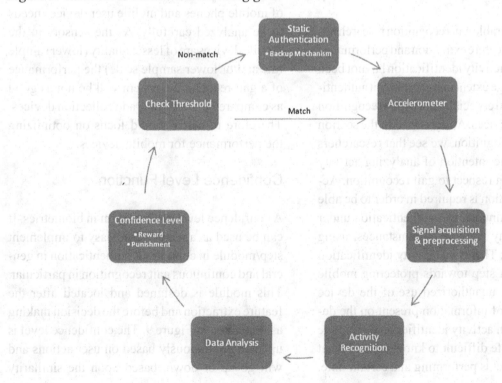

Evaluation of a Continuous Gait Authentication System

In this section we will describe in more detail how a continuous authentication system can be evaluated. In particular we will describe the changes in confidence level by introducing so-called "penalty-and-reward" functions. We will assume that the biometric data is collected from accelerometers in a mobile phone that is worn by a user while walking.

Activity Identification

Contributions within wearable gait recognition until now have only focused on the task of person identification where data was retrieved from dedicated external sensors.

One important issue in continuous authentication and gait recognition is to develop and evaluate algorithms to detect physical activities from data acquired using mobile devices (built-in sensors) worn on different parts of the body, which is also known as either *activity identification* or *activity recognition*.

Because wearable gait recognition research has had its focus on feature extraction and performance evaluation, the activity identification has not been analyzed to a large extent in wearable gait authentication before and especially not in gait recognition using mobile devices. As described in the section on Activity Recognition, we see that researchers have not had the intention of analyzing activity recognition with respect to gait recognition. Activity identification is required in order to be able to perform continuous gait authentication under normal everyday walking circumstances, using mobile devices. Therefore activity identification will be the first step towards protecting mobile devices against unauthorized use of the device and disclosure of information present on the device. Without an activity identifier on the mobile device, it is quite difficult to know exactly what activity a subject is performing at a certain time.

The gait recognition should only be functioning when the subject is physically active, and thus, the recognition should not be activated when the subject is passive (sitting down, standing, etc.).

Data Analysis

The data analysis part in continuous gait recognition is similar to the data analysis in static gait recognition. After walking activity has been identified, the walking signal has to be segmented and the segmented walking signal needs to be analyzed further. There are multiple ways of analyzing the data in wearable based gait recognition. Some approaches are described in the State of the Art section. The research on wearable sensor based gait recognition so far has only focused on "high grade" collection devices (high sample rate, large sample scale). The research on wearable sensor gait recognition using the accelerometer data from mobile phones or other mobile user devices does rarely exist. Sensor hardware (accelerometer, gyroscopes, etc.) on different mobile devices will be of different quality and therefore a broad selection of mobile phones and mobile user devices needs to be analyzed carefully. As the sensors in the mobile devices are of lesser quality (lower sample rate and/or lower sample scale) the performance of a gait recognition system will be not as good as compared to the high grade collection devices. Therefore research should focus on optimizing the performance for mobile devices.

Confidence Level Function

A confidence level is a new term in biometrics. It can be used as a realistic and easy to implement step/module in continuous authentication in general and continuous gait recognition in particular. This module is designed and located after the feature extraction and before the decision making as illustrated in Figure 9. The confidence level is updated continuously based on user actions and will go up or down, based upon the similarity between the current user action and the reference template. The limitation of static biometric analysis is that the authentication process is performed at the end of a full walking session and not during the session itself. In such a case we can only afterwards decide if the user was genuine or not, which is obviously too late. Therefore it is very important to introduce the idea of the confidence level function for continuous authentication.

Basically, a confidence level function is a function which updates a confidence value (C) for every captured feature during the walking session. The initial confidence value is set right after the static authentication and its value is 100.

Based on the distance between the current feature and the reference template, a decision rule is used to either increase or decrease the confidence value C. In particular, the confidence value will decrease each time the distance between the current feature and the reference template is outside the expected range, i.e. is above some pre-defined threshold. The value will increase each time this distance is below that pre-defined threshold. In other words the user should be punished when he/she makes mistakes (decreasing the confidence value) and he/she should be rewarded (increasing the confidence value) when he/she walks correctly. A setup for the confidence level function will look like follows:

$$C = \begin{cases} 100 & \text{initial value} \\ C - punishment & \text{mistake} \\ C + reward & \text{correct} \end{cases}$$

We should note that the confidence value C is initially set to 100 (100% confidence in the genuineness of the current user) and that it cannot rise above that. This means that in case of a reward the value of C increases, but is still bounded by 100. Similarly the confidence level value C cannot be lower than zero. The actual values C=100 and

C=0 indicate complete trust in the current user and complete distrust.

As mentioned before, there is a decision function that, based on the distance D between the current feature and the reference template, and based on a global threshold T decides whether the current action of the user was correct or wrong, i.e. if the user should be rewarded or punished. Generally speaking, if D≤T then the user is rewarded and if D>T he is punished. There are various ways to define a punishment or a reward. For example for the punishment, one solution could be to decrease the value C with a fixed constant. Another option could be to decrease C by the difference between the distance D and threshold T. Similar approaches can be taken for the reward. In fact there are no restrictions against combining a fixed reward value with a variable punishment.

In cases where data from an impostor are compared against a genuine user's reference template, the confidence level value is expected to generally keep decreasing. The impostor should be denied access after a relatively low number of user actions i.e. after a short walking time. This means that he cannot easily compensate his wrong walking by accidentally also walking correctly, i.e. walking as described in the reference template of the genuine user. However, when comparing data of a genuine user with its own template, the confidence level value should more or less fluctuate near the initialization value, meaning that wrong walking is easily compensated by correct walking.

Decision Rule

As described earlier in the section of static gait recognition a decision rule is based on a predefined threshold. The score value which is gained from the comparison-metric is compared to the threshold. Multiple decision rules could be implemented and applied. This mechanism can be easily translated to continuous gait authentication, by comparing the trust level to a pre-defined system threshold. If the value of the trust level C drops below a system threshold T_{trust}, then the system will lock out the user. Instead of using a system wide threshold could the system also be implemented with user defined thresholds. A user who is very stable in his way of walking could then have a higher personal threshold then a user who is less stable, i.e. is more likely to be punished for incorrect walking.

Backup Authentication Mechanism

When a user is locked out by the CA mechanism, a backup authentication mechanism should be activated. The user is rejected when the value of the confidence level C, as described in an earlier section, is under a certain system wide or personal threshold. This means that the system decides to deny the user further access and, thus, we enter a new state as illustrated in Figure 9. The state which will be entered is the static authentication state. This state must enable us to reset the confidence level in order to use the phone and the CA mechanism again. For example, if a user of a mobile phone gets rejected, the phone goes into the locked state. The user will now be able to enter the PIN code to open the phone from its locked state. Once the correct PIN code is entered, the user will return to the normal state and start with the highest trust level again.

Continuous Authentication: Multi Level Security

As described in the previous section we can use the trust level and a threshold to determine if a user needs to be locked out or not. This mechanism can actually be extended in such a way that Multi Level Security (MLS) can be provided. As mentioned before the value of the trust level C lies within the interval between 0 and 100. In the simple case a single threshold T is used such that the user gets locked out when C<T and stays logged in as long as C≥T. In principle a user can perform all actions as long as he is logged in.

The system can be extended such that we have multiple thresholds $T_0 < T_1 < \ldots < T_{n-1}$. For simplicities sake assume n=3 here, so we have three different thresholds and $T_0 < T_1 < T_2$. In this setting a user will be locked out of the system if the value of the trust level $C<T_0$ and he can perform all actions if $C≥T_2$. In case $T_0≤C<T_1$ then the user

Figure 10. Pyramid authentication: Continuous authorization and confidence level

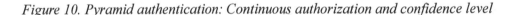

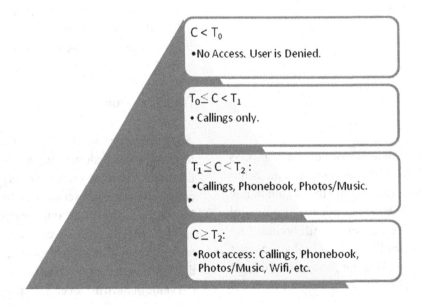

$C < T_0$
• No Access. User is Denied.

$T_0 ≤ C < T_1$
• Callings only.

$T_1 ≤ C < T_2$:
• Callings, Phonebook, Photos/Music.

$C ≥ T_2$:
• Root access: Callings, Phonebook, Photos/Music, Wifi, etc.

still will be logged on to the system, but he will not be able to perform all actions, for example he will only be able to make phone calls but he has no more access to any information stored on the phone. In case $T_1 \leq C < T_2$ then the user will be granted some more privileges besides making phone calls, but he will not have full access, for example he might then have access to data on the phone, but not be granted access to Wi-Fi.

As the value of C varies continuously the user will lose or regain access to particular privileges. Whenever a user wants to perform a particular action the CA system will check the value C of the trust level with the thresholds stored in the phone and decide if particular actions are allowed or not. Figure 10 illustrates an example of how the resources are related to the trust level.

CONCLUSION AND FUTURE WORK

Ensuring the correct identity of a user throughout a full session is important, especially for high security applications. In static biometric user authentication the authentication mechanism will make a decision about the correctness of the claimed user identity directly after the user has inputted his biometric feature. This decision is either accepting or rejecting this user, resulting in either access or not to the particular system. System performance is measured in terms of mistakes that are made by making the decision, i.e. in terms of FMR and FNMR.

The first difference for a continuous biometric user authentication mechanism is that the user is by default accepted due to the fact that his or her identity has been verified by a static authentication mechanism. A biometric CA mechanism will therefore only reject users if they have proven not to be the genuine user. In order to be able to measure the genuineness of the user we introduced trust levels and a way to adjust the trust level based on newly defined penalty and reward functions. The performance of a continuous authentication

system is measured in terms of how long it takes before an impostor is detected and locked out by the system.

In this chapter we focused on continuous user authentication using biometric gait recognition. In our approach gait is collected using wearable motion recording sensors attached to the person's body. One of the advantages of using WS-based gait recognition in continuous authentication is its unobtrusiveness. Whenever a user walks his identity is verified implicitly in the background without distracting the user from his normal activity. The proposed framework extends the traditional static authentication to account for periodic/continuous (re-)verification of identity. The proposed continuous authentication framework can easily be adjusted for other biometric modalities which are suitable for CA.

Future work will be to implement the proposed continuous gait authentication mechanism as an application in mobile phones and measure exact performances, i.e. the time it takes before impostor users are recognized as such by the CA mechanism and are locked out of the system.

REFERENCES

Ailisto, H. J., Lindholm, M., Mantyjarvi, J., Vildjiounaite, E., & Makela, S.-M. (2005). Identifying people from gait pattern with accelerometers. *Proceedings of the Society for Photo-Instrumentation Engineers, 5779*, 7–14.

Aminian, K., & Najafi, B. (2004). Capturing human motion using body-fixed sensors: outdoor measurement and clinical applications: Research articles. *Comput. Animat. Virtual Worlds, 15*(2), 79–94. doi:10.1002/cav.2

Aminian, K., Robert, P., Buchser, E., Rutschmann, B., Hayoz, D., & Depairon, M. (1999). Physical activity monitoring based on accelerometry: Validation and comparison with video observation. *Medical & Biological Engineering & Computing, 37*(3), 304–308. doi:10.1007/BF02513304

Annadhorai, A., Guenterberg, E., Barnes, J., Haraga, K., & Jafari, R. (2008). *Human identification by gait analysis.* Paper presented at the HealthNet '08: Proceedings of the 2nd International Workshop on Systems and Networking Support for Health Care and Assisted Living Environments, New York, NY, USA.

Bächlin, M., Schumm, J., Roggen, D., & Töster, G. (2009). *Quantifying gait similarity: User authentication and real-world challenge.* Paper presented at the ICB '09: Proceedings of the Third International Conference on Advances in Biometrics, Berlin, Heidelberg.

Bao, L., & Intille, S. (2004). *Activity recognition from user-annotated acceleration data.* Retrieved from http://citeseerx.ist.psu.edu/viewdoc/summary?doi=10.1.1.68.5133

BBC-News. (2008). *How can you identify a criminal by the way they walk?* Retrieved from http://news.bbc.co.uk/2/hi/uk_news/magazine/7348164.stm

Ben Abdelkader, C., Cutler, R., Nanda, H., & Davis, L. S. (2001). *EigenGait: Motion-based recognition of people using image self-similarity.* Paper presented at the AVBPA.

Bours, P., & Shrestha, R. (2010). *Eigensteps: A giant leap for gait recognition.* Paper presented at the 2nd International Workshop on Security and Communication Networks (IWSCN 2010), Karlstad, Sweden.

CanadaNews. (2008). *Forensic gait analysis points to accused.* Retrieved from http://www.canada.com/victoriatimescolonist/news/story.html?id=19d99f1a-bb4d-4d89-a92e-e7a583b1d14f.

Choudhury, T., Borriello, G., Consolvo, S., Haehnel, D., Harrison, B., & Hemingway, B. (2008). The mobile sensing platform: An embedded activity recognition system. *IEEE Pervasive Computing / IEEE Computer Society [and] IEEE Communications Society, 7*(2), 32–41. doi:10.1109/MPRV.2008.39

Coutaz, J., Crowley, J., Dobson, S., & Garlan, D. (2005). Context is key. *Communications of the ACM, 48*(3), 49–53. doi:10.1145/1047671.1047703

Derawi, M. O., Bours, P., & Holien, K. (2010). *Improved cycle detection for accelerometer based gait authentication.* Paper presented at the International Conference on Intelligent Information Hiding and Multimedia Signal Processing - Special Session on Advances in Biometrics.

Dong-Oh, K., Hyung-Jik, L., Eun-Jung, K., Kyuchang, K., & Jeunwoo, L. (2006). *A wearable context aware system for ubiquitous healthcare.* Paper presented at the Engineering in Medicine and Biology Society, 2006. EMBS '06. 28th Annual International Conference of the IEEE.

Farlex. (n.d.). *The free dictionary.* Retrieved from http://www.thefreedictionary.com/gait

Farrahi, K., & Gatica-Perez, D. (2008). *What did you do today? Discovering daily routines from large-scale mobile data.* Paper presented at the ACM International Conference on Multimedia (ACMMM). Retrieved from http://publications.idiap.ch/index.php/publications/showcite/farrahi:rr08-49

Foerster, F., & Fahrenberg, J. (2000). Motion pattern and posture: Correctly assessed by calibrated accelerometers. *Behavior Research Methods, Instruments, & Computers, 32*(3), 450–457. doi:10.3758/BF03200815

Foerster, F., Smeja, M., & Fahrenberg, J. (1999). Detection of posture and motion by accelerometry: A validation study in ambulatory monitoring. *Computers in Human Behavior, 15*(5), 571–583. doi:10.1016/S0747-5632(99)00037-0

Frank, J., Mannor, S., & Precup, D. (2010). *Activity and gait recognition with time-delay embeddings.*

Gafurov, D. (2008). *Performance and security analysis of gait-based user authentication.* Faculty of Mathematics and Natural Sciences, University of Oslo.

Gafurov, D., & Bours, P. (2010). Improved hip-based individual recognition using wearable motion recording sensor. In Kim, T.-H., Fang, W.-C., Khan, M. K., Arnett, K. P., Kang, H.-J., & Ślęzak, D. (Eds.), *Security technology, disaster recovery and business continuity* (*Vol. 122*, pp. 179–186). Berlin/Heidelberg, Germany: Springer. doi:10.1007/978-3-642-17610-4_20

Gafurov, D., Snekkenes, E., & Bours, P. (2010). *Improved gait recognition performance using cycle matching.* Paper presented at the 2010 IEEE 24th International Conference on Advanced Information Networking and Applications Workshops.

Henriksen, M., Lund, H., Moe-Nilssen, R., Bliddal, H., & Danneskiod-Samsøe, B. (2004). Test-retest reliability of trunk accelerometric gait analysis. *Gait & Posture, 19*(3), 288–297. doi:10.1016/S0966-6362(03)00069-9

Holien, K. (2008). *Gait recognition under non-standard circumstances.* Master thesis, Gjøvik Univeristy College.

Horprasert, T., Harwood, D., & Davis, L. (1999). *A statistical approach for real-time robust background subtraction and shadow detection.* Paper presented at the ICCV Frame-Rate WS.

Huang, B., Chen, M., Huang, P., & Xu, Y. (2007). *Gait modeling for human identification.* Paper presented at the International Conference on Robotics and Automation.

Hynes, M., Wang, H., & Kilmartin, L. (2009). Off-the-shelf mobile handset environments for deploying accelerometer based gait and activity analysis algorithms. *Conference Proceedings;... Annual International Conference of the IEEE Engineering in Medicine and Biology Society. IEEE Engineering in Medicine and Biology Society. Conference, 1,* 5187–5190.

Ibrahim, R. K., Ambikairajah, E., Celler, B., Lovell, N. H., & Kilmartin, L. (2008). *Gait patterns classification using spectral features.* Paper presented at the IET Irish Signals and Systems Conference (ISSC).

Iso, T., & Yamazaki, K. (2006). *Gait analyzer based on a cell phone with a single three-axis accelerometer.* Paper presented at the MobileHCI '06: Proceedings of the 8th Conference on Human-Computer Interaction with Mobile Devices and Services, New York, NY, USA.

Kale, A., Cuntoor, N., & Chellappa, R. (2002). *A framework for activity-specific human identification.* Paper presented at the Acoustics, Speech, and Signal Processing.

Kantz, H., & Schreiber, T. (2008). Nonlinear time series analysis. *The Economic Record, 84*(266), 396–397. doi:10.1111/j.1475-4932.2008.00502.x

Korpipää, P., Koskinen, M., Peltola, J., Mäkelä, S.-M., & Seppänen, T. (2003). Bayesian approach to sensor-based context awareness. *Personal and Ubiquitous Computing, 7*(2), 113–124. doi:10.1007/s00779-003-0237-8

Krumm, J., & Horvitz, E. (2006). Predestination: Inferring destinations from partial trajectories. In Dourish, P., & Friday, A. (Eds.), *UbiComp 2006: Ubiquitous Computing* (*Vol. 4206*, pp. 243–260). Berlin / Heidelberg, Germany: Springer. doi:10.1007/11853565_15

Larsen, P. K., Simonsen, E. B., & Lynnerup, N. (2008). Gait analysis in forensic medicine. *Journal of Forensic Sciences*, *53*(5), 1149–1153. doi:10.1111/j.1556-4029.2008.00807.x

Lee, C.-Y., & Lee, J.-J. (2002). Estimation of walking behavior using accelerometers in gait rehabilitation. *International Journal of Human-friendly Welfare Robotic Systems*, *3*, 32–36.

Lee, S.-W., & Mase, K. (2002). Activity and location recognition using wearable sensors. *IEEE Pervasive Computing / IEEE Computer Society [and] IEEE Communications Society*, *1*(3), 24–32. doi:10.1109/MPRV.2002.1037719

Lester, J., Choudhury, T., & Borriello, G. (2006). A practical approach to recognizing physical activities. In Fishkin, K., Schiele, B., Nixon, P., & Quigley, A. (Eds.), *Pervasive computing* (*Vol. 3968*, pp. 1–16). Berlin / Heidelberg, Germany: Springer. doi:10.1007/11748625_1

Liao, L., Fox, D., & Kautz, H. (2007). Extracting places and activities from gps traces using hierarchical conditional random fields. *The International Journal of Robotics Research*, *26*(1), 119–134. doi:10.1177/0278364907073775

Mantyjarvi, J., Lindholm, M., Vildjiounaite, E., Makela, S.-M., & Ailisto, H. A. (2005). *Identifying users of portable devices from gait pattern with accelerometers*. IEEE International Conference on Acoustics, Speech, and Signal Processing (ICASSP '05), 2, (pp. 973-976).

Mathie, M., Coster, A., Lovell, N., & Celler, B. (2003). Detection of daily physical activities using a triaxial accelerometer. *Medical & Biological Engineering & Computing*, *41*(3), 296–301. doi:10.1007/BF02348434

Mathie, M., Coster, A., Lovell, N., & Celler, B. (2004). Accelerometry: Providing an integrated, practical method for long-term, ambulatory monitoring of human movement. *Physiological Measurement*, *25*(2), R1. doi:10.1088/0967-3334/25/2/R01

Middleton, L., Buss, A. A., Bazin, A., & Nixon, M. S. (2005). *A floor sensor system for gait recognition*. Paper presented at the AUTOID '05: Proceedings of the Fourth IEEE Workshop on Automatic Identification Advanced Technologies, Washington, DC, USA.

Morris, S. J. (2004). *A shoe-integrated sensor system for wireless gait analysis and real-time therapeutic feedback*. Division of Health Sciences and Technology, Harvard University-MIT.

Mostayed, A., Kim, S., Mazumder, M. M. G., & Park, S. J. (2008). *Foot step based person identification using histogram similarity and wavelet decomposition*. Paper presented at the ISA '08: Proceedings of the 2008 International Conference on Information Security and Assurance (isa 2008), Washington, DC, USA.

Ng, J., Sahakian, A. V., & Swiryn, S. (2003). *Accelerometer-based body-position sensing for ambulatory electrocardiographic monitoring* (vol. 37). Arlington, VA: ETATS-UNIS: Association for the Advancement of Medical Instrumentation.

Nixon, M. S., Carter, J. N., Shutler, J., & Grant, M. (2002). New advances in automatic gait recognition. *Elsevier Information Security Technical Report*, *7*(4), 23–35. doi:10.1016/S1363-4127(02)00404-1

Nixon, M. S., Tan, T. N., & Chellappa, R. (2005). *Human identification based on gait*. Springer.

Niyogi, S. A., & Adelson, E. H. (1994). *Analyzing and recognizing walking gures in XYT*. In Conference of Computer Vision and Pattern Recognition.

Pärkkä, J., Ermes, M., Korpipää, P., Mäntyjärvi, J., Peltola, J., & Korhonen, I. (2006). Activity classification using realistic data from wearable sensors. *IEEE Transactions on Information Technology in Biomedicine*, *10*(1), 119–128. doi:10.1109/TITB.2005.856863

Rong, L., Jianzhong, Z., Ming, L., & Xiang, H. (2005). *Identification of individual walking patterns using gait acceleration*. In 1st International Conference in Bioinformatics and Biomedical Engineering, (pp. 543-546).

Rong, L., Jianzhong, Z., Ming, L., & Xiangfeng, H. (2007). *A wearable acceleration sensor system for gait recognition*. Paper presented at the Industrial Electronics and Applications, 2007. ICIEA 2007.

Sazonov, E. S., Bumpus, T., Zeigler, S., & Marocco, S. (2005). *Classification of plantar pressure and heel acceleration patterns using neural networks*. Paper presented at the International Joint Conference on Neural Networks, IJCNN '.

Sminchisescu, C., Kanaujia, A., Li, Z., & Metaxas, D. (2004). *Learning to reconstruct 3D human motion from Bayesian mixtures of experts. A probabilistic discriminative approach.*

Sprager, S., & Zazula, D. (2009). *Gait identification using cumulants of accelerometer data*. Paper presented at the SENSIG'09/VIS'09/MATERIALS'09: Proceedings of the 2nd WSEAS International Conference on Sensors, and Signals and Visualization, Imaging and Simulation and Materials Science, Stevens Point, Wisconsin, USA.

Streitz, N., & Nixon, P. (2005). The disappearing computer. *Communications of the ACM*, *48*(3), 32–35. doi:10.1145/1047671.1047700

Subramanya, A., Raj, A., Bilmes, J., & Fox, D. (2006). Recognizing activities and spatial context using wearable sensors. In *Proceedings of Uncerntainty in Artificial Intelligence*.

TimesOnline. (2006). *Aiming to catch criminals red-footed*. Retrieved from http://business.timesonline.co.uk/tol/business/law/article685365.ece

Vildjiounaite, E., Mäkelä, S.-M., Lindholm, M., Riihimäki, R., Kyllönen, V., Mäntyjärvi, J., & Ailisto, H. (2006). *Unobtrusive multimodal biometrics for ensuring privacy and information security with personal devices*. Paper presented at the Pervasive Computing Conference 2006.

Wang, L., Tan, T., Hu, W., & Ning, H. (2003). Automatic gait recognition based on statistical shape analysis. *IEEE Transactions on Image Processing*, *12*(9), 1120–1131. doi:10.1109/TIP.2003.815251

KEY TERMS AND DEFINITIONS

Biometric Sample: Raw data representing a biometric characteristic of an end-user as captured by a biometric system (for example the image of a fingerprint).

Comparison Score/Score: The level of similarity from comparing a biometric sample against a previously stored template.

Enrollment: The process of collecting biometric samples from a person and the subsequent preparation and storage of biometric reference templates representing that person's identity.

Equal Error Rate/EER: The error rate occurring when the decision threshold of a system is set so that the proportion of false rejections will be approximately equal to the proportion of false acceptances.

Gait: A particular way or manner on moving on foot.

Identification/Identify: The one-to-many process of comparing a submitted biometric sample against all of the biometric reference templates on file to determine whether it matches any of the templates and, if so, the identity of the enrollee whose template was matched. The biometric system using the one-to-many approach is seeking to find an identity amongst a database rather than verify a claimed identity.

Impostor: A person who submits a biometric sample in either an intentional or inadvertent attempt to pass him/herself off as another person who is an enrollee.

Template/Reference Template: Data, which represents the biometric measurement of an enrollee, used by a biometric system for comparison against subsequently submitted biometric samples.

Threshold/Decision Threshold: The acceptance or rejection of biometric data is dependent on the comparison score falling above or below the threshold. The threshold is adjustable so that the biometric system can be more or less strict, depending on the requirements of any given biometric application.

Verification/Verify: The process of comparing a submitted biometric sample against the biometric reference template of a single enrollee whose identity is being claimed, to determine whether it matches the enrollees' template.

Chapter 9
Keystroke Analysis as a Tool for Intrusion Detection

Daniele Gunetti
University of Torino, Italy

Claudia Picardi
University of Torino, Italy

ABSTRACT

The original dream of Keystroke Analysis was the same as that of other biometric techniques: replacing traditional authentication methods with techniques based on the analysis of the typing dynamics of users. Unfortunately, until now a sufficient level of accuracy and user friendliness for practical applications has not been achieved.

However, typing rhythms are available throughout an entire login session and, if we can perform Keystroke Analysis of free text, we can implement one of the best applications of continuous authentication: Intrusion Detection. In this case, an accuracy that is still not acceptable for access control can be more than sufficient as part of an Intrusion Detection policy, where (1) alarms that have been raised must in any case be validated by a human (e.g., a system administrator); (2) intrusions are normally detected joining together different techniques, in order to improve the resulting accuracy.

In this chapter we discuss the potentialities of Keystroke Analysis as a tool for Intrusion Detection and other security applications, and investigate experimentally how the accuracy of the analysis scales with the increase of the number of individuals involved, a fundamental issue if we want to add Keystroke Analysis to the set of tools that can be used to improve the security of our computers and networks.

DOI: 10.4018/978-1-61350-129-0.ch009

INTRODUCTION

There is an evident and growing interest for security applications based on biometric features, such as fingerprints, retina, iris, signature, palm and voiceprint (Jain et al. (eds.) 2008). The usual argument brought in favor of the use of biometric information for identity verification against more traditional techniques is that passwords (security based on *what you know*) can be forgotten or forged, and ID cards (*what you have*) can be lost or replicated, whereas biometric features (*what you are*) are unique and cannot be (easily) replicated, shared or stolen.

Within computer security, a natural biometric is represented by the dynamics shown by individuals when typing at the keyboard, and some peculiarities make keystroke analysis somewhat unique w.r.t. other biometrics. First, keystroke analysis is not intrusive, since users will be typing at the computer keyboard anyway. Second, it is inexpensive to implement, since the only sensor required is the keyboard itself. Third, keystroke patterns of an individual cannot be easily replicated or stolen by an impostor, even if such patterns are known. Finally, unlike other biometric features, typing rhythms are available throughout an entire login session (i.e., after an authentication phase has been passed, or fooled), since keystrokes exist as a mere consequence of users using computers.

The original dream of keystroke analysis was the same as that of other biometric techniques: replacing traditional authentication methods with the analysis of the typing dynamics of users. Unfortunately, such a dream has never become reality: although there have been a number of studies on the possibility of verifying personal identity through the analysis of the typing dynamics of short, pre-defined passphrases (e.g., Joyce and Gupta. (1990), Bleha et al. (1990), Brown and Rogers (1993), Obaidat and Sadoun (1997), Clarke et al. (2003), Clarke and Furnell (2007)), a sufficient level of accuracy and user friendliness for practical and commercial applications has

never been really achieved. Even when keystroke analysis is used not to replace, but to strengthen passwords (e.g., Reiter et al. (1999), Ong and Lai (2000), Revett et al. (2005), Chang (2005), Rodrigues et al. (2005), Hocquet et al. (2006), Mészáros et al. (2007)) one wonders whether a well-chosen password would be sufficient to reach the same level of security provided by a poor chosen password whose performance we try to improve by the analysis of typing rhythms of that password. All the above methods and systems show an error rate of a few percentage points. As a consequence, a well chosen password will always outperform any combinated technique, in terms of simplicity of implementation and false alarms.

However, the aforementioned peculiarities of typing rhythms, together with recent advances in the analysis of typing dynamics of free text, may suggest a change of perspective. Passwords will probably never be replaced by keystroke analysis, but the growth in the number of crimes perpetrated through and on computer and network resources, and on the Internet, call for new and improved security techniques to investigate and fight such illegal activities.

In this chapter we argue that computer and network intrusion detection, as well as identity tracing over anonymous Web-based resources, and password recovery, are only some of the possible situations where the analysis of typing rhythms may deserve a second chance.

BACKGROUND

Identifying users through the way they type on a keyboard is difficult, because keystrokes convey little information: just the time when keys are depressed and released. It is true that special keyboards may allow to measure additional features such as the acceleration or the energy impressed to the keystrokes, but such keyboards are normally not available, and are expensive. Moreover, recent sophisticated devices may use virtual keyboards where only digraph latency and keystroke duration could be easily monitored.

The problem with typing rhythms (as well as with many other behavioral biometrics) is that typing dynamics are only partially under the control of individuals, and can be greatly affected by transient psychological and physiological situations such as stress or illness. They show a certain degree of intrinsic instability even without any apparent reason: in fact, it is pretty difficult to control the number of milliseconds we hold down a key or the speed at which we move fingers on the keyboard when typing. For the same reason, it is also difficult to reproduce someone else's typing patterns. Such instability is magnified by the fact that typing patterns depend on the keyboard, on environmental conditions and, above all, on the entered text.

To mitigate the above problems, early research restricted the experiments to samples produced by entering fixed text. In what is considered the first paper on keystroke analysis, Gaines et al. (1980) report some results on identifying 7 secretaries who typed twice the same three passages of text (each one about 300–400 words long). Their study reached a *False Acceptance Rate* (FAR) of 0% and a *False Rejection Rate* (FRR) of 4%, using statistical significance tests on *digraph latencies*: the elapsed time between the release of a key and the depression of the next one.

Over the next twenty years various works exploited a variety of statistical, pattern matching, neural network, and other machine learning methods. The number of people involved in the experiments grew up to about 35–40 users and since, as we noted above, entering long pre-defined texts (both when building users' profiles and during the verification phase) is obviously annoying, input requirements were lowered from large passages down to short phrases or sets of words (such as name, surname and affiliation). Experimental results were however controversial: either the attained level of accuracy was far from being acceptable, or good performance was achieved

under very special conditions, which were hard to reproduce in real applications. (We refer to Bergadano et al. (2002) and Hempstalk (2009) for an in-depth description of various approaches to kesytroke analysis of fixed text.)

More recently, some researchers started to realize that, in practice, keystroke analysis cannot be performed with very short texts: collected timing data do not provide a sufficient amount of information to discriminate accurately among legal users and impostors. On the other hand, long predefined texts (as, e.g., in the experiments described in Umphress and Williams (1985), Leggett and Williams (1988), Bergadano et al. (2002)) that must be entered repeatedly to profile — and later to check — users' identity, are hardly acceptable. Thus, the only solution left is trying to exploit what stems from the normal use of computers: the keystroke dynamics of free text.

Unfortunately, the use of free text amplifies the instability of typing rhythms. In the first true investigation of the problem, using probabilistic weighted measures, Monrose and Rubin (2000) argue that "*while recognition based on free-text may be more desirable, free-text recognition was observed to vary greatly under operational conditions; the fact that the input is unconstrained, that the user may be uncooperative, and that environmental parameters are uncontrolled impose limitations on what can be achieved with free-text recognition*" (p. 11).

Nonetheless, more recent studies achieved some positive result. Dowland et al. (2001) monitored continuously four users for some weeks during their normal activity on computers running WindowsNT. Hence, the production of typing samples by the users is not constrained in any way. Users' profiles are determined by computing the mean and standard deviation of digraph latency; only digraphs that occur at least 50 times in different typing samples are kept. Nonetheless, profiles contain thousands of digraphs. A digraph occurring in a new sample U that must be classified is *valid* only if it comes within x standard deviations of its mean (with x varying from 0.5 to 2). U is then attributed to the user whose profile provides the largest number of valid digraphs. In this way, 50% of correct classification is achieved.

The experiments are refined in Dowland et al. (2002), where five users are involved, and a correct acceptance rate slightly below 60% is reached. No global information is given about the rejection rate of impostors. However, in the case of two users, when someone else's sample is compared to the user's profile, it is rejected in the 75% and 85% of the cases, respectively.

In a more recent study involving 35 users, Dowland and Furnell (2004) use esentially the same statistical method as above, and reach an optimum 4.9% FAR when setting in advance the FRR at 0%. The profiling phase requires collecting nearly 6 million keystrokes over three months of continuous monitoring.

The experiments of Nisenson et al. (2003) involve five users and 30 attackers, and are performed with a pretty small amount of typing data (each user provided three samples each one long roughly one line of free text). A classifier based on a modified compression technique (LZ78) is used, and samples are classified using a user specific threshold, reaching a FRR of 5.25% and an FAR of 1.13%.

In the next sections we describe (a revised version of) the approach to keystroke analysis of free text originally presented in Gunetti and Picardi (2005).

THE R+A APPROACH TO KEYSTROKE ANALYSIS

Most approaches to keystroke analysis work by comparing in some way the average typing speed of the same sequence of n consecutive typed keys (or n-graph) occurring in two samples. In most experiments, n = 2, and therefore the typing speed used is simply the digraph latency (in some cases together with the duration of the two keys). Un-

fortunately, because of the intrinsic instability of typing rhythms, such average speed is too coarse a measure to allow for an accurate discrimination among typists, and may actually blur other regularities hidden in the typing habits of users.

Characteristic typing patterns that are not recognized easily by just looking at the typing speed of n-graphs can however show up by comparing the typing speeds of different n-graphs, which can be called the *relative* typing speed of n-graphs. The basic idea can be easily grasped with an example. Suppose that in Alice's and Bob's profile there is a typing sample made by entering, respectively, the words *melting* and *selection*. Now, we are given a new typing sample X, made by entering the word *elastic* by Alice or Bob. Who typed X? The three typing samples have in common the 2-graphs *el* and *ti*. In X, *el* has been typed more slowly than *ti* (in short, *el>ti*). By looking at Alice's profile we know that entering digraph *el* more quickly than digraph *ti* (that is, *el<ti*) is in accordance with her typing style. On the contrary, Bob usually types *el* slower than *ti* (*el>ti*). As a consequence, we conclude that X comes from Bob. We have not considered the actual typing speeds of *el* and *ti* in X and in Alice's and Bob's profiles, just their relative typing speed.

The underlying assumption is that the typing speed of an individual may change for whatever reason, but we may expect the changes to affect all the typing characteristics in a similar way. One day, a headache causes Alice typing more slowly than usual, while a lot of coffee is going to make Bob nervous. Their typing speed will probably change, making any analysis based on the absolute typing speed of n-graphs very imprecise. On the contrary, the relative typing speed of Alice and Bob n-graphs is likely to remain unchanged, and useful to discriminate between the two: for Alice we still have *el<ti*, while for Bob we have *el>ti*. Much longer samples are used in the real case, and the analysis becomes more complicated: the typing speed of each n-graph must be compared with the typing speed of *all* the other *n*-graphs shared by two samples under comparison.

Note that the absolute typing speed of *n*-graphs should not be completely overlooked. A simple example explains why. Suppose that X has been provided by Bob or Claudia, and that in both their profiles, *el>ti*. In such cases, the actual typing speed of *el* and *ti* will help to discriminate between Bob and Claudia.

In the next section we describe two classes of distance measures ("R", for *Relative*, and "A", for *Absolute*, measures) originally described in Gunetti and Picardi (2005), that have been devised to compute the "distance" between two typing samples, and that try to capture formally what we have intuitively described above.

COMPUTING THE DISTANCE BETWEEN TWO TYPING SAMPLES

In the presented approach, the distance between two typing samples is always normalized in the interval [0..1], regardless of the particular combination of R and A measures used to compute it. An important consequence of this is that, actually, the approach can be used even with distance measures different from those described here, provided they can be normalized in the [0..1] interval. Just like we do with R and A measures, different distance measures can grasp different aspects of the typing dynamics of individuals. When combined together, such measures can provide a higher accuracy to authenticate users and to spot intruders. Intuitively, the more similar the typing patterns in two samples, the smaller their distance score, and we may expect two typing samples of an individual having a smaller distance score than two samples coming from different individuals.

"R" Measures

The idea of measuring the relative distance between typing samples can be formalized in what

have been called "R" measures (Gunetti & Picardi, 2005; Bergadano et al., 2002), as follows.

Given a vector V of K elements, a measure of the *disorder* of V w.r.t. its sorted counterpart V_s is given by the sum of the distances between the position of each element in V and the position of the same element in V_s. As an example, it is easy to see that the disorder of vector A = [2,5,1,4,3] w.r.t. A_s = [1,2,3,4,5] is: $(1 + 3 + 2 + 0 + 2) = 8$.

Clearly, a sorted array V_s has a disorder equal to 0, while a vector has the maximum disorder when its elements are in reverse order. The maximum disorder of a vector is given by:

$|V|^2/2$ (if $|V|$ is even); $(|V|^2 - 1)/2$ (if $|V|$ is odd).

Given a vector of K elements, we can normalize its disorder by dividing it by the value of the maximum disorder of a vector of K elements. In this way we can compare the disorder of vectors of different size. With this normalization, the disorder of any vector V falls between 0 (if V is ordered) and 1 (if V is in reverse order). The normalized disorder of vector A above is: $(1 + 3 + 2 + 0 + 2)/[(25 - 1)/2] = 8/12 = 0.66666$.

Now, let us consider two typing samples **T1** and **T2**. Suppose that, for each *n*-graph occurring in **T1** and **T2** (for *n*=2, *n*=3, etc.) we have available the corresponding typing speed, or, more precisely, the *n-graph time*: the time between the depression of the first and of the last (that is, the *n*th) key of the *n*-graph. Therefore, in the case of a 2-graph its time is computed by summing together the duration (or "dwell time") of the first keystroke and the elapsed time between the release of the first key and the depression of the second key (i.e., its latency, sometimes called the "fly time"). The time of a 3-graph is computed by summing together the durations of the first and second key, and the latency between the first and the second key and between the second and third key. In a similar way we can compute the time of a 4-graph (if a sample is sufficiently long, it is likely that a certain *n*-graph occurs more than once. In such cases, the *n*-graph is reported only once and the mean of the *n-graph time* of each occurrence is used). Clearly, a typing sample can be represented in terms of its 2-graphs (or digraphs), 3-graphs (trigraphs), 4-graphs (quadgraphs), and so on.

Moreover, let **T1** and **T2** be represented as two vectors sorted w.r.t. the *n-graph time* of their *n*-graphs. We may consider one of the two (e.g., **T1**) as the referring sorted array and we may compute the *Relative distance* between **T1** and **T2** w.r.t. the *n*-graphs they share (in short, R*n*(**T1, T2**)) as the normalized disorder of **T2** w.r.t. **T1**. In other words, if **T1** and **T2** share K *n*-graphs, the distance of **T2** from **T1** is the sum of the distances of each *n*-graph of **T2** w.r.t. the position of the same *n*-graph in **T1**, divided by the maximum disorder showed by an array of K elements; *n*-graphs not belonging to both samples are simply ignored. Clearly, R*n*(**T1, T2**) = R*n*(**T2, T1**) and, moreover, R*n* can be used to compute the distance between any two typing samples,

provided they share some *n*-graph (which is the case for texts sufficiently long—e.g., at least a line of text—and for *n* sufficiently small—e.g., *n* < 5). An example of this computation for 2-graphs is reported in Figure 1.

The relative distances between two typing samples, w.r.t. the digraphs, trigraphs, or longer *n*-graphs they share, provide different kinds of information about the similarities and differences between the two samples. This is particularly true in the case of free text. For example, the typing speed of a certain trigraph occurring in both samples may be influenced by the fact that the trigraph occurs in different contexts (that is, as part of different 4-graphs) in the two samples.

Hence, a more meaningful measure of the distance between two samples **T1** and **T2** may be obtained by combining R*n*(**T1, T2**) for different instances of *n*. That is:

$$R_{n,m}(\mathbf{T1}, \mathbf{T2}) = [R_n(\mathbf{T1}, \mathbf{T2}) + R_m(\mathbf{T1}, \mathbf{T2})]/2$$

Figure 1. Computing the R distance between two samples

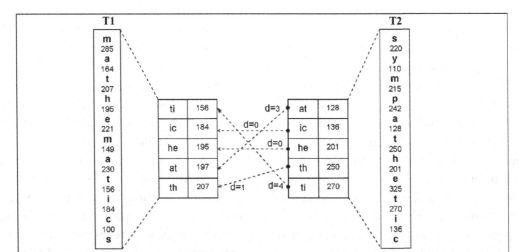

Steps for the computation of the *Relative distance* R2(**T1, T2**) between typing samples **T1**=**mathematics** and **T2**=**sympathetic** (between the characters of **T1** and **T2** are the corresponding 2-graph times in milliseconds):

1) only 2-graphs shared by **T1** and **T2** are considered
2) 2-graphs are sorted w.r.t. their typing speed (for 2-graphs occurring more than once, their mean speed is used)
3) the distance of **T1** and **T2** is computed as the sum of the distances of each 2-graph of **T1** w.r.t the position of the same 2-graph in **T2**. In our example we have = 3+0+0+1+4=8
4) 12 is the maximum possible distance between **T1** and **T2**, which is when the shared and sorted 2-graphs appear in reverse order in the two samples. Thus, 8/12 = 0.666 is the *Relative distance* R2(**T1, T2**) between **T1** and **T2**.

or, even:

$$R_{n,m,p}(\mathbf{T1}, \mathbf{T2}) = [R_n(\mathbf{T1}, \mathbf{T2}) + R_m(\mathbf{T1}, \mathbf{T2}) + R_p(\mathbf{T1}, \mathbf{T2})]/3$$

where, in the actual case, $n=2$, $m=3$, $p=4$.

Intuitively, the meaningfulness of a distance R_n between two samples **T1** and **T2** should be related to the number of n-graphs shared by the two samples. Hence, when combining different R distances, each should be weighted with the number of graphs used to compute it. However, the experiments presented in this chapter, performed with pretty more users and impostors than those in Gunetti and Picardi (2005), have shown that, actually, this weightening is essentially ininfluent. This is the reason why the definitions of $R_{n,m}$ and $R_{n,m,p}$ given above are simpler than those found in Gunetti and Picardi (2005).

"A" Measures

R measures work well to discriminate among individuals (Bergadano et al., 2002). However, as we noted before, the absolute typing speed of n-graphs cannot be completely overlooked. When the relative typing speed of n-graphs is not useful to discriminate between individual, the actual (or Absolute) typing speed may help.

Unlike R measures, A measures only take into consideration the absolute value of the typing speed of n-graphs in the samples that must be compared. The rationale of A measures is simple. Suppose a user can type on a keyboard exactly in the same way at all times. Then, a given n-graph is always typed at the same speed regardless of the entered text. Of course, this is virtually impossible, but we may reasonably expect two occurrences of a certain n-graph typed by the same individual, even in two different texts, to have *n-graph times* that are more similar than if the two texts have been entered by different individuals.

More formally, let $G_{T1,d1}$ and $G_{T2,d2}$ be the same n-graph occurring in two typing samples **T1** and

T2, with typing speed d1 and d2, respectively. We say that $G_{T1,d1}$ and $G_{T2,d2}$ are *similar* if $1 < \max(d1, d2)/\min(d1, d2) \leq t$ for some constant t greater than 1. The "A" distance between **T1** and **T2** w.r.t. the n-graphs they share and for a certain value of t is then defined as $A^t_n(\mathbf{T1}, \mathbf{T2}) = 1 - ($number of *similar* n-graphs between **T1** and **T2**)/(total number of n-graphs shared by **T1** and **T2**)

Note that, if there are no *similar* pairs of n-graphs in two typing samples, the computed distance is 1. If all n-graphs pairs are *similar*, the distance is 0. From the definition of A^t_n we see that two samples that share no n-graph have 1 as the maximum distance possible. On the contrary, the two samples will have the minimum distance w.r.t. any R measure. Actually, we do not worry for such extreme situations, since they are virtually impossible for sufficiently long samples. Consider for example our experiments, that involved 1151 typing samples with an average length of about 800 characters (the details of these experiments are described in the next section). Such samples can form $1150 \cdot 1151/2 = 661825$ different pairs. In such pairs we never found two samples sharing no 4-graphs, with a minimum number of about twenty 4-graphs shared by two samples (our experiments were performed using di, tri and quad-graphs. Hence, if two samples share one 4-graph, they certainly share at least one 3-graph and one 2-graph). Of course, if deemed necessary, an actual implementation of the method can easily take care of the case when two samples do not share any n-graph. For example, the computation of their distance can be avoided because meaningless.

In A measures n-digraphs are marked as *similar* in a way that resembles the way digraphs are marked as *accepted* or *invalid* in other approaches to keystroke analysis. However, we do not use standard deviations to define an interval of validity for n-graphs. On the contrary, we use a fixed ratio (t) between the typing speeds of n-graphs. As a consequence, even n-graphs occurring only once in both samples (so that for such n-graphs a true mean speed or standard deviation cannot be computed) can be compared. In this way we can exploit as much as possible all the available timing information, even in samples that do not have n-graphs repeated many times.

In the case of samples **T1** and **T2** of Figure 1, for digraphs and for $t = 1.25$ we have:

T1		T2	
197	**at**	128	$(197/128 = 1.539)$
195	**he**	201	$(201/195 = 1.030)$ (*similar*)
184	**ic**	136	$(183/136 = 1.345)$
207	**th**	250	$(250/207 = 1.207)$ (*similar*)
156	**ti**	270	$(270/156 = 1.730)$

And $A_2^{1.25}(\mathbf{T1}, \mathbf{T2}) = 1 - 2/5 = 0.6$.

Even in the case of A measures, for a given t, it is possible to compute a cumulative absolute distance between two samples w.r.t. n-graphs and m-graphs:

$$A_{n,m}^t(\mathbf{T1}, \mathbf{T2}) = [A_n^t(\mathbf{T1}, \mathbf{T2}) + A_m^t(\mathbf{T1}, \mathbf{T2})]/2$$

In a similar way, we may define $A_{n,m,p}^t(\mathbf{T1}, \mathbf{T2})$.

To make A measures working, a value for t must be chosen. Following Gunetti and Picardi (2005), when the first five volunteers of our experiments had provided their samples, we performed the classification task described in the next section, testing A_2^t for the following values of t: 1.025, 1.05, 1.10, 1.15, 1.20, 1.25, 1.33, 1.40. The best performance was achieved with $t = 1.05$. Note that it is possible that better outcomes could be reached for some value in the interval $[1.025 \div 1.10]$. Moreover, a different t may perform better for A_3^t and A_4^t. We did not bother to look for such particular values in order to avoid overfitting: a fine tuning of the method on a particular value for t in order to get the best results. Since in the outcomes presented in this chapter the value $t = 1.05$ has been used for all users' profile in all experiments, in the rest of the chapter we will omit it as the superscript of A measures. We note however that in real applications a different value t that performs better *for each legal user* can (and should) be found on the

basis of his/her typing profile: this will improve the ability of the system to discriminate between legal users and impostors.

R and A measures (or, for that matter, any other distance measure normalized in the interval $[0..1]$) can of course be combined together to achieve a more sophisticated discrimination power. Hence, for example, we may define:

$$d(\mathbf{T1}, \mathbf{T2}) = R_{2,3,4}A_2(\mathbf{T1}, \mathbf{T2}) = [R_{2,3,4}(\mathbf{T1}, \mathbf{T2}) + A_2(\mathbf{T1}, \mathbf{T2})]/2.$$

In fact, this is the distance measure that has been used for the experiments presented in this chapter. Of all the possible combinations of R and A measures, this is the one the has experimentally achieved the best performance. This is consistent with the findings of Gunetti and Picardi (2005), where different combinations of R and A measures were tested. The results of those tests can be summarized as follows:

1. R measures provide better performance than A measures. E.g., R_2 performs better than A_2, and R_3 performs better than A_3.
2. R measures computed on graphs of different length grasp well different aspects of the typing dynamics of di, tri and quad-graphs. That is, on the average $R_{2,3}$ performs better than R_2, and $R_{2,3,4}$ performs better than $R_{2,3}$ (with R_{24} and $R_{3,4}$ having a performance pretty similar to $R_{2,3}$).
3. Also A measures present a similar behavior, but it is much less evident. For example, $A_{2,3,4}$ performs only slightly better than A_2.
4. R and A measures combined together (such as, e.g., $R_{2,3,4}A_2$) work better than R or a A measures used separately.
5. because of point 3 above, the combination of different A measures is not worth the additional computational cost required. For example, measure $R_{2,3,4}A_{2,3}$ and $R_{2,3,4}A_{2,4}$ provide a slightly better FAR than $R_{2,3,4}A_2$, but a slightly worse FRR. $R_{2,3,4}A_{2,3,4}$ provides

more or less the same FAR of $R_{2,3,4}A_2$ but a worse FRR.

We refer to Gunetti and Picardi (2005) for a detailed discussion of the above points.

EXPERIMENTAL STUDIES

Gathering of the Samples

To perform our experiments, we asked 60 volunteers (all well-used to type on normal computer keyboards) to send us 15 messages from their computers, using an application that labeled each typed character with the time (in milliseconds) when the corresponding key was depressed. In our experiments, these people act as legal users of a hypothetical system. Each message had to be entered into a text area made of 12 lines of 65 characters each (for a total of 780 characters). However, people had not to enter exactly 780 characters, they could just stop when they had the "feeling" the form had been completed. On average, the samples provided have a length varying between 700 and 900 characters (for example, this very same paragraph is slightly more than 800 characters long). Under the same conditions, another 251 people were asked to provide just one typing sample. These individuals act as impostors that pretend to be one of the legal users of the system.

Since we wanted to test our system with samples produced in possibly different psychological and physiological conditions, volunteers could not provide more than one sample per day. In many cases, two or three weeks, or even more than one or two months passed between the production of two consecutive samples. Volunteers were completely free to choose when to provide a sample, and what to write. They were free to make typos, and to leave or correct them (by using the backspace key or the mouse, as preferred). Volunteers were free to pause in any moment when producing a sample, for whatever reason and as long as they wanted. No sample was rejected, for any reason. None of the people participating in the experiments was hired, or in any way paid for their assistance. All the volunteers were Italian and had to provide samples written in Italian. They were colleagues and PhD students or students in their last year of study.

Volunteers were asked to type the samples in the most natural way. They were completely free to choose what to write and the only limitations were of not typing the same word or phrase repeatedly in order to complete the form and not to enter the same text in two different samples (samples were checked to find unwanted repetitions). Volunteers were suggested to write about different subjects in each sample, such as family, vacations, job, movies, books, whatever they liked.

We chose to not control the way volunteers performed the experiment. Every day an email reminded each volunteer about the experiment, but people could of course ignore the reminder. Most volunteers used their own computers to provide the samples. Sometimes however, some people provided the sample from home or from computers located in another town. Thus, volunteers may have provided some samples with different keyboards. However, we don't know which samples were provided on which keyboards, and we have not tested our method with respect to the use of different keyboards.

User Authentication

In our experiments, the typing habits of a user are simply represented by a set of typing samples provided by that user. The set forms what is normally called the user's profile. Hence, suppose we have a set of users' profiles and a new typing sample provided by one of the users. We want to know who, among the users, provided the sample. We may use a distance measure $d(T1,T2)$ between samples such that, on the average, the distance between two samples of the same user is smaller than the distance between two samples provided by different users. As a consequence, if a user U provides a new sample X, the mean distance of X from (the samples in) U's profile is smaller than the mean distance of X from (the samples in) any other user's profile.

Hence, suppose we have three users' profile A, B and C, with, say, 4 typing samples in each profiles (e.g., in A we have samples $A1, A2, A3$ and $A4$). A new sample X must be classified among A, B and C. We may compute the mean distance (*md* for short) of X from each user's profile as follows:

$$md(A,X) = [d(A1,X) + d(A2,X) + d(A3,X) + d(A4,X)]/4;$$

$$md(B,X) = [d(B1,X) + d(B2,X) + d(B3,X) + d(A4,X)]/4;$$

$$md(C,X) = [d(C1,X) + d(C2,X) + d(C3,X) + d(A4,X)]/4.$$

X will be classified as belonging to the user whose profile provides the smallest mean distance.

The above classification rule is easily turned into an authentication procedure simply by marking the samples with an identity: a new sample X claimed to come from user A is authenticated as belonging to A if $md(A,X)$ is the smallest among all known users. Now, the system can be evaluated with respect to two kinds of mistakes it can make:

1. the percentage of cases in which a sample X from an unknown individual is erroneously attributed to one of the users of the system (that is, the *False Acceptance Rate -- FAR)*;
2. the percentage of cases in which a sample belonging to some user is not identified correctly (that is, the *False Rejection Rate -- FRR)*.

Note that, in the literature, the *FAR* and the *FRR* are sometimes replaced respectively by the *Impostor Pass Rate* and by the *False Alarm Rate*.

Unfortunately, a system adopting such a simple authentication rule would be easily fooled by an intruder. If there are, say, 20 users (and users' profiles) in the system, an unknown impostor that provides a sample pretending to be a legal user U has a chance out of 20 that the sample she provides is closer to U's profile than to any other profile known to the system.

Consider however the following. Suppose again that we have 3 users' profiles A, B and C (with 4 samples in each profile) and a new sample X that must be classified, and we have:

$$md(A,X)=0.420113; \quad md(B,X)=0.423543; \quad md(C,X)=0.425674.$$

And hence we decide that X belongs to user A. However, let us define $m(A)$ as the mean of the distances of the samples in A's profile. For example, if we have:

$$d(A1,A2) = 0.321843; \quad d(A1,A3) = 0.310029; \quad d(A2,A3) = 0.328765.$$

$$d(A1,A4) = 0.301456; \quad d(A2,A4) = 0.311198; \quad d(A3,A4) = 0.323783.$$

then:

$$m(A) = (0.321843 + 0.310029 + 0.328765 + 0.301456 + 0.311198 + 0.323783)/6 = 0.316179.$$

If X is provided by A, it is reasonable to expect it having a mean distance from A's profile close to $m(A)$ (in other words, $md(A,X) \approx m(A)$), which is not the case in our example. Therefore, though X is closer to A's profile than to any other user's profile, it cannot be recognized as belonging to A. To handle such cases, we reformulate the classification rule as follows: a new sample X claimed to belong to user A is authenticated as belonging to A if and only if:

1. $md(A,X)$ is the smallest with respect to any other user B and
2. $md(A,X)$ is *sufficiently* closer to $m(A)$ than to any other $md(B,X)$ computed by the system. Formally: $md(A,X) < m(A) + |k(md(B,X) - m(A))|$ for any user B, and for k such that $0 < k \leq 1$.

If a user A meeting the above rules cannot be found, X is rejected. By choosing a suitable value for k, we may have different trade-offs between FAR and FRR. Greater values of k will allow to cause less false alarms, but could let go unnoticed more impostors. Note that for $k = 1$, we have the original classification rule.

Now we have an operative rule that can be used to test the performance of our approach to user authentication. The 60 volunteers with 15 samples in their profile will act as legal users. In turn, each typing sample T of each legal user U will be used as an incoming sample, that should hopefully be acknowledged as belonging to U using the authentication rule described above and U's typing profile (that contains the remaining 14 samples provided by U). Moreover, T is used to attack all other 59 users in the system (note that when T, provided by U, is used to attack another legal user U1, U's profile is temporarily removed from the system before trying to authenticate T, so as to make the typing habits of U unknown to the system. Otherwise, T would very likely be recognized as belonging to the attacking user U, and not to the user under attack U1. Moreover, in this way we simulate the worst conditions for the system. In fact, each impostor's attack is now brought by someone *from the outside world—*

someone whose typing habits are completely unknown to the system). In this experiment the system is tested with $15 \cdot 60 = 900$ legal attempts and $900 \cdot 59 \cdot 15 = 796,500$ impostors' attacks. The outcomes of this experiment are reported in the first column of Table 1.

In the second column of Table 1 we show what happens to the system performance when, in the same setting of the first experiment, another 251 impostors (those volunteers who provided only one message) attack all the legal users of the system. In this case the number of impostors' attacks raises to $796,500 + 251 \cdot 900 = 1,022,400$. The third column of the table reports the outcomes of the authentication experiment performed using only the typing samples of the first 40 "users" and of the first 165 "impostors" who were able to provide all their samples (the numbers of the fourth column will be described in the next section). All FAR and FRR outcomes reported in Table I have been obtained using $d = R_{2,3,4}A_2$ and $k = 0.5$.

The Equal Error Rate (EER) reported in the last line of Table 1 refers to the case when FAR and FRR of the system are (at least roughly) equivalent, and is often used as a coarse estimate of the relative performance of different biometric techniques and systems. In our experiments, the EER is obtained with $k = 0.8$. While the EER of biometrics such as retina and iris scan is very small, the EER of fingerprint analysis is about 0.2%, and voiceprint and signature analysis show an average EER of about 2% (a comparison of the Equal Error Rate of different biometric techniques can be found, e.g., at: www.bio-tech-inc.com/bio.htm).

Table 1. Performance of our system for different numbers of legal users and impostors

number of Users/Impostors	60/60	60/311	40/205	20/311
FAR	0.007784%	0.010269%	0.0276%	0.0682%
FRR	3.5555%	3.5555%	3.1667%	2.6667%
EER	≈0.5%	≈0.5%	≈0.5%	≈0.5%

We discuss the numbers of Table 1 in the next section.

DISCUSSION AND FUTURE RESEARCH

The implementation of the authentication rule used in our experiments requires that an incoming new sample S declared as belonging to user U is confronted not only with U's profile, but with the profiles (and therefore with the samples in the profiles) of all users known to the system. This has two consequence on the scalability of our approach. First, the computational costs of our method increase with the number of users known to the system. Second, if two users have very similar typing habits, both could raise a false alarm when they are accessing their own account. The larger the number of legal users, the higher the chances of such a situation.

Both computational costs and the problem of users having very similar typing habits can be limited if we consider that a sample under analysis comes with a claimed identity. To limit computational costs, we do not actually need to compare a new sample with all users' profiles, but just with a subset of "reasonable" size (of course the subset must include the profile of the user the incoming sample is claimed to belong to). Selecting a number of profiles similar to those involved in our experiments will provide a similar level of accuracy (as more powerful multi-core CPUs are available, reaching a certain level of accuracy will require shorter and shorter time). When a system contains two users U1 and U2 with very similar typing habits, false alarms can be avoided by excluding the profile of U2 when authenticating a sample claimed to belong to U1. Of course, the system must "know" that U1 and U2 have similar typing habits, and this is easily achieved if the system has pre-computed the average distance between samples of U1 and U2, and checked whether such distance is similar to m(U1) or m(U2).

Note that, if U1 and U2 have very similar typing habits, and U2 attacks U1, he will be treated as an unknown individual and the attack will have some chances to succeed. However, in order for U2 to judge worth attacking U1, U2 *must know* that he and U1 have similar typing habits. Without this knowledge (which may not be easily acquired), U2 can only randomly choose the user to attack. It is fair to note that the above solution does not work well if many, or most of the users in the system, have similar profiles, and one may wonder how the space of profiles fills in as the number of users increases. This issue is addressed formally in Gunetti and Picardi (2005), with experimental evidence that the method can scale well beyond the number of users involved in our system. However, the outcomes of Table 1 provide another experimental evidence: when the number of users involved in the experiments grows of 50% (from 40 to 60 users), the FRR of the system only grows of about 11% (from 3.1667% to 3.5555%).

The fact that the authentication process of a sample involves the profiles of all users known to the system has a negative impact on the FRR of the system, but it also has a positive influence on its FAR. Indeed, a consequence of the definiton of our authentication rule is that an impostor has some chance to breach the system only if he chooses to attack a user with very similar typing habits. Without any knowledge on the typing habits of legal users, this can only happen by chance. Clearly, the larger the number of users involved in the authentication of a new sample, the lower the chances of this to happen. This is evident comparing the second and third columns of Table 1. When the number of legal users increases of 50% (from 40 to 60), the FAR shrinks more than 2.5 times, from 0.0276% to 0.010269% (and in spite of a number of attackers increased of about 1/3, from 205 to 311).

Following the same reasoning as above, when the number of legal users of the system is small, we may expect a better FRR and a worse FAR. The FRR will be better because there are less chances that two legal users have very similar typing habits, so as to fool the system. On the contrary, the FAR increases because an impostor has more chances of attacking the user with the typing habits most similar to those of the attacker. This is quite evident from the last column of Table I, where the experiments have been repeated using only 20 users selected randomly. As already observed, the accuracy of our system depends on the number of enrolled users. When a very small number of legal users is available, the system will show a very good FRR, but possibly a too high FAR. In such cases a simple solution is to use a smaller k (e.g., smaller than 0.5, as described in the section on user authentication), so as to rebalance the trade-off between FRR and FAR.

The European Standard for Access Control EN 50133-1 requires a commercial biometric system to have a FRR less than 1% and an FAR less than 0.001% (Polemi, 2000): the outcomes of our experiments are not very far from these numbers, and have been obtained without any particular form of overfitting or tuning of the system on the given data set. As we already observed, tuning is nevertheless possible by employing user-specific weights that would be highly recommended in any real application. The possibility of using free text means that we can get rid of an explicit enrollment phase, that is clearly perceived as an annoying burden by users. For true security applications, one might want to profile users in a protected environment, so as to avoid the introduction of false samples. However, users will still be free to keep on doing their normal job. We believe that the above characteristics may suggest new perspectives to the practical applications of keystroke analysis in the field of computer security. We suggest some of them in the following sections.

Intrusion Detection

The ability to perform keystroke analysis of free text allows to analyze the typing habits of individuals in a transparent way, while users attend to their usual tasks. Hence, if the keystroke analysis system (KAS for short, in the following) notices that a monitored account is producing typing dynamics different from those in the typing profile of the account's owner, an intrusion is going on (of course, we cannot consider the case where the same account is legally used by more users). In other words, we may use the KAS as (part of) an intrusion detection system (IDS for short). In particular we are performing a form of *anomaly detection*: the individual whose account is under observation is not behaving as expected.

Clearly, keystroke analysis (and possibly any other technique) is to all extent useless if the intruder just enters a few keystrokes (e.g., a short command) and logs out. More likely, the impostor will try to go unnoticed as long as possible, possibly through more than one login session, while stealing information and using illegally system resources, therefore producing a sufficient amount of typing information to be analyzed. In principle, the KAS can be used alone as an intrusion detection system, e.g., by implementing a form of continuous authentication (indeed, intrusion detection is one of the key applications of continuous authentication). However, more realistically it should be added to the set of tools available to detect intrusions. In fact, any intrusion detection technique is prone to make some mistake: it can let go unnoticed some intrusion and it produces a number of false alarms. This last issue is, in particular an endemic problem of IDSs based on anomaly detection (McHugh, 2000): legal users may change their habits, and what was first a normal behavior can become an anomaly, in this way causing the IDS to raise a (false) alarm.

Here is where keystroke analysis can be particularly effective. Axelsson (1999) observes that an IDS requires a FRR largely lower than 0.1% to be effective. As a quantitative example, reworked from McHugh (2000), let us have an IDS with a 0% FAR and a 0.005% FRR. The IDS must analyze, say, 10,000,000 login sessions where 1 out of 100,000 of such sessions was a true intrusion. The IDS has a 0% FAR, therefore all 100 true intrusions are detected. However, the IDS will also raise 500 false alarms. Suppose now the IDS is endowed with a KAS with an FAR = FRR of 0.5% (e.g., the EER shown by our system in the above experiments), and that, every time an alarm is raised by the IDS for a particular account, we have a sufficient amount of keystroke data generated by that account to let the KAS intervene. Then, the FRR of the IDS+KAS shrinks to 0.000025%, while the FAR grows to 0.5%. In our example, the false alarms raised will now be about two or three, and possibly all 100 intrusion will still be detected.

A natural objection to the use of a KAS as an aid to IDS based on anomaly detection is that also typing habits change, magnifying the false alarm rate of the IDS. We note that, on the one hand, typing skills improve up to a certain point, and then they tend to stabilize. On the other hand, users' profiles can be updated substituting old typing samples with newer ones. Actually, the use of new applications, new computers, new operating systems, as well as different duties and tasks assigned are much more important sources of anomalies.

Keystroke analysis can be particularly useful in case of stolen/cracked passwords. In principle, the KAS can be used to check the identity of logged users at regular intervals. For example, every time a certain user has entered a given amount of, say, 250 or 500 keystrokes, the KAS can be run to include the new data available in the analysis. As more keystrokes are available, the analysis becomes more accurate, until the KAS can come to a conclusion whether the individual under observation is a legal user or an impostor. However, if the computational resources avail-

able are limited, typing data collected during users' connection to the system do not need to be analyzed in real time, but, e.g., overnight on all accounts accessed the previous day or, for a given account, after logout. When the KAS detects a typing anomaly (i.e., a potential intrusion) for a certain account, the legal user of the account could simply be required to change his password. A FRR of 0.5 or 1% would not be a true problem, and could also be beneficial: users will have to update their passwords from time to time, something that is reccomendable in any case. In a system with about 100 users that connect to the system once or twice per day, about 1 or 2 false alarms will be raised each day, on average.

We believe that the approach to keystroke analysis described in this chapter is particularly suitable for intrusion detection. First, although relatively long samples are required to provide a good level of accuracy, such samples need not to be produced in a unique, continuous typing session. Long samples can even be built by merging together the very short samples that are produced, e.g., when an URL is typed at the browser navigation bar or when a Unix command is entered. Note that samples even longer than 800 characters can be formed in this way, thus reaching outcomes even better that those presented here (e.g., as shown in Gunetti and Picardi, 2005).

Second, discrimination among individuals is possible even when samples are written in a language different from the one they used to form their typing profile (the presented approach has been tested with samples written in English and in Italian (Gunetti et al., 2005b)). This ability is important since, for example, more and more people use their own language when communicating with locals, but use English as the "Lingua Franca" to communicate with the rest of the world.

Third, it has been shown experimentally (Gunetti et al., 2005a) that the method works even when a long time (more than one year and a half, in the experiments) has passed since the formation of users' profiles. This proves that the typing habits of users, once stabilized, tend to remain unchanged even in the long term, which is important to limit false alarms.

Identity Tracing in Cyberspace

Various forms of cybercrime are conducted through the exchange of anonymous messages over a variety of Web-based channels such as e-mail, Web sites, Internet newsgroups and chat rooms. People do not have to provide their real identity on the Web, so that investigating cybercrime requires some way to trace individuals' identity over the Net. Keystroke analysis of online messages offers a possible aid, if anonymous Web servers provide some form of keystroke monitoring. In such a case, the analysis and comparison of the typing rhythms of messages coming from different anonymous accounts and web connections can be helpful to decide if such messages have been written by the same individual, (without actually identifying the author, unless a profile of his/her typing habits is available) or at least to direct investigations on a subset of the individuals under observation. Table 2 reports the accuracy of the system that, on the basis of their distance score, tries to decide if two anonymous messages have been typed by the same or by different individuals (even in this experiment the distance used is $R_{2,3,4}A_2$ and the system is tuned to have a similar performance on pairs of samples from the same and different individuals.) To trace criminal identity in cyberspace investigations, keystroke analysis can of course be combined with other techniques, such as for example authorship identification based on analyzing stylistic features of online messages (Li et al., 2006).

Password Recovery

The proliferation of password-protected services, both within internal computing systems and on the Internet, requires users to set and remember more and more passwords. Unfortunately, passwords

Table 2. Performance of the system in deciding if two samples have been typed by the same or by different individuals

n. of characters in each sample (n. of individuals)	≈800 (60 individuals)	≈800 (311 individuals)
Total number of pairs of samples from the same individual % of correct decisions	6300 91.619%	6300 92.095%
Total number of Pairs of samples from different individuals % of correct decisions	398250 91.595%	655525 91.748%

that are easy to remember are often also easy to crack. Conversely, hard to crack passwords are often easy to forget, so that some form of password recovery is required. Lost and forgotten passwords are now a well known-problem (BBC News online, 2000). According to a much cited study of Gartner Group, 40% of all help desk calls are for forgotten passwords, and each year companies spend up to $200-$300 per user trying to maintain secure passwords.

When a system administrator or help-desk operator is not immediately available, keystroke analysis can be used as an alternative authentication method, if a typing profile of the legal users of the service is available. The use of long texts in the re-authentication process (say, at least 1000 keystrokes, that may need a few minutes to be entered) will assure a sufficient level of accuracy and will discourage potential intruders (virtually, passwords should not be lost frequently, so that the inattentive user would not be annoyed frequently with the recovery procedure).

CONCLUSION

Many interesting issues in the research about keystroke analysis are still open. One of the most important is, of course, improving the accuracy of the various methodologies w.r.t. the amount of information (that is, keystrokes) available. Recent studies are providing very useful insight on this issue (e.g., Hempstalk, (2009)). An equally important point is trying to understand how methods behave with the increase in the number of individuals (both users and impostors) involved in the analysis.

Only a KAS able to provide a good level of accuracy even when confronted with some hundreds users and some thousands (ore more) potential impostors will be of practical use. Therefore, one may wonder how statistically meaningful are the outcomes of experiments conducted on a bunch of, say, 30 to 50 users, as it is common in the literature on keystroke analysis. Studies on the statistical significance of biometric experiments abound, and we refer to Wayman (2000) for a comprehensive treatment of the subject (see also Bergadano et al. (2003) for a study of different techniques).

However, we agree with the position of J. L. Wayman, Director of the U.S. National Biometric Test Center. Wayman (2000) admits *"our inability to predict even approximately how many tests will be required to have 'statistical confidence' in our results. We currently have no way of accurately estimating how large a test will be necessary to adequately characterize any biometric device in any application, even if error rates are known in advance"* (p. 14*)*. As is sadly common in experimental science, the number of different users and samples gathered to test a system are not decided on the basis of pre-defined confidence intervals but, more realistically, by the amount of resource, time, and budget available (Wayman, 1999). Of course, once a system has been tested, it is then possible to estimate the uncertainty of its error rates with various methods, but such estimates will have to be taken *cum grano salis*, because of the many sources of variability that influence biometric features (Mansfield & Wayman, 2002). This is even truer in the case of an unstable biometric such as keystroke dynamics: the only way to evaluate a method for kesytroke analysis is to test it with as many users and impostors as possible. The number of parameters that may influence keystroke dynamics is so high that any statistical evaluation of the system will be of limited use.

The rapid increase of ubiquitous electronic communications, and the pervasive presence of computers and computer networks in many aspects of our life has been unfortunately accompanied by a corresponding growth of illegal activities. Such activities include computer and network intrusions, Internet frauds, cyber piracy, and online distribution of illegal material. Moreover, criminal and terrorist groups use the cyberspace to conduct their crimes, exploiting the anonymity of the Net to exchange messages and information. Computing resources can be themselves the objective of terrorist attacks.

We are well-aware that the use of biometric technologies in security applications does not come without economical and social costs (for example, privacy is a fundamental issue within biometric applications in general, and for keystroke analysis in particular (Volokh, E. (2000); Chandra and Calderon (2005)). Nonetheless, we believe that an accurate form of identity verification based on the analysis of the typing rhythms of free text can be added to the set of tools available to answer to the increasing demand for security of our times.

REFERENCES

Axelsson, S. (1999). The base-rate fallacy and its implications for the difficulty of intrusion detection. In *Proceedings of the 6th ACM Conference on Computer and Communication Security*. Singapore.

BBC News online (2000). *You must remember this... that and other*. Retrieved from http://news.bbc.co.uk/1/hi/uk/720976.stm

Bergadano, F., Gunetti, D., & Picardi, C. (2002). User authentication through keystroke dynamics. *ACM Transactions on Information and System Security, 5*(4), 367–397. doi:10.1145/581271.581272

Bergadano, F., Gunetti, D., & Picardi, C. (2003). Identity verification through dynamic keystroke analysis. *Journal of Intelligent Data Analysis, 7*(5).

Bleha, S., Slivinsky, C., & Hussein, B. (1990). Computer-access security systems using keystroke dynamics. *IEEE Transactions on Pattern Analysis and Machine Intelligence PAMI, 12*, 1217–1222. doi:10.1109/34.62613

Brown, M., & Rogers, S. J. (1993). User identification via keystroke characteristics of typed names using neural networks. *International Journal of Man-Machine Studies, 39*, 999–1014. doi:10.1006/imms.1993.1092

Chandra, A., & Calderon, T. (2005). Challenges and constraints to the diffusion of biometrics in Information Systems. *Communications of the ACM, 48*(12), 101–106. doi:10.1145/1101779.1101784

Chang, W. (2005). Keystroke biometric system using wavelets. In *Advances in Biometrics, Lecture Notes in Computer Science, 3832*. Berlin, Germany: Springer.

Clarke, N., & Furnell, S. (2007). Authenticating mobile phone users using keystroke analysis. *International Journal of Information Security, 6*(1).

Clarke, N., Furnell, S., Lines, B., & Reynolds, P. (2003). Using keystroke analysis as a mechanism for subscriber authentication on mobile handsets. In *Proceedings of the 18th Conference on Information Security. (IFIP/SEC 2003)*. Athens, Greece: Kluwer.

Dowland, P., & Furnell, S. (2004). A long-term trial of keystroke profiling using digraph, trigraph and keyword latencies. In *Proceedings of IFIP/SEC 2004 - 19th International Conference on Information Security*, (pp. 4275– 4289).

Dowland, P., Furnell, S., & Papadaki, M. (2002). Keystroke analysis as a method of advanced user authentication and response. In *Proceedings of the 17th IFIP/SEC 2002 Conference*. Cairo, Egypt: Kluwer.

Dowland, P., Singh, H., & Furnell, S. (2001). A preliminary investigation of user authentication using continuous keystroke analysis. In *Proceedings 8th IFIP Annual Working Conference on Information Security Management and Small System Security*. Las Vegas, Nevada.

Gaines, R., Lisowski, W., Press, S., & Shapiro, N. (1980). *Authentication by keystroke timing: Some preliminary results*. Technical Report R-256-NSF, Rand Corporation.

Gunetti, D., & Picardi, C. (2005). Keystroke analysis of free text. *ACM Transactions on Information and System Security, 8*(3), 312–347. doi:10.1145/1085126.1085129

Gunetti, D., Picardi, C., & Ruffo, G. (2005a) Dealing with different languages and old profiles in keystroke analysis of free text. In S. Bandini, (Ed.), *Proceedings of the Ninth Congress of the Italian Association for Artificial Intelligence (AI*IA-2005)*, (LNCS 3673, pp. 347–358). Milan, Italy: Springer-Verlag.

Gunetti, D., Picardi, C., & Ruffo, G. (2005b). Keystroke analysis of different languages: A case study. In A. F. Famili, J. N. Kok, J. M. Pena, A. Siebes, & A. Feelders, (Eds.), *Proceedings of the Sixth Symposium on Intelligent Data Analysis (IDA 2005)*, (LNCS 3646, pp. 133–144). Madrid, Spain: Springer-Verlag.

Hempstalk, K. (2009). *Continuous typist verification using machine learning*. PhD Thesis, University of Wakaito, Hamilton, New Zealand.

Hocquet, S., Ramel, J., & Carbot, H. (2006). Estimation of user specific parameters in one-class problems. In *Proceedings of the 18th International Conference on Pattern Recognition (ICPR'06)* volume 4. Washington, DC: IEEE Computer Society.

Jain, A. K., Flynn, P., & Ross, A. A. (Eds.). (2008). *Handbook of biometrics*. Springer. doi:10.1007/978-0-387-71041-9

Joyce, R., & Gupta, G. (1990). User authorization based on keystroke latencies. *Communications of the ACM, 33*(2), 168–176. doi:10.1145/75577.75582

Leggett, J., & Williams, G. (1988). Verifying identity via keystroke characteristics. *International Journal of Man-Machine Studies, 28*(1), 67–76. doi:10.1016/S0020-7373(88)80053-1

Li, J., Zheng, R., & Chen, H. (2006). From fingerprint to writeprint. *Communications of the ACM, 49*(4), 77–82. doi:10.1145/1121949.1121951

Mansfield, A. J., & Wayman, J. L. (2002). *Best practices in testing and reporting performances of biometric devices*. Deliverable of the Biometric Working Group of the CESG Gov. Communication Headquarters of the United Kingdom. National Physical Laboratory, Report CMCS 14/02. Teddington, United Kingdom. Retrieved from www.cesg.gov.uk/technology/biometrics/media/Best%20Practice.pdf

McHugh, J. (2000). Testing intrusion detection systems. *ACM Transactions on Information and System Security, 3*(4), 262–294. doi:10.1145/382912.382923

Mészáros, A., Bankó, Z., & Czúni, L. (2007). Strengthening passwords by keystroke dynamics. *IEEE International Workshop on Intelligent Data Acquisition and Advanced Computing Systems: Technology and Applications*. Dortmund, Germany

Monrose, F., & Rubin, A. (2000). Keystroke dynamics as a biometric for authentication. *Future Generation Computer Systems, 16*(4), 351–359. doi:10.1016/S0167-739X(99)00059-X

Nisenson, M., Yariv, I., El-Yaniv, R., & Meir, R. (2003). Towards behaviometric security systems: Learning to identify a typist. In *Proceedings of the 7th European Conference on Principles and Practice of Knowledge Discovery in Databases (ECML/PKDD)*. Berlin, Germany: Springer-Verlag.

Obaidat, M. S., & Sadoun, B. (1997). Verification of computer users using keystroke dynamics. *IEEE Transactions on Systems, Man, and Cybernetics. Part B, Cybernetics, 27*(2), 261–269. doi:10.1109/3477.558812

Ong, C., & Lai, W. (2000). Enhanced password authentication through typing biometrics with the k-means clustering algorithm. In *Proceedings of the Seventh International Symposium on Manufacturing with Applications*. Hawaii, USA.

Polemi, D. (2000). *Biometric techniques: Review and evaluation of biometric techniques for identification and authentication, including an appraisal of the areas where they are most applicable*. Technical report, Report prepared for the European Commission DG XIII - C.4 on the Information Society Technologies, (IST) (Key action 2: New Methods of Work and Electronic Commerce). Retrieved from www.cordis.lu/infosec/src/stud5fr.html

Reiter, M. K., Monrose, F., & Wetzel, S. (1999). Password hardening based on keystroke dynamics. In *Proceedings of the 6th ACM Conference on Computer and Communications Security*, (pp. 73–82). Singapore. New York, NY: ACM.

Revett, K., Magalhães, S., & Santos, H. (2005). Enhancing login security through the use of keystroke input dynamics. In *Advances in Biometrics, Lecture Notes in Computer Science, 3832*. Berlin, Germany: Springer.

Rodrigues, R., Yared, G., Costa, C., Yabu-Uti, J., Violaro, F., & Ling, L. (2005). Biometric access control through numerical keyboards based on keystroke dynamics. In *Advances in Biometrics, Lecture Notes in Computer Science, 3832*. Berlin, Germany: Springer.

Umphress, D., & Williams, G. (1985). Identity verification through keyboard characteristics. *International Journal of Man-Machine Studies, 23*, 263–273. doi:10.1016/S0020-7373(85)80036-5

Volokh, E. (2000). Personalization and privacy. *Communications of the ACM, 43*(8), 84–88. doi:10.1145/345124.345155

Wayman, J. L. (1999, April). *Fundamentals of biometric authentication technologies*. Paper presented at the CardTech/SecurTech Conference. Bethesda, MD.

Wayman, J. L. (Ed.). (2000). *National Biometric Test Center: Collected works 1997-2000*. Biometric Consortium of the U.S. Government interest group on biometric authentication. San Jose State University, CA. Retrieved from www.engr.sjsu.edu/biometrics/nbtccw.pdf

Chapter 10

Personal Identification and Authentication Based on Keystroke Dynamics in Japanese Long–Text Input

Toshiharu Samura
Akashi National College of Technology, Japan

Haruhiko Nishimura
University of Hyogo, Japan

ABSTRACT

We have investigated several characteristics of keystroke dynamics in Japanese long-text input. We performed experiments with 189 participants, classified into three groups according to the number of letters they could type in five minutes. In this experimental study, we extracted feature indices from the keystroke timing for each alphabet letter and for each two-letter combination composed of a consonant and vowel in Japanese text. Taking into account two identification methods using Weighted Euclidean Distance (WED) and Array Disorder (AD), we proposed a hybrid model for identifying individuals on the basis of keystroke data in Japanese long-text input. By evaluating the identification performance of individuals in the three groups, the effectiveness of the method was found to correspond to the typing skill level of the group.

INTRODUCTION

Timing data for keystrokes follows a fixed pattern, and biometric measures that use such data are called keystroke dynamics. Keystroke dynamics has two features that differentiate it from other forms of biometric measures. First, keystroke dynamics can be measured using only a keyboard; special equipment, such as fingerprint and retinal scanners, is not required. Second, this biometric measuring system has applications other than ac-

DOI: 10.4018/978-1-61350-129-0.ch010

cess authorization, such as investigation into the identity of malicious users who attempt to gain unauthorized access to computer systems.

Most previous research on keystroke dynamics has focused on user authentication during login, using not only information about a series of input characters for password recognition, but also keystroke dynamics as part of the authentication process (Umphress & Williams, 1985; Leggett & Williams, 1988; Joyce & Gupta, 1990; Kasukawa et. al., 1992; Kotani, Norioka & Horii, 2005; Obaidat & Sadoun, 1999; Bender & Pankanti, 2007; AdmitOneSecurity, 2010). Short words such as passwords, however, generally do not contain sufficient keystroke information for such dynamics to enable user recognition, resulting in a lower verification rate in comparison with fingerprint or retinal scans. Keystroke dynamics is therefore most often used as a complementary check in password recognition.

Similar to handwriting analysis and voice printing, another use of keystroke dynamics is feature analysis related to human behavior. This study focuses on identification and authentication from the point of view of using keystroke dynamics related to human behavior. Here, we consider the use of an analytic method that captures individual characteristics through the input of completely different phrases, rather than using repeated input of a short word for password verification. By using sentences of a certain length, it is possible to obtain sufficient information for deriving dynamics statistically. Little research has been performed on the keystroke dynamics of such long-text input, and this has only recently become the subject of academic discussion (Monrose & Rubin, 2000; Bergadano, Gunetti & Picardi, 2002; Gunetti & Picardi, 2005; Curtin et. al., 2006; Villani et.al., 2006; Ahmed & Traoré,2008; Samura & Nishimura, 2008; Samura & Nishimura, 2009a; Samura & Nishimura, 2009b; Tappert, Villani & Cha, 2009; Samura & Nishimura, 2010; Samura & Nishimura, 2011).

In the present study, we propose a method for feature index extraction and identification that enables identification of individuals through long-text input as a fundamental topic in keystroke dynamics research. Here, we use keystroke timing for single character and paired character sequences when the user is inputting Latin characters. For identification methods, we use our previously proposed Weighted Euclidean Distance (WED) method (Samura & Nishimura, 2009a; Samura & Nishimura, 2009b), the Array Disorder (AD) method proposed by Gunetti et al. (Bergadano, Gunetti & Picardi, 2002; Gunetti & Picardi, 2005), and a hybrid method that compares given keystroke data using both the WED and AD methods, as well as a combination of the two (Samura & Nishimura, 2010a). While the WED method evaluates the magnitude of differences in feature indices, the AD method evaluates ranking patterns of feature indices. The difference in these approaches leads to significantly higher identification rates for participants with low typing skill when using the WED method in comparison with the AD method. On the other hand, as pointed out by Gunetti et al., relative ranking patterns are resistant to the effects related to differences in input environment (e.g., differing keyboards) and physical or emotional states; thus, in some cases the AD method should be more effective than the WED method. This chapter presents a large-scale study involving 189 participants. We compare the WED and AD methods, and introduce and evaluate a hybrid method that complementarily incorporates the strengths of both.

Keystroke Data and Extraction of Feature Indices

Consider a situation in which a user inputs text of a given length. During keyboard entry, the system performs background measurements of key press and release times. Figure 1 shows example data on Japanese hiragana input by entering combinations of Latin letters. The first field shows the typed let-

Figure 1. Example of keystroke data

b,	p,	1197417770648
a,	p,	1197417770733
b,	r,	1197417770791
i,	p,	1197417770816
a,	r,	1197417770823
i,	r,	1197417770872
k,	p,	1197417770972
k,	r,	1197417771039
i,	p,	1197417771112
i,	r,	1197417771167

ter, the second field shows the key press ("p") or release ("r"), and the third field shows the UNIX system time of the event (millisecond precision).

Measurements can be performed to acquire such keystroke data by using keystrokes for either single alphabet letters or letter pairs. While a relatively large amount of previous research has focused on letter pairs (Bergadano, Gunetti & Picardi, 2002; Gunetti & Picardi, 2005), there has been relatively little research examining both single letter and letter pairs (Curtin et. al., 2006; Villani et.al., 2006; Samura & Nishimura, 2008; Samura & Nishimura, 2009a; Samura & Nishimura, 2009b; Tappert, Villani & Cha, 2009; Samura & Nishimura, 2010a; Samura & Nishimura, 2010b). When typing in English, certain combinations of three letters or more frequently occur, for example, "the" and "tion"; however, because Japanese typing involves the input of hiragana characters (formed from either a single vowel letter or a consonant-vowel letter pair), particular combinations of three or more letters occur infrequently. This study therefore does not address feature indices for combinations of three or more letters.

The notation *1pr* in Figure 2 indicates the time from press to release of a single key, and is referred to below as key press duration. The notation *2rr* in Figure 2 indicates the time from the release of one key to the release of the following key when typing a consonant-vowel pair. The time from release of the first key to the time of pressing the following key (*2rp*) and the time from pressing the first key to pressing the second key (*2pp*) are also considered. Furthermore, *2pr1* indicates the time from pressing the first key to releasing the next key, *2pr2* indicates the key press duration when typing the second (vowel) key, and *2pr3* indicates the key press duration when typing the first (consonant) key. As shown in Table 1, the average and standard deviation of each of the seven measures described above are used as the feature indices for identification of individuals.

These measurements are, however, not independent of each other; for example, $2pp = 2pr3 + 2rp$. Therefore, *2pp* might seem to be unnecessary for evaluation, but the evaluation of *2pp* corresponds to the evaluation of the correlation between *2pr3* and *2rp* because in general $(2pp.sd)^2 = (2pr3.sd)^2 + (2rp.sd) - 2((2pr3 \cdot 2rp).av - 2pr3.av \cdot 2rp.av)$. Furthermore, the use of multiple feature indices ensures highly robust data processing.

Figure 2. Keystroke measurements for a single letter (above) and a letter pair (below)

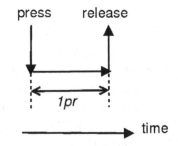

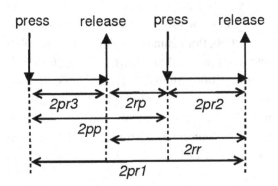

Table 1. Feature indices of keystroke

Notation	Description
1pr	Average (*1pr.av*) and standard deviation (*1pr.sd*) of key press duration for Latin alphabet single letters of **a** to **z**.
2rr	Average (*2rr.av*) and standard deviation (*2rr.sd*) of release to release transition time between consonant-vowel letter pairs.
2rp	Average (*2rp.av*) and standard deviation (*2rp.sd*) of release to press transition time between consonant-vowel letter pairs.
2pp	Average (*2pp.av*) and standard deviation (*2pp.sd*) of press to press transition time between consonant-vowel letter pairs.
2pr1	Average (*2pr1.av*) and standard deviation (*2pr1.sd*) of press to release transition time between consonant-vowel letter pairs.
2pr2	Average (*2pr2.av*) and standard deviation (*2pr2.sd*) of key press duration for the second letter of consonant-vowel letter pairs.
2pr3	Average (*2pr3.av*) and standard deviation (*2pr3.sd*) of key press duration for the first letter of consonant-vowel letter pairs.

When the feature indices are taken as *x*, the final identification function can be standardized as shown by the following equation:

$$x' = \frac{x - x_{\min}}{x_{\max} - x_{\min}} \quad (0 \leq x' \leq 1) \tag{1}$$

Here, $x_{\min}$ and $x_{\max}$ are the minimum and maximum values obtained from the measurements of feature index *x* in all participants. This formula was previously introduced by Curtin et al. (2006), and we followed this standardization to ensure that our case of Japanese texts could be compared with the case of English texts by Curtin et al.

As a statistical normalization method, the standard normal distribution with a mean of 0 and a standard deviation of 1 is well known. The formula for a normal distribution for an original value of feature index *x* is as follows:

$$x' = \frac{(x - \bar{x})}{\sigma} \tag{2}$$

where $\bar{x}$ is the mean, and σ is the standard deviation of the original normal distribution. Comparing Equation (1) and (2), we can see that $(x_{\max} - x_{\min})$ corresponds to σ and both equations exhibit a similar trend: when one increases (resp. decreases), the other increases (resp. decreases) accord-

ingly. Therefore, in practical use, the above two standardizing equations are considered to have little difference between them.

METHOD OF IDENTIFICATION

Profiles are created through extraction of feature indices for each typist (A, B, C, ···) using multiple (*N*) documents. The profile collection is then used to determine the typist who input an unknown document. In this section, we first describe the WED method (Samura & Nishimura, 2009a; Samura & Nishimura, 2009b) and the AD method (Bergadano, Gunetti & Picardi, 2002; Gunetti & Picardi, 2005) for comparison of the feature indices for the unknown document and subsequent comparison with each profile. Then, we describe the hybrid method that we propose (Samura & Nishimura, 2010a).

Weighted Euclidean Distance Method

Taking the first profiling document of Typist A as doc*A1*, the profiling document of each participant can be represented as doc*A1*, doc*A2*, ···, doc*AN*, doc*B1*, doc*B2*, ···, doc*BN*, doc*C1*, ···. An unknown document is represented as doc*UK*. The squared

WED WED^2 (doc*A1*, doc*UK*) used as the identification function is given by the following equation:

$$WED^2\left(docA1, docUK\right) = \frac{1}{m}\sum_{\alpha=1}^{m}\left(\frac{1}{n_\alpha}\right)\sum_{i=1}^{n_\alpha}\left(k_{\alpha(i)} - r_{\alpha(i)}\right)^2$$

(3)

The index $\alpha(=1,2,\cdots)$ of the feature indices is then *1pr.av*, *1pr.sd*, $\cdots$. Furthermore, *m* is the number of contributing feature indices, $\alpha(i)$ indicates the feature index α for the *i* th character (single letter or letter pair), and n_α is the number of characters therein. n_α will vary greatly with respect to the number of characters compared when, for example, taking the keystroke feature indices for single letters and those for two-letter combinations. $k_{\alpha(i)}$ is the $\alpha(i)$ feature index standardized according to Equation (1) for a profiling document (e.g., doc*A1*), and $k_{\alpha(i)}$ is that for $\alpha(i)$ of an unknown document (doc*UK*). The WED is normalized to 0~1 using the weightings $1/m$ and $1/n_\alpha$.

During actual feature index extraction, a lower threshold N_{TH} for the number of occurrences of each character type (single letter and letter pair) and an upper threshold T_{TH} for key press duration other than *2pr1* are introduced. As a result, when comparing $k_{\alpha(i)}$ and $r_{\alpha(i)}$, there can be loss of *k-r* pair feature indices for a given input document in accordance with the setting of the lower threshold N_{TH} for that document. In cases where the keystroke feature indices for all *k-r* pairs in a given document are missing, then the document is removed from consideration for the participant.

Figure 3 illustrates the *2pp.av* feature indices for two documents, namely, doc*A1* and doc*UK*. For the five *2pp.av* letter pairs common to the two documents, the squared WED is given by the following equation:

$$WED^2_{2pp.av}\left(docA1, docUK\right) =$$
$$[(0.21 - 0.11)^2 + (0.10 - 0.13)^2 + (0.39 - 0.32)^2$$
$$+ (0.30 - 0.10)^2 + (0.22 - 0.18)^2] / 5$$

(4)

Figure 3. Illustration of the weighted euclidean distance (WED) method for remaining letter pairs and their standardized values of 2pp.av in docA1 and docUK, where there are five letter pairs in common between them

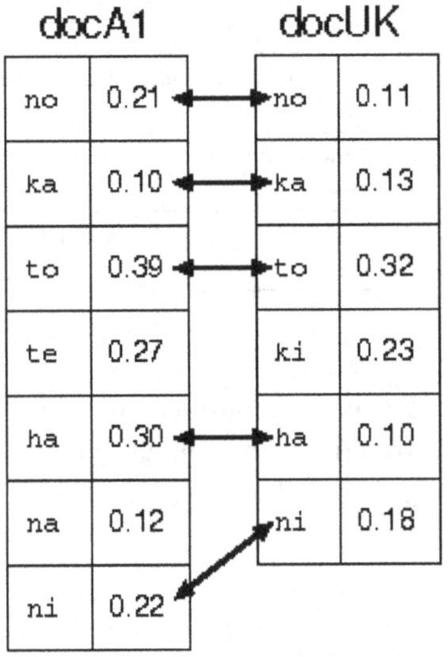

Identification is performed using the nearest-neighbor classification rule (Figure 4). In other words, comparisons are performed between the unknown document and each of the profile documents, and the typist of the profile document that gives the lowest value is taken to be the typist of the unknown document. For example, given five profile documents (*A1~A5*) for a given participant (Typist A), we can expect that if Typist A also typed the unknown document then its value will be close to one of the five states of Typist A *A1~A5*.

Array Disorder Method

The AD method, which is called the "R-measure" in Bergadano, Gunetti and Picardi (2002) and in Gunetti & Picardi(2005), but referred to as the Array Disorder in the present study, ranks characters according to their feature index values, and evaluates the disorder of the rankings. Standardized feature indices are sorted in increasing order, the difference in rankings of each are compared,

Figure 4. Personal identification by nearest-neighbor classification rule with squared WED

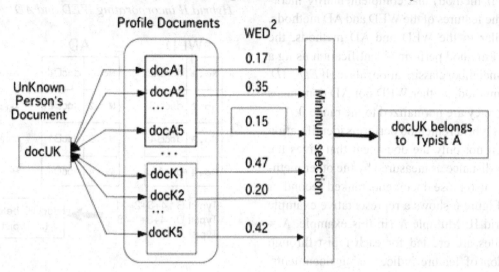

and the totals of each are taken as the distance. As in the case of the WED method, missing feature indices of character pair keystroke are not considered during the comparison. When n_a characters are used to compare a feature index α, if n_a is even then the distance is divided by $n_a^2 / 2$; if n_a is odd then the distance is divided by $(n_a^2 - 1)/2$. Finally, the value is normalized to the range 0~1 by dividing the value by the number of contributing feature indices m.

Figure 5 shows the feature index values from Figure 3 rearranged in increasing order. The sum of the difference in rankings of each character (the d value in the figure) is normalized, resulting in the following calculation of the AD value:

$$AD_{2pp.av}\left(docA1, docUK\right) = \frac{1}{(5^2 - 1)^2}\left[3 + 0 + 2 + 0\right]$$

$$(5)$$

Identification under the AD method uses the nearest-neighbor classification rule, as in the case of the WED method.

Hybrid Method

In contrast to the WED method, which evaluates the magnitude of differences in feature index values between documents, the AD method focuses on differences between documents in ranking patterns of the feature indices. This study introduces two hybrid methods (the Hybrid I method and the

Figure 5. Illustration of array disorder (AD) method for the example in Figure 3

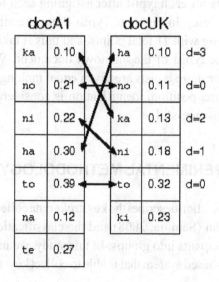

Hybrid II method) that complementarily incorporate the features of the WED and AD methods.

Similar to the WED and AD methods, the Hybrid I method performs identification using a nearest-neighbor classification rule for *WED+AD*. In this method, neither WED nor AD dominates because they are normalized to the range 0~1.

The Hybrid II method performs identification based on not only the document that gives the shortest distance as measured by the other methods, but also those documents ranked second or lower. Figure 6 shows a representative example in Hybrid II. Multiple *N* (in this example, *N* = 5) profiles are created for each typist through extraction of feature indices using documents. The table on the left shows the results of the WED method, comparing each of the unknown documents (doc*UK*) and sorting them into a proximity list (ranked 1~(*N*-1)) that begins with the document with the shortest distance. In this example, the second profile document of Typist B (doc*B2*) has the shortest distance, followed by the third profile document typed by Typist D (doc*D3*). The table on the right shows the results of the AD method, and similarly is a proximity list according to distances found using this method. Overall evaluation is performed by assigning four ranking points to the profile document in the first position (the nearest document), and totaling the points for each typist after assigning each to the four ranks. In Figure 6, Typist B has the highest ranking with 11 total points, and thus is taken to be the typist of the unknown document. When two or more typists are given equal rankings for the first position, identification is considered to be unsuccessful.

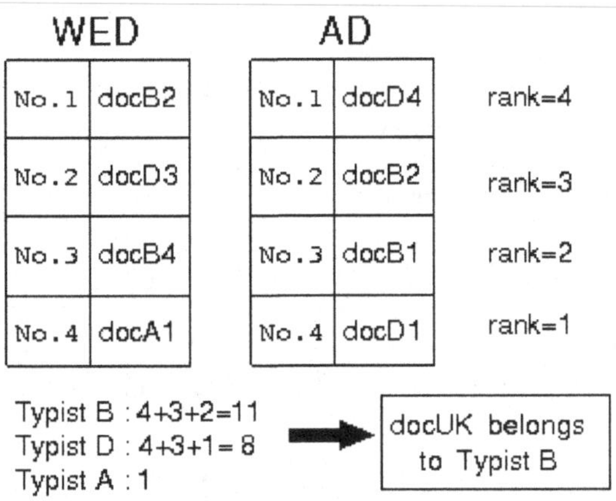

EXPERIMENTAL METHODOLOGY

This section describes the keystroke data collection system (Samura, 2008) and the classification of participants into groups. In this study, we used a web-based system that is able to collect keystroke

Figure 6. Illustration of identification method by Hybrid II incorporating WED and AD

data from a large number of participants in a single experiment. The system uses typing support software that was familiar to the participants, thereby lowering effects related to unfamiliarity and nervousness. Figure 7 shows a screenshot of the software interface used in this study.

The document display screen allows participants who are skilled typists to input text while viewing the Japanese text displayed in the upper row. Less skilled typists can type while viewing the Latin alphabet text displayed in the middle row. Latin alphabet text is removed from the screen as it is typed, allowing confirmation of mistyped characters. The top row displays the number of keystrokes, the number of errors, and the amount of time remaining. Because this experiment focuses only on Latin alphabet input keystroke, by design Latin character input is not converted into Japanese kanji characters.

While participants are typing, browser-embedded JavaScript code records character input, key press times, and key release times. Times are recorded using UNIX times (millisecond precision). Recorded data were sent to a server using Ajax. Participants input data during 5-min sessions separated by at least one week. Lower thresholds for single letters and letter pairs, N_{TH}, were set at 3 occurrences (N_{TH}=3), and key press

Figure 7. Screenshot of interface of keystroke data collecting system

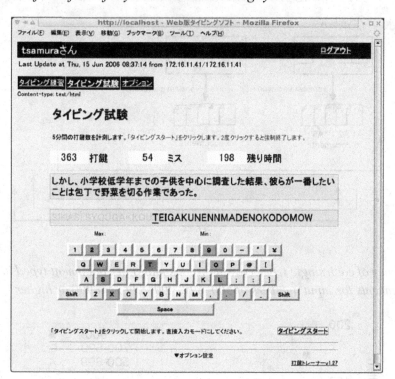

duration T for keystrokes other than *2pr1* were set at 300 ms or less ($T<T_{TH}$=300). We explain the appropriateness of these values in section "User Identification" 6.1.

Analysis was performed after dividing participants into three groups according to the number of letters that they could type in 5 min: G500 for those who could type at least 500 letters, G700 for those who could type at least 700 letters, and G900 for those who could type at least 900 letters. Table 2 shows the number of participants in each category.

Table 2. Group classification of participants

Group	G500	G700	G900
Number of input letters (5 min)	≥500	≥700	≥900
Number of Participants	189	127	88
Number of all documents(1 set)	945	635	440

The number of documents obtained from each participant varied from 5 to 18. As shown in Figure 8, the number of documents from each user was set to 5 by choosing 5 documents at random from those created by participants who typed an excess number of documents. Analysis was performed taking, as a single set, the number of documents equal to 5 times the number of participants. To account for possible bias in document selection, analysis was performed five times on 5 similar document sets.

We next describe the basic features (statistics) of the documents examined. The documents were divided into three groups according to the number of letters they contained: 500 to 699 letters, 700 to 899 letters, and 900 or more letters. Figures 9 and 10, respectively, show the average number of occurrences of single letters (vowel or consonant) and letter pair combinations (consonant plus vowel) for the most common twenty occurrences,

Figure 8. Procedure for preparing document sets

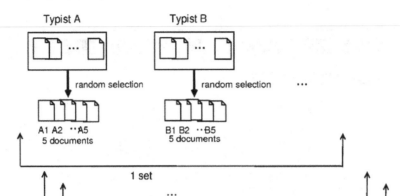

Figure 9. Frequency of each single letter (vowel or consonant) per document typed in 5 min, averaged for all input documents for input numbers of 500–699, 700–899, and 900 or higher

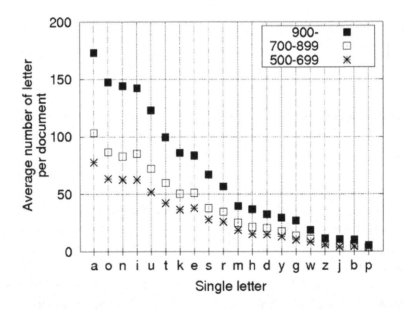

ranked in decreasing order of the occurrences in those documents containing more than 900 letters.

The number of letter pair occurrences is much lower than that of the single letter occurrences, and the probability of a missing pair increases with lower ranking. As can be seen from the graphs, for those typists with input rates of 500-699 letters there will be many letter pairs for which the occurrence count is below the lower threshold $N_{TH}=3$.

As an indicator of the expected values for each of the feature indices listed in Table 1, Figure 11 shows the average and standard deviation values for all documents for the groups G500, G700, and G900. The figure shows a trend of longer times for each feature index for the groups demonstrating lower typing skill. This is a consequence of the fact that typists with poor typing skills take longer to type letters than those with better typing skills.

Figure 10. Frequency of each letter pair (consonant plus vowel) per document typed in 5 min, averaged for all input documents for input numbers of 500–699, 700–899, and 900 or higher

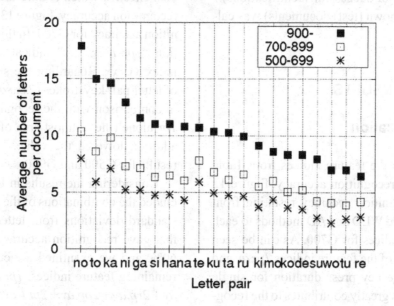

Figure 11. Average and standard deviation values of the feature indices in Table 1 for all input documents for each group of participants

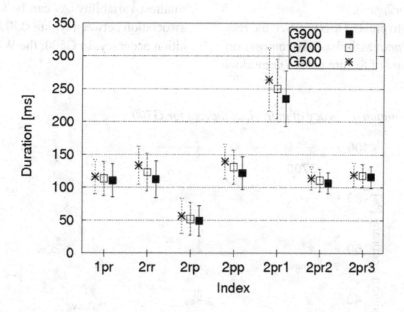

The leave-one-out cross validation method was use for evaluation of the identification. Under this method, one participant's document was removed and treated as the unknown (test) document, doc*UK*. In the case where the typist of the candi-

date profile document was matched with the typist of the unknown (test) document, the identification was classified as a success; otherwise, the identification was classified as a failure. Such validation was performed in turn on each document used in the study, and the recognition accuracy (number of successful identifications) / (number of unknown (test) documents) was calculated.

ANALYSIS RESULTS

User Identification

We first discuss the feature indices from Table 1 that improve recognition accuracy. Figure 12 shows the recognition accuracy resulting from application of the WED and AD methods to each of the feature indices for G700. As can be seen from the results of the feature indices *1pr.av* and *2pr3.av*, average key press duration for single letter keystrokes greatly contributes to the recognition accuracy. On the other hand, there was not a large contribution from the standard deviation in the case of letter pair keystrokes (*2xx.sd*: *xx* = *rr, pr1, pp, pr1,pr2, pr3*).

In this study, to prevent loss we used the relatively common *1pr.av* as the basis for comparison, comparing the case of feature index *1pr.av* alone

with cases including other feature indices. We then checked which feature indices improve the recognition accuracy. Figure 13 shows the recognition accuracy for G700. In this figure, the notation "*1pr.av+xxx.xx*" indicates the addition of index *xxx.xx*. Regarding the standard deviation of letter pair keystrokes (*2xx.sd*), we can see that in comparison with the recognition accuracy of *1pr* alone (the leftmost area of the graph), each addition lowered the value. We found similar results for G500 and G900.

Considering the results in Figure 13, we excluded the combinations of the feature indices of standard deviations from letter pair keystrokes that gave recognition accuracy less than about 60%, and we examined the combination of all remaining feature indices, *1pr.av* + *1pr.sd* + *2rr.av* + *2rp.av* + *2pp.av* + *2pr1.av* + *2pr2.av* + *2pr3.av*. The results are shown in Figure 14. For every group, the hybrid methods (Hybrid I and Hybrid II) gave the highest recognition accuracy with the smallest variability. As can be seen, there is an association between typing skill level and recognition accuracy. In G500, the WED method had

Figure 12. Recognition accuracy of individual indices for G700

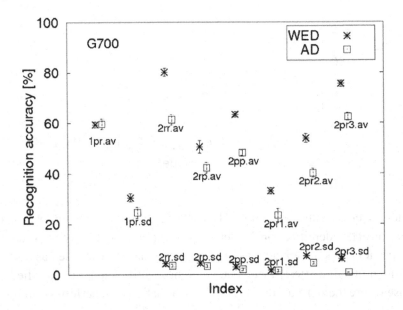

Figure 13. Recognition accuracy of the combination of 1pr.av and other indices for G700

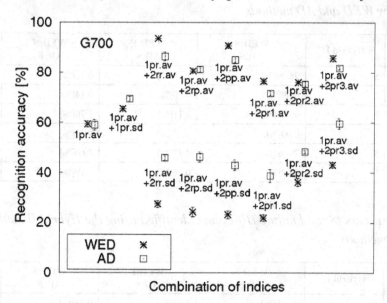

Figure 14. Recognition accuracy of feature combination 1pr.av + 1pr.sd + 2rr.av + 2rp.av + 2pp.av + 2pr1.av + 2pr2.av + 2pr3.av for the three groups

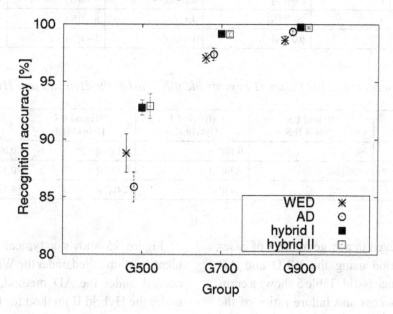

significantly higher recognition accuracy than the AD method.

Table 3 (Hybrid I) and Table 4 (Hybrid II) show the identification success (S) and failure (F) ratios of the hybrid methods in comparison with the WED and AD methods. In cases where both

the WED and AD methods succeeded in identification, the hybrid method also succeeded in almost all cases. In addition, the hybrid methods successfully resulted in identification in a large majority of cases where one of the WED or AD methods failed. Furthermore, the hybrid methods

Table 3. Ratio of success (S) and failure (F) events identified using the Hybrid I method for S and F events identified by WED and AD methods

Group	Hybrid I	WED:S AD:S	WED:F AD:S	WED:S AD:F	WED:F AD:F
G900	S	98.09[%]	1.18[%]	0.32[%]	0.18[%]
	F	0.09[%]	0.00[%]	0.14[%]	0.00[%]
G700	S	95.06[%]	2.11[%]	1.76[%]	0.25[%]
	F	0.00[%]	0.22[%]	0.25[%]	0.35[%]
G500	S	79.09[%]	4.42[%]	7.60[%]	1.65[%]
	F	0.02[%]	0.76[%]	2.10[%]	4.36[%]

Table 4. Ratio of success (S) and failure (F) events identified using the Hybrid II method for S/F cases by WED and AD methods

Group	Hybrid II	WED:S AD:S	WED:F AD:S	WED:S AD:F	WED:F AD:F
G900	S	98.18[%]	1.05[%]	0.36[%]	0.14[%]
	F	0.00[%]	0.14[%]	0.09[%]	0.04[%]
G700	S	94.96[%]	2.05[%]	1.86[%]	0.25[%]
	F	0.09[%]	0.28[%]	0.16[%]	0.35[%]
G500	S	79.05[%]	4.15[%]	8.21[%]	1.38[%]
	F	0.06[%]	1.04[%]	1.48[%]	4.63[%]

Table 5. Ratio of success (S) and failure (F) events identified using the Hybrid I and Hybrid II methods

Group	Hybrid I:S Hybrid II:S	Hybrid I:F Hybrid II:S	Hybrid I:S Hybrid II:F	Hybrid I:F Hybrid II:F
G 900	99.59[%]	0.18[%]	0.13[%]	0.09[%]
G 700	98.80[%]	0.38[%]	0.32[%]	0.50[%]
G 500	90.33[%]	2.43[%]	2.46[%]	4.78[%]

were successful even in a large number of cases where identification using the WED and AD methods was unsuccessful. Table 5 shows a comparison of the success and failure ratios of the Hybrid I and Hybrid II methods. From that table, we can see that in cases where the Hybrid I method was successful, the Hybrid II method was also successful. In cases where one of the methods was unsuccessful, the other case shows similar failure rates.

Figure 15 shows a typical example where identification failed under the WED method, succeeded under the AD method, and succeeded under the Hybrid II method for G700. Figure 16 shows a typical example where identification failed under both the WED method and the AD method, but succeeded under the Hybrid II method for G700. Here, we can see a situation where additive evaluation across the top four ranks leads to successful identification. Figure 17 shows an example of a case where identification was

Figure 15. Example of successful identification using the Hybrid II method in the case of success by WED and failure by AD

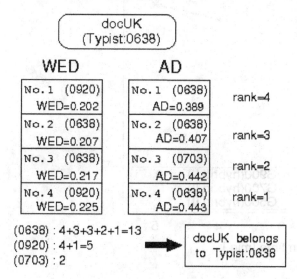

Figure 16. Example of successful identification using the Hybrid II method in the case of failure by both WED and AD

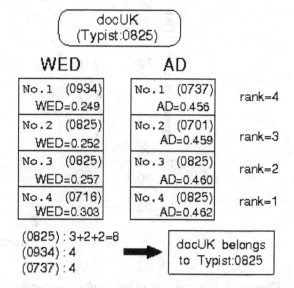

successful under both the WED and AD methods, but failed under the Hybrid II method for G700. As can be seen, identification failed because two typists received the same score for the first rank.

As shown in Figure 10, when the number of typed letters falls to 700 or less, the number of occurrences of letter pairs frequently falls below the lower threshold N_{Th}=3. Nonetheless, the recognition accuracy of the hybrid methods for G700 was greatly improved at 99.3%, indicating that identification can be performed if the typist is of at least beginner skill (able to type most characters without looking at the keyboard).

We next discuss the appropriateness of the selected values for the typing time for each document, the lower threshold N_{TH} for occurrence, and the upper threshold N_{TH} for key press duration. Figure 18 shows the effects of increasing the typing time on recognition accuracy. As can be seen, the value levels off at approximately 5 min.

In this study we set the lower threshold for occurrence of single letters and letter pairs to 3 (N_{Th}=3). Figure 19 shows the dependence of recognition accuracy on the lower threshold N_{TH} for

occurrence. As one can see, the recognition accuracy is high in the area around a value of 3. The recognition accuracy decreases when N_{TH} increases because the number of contributing characters n_a for evaluation decreases.

Figure 17. Example of unsuccessful identification using the Hybrid II method in the case of successful identification by both WED and AD

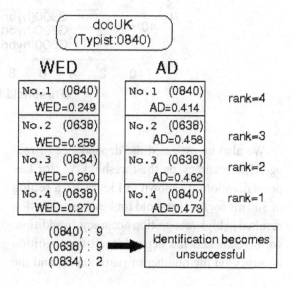

Figure 18. Dependence of recognition accuracy on input duration of document (1–5 min)

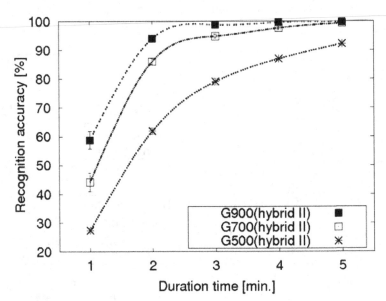

Figure 19. Dependence of recognition accuracy on threshold for letter occurrence (N_{TH}=2~20)

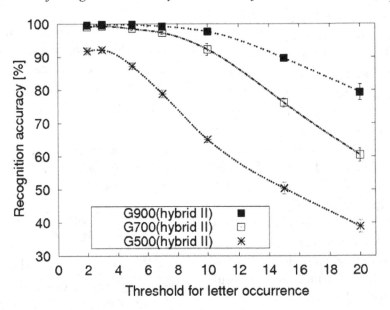

We also investigated the dependence of recognition accuracy on the threshold N_{TH} for key press duration. As shown in Figure 20, a setting of 300 ms for the threshold for key press duration resulted in high recognition accuracy. In addition, we investigated the dependence of recognition accuracy on the number of participants, and the results are shown in Figure 21. We found that recognition accuracy increased as the number of participants decreased; moreover, the resulting decreases in the number of unknown (test) documents led to an increase in the margin of error. The results indicate an approximate recognition accuracy of 95% for the G500 group with a num-

Figure 20. Dependence of recognition accuracy on threshold for key press duration (T_{TH}=200~1500)

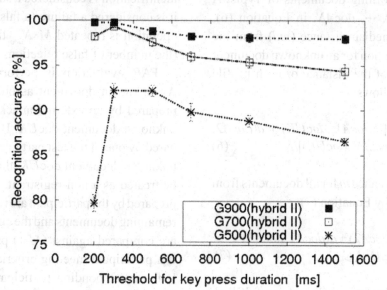

Figure 21. Dependence of recognition accuracy on the number of participants

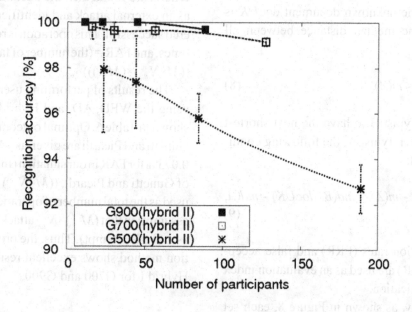

ber of participants similar to the G700 and G900 groups (approximately 100). When the number of participants increases above that of the presented data, the recognition accuracy is reduced, but the rate of reduction is expected to be gradual.

User Authentication

In this section, we further consider the case where doc*UK* contains a typing sample from a person completely unknown to the system. For this case, we used the method of Gunetti & Picardi (2005) to evaluate user authentication.

Taking the profiling documents of Typist A as doc$A1$, doc$A2$, $\cdots$, docAN, in Equation (6), we express the median distance (*md*) from the identification function for an unknown document docUK in terms of the distance of each profile document *d* as follows:

$$md(A, docUK) = [d(docA1, docUK) + d(docA2, docUK) + \cdots + d(docAN, docUK)]/N \qquad (6)$$

The median distance *m* for all documents from typist A is given by Equation (7):

$$m(A) = d(docA1, docA2) + d(docA1, docA3) + \cdots + d(docA(N-1), docAN)/_N C_2 \qquad (7)$$

When the following conditions are fulfilled, an unknown document docUK is taken to belong to A. The median distance *md*(A,docUK) between Typist A and the unknown document docUK is shorter than the median distance between all other typists.

$$md(A, docUK) < m(A) \qquad (8)$$

Or taking Typist B to have the next shortest value of *md* after Typist A, the following condition is satisfied:

$$md(A, docUK) - m(A) \leq md(B, docUK) - md(A, docUK) \qquad (9)$$

False rejection rates (FRR) and false acceptance rates (FAR) are used as an evaluation index of user authentication.

In this study, as shown in Figure 8, each set contained *M* participants (G500, G700, and G900 in Table 2), each having $N_{doc} = 5$ profiling documents. FRR evaluation is performed as follows. As in the leave-one-out cross validation method, a document is removed from the test documents of a participant, and is taken as the unknown document docUK. If the conditions above match with the typist of the unknown document then the identification is considered a success; otherwise, it is considered a failure (a false rejection). This operation is repeated $M \times N_{doc}$ times, and FRR = (the number of false rejections/$(M \times N_{doc})$) $\times 100$.

FAR evaluation is performed as follows. An unknown document assumed to have been prepared by an external attacker is used as the unknown document docUK. If a document prepared by one of the test participants is used as the unknown document docUK, that participant will be treated as a non-registrant, so all documents prepared by the participant are removed. Next, the remaining documents and the unknown document are compared against (*M*-1) participants to see if a participant meeting criteria above is found. If the corresponding participant is found, then the authentication is considered a failure (false acceptance), and if no participants fulfilling the criteria are found then the document is classified as an external attack and identification is considered successful. This operation is repeated $M \times N_{doc}$ times, and FAR = (the number of false acceptance/$((M \times N_{doc}) \times (M-1))) \times$.

The results of performing user authentication using the WED, AD, and Hybrid I methods are shown in Table 6. Optimal outcomes according to Gunetti and Picardi are given as 4.8% for FRR and 0.073% for FAR in our situation (In the calculations of Gunetti and Picardi, $((M \times N_{doc}) \times (M-1) \times N_{doc})$ is used as the total number of operations based on the assumption that $(M-1) \times N_{doc}$ attacks are performed as a single attempt). Thus, the present identification method shows excellent results when using Hybrid I for G700 and G900.

CONCLUSION

We investigated a method for identification of individuals using keystroke data from long-text input. Specifically, we proposed 14 feature indices related to the typing of single letters and consecutive letter pairs using Latin alphabet input, confirmed improvements in recognition

Table 6. Results of user authentication for three groups when using the feature combination 1pr.av + 1pr. sd + 2rr.av + 2rp.av + 2pp.av + 2pr1.av + 2pr2.av + 2pr3.av in the WED, AD and Hybrid I methods

G900			
Method	WED	AD	Hybrid I
No. of false rejections No. of false acceptance	25.6±4.4 8.0±2.2	11.8±1.8 5.8±1.6	9.4±1.5 6.0±3.0
FRR (%) FAR (%)	5.82±1.00 0.0209±0.0058	2.68±0.41 0.0152±0.0043	2.14±0.34 0.0157±0.0078
G700			
Method	WED	AD	Hybrid I
No. of false rejections No. of passed acceptance	45.6±3.04 19.2±4.8	32.6±1.95 8.6±3.7	19.4±4.72 8.6±3.1
FRR (%) FAR (%)	7.18±0.48 0.0240±0.0060	5.13±0.31 0.0108±0.00469	3.06±0.74 0.0108±0.0039
G500			
Method	WED	AD	Hybrid I
No. of false rejections No. of passed acceptance	98.0±2.3 57.6±7.5	92.4±8.0 34.2±6.2	75.4±3.6 29.8±11.3
FRR (%) FAR (%)	10.37±0.24 0.0324±0.0042	9.78±0.85 0.0193±0.0035	7.98±0.38 0.0168±0.0064

related to the use of 8 of those feature indices, and constructed an associated evaluation index. For the identification method, we introduced a hybrid method that incorporates the AD method proposed by Gunetti et al. into the WED method that we previously proposed, and experimentally confirmed the improved recognition accuracy for the hybrid method.

By performing a large-scale experiment involving 189 participants, we were able to obtain new results that compare identification performance between groups of users with differing typing skill levels. We found that our method had recognition accuracy rates of over 99% for participants able to type at least 140 letters per minute (G700 and G900). We also found that variation due to profile selection was small. We confirmed that recognition accuracy was over 95% even for group G500 with fewer than 100 participants. While this study used Japanese text input in its investigation, the feature indices and identification methods used can also be applied to other languages.

Finally, we would like to close with a discussion of possible applications of keystroke dynamics. In previous research, keystroke dynamics have generally been consider to be a supplementary security measure used in conjunction with password authentication during system logins to prevent unauthorized access. Additional incorporation of keystroke dynamics for long-text input can be used for continuous system monitoring for unauthorized users after login occurs. Specific examples include the introduction of an keystroke dynamics system to e-Learning materials and online tests to detect impersonation and unauthorized access (Ahmed & Traoré, 2008; Tappert, Villani & Cha, 2009). The inclusion of encoded keystroke data in e-mails could also be used in place of digital signatures.

We used the method of Gunetti and Picardi to determine the recognition accuracy for user authentication, but we plan to examine other methods in future studies. Furthermore, there are many areas for further research related to factors that must be considered for practical use, such as using different keyboards, and the unfamiliarity and nervousness of users. We hope to address these topics in future studies.

REFERENCES

AdmitOne Security Inc. (2010). *Home*. Retrieved September 2010, from http://www.admitonesecurity.com/

Ahmed, A. A. E., & Traoré, I. (2008). Employee surveillance based on free text detection of keystroke dynamics. In Gupta, M., & Sharman, R. (Eds.), *Handbook of research on social and organizational liabilities in information security* (pp. 47–63). Hershey, PA: Idea Group Publishing. doi:10.4018/978-1-60566-132-2.ch003

Bender, S., & Postley, H. (2007). *Key sequence rhythm recognition system and method.* (US Patent US7206938), US Patent Office.

Bergadano, F., Gunetti, D., & Picardi, C. (2002). User authentication through keystroke dynamics. *ACM Transactions on Information and System Security, 5*(4), 367–397. doi:10.1145/581271.581272

Curtin, M., Tappert, C., Villani, M., Ngo, G., Simone, J., St. Fort, H., & Cha, S.-H. (2006). *Keystroke biometric recognition on long-text input: A feasibility study.* The 2006 IAENG International Workshop on Scientific Computing and Computational Statistics.

Gunetti, D., & Picardi, C. (2005). Keystroke analysis of free text. *ACM Transactions on Information and System Security, 8*(3), 312–347. doi:10.1145/1085126.1085129

Joyce, R., & Gupta, G. (1990). User authorization based on keystroke latencies. *Communications of the ACM, 33*(2), 168–176. doi:10.1145/75577.75582

Kasukawa, M., Mori, Y., Komatsu, K., Akaike, H., & Kakuda, H. (1992). An evaluation and improvement of user authentication system based on keystroke timing data. [in Japanese]. *Transactions of Information Processing Society of Japan, 33*(5), 728–735.

Kotani, K., Norioka, Y., & Horii, K. (2005). Construction and evaluation of keystroke authentication system using the numerical keypad. [in Japanese]. *The Transaction of Human Interface Society, 7*(1), 149–156.

Leggett, J., & Williams, G. (1988). Verifying identity via keystroke characteristics. *International Journal of Man-Machine Studies, 28*(1), 67–76. doi:10.1016/S0020-7373(88)80053-1

Monrose, F., & Rubin, A. (2000). Keystroke dynamics as a biometric for authentication. *Future Generation Computer Systems, 16*, 351–359. doi:10.1016/S0167-739X(99)00059-X

Obaidat, M. S., & Sadoun, B. (1999). Keystroke dynamics based authentication. In Jain, A. K., Bolle, R., & Pankanti, S. (Eds.), *Biometrics: Personal identification in networked society* (pp. 213–230). Springer.

Samura, T. (2008). A Web-based typing learning system that supports Japanese text. [in Japanese]. *Journal of Education in the College of Technology, 31*, 471–476.

Samura, T., & Nishimura, H. (2008). Performance analysis of personal identification by keystroke data in free text typing. [in Japanese]. *Proceedings of SICE Symposium on Systems and Information, 2008*, 59–64.

Samura, T., & Nishimura, H. (2009a). Personal identification by keystroke dynamics in Japanese free text typing. *Transactions of the Institute of Systems* [in Japanese]. *Control and Information Engineers, 22*(4), 145–153. doi:10.5687/iscie.22.145

Samura, T., & Nishimura, H. (2009b). Keystroke timing analysis for individual identification in Japanese free text typing. *Proceedings of ICROS-SICE International Joint Conference, 2009*, 3166–3170.

Samura, T., & Nishimura, H. (2010a). A hybrid model for individual identification based on keystroke data in Japanese free text typing. [in Japanese]. *Transactions of the Society of Instrument and Control Engineers, 46*(11), 676–684.

Samura, T., & Nishimura, H. (2011). Keystroke dynamics for individual identification in Japanese free text typing. *SICE Journal of Control. Measurement and System Integration, 4*(2), 172–178.

Tappert, C. C., Villani, M., & Cha, S. (2009). Keystroke biometric identification and authentication on long-text input. In Wang, L., & Geng, X. (Eds.), *Behavioral Biometrics for Human Identification: Intelligent Applications* (pp. 342–367). Medical Information Science Reference. doi:10.4018/978-1-60566-725-6.ch016

Umphress, D., & Williams, G. (1985). Identity verification through keyboard characteristics. *International Journal of Man-Machine Studies, 23*, 263–273. doi:10.1016/S0020-7373(85)80036-5

Villani, M., Tappert, C., Ngo, G., Simone, J., St. Fort, H., & Cha, S.-H. (2006). Keystroke biometric recognition studies on long-text input under ideal and application-oriented conditions. *Proceedings of the 2006 Conference on Computer Vision and Pattern Recognition Workshop*, C3-1.

Chapter 11

Continuous User Authentication Based on Keystroke Dynamics through Neural Network Committee Machines

Sérgio Roberto de Lima e Silva Filho
Bry Tecnologia S.A., Brazil

Mauro Roisenberg
Federal University of Santa Catarina, Brazil

ABSTRACT

This chapter proposes an authentication methodology that is both inexpensive and non-intrusive and authenticates users continuously while using a computer keyboard. This proposed methodology uses neural network committee machines. The committee consists of several independent neural networks trained to recognize a behavioral biometric characteristic: user's typing pattern. Continuous authentication prevents potential attacks when users leave their desks without logging out or locking their computer session. Some experiments were conducted to evaluate and to calibrate the authentication committee. Best results show that a 0% FAR and a 0.15% FRR can be achieved when different thresholds are used in the system for each user. In this proposed methodology, capture system does not need to concern about typing errors in the text. Another feature of this methodology is that new users can be easily added to the system, with no need to re-train all neural networks involved.

INTRODUCTION

Currently, lots of people are using computers and their networks in order to simplify their lives, get remote services and stay connected with other people. So, users are increasing their dependency on computers and Internet (Monrose & Rubin, 1997; Obaidat, 1995; Obaidat & Sadoun, 1997). Such dependency results in more critical informa-

DOI: 10.4018/978-1-61350-129-0.ch011

tion being stored in computers that become a prime target for frequent attacks. Those attacks may cause some serious problems such as classified documents being disclosed and critical information being deleted, falsified or stolen (Anagun & Cin, 1998; Capuano, Masella, Miranda & Salerno, 1999; Obaidat, 1995; Obaidat & Sadoun, 1997).

Many users do not concern enough or do not know the dangers of the misuse of personal, confidential or critical information stored in their computers. So, imagine a user that stores a bank account password into a file on the computer. An unauthorized person can gain access to this computer, get the password and use the Internet banking to transfer money to another account. Same problem occurs when a credit card number is stored in the computer. Intruders could use credit card number to buy what they want via online shops.

In order to assure that only valid users will be able to access computer resources and the information stored in them, authentication mechanisms try to prevent non-authorized users to disguise themselves as valid users and then access those restricted resources (Brown & Rogers, 1993; Coltell, Bada & Torres, 1999; Monrose, Reiter & Wetzel, 1999; Obaidat & Sadoun, 1997).

User authentication mechanisms are a very promising area of research and in recent years many authentication mechanisms have been proposed. However, those schemes have a common drawback as they only authenticate a user at the login procedure. If a user leaves the desk without logging out or locking computer session, an intruder has an occasion to use the system (Coltell, Bada & Torres, 1999).

An authentication scheme that overcomes such deficiency must continuously authenticate the user who is using the computational resource. So, users are authenticated all the time, starting at the very moment they access the resources to the moment they are no longer using the computer. If users have to leave their desks for a short break or to attend a meeting, they do not have to worry

about non-authorized access to the computer because it will remain protected from any attack of non-authorized people.

Analyzing which feature should be used to provide that continuous authentication, we can conclude that continuous authentication is impracticable using passwords because would be extremely tiring for the user having to repeatedly typing same password to get access to computer. Same problem occurs when a smartcard is used for authentication. If a system asks all the time for a smartcard to authenticate the user, it probably would cause the user to leave the smartcard connected to the computer. On the occasion of an oversight, an intruder could gain access to the system.

Given these drawbacks for conventional authentication features to be used in a continuous authentication mechanism, many researchers have considered using biometric characteristics in continuous authentication schemes. However, in a continuous authentication environment we can discard some biometric characteristics that have been commonly used in a human authentication context, like fingerprint recognition, eye scan of iris or retina, voice recognition, face recognition using the geometry of the face and signature dynamics. For example, it would be totally impractical for a user to constantly put the thumb in a fingerprint reader or continuously talk in a speech recognizer.

Looking for an appropriate biometric characteristic to be used continuously, we found that two behavioral characteristics are present most of the time a user is using a computational resource: keystroke and mouse usage dynamics. As keyboard and mouse devices are constantly used for interacting with the system, their dynamics can be used as viable features for user authentication throughout the work session even after the access control phase has been passed (Bergadano, Gunetti & Picardi, 2002).

Therefore, the objective of this study is to investigate and develop a user authentication methodology that will be secure, inexpensive, and continuous. In this study, keystroke dynamics behavioral characteristic was chosen because it seems to be appropriate to continuous authentication, besides its inexpensive cost, once there is no need to use any other biometric capture device than an ordinary keyboard. The system has also a non-intrusive characteristic, that is, users do not feel uncomfortable typing data on a keyboard. If intruders try to access the computing system, they will not be denied access as typing pattern will no more be compatible with the pattern expected from the legitimate user. As a result, the system can lock all resources until achieving a successful authentication for the true user.

Another practical behavioral biometric characteristic for continuous authentication would be the analysis of user's mouse usage pattern to supplement the keyboard pattern analysis. This choice would be very interesting because the use of mouse devices is common nowadays, but this chapter is restricted to the study of keystroke dynamics.

The continuous authentication by keystroke dynamics is clearly a pattern recognition problem, and more specifically, a pattern classification problem. Neural pattern recognition approach seems to be an appealing methodology to tackle this problem. According to Monrose & Rubin (1997) some neural network models present high performance results, however, the same author emphasizes that each time a new user is registered in the system all neural networks involved must be retrained.

In this work we propose an authentication structure of Artificial Neural Networks (ANN), grouped in a committee machine. The committee consists of several independent neural networks. For any given user that wants to be authenticated to the system, each network of the committee is trained to recognize if the presented typing pattern belongs to that user against to some other user registered in the system. During the operation, the decisions of each of the networks of the committee

are combined and, if a given threshold is reached, then the user is authenticated by the system. Moreover, this authentication is done throughout the whole system operation time. Further on the excellent performance in user authentication, other feature of this methodology is that new users can be easily added to the system, with no need to re-train all Neural Networks involved.

False Rejection Rate (FRR) and False Acceptance Rate (FAR) were used to measure the performance of this biometric system. FRR indicates how many true users were considered intruders by the system while the FAR express how many non-authorized users were accepted by the biometric system (Obaidat & Sadoun, 1997). When FAR is too high that indicates the system is very susceptible to intrusion indicating a failure in security system. On the other hand, high FRR indicates the amount of frustration among system users. The problems is that FRR and FAR are roughly inversely proportional and reducing a particular rate causes an increase in the other. Thus biometric systems must have thresholds to control error rates in order to optimizing relationship between the two rates, allowing the system to accept and reject users in an acceptable percentage.

The remaining part of this chapter is organized as follows: next section is a brief summary of keystroke dynamics and related works in the area. The following sections show Artificial Neural Networks and Committee Machines theory respectively. The methodology proposed to authenticate users is explained later. After these sections, experiments and results over this methodology and future research directions are presented. Finally, the last section presents conclusions of this work.

BACKGROUND

In the 19th century, observation of telegraph operators showed that each operator had a distinct pattern of keying messages over telegraph lines and that those operators could recognize who was typing simply by listening to keyed messages characteristics. According to Joyce & Gupta (1990) "the same neurophysiological factors that make a written signature unique are also exhibited in a users' typing pattern. When a person types on a keyboard, he/she leaves a digital signature in the form of keystrokes latencies" (p. 168).

Many characteristics can be analyzed about a user's keystroke dynamics, such as latency between keystrokes, time pressing a keystroke, correlation, pressure on the keyboard, full speed typing, frequency errors and corrections typing errors, and many others. Therefore, when someone is typing texts, all information typed can be watched in order to extract the rhythm of keystroke latencies. Afterwards, users can be authenticated by this rhythm.

In order to determine the users' profile, initially they are requested to enter a chosen sample sentence a certain number of times. Later, this profile will be used to authenticate the user to the system. When identity verification of a user that requires access to computer resources is done at the login time, this approach is often referred to as static keystroke analysis or static method. On the other hand, the situation where profile information is used to continuously authenticate the user throughout all the time the keyboard is used during a work session is known as continuous approach or dynamic keystroke analysis (Bergadano, Gunetti & Picardi, 2002). Most studies about keystroke dynamics use static authentication method and in most cases the password is analyzed to verify user's identity.

In 1990, Joyce & Gupta (1990) developed a study addressing authentication using static approach at login time. Here, login name, password, user's first and last name information from 33 users were collected 8 times to provide the profiles and 5 times to test the model. The keystroke characteristic studied was the latency between digraphs, using a statistical model as classifier. That model resulted in an FAR of 0.25% and an FRR of 16.67%.

Recently, many studies about this theme of keystroke dynamics were conducted. In 1980, Gaines et al. (1980) published a work about using keystroke dynamics to authenticate a group of seven secretaries using statistical methods. Gaines used three texts from 300 to 400 words each, collecting each one of them twice, making the second collection four months after the first one. Latency between a pair of consecutive keystrokes, called digraphs, was used as a measurement characteristic, but only digraphs that occurred more than 10 times. Gaines method generated an FAR of 0% and an FRR of 4%.

After those studies, many others were developed such as in Obaidat (1995) and Obaidat & Sadoun (1997), where authors reached a result of 100% user classification using several classifiers, both statistical and neural with some classification methods based on neural networks.

Other studies using keystroke dynamics as a user authentication method can be cited, the majority of them using static authentication approach. Those studies can be seen in (Anagun & Cin, 1998; Bleha, Slivinsky & Hussien, 1990; Brown & Rogers, 1993; Capuano, Masella, Miranda & Salerno, 1999; Joyce & Gupta, 1990; Monrose, Reiter & Wetzel, 1999; Obaidat, 1995; Obaidat & Sadoun, 1997). Continuous detection approaches are described in Gaines et al. (1980), Gunetti and Picardi (2005) and Monrose and Rubin (1997). In Coltell, Bada and Torres (1999), both authentication forms are studied. Other interesting studies are: Bergadano, Gunetti and Picardi (2002) that focuses on fixed text detection and uses correlation between keystrokes as a measurement characteristic; and Monrose, Reiter & Wetzel (1999) that proposes a secure password system using keystroke dynamics and also shows that it is possible to develop a file cryptography model based on user's keystroke dynamics information.

As mentioned earlier, mouse usage pattern analysis is another behavioral biometric characteristic that can be used to authenticate users on a computer. Just as keystroke dynamics, user authentication through mouse usage patterns can be performed by a static or dynamic method.

In Aksar and Artun (2009), a static approach of mouse usage patterns is implemented in order to replace the mechanism for login/password. The authors collected features from nine paths between seven squares displayed consecutively on the screen. Results were 5.9% of FAR and FRR of 5.9% using 10 users to test this biometric system.

In Ahmed and Traoré (2007), a dynamic approach to identify user via mouse usage patterns has been implemented. Mouse movements were captured transparently during the use of 22 users, while they performed their routine tasks. These samples were divided into sessions that were later used to verify the accuracy of this biometric system. Main experiment results presented a FAR of 2.4649% and a FRR of 2.4614%.

More recently, some studies started to examine keystroke dynamics on mobile devices, since its use has grown year after year. The same computer authentication problems can also be noted for mobile devices. Some research in this area can be seen in Clarke and Furnell (2007) where experiments were conducted by typing PINs, telephone numbers and text messages. In this study 30 users tested the system and even showed a mean error rate below 5%.

Also in Clarke and Furnell (2007), there is a discussion about complexities of successfully discriminating between users because a single user may incorporate a fairly large spread of latencies values.

Likewise, when entering a text through a keyboard, latency between keystrokes is not a fixed number but a set of values that follow some frequency distribution. User data is compound by the mean and absolute deviation calculated from the latency time between every two keys obtained from user samples. An idea about the kind of problem that needs to be solved can be seen in Figure 1. There we can clearly see that this is a problem where there are overlaps of patterns in the classification patterns and establishing thresholds is extremely complex. In this case, latency observed between two fixed keys may not be enough to clearly determine to which class or to which user a particular latency belongs to. Moreover, the frequency distributions for each two different keys follow different distributions for each user. Thus, the problem of pattern classification extends to an N^N dimension, where N is the number of different keys on a keyboard.

About classification techniques employed, we would find mostly statistical methods, neural networks, and fuzzy logic, among others. Neural network approaches using back-propagation

Figure 1. A schematic example of two-dimensional vector (X1, X2) belonging to 4 classes in order to illustrate the difficulty in establishing an threshold between classes

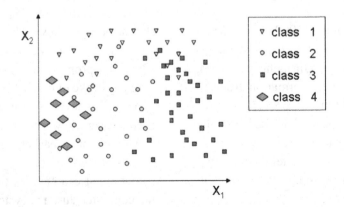

models present high performance results, however each time a new user is introduced into the system the neural networks must be re-trained (Monrose & Rubin, 1997).

ARTIFICIAL NEURAL NETWORKS (ANN)

ANNs are composed by interconnected simple computational units called neurons. The role of a neuron is to map multiple input signals into one output. These inputs can be either signals from out of the network or outputs from other neurons. To perform this input-output mapping, each neuron uses an activation function, usually sigmoid, hyperbolic tangent or even linear (Barreto, 2000).

Neurons are organized into layers where each neuron is fully connected with each neighboring layers neuron. Multilayer perceptron (MLP) networks can have more than one hidden layer, but a single hidden layer is capable of approximating any continuous, multivariate function to any desired degree of accuracy (Haykin 1999).

In MLP networks, each hidden layer neuron calculates its activation through the equation:

$$a_j^h = f^h(\sum_{i=1}^{n} w_{ij}^h x_i^q + b_j) \qquad (1)$$

where a_j^h is the output for the jth neuron in the hidden layer for an input x_i^q, w_{ij}^h is the ith weight of the neuron j, b_j is the bias term for the neuron j and $f^h(.)$ is the activation function. Similarly, the equation for the output layer is:

$$a_k^o = f^o(\sum_{i=1}^{j} w_{ki}^o a_i^h + b_k) \qquad (2)$$

where a_k^o is the output for the kth neuron in the output layer.

ANNs have very interesting organizational principles such as learning, generalization, adaptability, fault tolerance and distributed representation in a network of weights where nodes are artificial neurons. Main characteristics of ANN are their ability to learn complex nonlinear input-output relationships, using sequential training procedures and adapting themselves to the data.

Figure 2 represents an Artificial Neural Network containing three input neurons, two intermediate neurons and two output neurons. All input neurons are connected to all intermediate neurons through synaptic connections (weights) and all intermediate neurons are also connected to all output neurons through synaptic connections.

In pattern classification tasks, ANNs are often used to model decision threshold with a good generalization performance through a model with

Figure 2. Artificial neural network sample

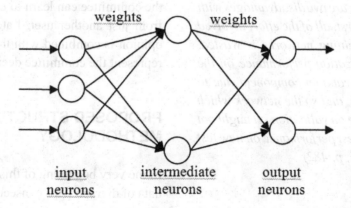

an intermediate degree of complexity. However, in the specific case of keystroke dynamics, the degree of freedom variables problem is quite high and overlapping patterns can occur frequently when analyzing a few pairs of keys. Thus, using a single ANN, performance is unsatisfactory given the complexity of user authentication through keystroke dynamics.

Later in this work, we present ANNs configuration used as well as training stage parameters.

COMMITTEE MACHINES

When a task is too complex, the best thing to do is to divide it into smaller and simpler tasks and combine solutions in order to solve the whole task. Haykin (2001) states that this is the principle of "divide and conquer" (p. 373) often used in Engineering.

Haykin (1999) states that, in supervised learning, computational simplicity is reached by sharing learning tasks among a number of experts that, by their time, divide input space into a set of subspaces. That expert combination constitutes a committee machine.

According to Bishop (1995):

"it is common practice in the application of neural networks to train many different candidate networks and then to select the best, on the basis of performance on an independent validation set for instance, and to keep only this network and to discard the rest. There are two disadvantages with such an approach. First, all of the effort involved in training the remaining networks is wasted. Second, the generalization performance on the validation set has a random component due to the noise on the data, and so the network which had best performance on validation set might not be the one with the best performance on new test data". (Bishop, 1995, p. 482)

So, committee machines are expected to produce better results than using any expert individually, because they combine knowledge from several experts to reach a decision. Committee machines can be categorized in: static structures and dynamic structures (Haykin, 1999).

In static structures, combination mechanism between experts does not depend on input data. This category can also be classified in: ensemble average, where global output is a result of linear combination of each specialist outputs; and reinforcement, where a weak learning algorithm can learn how to reach a higher accuracy.

Dynamic structures involve input data in each expert output combination mechanism to generate the global output. This category can also be divided into 2 methods: mixture of experts, where answers from experts are non-linearly linked by only one gating network; and hierarchical mixture of experts, where several gating networks are disposed hierarchically in order to link non-linearly each expert outputs. Dynamic structures can also be seen as modular networks.

In the method of ensemble average a number of specialists are trained differently sharing the same input data and outputs produced by each one of these experts should be combined to produce a global output. In our work we used an adapted version of the ensemble average mechanism where each expert is trained with different input data (Figure 3). Instead of using a single large structure capable of differentiating the user template from all other users, we proposed that each specialist in the committee can learn to differentiate the user from just another user. Later, each specialist's opinion is combined with the others in order to represent the committee decision.

PROPOSED STRUCTURE AND METHODOLOGY

In the very beginning of this study, we collected data of digraph (two consecutive keystrokes) la-

Figure 3.Committee machine based on ensemble average

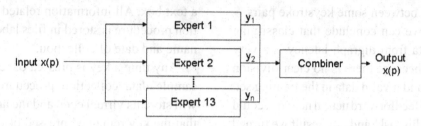

tency time from some volunteers and analyzed its variability and frequency distribution in order to understand the complexity of the pattern recognition problem and to help choosing an appropriate methodology to tackle the problem.

Figure 4 shows some samples of the latency between two consecutive keystrokes (digraph of characters 32-37) for fourteen different users. In the figure we can see that considering one user as a valid sample and all other user as invalid samples, there are intersections in data set. These intersections make it virtually impossible for a single ANN trained with those samples to correctly classify the sample as valid or invalid when a given latency time between those keystrokes is presented to it. When more users are introduced in the neural pattern classifier system, the neural network performance quickly degrades. Looking in the literature for similar works that propose

the use of neural classifiers to authenticate users by keystrokes (Anagun & Cin, 1998; Brown & Rogers, 1993), we see that this problem does not appear because often too small amounts of texts and therefore, digraphs were analyzed. With continuous authentication and the use of large amounts of data for training the system, this problem tends to worsen. Tests with a single ANN structure to represent a user template shows that only 11.5% of data from a test set were correctly classified proving the inefficiency of this proposed structure.

Still looking at the Figure 4, which shows the latency time of a keystroke digraph between many users, we can observe that two or more of them frequently have very similar frequency distribution for that digraph. In the same figure we can observe that user 6 and user 10 have a similar latency. Furthermore, for almost all the digraphs

Figure 4. Latency time of 14 users for a given digraph

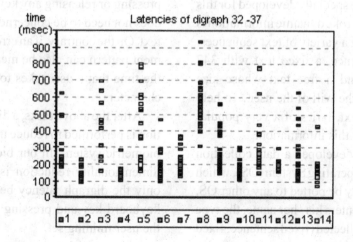

analyzed we observed that 2 or more users had similar latency between some keystroke pairs.

Therefore, we can conclude that classifying users using data from digraph latency is a very complex task, because there is no clear division between valid and invalid data in the training set. So, an ordinary feedforward neural network could not be used in this task, and as a result we turned to the concept of committee machines looking for a solution to this issue.

Our proposed methodology for user authentication through keystroke dynamics consists of by data collection, user template generation and neural experts training at this stage,, the system can operate in a verification stage, where it can be used to authenticate or invalidate a given user according with the templates generated in the first stage. The neural structure of the system is composed of a set of committee machines, where each committee machine is used to represent a user template. Below we explain these 2 stages of the biometric system.

Enrollment and Training Template User Stage

Data Acquisition and Dimensionality Reduction

In the first stage of the biometric system, sample data is collected from all users. The data is collected using software specially developed for this purpose. User's keystroke dynamic information is collected by entering a variety of text sequences: a 32-character sentence, a fixed text with 347 characters length and a free text whose size varies according to the will of the user.. To help memorizing fixed text, lyrics of a very popular song was chosen for this information.

In this work we developed a data collection tool for Windows® Operating System (OS), which however, could easily be ported to any other OS. In this tool the user enters his / her name, the type of text that will be collected (fixed sentence, fixed

text or free text) and then types the sample text in a text box. All information related to the collection procedure is stored in files labeled with user name and date of collection.

Any time a key is pressed or released during sample data collection procedure, the system will store its virtual code and the amount of time that the key remained pressed or released. With this information it is possible to calculate any measure of latency between keystrokes: latency between pressing two keys in succession, pressing and releasing the same key or any other action involving the latency between one or more keys. Thus the biometric system could use any of the characteristics of the latency between keystrokes.

Given that we are particularly interested in the latency time between digraphs, while collecting this measurement our system normalizes and filters the collected data in order to discard interruptions in typing. The latency values between keys are normalized between -1 and 1 considering that the minimum value is 0ms and the maximum is 600ms. This maximum value adopted for the latency was obtained by analyzing frequencies of the latency times between keystrokes of all users, which showed that 95% of digraphs have latency less than 600ms. Latencies greater than 600ms were considered as interruptions in typing and hence were discarded from the neural network training set.

Once a recording event action is triggered by pressing or releasing any key, the capture system does not need to be concerned about errors in the text. On the contrary, if an error occurs, the adjustment pattern can also be measured by analyzing the time that a user takes to delete one or more characters.

After the above tasks, a dimensionality reduction is performed to reduce the cost of processing biometric system. In our biometric system, this dimensionality reduction is achieved by using only the digraph latency between pressing first keyboard key and pressing second key to form the user training set.

Training Set Construction

After users have entered the three types of texts in the data collection tool several times a day and for several days (typically six days), we have a number of samples considered sufficiently representative to form the training set for the neural system.

A user profile based on the training set submitted to the committee machine is constructed from the sample files containing the times collected for the user keystrokes, as follows:

Let x and y two be keys in the keyboard and t^{xy} be the latency time between those keys, the mean latency between x and y is calculated as:

$$\mu^{xy} = \frac{1}{N} \sum_{i=1}^{n} t_i^{xy} \qquad (3)$$

where n is the number of occurrences of the xy digraph in the user samples.

The training set of a user W is represented by a vector Z_w of size s whose elements are ordered triples, as shown in Equation 4.

$$Z_W = [(x_1, y_1, \mu^{x_1 y_1}), (x_1, y_2, \mu^{x_1 y_2}), ..., (x_n, y_n, \mu^{x_n y_n})] \qquad (4)$$

where x_i and y_j are the virtual code of the digraphs keys and $\mu^{x_i y_j}$ is the mean latency time between them.

Neural Network Committee Machine Training

Once the training sets (TS) of all users that want to be registered in the authentication system are prepared, the committee machine that represents each user template and that is capable to authenticate them as legitimate users must be created and trained.

The standard structure of committee machines by ensemble average provides that all inputs of networks are the same. However, in our committee machine, each neural network training set that composes the committee machine that represents a given user template is distinct. This makes each neural network in the committee specialized in validating a given user against just another user, i.e., suppose there are U users registered in the system, the committee machine created for authenticating user W will consist of U-1 networks. Each of these networks will be trained with the training set Z_w of user W, for which the expected network output is 1 (legitimate), and the training set Z_Y of another user Y, for which the expected network output is -1 (intruder). An example of a committee machine responsible for validating user 1 against 13 other registered users in the authentication system can be seen in Figure 5.

The neural networks in the committee are feedforward neural networks trained with backpropagation. They have 513 input neurons, one hidden layer with 10 neurons and a single output neuron. The activation function of the neurons is hyperbolic tangent. The inputs of each neural

Figure 5. Committee machine framework with the user 1 template

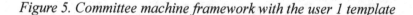
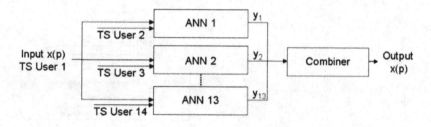

network are coded as follows: the first 256 input neurons encodes the first digraph key pressed while the next 256 input neurons encodes the second digraph key pressed, finally the last input neuron (neuron named latency) receives the normalized value of the mean latency time between the keystrokes. Imagine, for example, that a case in the training set contains the mean time latency of 76 ms between digraphs 84 and 69, then the neurons 84, 325 (256+69) will be activated with

value 1 and the neuron 513 will be activated with -0.746 (the value 76 normalized between -1 and 1). All other input neurons will have the value 0. This coding scheme was chosen after tests with some coding alternatives and it was the one that presented the best results in ANNs training. Figure 6 shows how the above example is coded and presented to ANNs highlighting the activated neurons.

Figure 6. Example of verification procedure for the word "test"

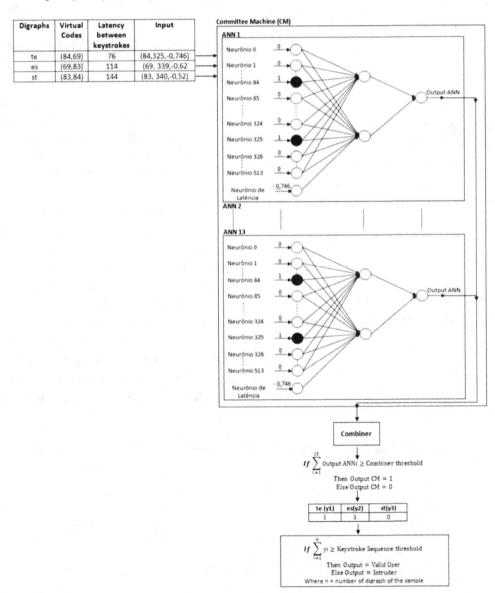

During the training step while a set of *U-1* ANNs sharing the same topology are trained individually in order to represent the user template, we can imagine that the mean latency time between two given users can be the same for some digraphs, what lead some neural networks to be incapable of distinguishing the valid user by looking at just one digraph. Once the committee machine framework takes into account a set of experts, we expect that other neural networks belonging to the committee do not experience same limitation for the same specific digraph and by this way, any ambiguity can be solved. Other problem can occur during the authentication system operation step, where the acquired time latency for a given digraph, while user is typing, will not match exactly the mean latency time used to train the committee machine that represents the user template. These problems can be minimized by assigning an appropriate threshold value to the committee combiner output. This value represents the minimum number of neural networks that compose the committee whose decision correctly classifies the latency time between digraphs as belonging to the valid user. Experiments made to find the appropriate threshold value are presented and discussed later in this text.

After all users *U* have been enrolled in the biometric system, a total amount of *U.(U-1)* neural networks would have been trained and the system will be ready to operate in the Verification Stage, trying to identify whether a given keystroke sequence belongs or not to a defined user template.

Verification Stage

When operating in the verification stage, the committee machine authentication system tries to verify if a given keystroke sequence really belongs to the claimed user identity. In this biometric system stage, a keystroke sequence from the user that wants to be validated is collected, the time latency between keystrokes is extracted, normalized and presented along the digraphs to the user committee machine, so that the system can check whether the sequence really belongs to the true user or to an intruder.

The outcome of the authentication system regarding the authenticity of the user using the keyboard is based on two decisions to make:

1. How many neural networks of the host committee should accept the latency for a given digraph as belonging to the user actually specified? This threshold represents the combiner of the committee machine and is called *"combiner threshold"*; and
2. What must be the minimum percentage of digraphs classified as valid by the committee machine in the keystroke sequence, here called *"keystroke sequence threshold"*?

Thus, the system must check whether a keystroke sequence really belongs to the true user even if the committee machine fails in correctly classify a number of users' digraph latencies, due to lack of digraph information during the neural network training or inconsistent typing rhythm during a short period of time.

For instance, by setting up the *combiner threshold* to 8 and the *keystroke sequence threshold* to 50%, if a given digraph latency is considered belonging to the valid user by at least 8 ANNs of the committee machine and if this occurs in at least 50% of the digraphs in the sequence, then user will successfully be authenticated by the system. Otherwise, the sequence will be flagged as belonging to an intruder. The strictness or flexibility in defining those thresholds imply in different and opposite FAR and FFR rates, resulting in a more or less secure biometric system.

Another expected advantage of using this two-step validation approach is the system robustness in dealing with typing errors or digraphs not belonging to the training set when they are presented in the keystroke sequence. This comes from the fact that a user will not be blocked by the system until the number of digraphs considered invalid in the sequence exceeds defined thresholds.

Figure 6 shows an example of system operation during the verification stage where the word "test" is used as a keystroke sequence to verify user identity. The first table in Figure 6 illustrates how digraphs and their latency are treated and encoded to represent input data to the committee machine. It also shows how the ANN neurons are activated and how each ANN outputs are combined in the committee machine. After this, the *combiner threshold* is applied to decide if the digraph presented to the committee machine is a valid (1) or a false sample (0). Finally, after all digraphs of the keystroke sequence have been presented to the committee machine, their output sequence is verified to test if the *keystroke sequence threshold* is met by the sequence. If this threshold is met, then the keystroke sequence belongs to a valid user, otherwise it belongs to an intruder.

A discussion and some experiments regarding a methodology to find appropriate values for both thresholds are presented in the next section.

EXPERIMENTS AND RESULTS

Before presenting the results of the experiment conducted to test the proposed biometric system, some important aspects of the biometric system construction and a description of training and test sets must be presented.

Users Analyzed: A group of 20 users were analyzed; no special characteristic like typing training was required. Those users were divided into 2 groups. Group 1 involved 14 users who after providing training data, were all enrolled in the system. The users also provided test samples in order to check system effectiveness. On the other hand, group 2 involved 6 users, whose data were used only to test the biometric system, acting as "intruders". Those are essential to check system effectiveness related to false acceptance.

Amount of Samples, Training Sets and Test Sets: Users typed the three target information 5 times each collecting day. Group 2 users performed that procedure only once while group 1 users repeated that six distinct days.

As we consider in our experiments that users from group 1 must be enrolled in the authentication system, their samples will be divided in training sets and test sets. Odd samples of each day make the training set while even collections make the test set.

Therefore, each group 1 user had, for each target information, a training set composed of 18 samples and a test set composed of 12 samples. On the other hand, group 2 users provided only 5 samples of each target information to test the system.

Training sets of each user belonging to group 1 were used to create a user individual template.

Artificial Neural Network: For classification purposes, a direct ANN was implemented with back-propagation learning algorithm using the hyperbolic tangent as output function. The network shows bias in input layer and intermediate layer. We can configure the number of input neurons, number of neurons in the hidden layer, learning coefficient and the number of iterations of the ANN.

The network always uses only one neuron in the output layer. When the output value of the output neuron is greater than or equal to zero the input data presented to the network is considered valid, otherwise it is considered as data coming from intruders.

Experiments

In order to check the performance of the proposed methodology and assess the influence of appropriately setting both committee machine *combiner threshold* and *keystroke sequence threshold*, we describe and report three experiments that were performed. In the first experiment we used fixed thresholds in committee machines classifiers while fixed sentence and fixed text samples were used to test the performance of the committee machines. In the second experiment the same samples were used to test the committee machine classifier while both thresholds were variable for each user. The last experiment was conducted using free text and fixed text information to create the user's template, and committee machines with fixed thresholds and variable thresholds for each user was tested.

In all experiments, each artificial neural network was configured with 513 neurons in input layer, 10 neurons in the intermediate layer and one neuron in the output layer. For training procedure, the neural network performed 5,000 iterations with learning coefficient of 0.065. The training algorithm was back-propagation using hyperbolic tangent as output function. The network shows bias in the input and intermediate layers. These settings were defined after conducting experiments to find best settings for artificial neural network.

Experiment 1: Representing a User by Committee Machines Using the Same Thresholds for Each User

This experiment uses the committee machine proposed in this study to solve the issue of recognizing user keystroke patterns by analyzing user data matched in pairs.

In order to check the effectiveness of using committee machines, this experiment was divided into 2 steps: user analysis by fixed sentence data training set, and user analysis based on fixed text data training set. In this experiment, the committee machines thresholds for all users are set at the same value.

As proposed in the methodology, each user had 13 ANNs trained. Outputs from each ANN are combined so that results can be assessed as valid or not according to the thresholds used for the committee machine framework.

After the training procedure, each test sample from each valid user was presented to trained committee machine in order to evaluate system false

rejection rate (FRR). A set of 170 valid samples were used for this purpose. In order to evaluate system false acceptance rate (FAR), 2,210 test samples were used from each of the 13 users of group 1, whose training sets were used to train each committee machine ANN, along with 490 test samples collected from group 2 users.

Since FAR is broadly inversely proportional to FRR, we must choose threshold values that allow reaching an acceptable result for both rates that assess system effectiveness. This is important because if the system uses high values for both thresholds, most intruders will be rejected but valid users can also be rejected. If the system uses low values for both thresholds, most valid users will never be rejected by the system but intruders can also be accepted.

This experiment yielded the following results (Table 1).

In the fixed sentence (32-character sentence) analysis step, the best results were obtained using *combiner threshold* set to 8 and keystroke sequence threshold equal 65%. In the fixed text (fixed text with 347 characters length) analysis step, the best results were obtained by setting *combiner threshold* to 9 and *keystroke sequence threshold* to 55% or more of sample digraph latencies.

An important issue is analyzing the results of the fixed text analysis step using the best thresholds (*combiner threshold* = 8 and *keystroke sequence threshold* = 65% latencies) of fixed sentence analysis step. Using those thresholds in the fixed text analysis step, experiment resulted in an FRR of 2.35% and an FAR of 2.09%. That improvement in data classification when comparing to fixed sentence analysis is due mostly to a larger amount of data analyzed at fixed text

Table 1. Experiment 1 results

Fixed Sentence		Fixed Text	
FAR	FRR	FAR	FRR
3.77%	4.11%	1.67%	0.58%

step. More data analyzed make the occurrence of more digraphs possible and, therefore, makes the training set more consistent.

To determine the best thresholds to be used, we tested *combiner threshold* value varying from 1 to 13 and *keystroke sequence threshold* value varying from 5% to 95%. We could observe that the best classification results occur when using intermediate values for thresholds or using one threshold with a high value and the other one with a low value. Therefore, the biometric system will reach higher effectiveness when there is a switch between thresholds set to reject intruders and accept most valid users. This becomes necessary due to the inversely proportional characteristic of the relation between both effectiveness measures, FRR and FAR.

Experiment 2: User Representation by Committee Machines Using Distinct Thresholds for Each User

This experiment was performed using the same results of Experiment 1 but, instead of using a fixed threshold for all users, this experiment proposed to use distinct thresholds for each user.

As in the previous experiment, both fixed sentence and fixed text target information were analyzed.

This experiment reached to the results shown in Table 2.

Analyzing Table 2 we can observe that, in fixed sentence analysis, 6 users were perfectly classified by using distinct thresholds for each user. In addition, we can note that only one valid user was incorrectly classified by the system. Regarding FAR, only the 6 perfectly classified users could not be mistaken for other users.

When the classifier used fixed text samples, there is a more significant improvement in system results. Table 2 shows that all users (13 users) were perfectly classified and that the system misclassified only one user (user 14).

Results obtained in this experiment show a significant improvement compared to Experiment 2, which yielded a FRR of 4.11% and a FAR of 3.77% in fixed sentence analysis and an FRR of 0.58% and an FAR of 1.67% in fixed text analysis.

Again, we tested *combiner threshold* value varying from 1 to 13 and *keystroke sequence threshold* value varying from 5% to 95% to find the combination that shows the best results. In this experiment it was found that different users have different best thresholds values.

Experiment 3: Using Free Text and Fixed Text to Create the User Template

This experiment follows the same characteristics as the previous ones, the only difference being that here we used samples of fixed text and free text as a training set for the ANNs. To check effectiveness of this experiment, we analyzed test sets of fixed text. The goal of this experiment is verifying whether when we type texts independently, i.e.

Table 2. Experiment 2 results

User	Fixed Sentence		Fixed Text	
	FAR	FRR	FAR	FRR
User 1	0%	0%	0%	0%
User 2	1.55%	0%	0%	0%
User 3	0%	0%	0%	0%
User 4	0%	0%	0%	0%
User 5	0%	0%	0%	0%
User 6	2.07%	0%	0%	0%
User 7	0.52%	16.66%	0%	0%
User 8	2.07%	0%	0%	0%
User 9	0%	0%	0%	0%
User 10	1.55%	0%	0%	0%
User 11	1.04%	0%	0%	0%
User 12	0%	0%	0%	0%
User 13	2.07%	0%	0%	0%
User 14	3.63%	0%	2.13%	0%
Total	1.04%	1.18%	0.15%	0%

free from need to copy a pre-determined text, user pattern remains constant.

This experiment was divided into 2 steps: tests with same thresholds for all users in their committee machines and tests with user representation by committee machines using distinct thresholds for each user.

This experiment yielded the following results.

In the first stage of this experiment we used a user representation by committee machines using the same thresholds for each user. Best results were obtained when *combiner threshold* is set to 6 and *keystroke sequence threshold* is set to 80%. For these thresholds, the system yields a FRR of 1.76% and a FAR of 3.23%

It is important to observe that compared to the error rate for the best threshold values of Experiment 1 (*combiner threshold* = 8 and *keystroke sequence threshold* = 65%), there is a deterioration in the system effectiveness. A possible explanation for this may be that many times people when typing free information were undecided about what to write. This problem caused much more interruptions in free text typing than in typing a predefined text. Another possibility is that when a user is typing free text, probably, much more typing errors occurs and the number of typed digraphs increases requiring a larger training set to train ANNs.

In the second stage of the experiment, which uses user representation by committee machines using distinct thresholds for each user, the system yields a FRR of 0% and a FAR of 0.27%. Again, the use of different thresholds on committee machines shows an improvement in rates of classification of the users.

FUTURE RESEARCH DIRECTIONS

One improvement to be made in our system is testing committee machine with other characteristics combined with latency between two consecutive keystrokes. Also, in our study, free text informa-tion collected from users was used to test user's templates created with fixed text information collected from these users. In this scenario, the system experienced a slight decrease in performance but continued to have good performance compared to related work. As future work, we intend to use only free text information to create user's templates since this scenario is closer to the practical use of computer, while users are performing their routine tasks. Also, in future works we need to verify how increasing training set including more digraphs in it could affect the system performance.

Another improvement to be implemented in our system in the future is the use of the concept of sessions presented by Ahmed and Traoré (2007) for validating users' data. This concept is important because our current system considers all data from a given sample to classify user as a legitimate user or an intruder. Using sessions makes possible to block computer resources in a smaller time frame than using validation based on all data.

Regarding committee machine, user's template for each user is currently comprised by *U-1* artificial neural networks. New experiments must be performed to identify how many artificial neural networks are necessary to compose one committee machine that can learn classifying patterns of user keystroke dynamics, independently of the number of users registered in the system. This analysis is essential to define if the biometric system is scalable with respect to number of enrolled users and with respect to the operational cost of the biometric system. The goal of this experiment will be to investigate whether a committee machine with a small number of artificial neural networks combining data from the user that is the owner of the template and data from other users may have good results. This would allow forming the committee machine with a fixed number of ANNs and remove the need for having *U-1* ANNs. This results in cost reduction for training, reduction in the size of user's template and in the scalability of using the system when hundreds of users are enrolled in the biometric system.

Finally, our biometric system was tested by a few users when compared with the practical applications of real world. So, experiments with a larger amount of users would be necessary to ensure the robustness and security of the system when used by hundreds or thousands of users

CONCLUSION

From this study we can conclude that it is possible to develop a secure, inexpensive, and continuous authentication method by analyzing the behavioral characteristics of the user keystroke dynamics using committee machines as classifiers.

We can observe that using only one ANN as a classifier might not be appropriate due to the occurrence of ambiguous data in the training set. However, the results obtained using ANNs in an adaptation of committee machines show that it is possible to classify a user as a true user or as an intruder with accuracy comparable with other studies about the subject.

Classification experiments using committee machines show that using a pair of fixed thresholds for all the users, the system yielded a FRR of 4.11% and a FAR of 3.77% when ANNs were trained and tested using fixed sentence samples. When target information used was fixed text, results obtained were a FRR of 0.58% and a FAR of 1.67%. Finally, when we used free text and fixed text for training and fixed text to test, committee machine results were a FRR of 1.76% and a FAR of 3.23%

Using pairs of distinct thresholds for each user, the system achieved a FRR of 1.18% and a FAR of 1.04% for fixed sentence analysis, and a FRR of 0% and a FAR of 0.15% for fixed text analysis. When using free text and fixed text for training and fixed text to verify the performance, committee machines results were a FRR of 0% and a FAR of 0.27%.

From those results we can conclude that the system effectiveness is improved using distinct thresholds for each user. Other conclusion is that using free text in training sets of committee machines caused a slight decrease in performance in the system but does not invalidate its performance.

Analysis of efficacy rates in this study shows that the results of those experiments are very good compared to other works in the area. However, categorizing this work more more or less efficient than the others would be a mistake because of the difference between collected information and number of users involved in the different studies.

When any correction keys were pressed, latency between those keys was also collected. Hence typographical correction is treated just like correct data typing, with no special treatment.

Many studies in this research area show the need to re-train ANNs whenever a new user is added to the system as a major negative factor of using ANNs for authentication. This is the primary contribution of this study, because it shows that using committee machines there is no such need to re-train ANNs. When a new user has to be added to the proposed authentication system, we only have to train the ANNs that will constitute that user's committee machine and a new ANN for the committee machines of all the other users. After training all ANNs we only have to modify the configuration of the committee machine classifier so that it can take into account one more ANN.

REFERENCES

Ahmed, A. A. E., & Traoré, I. (2007). A new biometric technology based on mouse dynamics. *IEEE Transactions on Dependable and Secure Computing, 4*(3), 165–179. doi:10.1109/TDSC.2007.70207

Aksari, Y., & Artuner, H. (2009). *Active authentication by mouse movements*. In The 24th International Symposium on Computer and Information Sciences, ISCIS 2009, (pp. 571–574). Guzelyurt, Turkey.

Anagun, A. S., & Cin, I. (1998). A neural network based computer access security system for multiple users. *Computers & Industrial Engineering, 35*(1-2), 351–354. doi:10.1016/S0360-8352(98)00092-8

Barreto, J. M. (2000). *Inteligência Artificial no limiar do Século XXI: Abordagem Híbrida - simbólica, conexionista e evolutiva* (2nd ed.). Florianópolis, Santa Catarina: Duplic Prest. Serviços.

Bergadano, F., Gunetti, D., & Picardi, C. (2002). User authentication through keystroke dynamics. *ACM Transactions on Information and System Security, 5*(4), 367–397. doi:10.1145/581271.581272

Bishop, C. (1995). *Neural networks for pattern recognition*. Cambridge, UK: Oxford University Press.

Bleha, S., Slivinsky, C., & Hussien, B. (1990). Computer-access security systems using keystroke dynamics. *IEEE Transactions on Pattern Analysis and Machine Intelligence, 12*(12), 1217–1222. doi:10.1109/34.62613

Brown, M., & Rogers, S. J. (1993). User identification via keystroke characteristics of typed names using neural networks. *International Journal of Man-Machine Studies, 39*(6), 999–1014. doi:10.1006/imms.1993.1092

Capuano, N., Masella, M., Miranda, S., & Salerno, S. (1999). User authentication with neural networks. In *Proceedings of the 5th International Conference on Engineering Applications of Neural Networks EANN'99,* (pp. 200-205). Warsaw, Poland.

Clarke, N. L., & Furnell, S. M. (2007). Advanced user authentication for mobile devices. *Computers & Security, 26*(2), 109–119. doi:10.1016/j.cose.2006.08.008

Coltell, O., Bada, J. M., & Torres, G. (1999). Biometric identification system based in keyboard filtering. In *Proceedings of XXXIII Annual IEEE International Carnahan Conference on Security Technology,* (pp. 203-209). Madrid, Spain.

Gaines, R., Lisowski, W., Press, S., & Shapiro, N. (1980). *Authentication by keystroke timing: Some preliminary results*. Rand Report R-256-NSF. Rand Corporation.

Gunetti, D., & Picardi, C. (2005). Keystroke analysis of free text. [ACM TISSEC]. *ACM Transactions on Information and System Security, 8*(3), 312–347. doi:10.1145/1085126.1085129

Haykin, S. (1999). *Neural networks: A comprehensive foundation*. Upper Saddle, NJ: Prentice-Hall, Inc.

Joyce, R., & Gupta, G. (1990). Identity authentication based on keystroke latencies. *Communications of the ACM, 33*(2), 168–176. doi:10.1145/75577.75582

Monrose, F., Reiter, M. K., & Wetzel, S. (1999). Password hardening based on keystroke dynamics. In *Proceedings of the 6th ACM conference on Computer and Communications Security CCS99,* (pp. 73-82). Singapore.

Monrose, F., & Rubin, A. D. (1997). Authentication via keystroke dynamics. In *Proceedings of the 4th ACM Conference on Computer and Communications Security CCS97,* (pp. 48-56). Zurich, Switzerland.

Obaidat, M. S. (1995). A verification methodology for computer systems users. In *Proceedings of the 1995 ACM Symposium on Applied Computing,* (pp. 258-262). Nashville, Tennessee, United States.

Obaidat, M. S., & Sadoun, B. (1997). Verification of computer uses using keystroke dynamics. *IEEE Transactions on Systems, Man, and Cybernetics. Part B, Cybernetics, 27*(2), 261–269. doi:10.1109/3477.558812

ADDITIONAL READING

Alexandre, T. J. (1997). Biometrics on smart cards: An approach to keyboard behavioral signature. *Future Generation Computer Systems - Special issue on smart cards, 13*(1), 19–26.

Araújo, L. C. F. (2004). *Uma Metodologia para Autenticação Pessoal baseada em Dinâmica da Digitação*. Master's dissertation, Universidade Estadual de Campinas, São Paulo, Brazil.

Araujo, L. C. F., Sucupira, L. H. R., Jr., Lizarraga, M. G., Ling, L. L., & Yabu-Uti, J. B. T. (2003). A fuzzy logic approach in typing biometrics user authentication. In *Proc. 1st Indian Int. Conf. Artificial Intelligence*, (pp. 1038–1051). Hyderabad, India.

Araujo, L. C. F., Sucupira, L. H. R. Jr, Lizarraga, M. G., Ling, L. L., & Yabu-Uti, J. B. T. (2005). User authentication through typing biometrics features. *IEEE Transactions on Signal Processing, 53*(2), 851–855. doi:10.1109/TSP.2004.839903

Christodoulakis, S. (1980). An Interactive Pattern Recognition. In *Proceedings of the 11th SIGCSE Technical Symposium on Computer Science Education*, (pp. 184). Kansas City, Missouri, United States.

Clarke, N. L., & Furnell, S. M. (2006). Authenticating mobile phone users using keystroke analysis. *International Journal of Information Security, 6*(1), 1–14. doi:10.1007/s10207-006-0006-6

Filho, S. R. L. S. (2005). *Autenticação Contínua pela Dinâmica da Digitação usando Máquinas de Comitê*. Master's dissertation, Universidade Federal de Santa Catarina, Santa Catarina, Brazil.

Guven, A., & Sogukpinar, I. (2003). Understanding users keystroke patterns for computer access security. *Computers & Security, 22*(8), 695–706. doi:10.1016/S0167-4048(03)00010-5

Hocquet, S., Ramel, J. Y., & Cardot, H. (2004). Users Authentication by a study of human computer interactions. In *8th Annual (Doctoral) Meeting on Health, Science, and Technology.*

Hyrayama, V. (2004). *Classificador de Qualidade de Álcool Combustível e Poder Calorífico de Gás GLP*. Master's dissertation, Universidade de São Paulo, São Paulo, Brazil.

Ilonen, J. (2005). *Keystroke Dynamics*. Lecture presented at the Advanced Topics in Information Processing Lectures, Lappeeranta University of Technology, Lappeeranta, Finland. Retrieved on July, 24, 2005, from http://www.it.lut.fi/kurssit/03-04/010970000/seminars/Ilonen.pdf.

Jain, A. K., Duin, R. P. W., & Mao, J. (2000). Statistical pattern recognition: A review. *IEEE Transactions on Pattern Analysis and Machine Intelligence, 22*(1), 4–37. doi:10.1109/34.824819

Lammers, A., & Langenfeld, S. (1991). Identity Authentication Based on Keystroke Latencies Using Neural Networks. *Journal of Computing Sciences in Colleges, 6*(5), 48–51.

Lee, J. W., Choi, S. S., & Moon, B. R. (2007). An evolutionary keystroke authentication based on ellipsoidal hypothesis space. In *Proceedings of GECCO 2007: Genetic and Evolutionary Computation Conference*, (pp. 2090-2097). London, England.

Lin, D. T. (1997). Computer-Access Authentication with Neural Network Based Keystroke Identity Verification. In *IEEE International Conference on Neural Networks - Conference Proceedings, 1*, (pp. 174-178).

Liu, S., & Silverman, M. (2001). A Practical Guide to Biometric Security Technology. *IT Professional*, *3*(1), 27–32. doi:10.1109/6294.899930

Mahar, D., Napier, R., Wagner, M., Laverty, W., Henderson, R. D., & Hiron, M. (1995). Optimizing digraph-latency based biometric typist verification systems: inter and intra typist differences in digraph latency distributions. *International Journal of Human-Computer Studies*, *43*(4), 579–592. doi:10.1006/ijhc.1995.1061

Miller, B. (1994). Vital signs of identity. *IEEE Spectrum*, *31*(2), 22–30. doi:10.1109/6.259484

Monrose, F., & Rubin, A. D. (2000). Keystroke Dynamics as a Biometric for Authentication. *Future Generation Computer Systems*, *16*(4), 351–359. doi:10.1016/S0167-739X(99)00059-X

Mroczkowski, P. (2004). *Identity Verification using Keyboard Statistics*. Master's dissertation, Linköping Institute of Technology, Linköping, Sweden.

Obaidat, M. S., & Macchairolo, D. T. (1993). An On-Line Neural Network System for Computer Access Security. *IEEE Transactions on Industrial Electronics*, *40*(2), 235–242. doi:10.1109/41.222645

Obaidat, M. S., & Macchairolo, D. T. (1994). A Multilayer Neural Network System for Computer Access Security. *IEEE Transactions on Systems, Man, and Cybernetics*, *24*(5), 806–813. doi:10.1109/21.293498

Obaidat, M. S., & Saudon, B. (1997). A Simulation Evaluation Study of Neural Network Techniques to Computer User Identification. *Information Sciences: an International Journal*, *102*(1-4), 239–258.

Ord, T., & Furnell, S. M. (2000). User authentication for keypad-based devices using keystroke analysis. In *Proceedings of the Second International Network Conference*, (pp. 263-272). Plymouth, UK.

Ru, W. G., & Eloff, J. H. P. (1997). Enhanced Password Authentication through Fuzzy Logic. *IEEE Expert: Intelligent Systems and Their Applications*, *12*(6), 38–45.

Shakshuki, E., Luo, Z., & Gong, J. (2005). An agent-based approach to security service. *Journal of Network and Computer Applications*, *28*(3), 183–208. doi:10.1016/j.jnca.2004.06.004

Song, D., Venable, P., & Perrig, A. (2010). *User Recognition by Keystroke Latency Pattern Analysis*. Retrieved on September, 07, 2010, from http://citeseerx.ist.psu.edu/-viewdoc/download?doi=10.1.1.37.7619&rep=rep1&type=pdf.

Sung, K. S., & Cho, S. (2006). GA SVM Wrapper Ensemble for Keystroke Dynamics Authentication. In: *International Conference on Biometrics*, (pp. 654-660). Hong Kong.

Yu, E., & Cho, S. (2004). Keystroke dynamics identity verification – its problems and practical solutions. *Computers & Security*, *23*(5), 428–440. doi:10.1016/j.cose.2004.02.004

KEY TERMS AND DEFINITIONS

Artificial Neural Networks: Artificial Neural Networks can be seen as a large number of interconnected simple processors, forming a parallel computational system that attempt to use some organizational principles such as learning, generalization, adaptability, fault tolerance and distributed representation in a network of weights where nodes are the artificial neurons.

Authentication: Act of identifying or verifying data authenticity and veracity to prevent that unauthorized users obtain access to the systems.

Biometric Behavioral Characteristic: Those are characteristics related to behavior that can be used to represent a person such as: voice, signature, keystroke dynamics, etc.

Biometrics: is the science that study life being measured. In computational systems, Biometrics is the measurement of any physical or behavioral feature that allows unique identification of an individual.

Committee Machine: This is a combination of expert systems that, grouped in a committee, can make a decision.

False Acceptance Rate: The rate that measures the number of intruders accepted by a biometric system.

False Rejection Rate: The rate that measures the number of legitimate users considered intruders by a biometric system.

Keystroke Dynamics: This is a behavioral biometric feature that identifies an individual through their keyboard typing pattern.

Pattern Recognition: This is the process of classifying data or objects by analyzing their characteristics and observing their similarities.

Compilation of References

AdmitOne Security Inc. (2010). *Home*. Retrieved September 2010, from http://www.admitonesecurity.com/

Ahmed, A. A. E., & Traoré, I. (2007a). A new biometrics technology based on mouse dynamics. *IEEE Transactions on Dependable and Secure Computing*, 4(3), 165–179. doi:10.1109/TDSC.2007.70207

Ahmed, A. A. E., & Traoré, I. (2008). Employee surveillance based on free text detection of keystroke dynamics . In Gupta, M., & Sharman, R. (Eds.), *Handbook of research on social and organizational liabilities in information security* (pp. 47–63). Hershey, PA: Idea Group Publishing. doi:10.4018/978-1-60566-132-2.ch003

Ahmed, A. A. E., & Traoré, I. (2007b). Behavioral biometrics for online computer user monitoring . In Yanushkevich, S. (Eds.), *Image pattern recognition: Synthesis and analysis in biometrics* (pp. 141–161). World Scientific Publishing. doi:10.1142/9789812770677_0010

Ahmed, A. A. E., & Traoré, I. (2005a). Detecting computer intrusions using behavioral biometrics. *Proceedings of 3rd Ann. Conf. on Privacy, Security, and Trust* (pp. 91-98). St. And. NB, Canada.

Ahmed, A. A. E., & Traoré, I. (2005b). Anomaly intrusion detection based on biometrics. *Proceedings of 6th IEEE Information Assurance Workshop, 15-17 June*. West Point, New York, USA.

Ahmed, A. A. E., Traoré, I., & Almulhem, A. (2008b). *Digital fingerprinting based on keystroke dynamics*. International Symposium on Human Aspects of Information Security & Assurance (HAISA 2008) (pp. 94-104). Plymouth, UK.

Ailisto, H. J., Lindholm, M., Mantyjarvi, J., Vildjiounaite, E., & Makela, S.-M. (2005). Identifying people from gait pattern with accelerometers. *Proceedings of the Society for Photo-Instrumentation Engineers*, 5779, 7–14.

Aksari, Y., & Artuner, H. (2009). *Active authentication by mouse movements*. In The 24th International Symposium on Computer and Information Sciences, ISCIS 2009, (pp. 571–574). Guzelyurt, Turkey.

Aleksandrowicz, A., & Leonhardt, S. (2007). Wireless and non-contact ECG measurement system – The Aachen SmartChair. *Acta Polytechnica . Journal of Advanced Engineering*, 47(4–5), 68–71.

Altinok, A., & Turk, M. (2003). Temporal integration for continuous multimodal biometrics. *Proc. Workshop on Multimodal User Authentication*, (pp. 131–137).

Aly, M. A. M. (2009). *A framework for integrating drivers' affective states in GISs using biosignals in a vehicle*. Master thesis, International School of Informatics, Johannes Kepler University Linz, Hagenberg.

Aminian, K., & Najafi, B. (2004). Capturing human motion using body-fixed sensors: outdoor measurement and clinical applications: Research articles. *Comput. Animat. Virtual Worlds*, 15(2), 79–94. doi:10.1002/cav.2

Aminian, K., Robert, P., Buchser, E., Rutschmann, B., Hayoz, D., & Depairon, M. (1999). Physical activity monitoring based on accelerometry: Validation and comparison with video observation. *Medical & Biological Engineering & Computing*, 37(3), 304–308. doi:10.1007/BF02513304

Anagun, A. S., & Cin, I. (1998). A neural network based computer access security system for multiple users. *Computers & Industrial Engineering*, 35(1-2), 351–354. doi:10.1016/S0360-8352(98)00092-8

Annadhorai, A., Guenterberg, E., Barnes, J., Haraga, K., & Jafari, R. (2008). *Human identification by gait analysis.* Paper presented at the HealthNet '08: Proceedings of the 2nd International Workshop on Systems and Networking Support for Health Care and Assisted Living Environments, New York, NY, USA.

Araujo, L. C. F., Sucupira, L. H. R., Lizarraga, M. G., Ling, L. L., & Yabu-Uti, J. B. T. (2005). User authentication through typing biometric features. *IEEE Transactions on Signal Processing, 53*(2), 851–855. doi:10.1109/TSP.2004.839903

Arnrich, B., Setz, C., La Marca, R., Tröster, G., & Ehlert, U. (2010). What does your chair know about your stress level? *IEEE Transactions on Information Technology in Biomedicine, 14*(2), 207–214. doi:10.1109/TITB.2009.2035498

Axelsson, S. (1999). The base-rate fallacy and its implications for the difficulty of intrusion detection. In *Proceedings of the 6th ACM Conference on Computer and Communication Security.* Singapore.

Azzini, A., Marrara, S., Sassi, R., & Scotti, F. (2008). A fuzzy approach to multimodal biometric continuous authentication. *Fuzzy Optimization and Decision Making, 7*, 243–256. doi:10.1007/s10700-008-9034-1

Azzini, A., & Marrara, S. (2008). Impostor users discovery using a multimodal biometric continuous authentication fuzzy system . In Lovrek, I. (Eds.), *KES 2008, Part II, LNAI 5178* (pp. 371–378). Berlin/Heidelberg, Germany: Springer-Verlag.

Bächlin, M., Schumm, J., Roggen, D., & Töster, G. (2009). *Quantifying gait similarity: User authentication and real-world challenge.* Paper presented at the ICB '09: Proceedings of the Third International Conference on Advances in Biometrics, Berlin, Heidelberg.

Bao, L., & Intille, S. (2004). *Activity recognition from user-annotated acceleration data.* Retrieved from http://citeseerx.ist.psu.edu/viewdoc/summary?doi=10.1.1.68.5133

Barnett, M., Leino, R. M., & Schulte, W. (2005). The SPEC# programming system: An overview. *Construction and Analysis of Safe, Secure and Interoperable Smart devices (CASSIS) 2004* [Springer.]. *LNCS, 3362*, 49–69.

Barreto, J. M. (2000). *Inteligência Artificial no limiar do Século XXI: Abordagem Híbrida - simbólica, conexionista e evolutiva* (2nd ed.). Florianópolis, Santa Catarina: Duplic Prest. Serviços.

BBC News online (2000). *You must remember this... that and other.* Retrieved from http://news.bbc.co.uk/1/hi/uk/720976.stm

BBC-News. (2008). *How can you identify a criminal by the way they walk?* Retrieved from http://news.bbc.co.uk/2/hi/uk/_news/magazine/7348164.stm

Beizer, B. (1995). *Black-box testing: Techniques for functional testing of software and systems.* New York, NY: Wiley.

Belhumeur, P. N., Hespanha, J. P., & Kreigman, D. J. (1997, July). Eigenfaces vs. Fisherfaces: Recognition using class specific linear projection. *IEEE Transactions on Pattern Analysis and Machine Intelligence, 19*(7), 711–720. doi:10.1109/34.598228

Bellak, L. (1994). The schizophrenic syndrome and attention deficit disorder: Thesis, antithesis, and synthesis? *American Psychologist, 49*, 25-29.

Ben Abdelkader, C., Cutler, R., Nanda, H., & Davis, L. S. (2001). *EigenGait: Motion-based recognition of people using image self-similarity.* Paper presented at the AVBPA.

Bender, S., & Postley, H. (2007). *Key sequence rhythm recognition system and method.* (US Patent US7206938), US Patent Office.

Benovoy, M., Cooperstock, J. R., & Deitcher, J. (2008). Biosignals analysis and its application in a performance setting – Towards the development of an emotional-imaging generator. *Biosignals, 1*, 253–258.

Bergadano, F., Guneti, D., & Picardi, C. (2002). User authentication through keystroke dynamics. *ACM Transactions on Information and System Security, 5*(4), 367–397. doi:10.1145/581271.581272

Bergadano, F., Gunetti, D., & Picardi, C. (2003). Identity verification through dynamic keystroke analysis. *Journal of Intelligent Data Analysis, 7*(5).

Bhattacharyya, D., Ranjan, R., Alisherov, A., & Choi, M. (2009). Biometric authentication: A review. *International Journal of u-and e-Service . Science and Technology, 2*(3), 13–28.

Biel, L., Petterson, O., & Stork, D. (2001). ECG analysis: A new approach in human identification. *IEE Transactions on Instrumentation and Measurement, 50*(3), 808–812. doi:10.1109/19.930458

Bishop, C. (1995). *Neural networks for pattern recognition*. Cambridge, UK: Oxford University Press.

Bleha, S., Slivinsky, C., & Hussien, B. (1990). Computer-access security systems using keystroke dynamics. *IEEE Transactions on Pattern Analysis and Machine Intelligence, 12*(12), 1217–1222. doi:10.1109/34.62613

Bleha, S. A., Knopp, J., & Obadiat, M. S. (2002). Performance of the perceptron algorithm for the classification of computer users. *Proceedings of the ACM/SIGAPP Symposium on Applied Computing*. New York, NY: ACM Press.

Blobel, P., Zvanmi, L., & Aka, B. (2008). Estimation of mental stress levels based on heart rate variability and stress factor in mobile settings. In *CeHR E-Health Conference Proceedings 2007: Combining Health Telematics, Telemedicine, Biomedical Engineering and Bioinformatics to the Edge*. Akademische Verlagsgesellschaft.

Bobick, A. F. (1997). Movement, activity and action: The role of knowledge in the perception of motion. *Philosophical Transactions of the Royal Society B . Biological Sciences, 352*(1358), 1257–1265. doi:10.1098/rstb.1997.0108

Boswer, B. E., Guyon, I. M., & Vapnik, V. N. (1992). *A training algorithm for optimal margin classifiers*. 5th Annual Workshop on Computational Learning Theory (pp. 144-152).

Bours, P., & Shrestha, R. (2010). *Eigensteps: A giant leap for gait recognition*. Paper presented at the 2nd International Workshop on Security and Communication Networks (IWSCN 2010), Karlstad, Sweden.

Bowyer, K. W., Hollingsworth, K., & Flynn, P. J. (2008). Image understanding for iris biometrics: A survey. *Computer Vision and Understanding, 110*, 281–307. doi:10.1016/j.cviu.2007.08.005

Braff, D. L., & Freedman, R. (2002). Endophenotypes in studies of the genetics of schizophrenia . In Davis, K. L., Charney, D. S., Coyle, I. T., & Nemeroff, C. (Eds.), *Neuropharmacology: The fifth generation of progress* (pp. 703–716). Philadelphia, PA: Lippincott Williams, & Wilkins.

Brown, M., & Rogers, S. J. (1993). User identification via keystroke characteristics of typed names using neural networks. *International Journal of Man-Machine Studies, 39*(6), 999–1014. doi:10.1006/imms.1993.1092

Burges, C. J. C. (1998). A tutorial on support vector machines for pattern recognition. *Data Mining and Knowledge Discovery, 2*(2), 121–167. doi:10.1023/A:1009715923555

Cacioppo, J. T., Bernsten, G. G., Larsen, J. T., Poehlmann, K. M., & Ito, T. A. (2000). The pyschophysiology of emotion . In Lewis, M., & Haviland-Jones, J. M. (Eds.), *The handbook of emotion* (2nd ed., pp. 173–191). New York, NY: Guilford Press.

Calderon, T. G., Akhilesh, C., & Cheh, J. (2006). Modeling an intelligent continuous authentication system to protect financial information resources. *International Journal of Accounting Information Systems, 7*(2), 91–109. doi:10.1016/j.accinf.2005.10.003

Camus, T. A., & Wildes, R. P. (2002). *Reliable and fast eye finding in close-up images*. In International Conference on Pattern Recognition (pp. 389-394).

CanadaNews. (2008). *Forensic gait analysis points to accused*. Retrieved from http://www.canada.com/victoriatimescolonist/news/story.html?id=19d99f1a-bb4d-4d89-a92e-e7a583b1d14f.

Capuano, N., Masella, M., Miranda, S., & Salerno, S. (1999). User authentication with neural networks. In *Proceedings of the 5th International Conference on Engineering Applications of Neural Networks EANN'99*, (pp. 200-205). Warsaw, Poland.

Carrillo, C. (2003). *Continuous biometric authentication for authorized aircraft personnel: A proposed design*. Master's thesis, Naval Postgraduate School.

Chan, A. D. C., Hamdy, M. M., Badre, A., & Badee, V. (2008). Wavelet distance measure for person identification using electrocardiograms. *IEEE Transactions on Instrumentation and Measurement, 57*(2), 248–253. doi:10.1109/TIM.2007.909996

Chandra, A., & Calderon, T. (2005). Challenges and constraints to the diffusion of biometrics in Information Systems. *Communications of the ACM, 48*(12), 101–106. doi:10.1145/1101779.1101784

Chang, W. (2005). Keystroke biometric system using wavelets . In *Advances in Biometrics, Lecture Notes in Computer Science, 3832*. Berlin, Germany: Springer.

Cheng, S. Y., Park, S., & Trivedi, M. M. (2005). Multiperspective thermal IR and video arrays for 3D body tracking and driver activity analysis. In *Proceedings of the 2005 IEEE Computer Society Conference on Computer Vision and Pattern Recognition (CVPR '05)*, (p. 3), Washington, DC: IEEE Computer Society.

Choras, M. (2009). Ear biometrics . In Zi Li, S. (Ed.), *Encyclopedia of biometrics* (pp. 233–241). doi:10.1007/978-0-387-73003-5_173

Choudhury, T., Borriello, G., Consolvo, S., Haehnel, D., Harrison, B., & Hemingway, B. (2008). The mobile sensing platform: An embedded activity recognition system. *IEEE Pervasive Computing / IEEE Computer Society [and] IEEE Communications Society, 7*(2), 32–41. doi:10.1109/MPRV.2008.39

Clarke, N., & Furnell, S. (2007). Authenticating mobile phone users using keystroke analysis. *International Journal of Information Security, 6*(1).

Clarke, N. L., & Furnell, S. M. (2007). Advanced user authentication for mobile devices. *Computers & Security, 26*(2), 109–119. doi:10.1016/j.cose.2006.08.008

Clarke, N., Furnell, S., Lines, B., & Reynolds, P. (2003). Using keystroke analysis as a mechanism for subscriber authentication on mobile handsets. In *Proceedings of the 18th Conference on Information Security. (IFIP/SEC 2003)*. Athens, Greece: Kluwer.

Clifford, G. D., Azuaje, F., & McSharry, P. (2006). *Advanced methods and tools for ECG data analysis*. Norwood, MA: Artech House, Inc.

Coltell, O., Bada, J. M., & Torres, G. (1999). Biometric identification system based in keyboard filtering. In *Proceedings of XXXIII Annual IEEE International Carnahan Conference on Security Technology*, (pp. 203–209). Madrid, Spain.

Coull, S. E., & Szymanski, B. K. (2008). Sequence alignment for masquerade detection. *Computational Statistics & Data Analysis, 52*(8).

Coull, S., Branch, J., Szymanski, B., & Breimer, E. (2003). Intrusion detection: A bioinformatics approach. *Proceedings of the Nineteenth Annual Computer Security Applications Conference*, (pp. 24-34). Las Vegas, NV.

Coutaz, J., Crowley, J., Dobson, S., & Garlan, D. (2005). Context is key. *Communications of the ACM, 48*(3), 49–53. doi:10.1145/1047671.1047703

Crider, A., Kremen, W. S., Xian, H., Jacobson, K. C., Waterman, B., & Eisen, S. A. (2004). Stability, consistency, and heritability of electrodermal response lability in middle-aged male twins. *Psychophysiology, 41*(4), 501–509. doi:10.1111/j.1469-8986.2004.00189.x

Curio, G., & Mueller, K. R. (2007). *Contactless ECG system for emergencies. Press release*. Berlin: Charity, Berlin and Fraunhofer Institute FIRST.

Curtin, M., Tappert, C., Villani, M., Ngo, G., Simone, J., St. Fort, H., & Cha, S.-H. (2006). *Keystroke biometric recognition on long-text input: A feasibility study*. The 2006 IAENG International Workshop on Scientific Computing and Computational Statistics.

Dalageorgou, C., Ge, D., Jamshidi, Y., Nolte, I. M., Riese, H., & Savelieva, I. (2007). Heritability of QT interval: How much is explained by genes for resting heart rate? *Journal of Cardiovascular Electrophysiology, 19*(4), 386–391. doi:10.1111/j.1540-8167.2007.01030.x

Dash, M., & Liu, H. (1997). Feature selection for classification. *Intelligent Data Analysis, 1*, 131–156. doi:10.1016/S1088-467X(97)00008-5

Daugman, J. (2004). How iris recognition works. *IEEE Transactions on Circuits and Systems for Video Technology, 14*(1), 21–30. doi:10.1109/TCSVT.2003.818350

de Lima e Silva Filho. S. R., & Roisenberg, M. (2006). Continuous authentication by keystroke dynamics using committee machines. In S. Mehotra, et al. (Eds.), *ISI 2006, LNCS 3975* (pp. 686-687). Berlin/Heidelberg, Germany: Springer-Verlag.

De Looze, M., Kuijt-Evers, L., & Van Dieen, J. (2003). Sitting comfort and discomfort and the relationships with objective measures. *Ergonomics*, *46*(10), 985–997. doi:10.1080/0014013031000121977

De Oliveira, M. V. S., Kinto, E. A., Hernandez, E. D. M., & de Carvalho, T. C. M. (2005). User authentication based on human typing patterns with artificial neural networks and support vector machines. *XXV Congresso de Sociedade Brasileira de Computacao*, (pp. 484-493).

de Ru, W. G., & Eloff, J. H. P. (1997). Enhanced password authentication through fuzzy logic. *IEEE Expert*, *12*(6), 38–45. doi:10.1109/64.642960

DeLoney, C. (2008). *Person identification and gender recognition from footstep sound using modulation analysis.* (Technical Report TR 2008-17), University of Maryland. Retrieved December 28, 2010, from http://drum.lib.umd.edu/bitstream/1903/8379/3/DeLoney.pdf

Denning, D. E., & Neumann, P. G. (1985). *Requirements and model for IDES - A real-time intrusion detection system. Technical report, Computer Science Laboratory.* Menlo Park, CA: SRI International.

Derawi, M. O., Bours, P., & Holien, K. (2010). *Improved cycle detection for accelerometer based gait authentication.* Paper presented at the International Conference on Intelligent Information Hiding and Multimedia Signal Processing - Special Session on Advances in Biometrics.

Docter, R. F., & Friedman, L. F. (1965). Thirty-day stability of spontaneous galvanic skin responses in man. *Psychophysiology*, *2*(4), 311–315. doi:10.1111/j.1469-8986.1966.tb02659.x

Dong-Oh, K., Hyung-Jik, L., Eun-Jung, K., Kyuchang, K., & Jeunwoo, L. (2006). *A wearable context aware system for ubiquitous healthcare.* Paper presented at the Engineering in Medicine and Biology Society, 2006. EMBS '06. 28th Annual International Conference of the IEEE.

Dorigo, M., Gambardella, L. M., Birattari, M., Martinoli, A., Poli, R., & Stützle, T. (2006). *Ant colony optimization and swarm intelligence.* 5th International Workshop ANTS, LNCS 4150, Springer Verlag.

Dowland, P., & Furnell, S. (2004). A long-term trial of keystroke profiling using digraph, trigraph and keyword latencies. In *Proceedings of IFIP/SEC 2004 - 19th International Conference on Information Security*, (pp. 4275– 4289).

Dowland, P., Furnell, S., & Papadaki, M. (2002). Keystroke analysis as a method of advanced user authentication and response. In *Proceedings of the 17th IFIP/SEC 2002 Conference.* Cairo, Egypt: Kluwer.

Dowland, P., Singh, H., & Furnell, S. (2001). A preliminary investigation of user authentication using continuous keystroke analysis. In *Proceedings 8th IFIP Annual Working Conference on Information Security Management and Small System Security.* Las Vegas, Nevada.

Duin, R. P. W., & Tax, D. M. J. (2000). Experiments with classifier combining rules. *Proc. First Workshop Multiple Classifier Systems*, (pp. 16-29).

Edelberg, R. (1971). Electrical properties of skin . In Elden, H. R. (Ed.), *A treatise of the skin* (*Vol. 1*, pp. 519–551). New York, NY: Wiley.

Erzin, E., Yemez, Y., Tekalp, A. M., Ercil, A., Erdogan, H., & Abut, H. (2006). Multimodal person recognition for human-vehicle interaction. *IEEE MultiMedia*, *13*(2), 18–31. doi:10.1109/MMUL.2006.37

Farlex. (n.d.). *The free dictionary.* Retrieved from http://www.thefreedictionary.com/gait

Farrahi, K., & Gatica-Perez, D. (2008). *What did you do today? Discovering daily routines from large-scale mobile data.* Paper presented at the ACM International Conference on Multimedia (ACMMM). Retrieved from http://publications.idiap.ch/index.php/publications/showcite/farrahi:rr08-49

Fawcett, T., & Provost, F. (1999). Activity monitoring: Noticing interesting changes in behavior. *Proceedings of the Fifth International Conference on Knowledge Discovery and Data Mining* (pp. 53-62).

Fisher, R. A. (1936). The use of multiple measures in taxonomic problems. *Annals of Eugenics*, *7*, 179–188. doi:10.1111/j.1469-1809.1936.tb02137.x

Flior, E., & Kowalski, K. (2010). *Continuous biometric user authentication in online examinations*. Seventh International Conference on Information Technology: New Generations (ITING), Las Vegas Nevada, USA, 12-14 April, 2010, 2010, (pp. 488-492).

Foerster, F., & Fahrenberg, J. (2000). Motion pattern and posture: Correctly assessed by calibrated accelerometers. *Behavior Research Methods, Instruments, & Computers*, *32*(3), 450–457. doi:10.3758/BF03200815

Foerster, F., Smeja, M., & Fahrenberg, J. (1999). Detection of posture and motion by accelerometry: A validation study in ambulatory monitoring. *Computers in Human Behavior*, *15*(5), 571–583. doi:10.1016/S0747-5632(99)00037-0

Forsen, G., Nelson, M., & Staron, R. (1977). Personal attributes authentication techniques . In Griffin, A. F. B. (Ed.), *RADC report RADC-TR-77-1033*.

Frank, J., Mannor, S., & Precup, D. (2010). *Activity and gait recognition with time-delay embeddings*.

Freund, Y., & Schapire, R. E. (1995). A decision-theoretic generalization of online learning and an application to boosting.

Gafurov, D. (2008). *Performance and security analysis of gait-based user authentication*. Faculty of Mathematics and Natural Sciences, University of Oslo.

Gafurov, D., & Bours, P. (2010). Improved hip-based individual recognition using wearable motion recording sensor . In Kim, T.-H., Fang, W.-C., Khan, M. K., Arnett, K. P., Kang, H.-J., & Ślęzak, D. (Eds.), *Security technology, disaster recovery and business continuity* (Vol. 122, pp. 179–186). Berlin/Heidelberg, Germany: Springer. doi:10.1007/978-3-642-17610-4_20

Gafurov, D., & Snekkeness, E. (2009). Gait recognition using wearable motion recording sensors. *Eurasip Journal on Advances in Signal Processing*, vol. 2009, Article ID 415817 (16 pages), Hindawi Publishing Corporation.

Gafurov, D., Snekkenes, E., & Bours, P. (2010). *Improved gait recognition performance using cycle matching*. Paper presented at the 2010 IEEE 24th International Conference on Advanced Information Networking and Applications Workshops.

Gaines, R., Lisowski, W., Press, S., & Shapiro, N. (1980). *Authentication by keystroke timing: Some preliminary results*. Technical Report R-256-NSF, Rand Corporation.

Gamboa, H., & Fred, A. (2003). An identity authentication system based on human computer interaction behavior. *Proceedings of 3rd International Conference on Pattern Recognition in Information Systems*.

Garcia, J. (1986). *Personal identification apparatus*. (Patent Number 4.6X.334). Washington, DC: US Patent and Trademark Office.

Garg, A., Rhalkar, R., Upadhyaya, S., & Kwiat, K. (2006). Profiling users in GUI based systems for masquerade detection. *Proceedings of the 2006 IEEE Workshop on Information Assurance* (pp. 48-54). West Point, NY.

Giles, E. (1970). Discriminant function sexing of the human skeleton . In Stewart, T. D. (Ed.), *Personal identification in mass disasters* (pp. 99–109). Washington, D.C.: Smithsonian Institution.

Gilmore, C. S., Malone, S. M., & Iacono, W. G. (2010). Brain electrophysiological endophenotypes for externalizing psychopathology: A multivariate approach. *Behavior Genetics*, *40*(2), 186–200. doi:10.1007/s10519-010-9343-3

Goecks, J., & Shavlik, J. (1999). Automatically labeling Web pages based on normal user actions. *Procedings of the IJCAI Workshop on Machine Learning for Information Filtering*.

Gottesman, H., & Shields, J. (1972). *Schizophrenia and genetics: A twin study vantage point*. New York, NY: Academic Press.

Gottesmann, I. I. (2003). The endophenotype concept in psychiatry: Etymology and strategic intentions. *The American Journal of Psychiatry*, *160*(4), 636–645. doi:10.1176/appi.ajp.160.4.636

GPSBabel. (2010). *Convert, upload, download data from GPS and map programs*. Retrieved December 28, 2010, from http://www.gpsbabel.org/

Guneti, D., & Picardi, C. (2005). Keystroke analysis of free text. *ACM Transactions on Information and System Security*, *8*(3), 312–347. doi:10.1145/1085126.1085129

Gunetti, D., Picardi, C., & Ruffo, G. (2005a) Dealing with different languages and old profiles in keystroke analysis of free text. In S. Bandini, (Ed.), *Proceedings of the Ninth Congress of the Italian Association for Artificial Intelligence (AI*IA-2005)*, (LNCS 3673, pp. 347–358). Milan, Italy: Springer-Verlag.

Guo, Z., Zhang, L., & Zhang, D. (2010). *Feature band selection for multispectral palmprint recognition.* International Conference on Pattern Recognition (pp. 1–4).

Hamdy, O., & Traoré, I. (2009). New physiological biometrics based on human cognitive factors. *Proceedings of the International Conference on Complex, Intelligent, and Software Intensive Systems (CISIS)*, Fukoka, Japan, (pp. 910-917).

Hansell, N. K., Wright, M. J., Geffen, G. M., Geffen, L. B., Smith, G. A., & Martin, N. G. (2001). Genetic influences on ERP slow wave measures of working memory. *Behavior Genetics*, *31*(6), 603–614. doi:10.1023/A:1013301629521

Hao, Y., Sun, Z., & Tan, T. (2007). Comparative studies on multispectral palm image fusion for biometrics. *Asian Conference on Computer Vision, 2*, (pp. 12–21).

Hao, Y., Sun, Z., Tan, T., & Ren, C. (2008). *Multi spectral palm image fusion for accurate contact free palmprint recognition.* 15th International Conference on Image Processing, (pp. 281 – 284).

Hashia, S. (2004). *Authentication by mouse movements.* San Jose State University.

Haykin, S. (1999). *Neural networks: A comprehensive foundation.* Upper Saddle, NJ: Prentice-Hall, Inc.

Hempstalk, K. (2009). *Continuous typist verification using machine learning.* PhD Thesis, University of Wakaito, Hamilton, New Zealand.

Henriksen, M., Lund, H., Moe-Nilssen, R., Bliddal, H., & Danneskiod-Samsøe, B. (2004). Test-retest reliability of trunk accelerometric gait analysis. *Gait & Posture*, *19*(3), 288–297. doi:10.1016/S0966-6362(03)00069-9

Hetzel, W. C. (1998). *The complete guide to software testing* (2nd ed.). Wellesley, MA: QED Information Sciences.

Hocquet, S., Ramel, J. Y., & Cardot, H. (2004). Users authentication by a study of human computer interaction. *Proc. Eighth Ann. (Doctoral) Meeting on Health, Science and Technology*.

Hocquet, S., Ramel, J., & Carbot, H. (2006). Estimation of user specific parameters in one-class problems. In *Proceedings of the 18th International Conference on Pattern Recognition (ICPR'06)* volume 4. Washington, DC: IEEE Computer Society.

Holien, K. (2008). *Gait recognition under non-standard circumstances.* Master thesis, Gjøvik Univeristy College.

Horprasert, T., Harwood, D., & Davis, L. (1999). *A statistical approach for real-time robust background subtraction and shadow detection.* Paper presented at the ICCV Frame-Rate WS.

Huang, B., Chen, M., Huang, P., & Xu, Y. (2007). *Gait modeling for human identification.* Paper presented at the International Conference on Robotics and Automation.

Hurley, D., Arbab-Zavar, B., & Nixon, M. (2008). The ear as a biometric. In S. Zi Li (Ed.), *Handbook of biometrics*, (pp. 131–150). Springer Science+Business Media.

Hussain, B., McLaren, R., & Bleha, S. (1989). An application of fuzzy algorithms in a computer access security system. *Pattern Recognition Letters*, *9*, 39–43. doi:10.1016/0167-8655(89)90026-3

Hynes, M., Wang, H., & Kilmartin, L. (2009). Off-the-shelf mobile handset environments for deploying accelerometer based gait and activity analysis algorithms. *Conference Proceedings; ... Annual International Conference of the IEEE Engineering in Medicine and Biology Society. IEEE Engineering in Medicine and Biology Society. Conference*, *1*, 5187–5190.

IBIA. (2010). *International Biometrics & Identification Association* (IBIA). Retrieved December 28, 2010, from http://www.ibia.org/

Ibrahim, R. K., Ambikairajah, E., Celler, B., Lovell, N. H., & Kilmartin, L. (2008). *Gait patterns classification using spectral features.* Paper presented at the IET Irish Signals and Systems Conference (ISSC).

Intersense. (2010). *Precision motion tracking solutions – InertiaCube.* Retrieved December 28, 2010, from http://www.intersense.com/categories/18/

Iso, T., & Yamazaki, K. (2006). *Gait analyzer based on a cell phone with a single three-axis accelerometer.* Paper presented at the MobileHCI '06: Proceedings of the 8th Conference on Human-Computer Interaction with Mobile Devices and Services, New York, NY, USA.

Israel, S., Irvine, J., Cheng, A., Wiederhold, M., & Wiederhold, B. (2005). ECG to identify individuals. *Pattern Recognition, 38*(1), 133–142. doi:10.1016/j.patcog.2004.05.014

Jagadeesan, H., & Hsiao, M. (2009). A novel approach to design of user re-authentication systems. *Proceedings of the IEEE Conference on Biometrics: Theory, Applications and Systems,* (pp. 379-384).

Jain, A. K., Flynn, P., & Ross, A. (2007). *Handbook of biometrics.* Springer-Verlag.

Jain, A., Griess, F., & Connell, S. (2002). Online signature verification. *Pattern Recognition, 35,* 2963–2972. .doi:10.1016/S0031-3203(01)00240-0

Jain, A. K., Flynn, P., & Ross, A. A. (Eds.). (2008). *Handbook of biometrics.* Springer. doi:10.1007/978-0-387-71041-9

Joachims, T. (1999). Making largescale SVM learning practical . In Scholkopf, B., Burges, C. J. C., & Smola, A. J. (Eds.), *Advances in kernel methods- Support vector learning.* MIT Press.

Joyce, R., & Gupta, G. (1990). User authorization based on keystroke latencies. *Communications of the ACM, 33*(2), 168–176. doi:10.1145/75577.75582

Joyce, R., & Gupta, G. (1990). Identity authentication based on keystroke latencies. *Communications of the ACM, 33*(2), 168–176. doi:10.1145/75577.75582

Kale, A., Cuntoor, N., & Chellappa, R. (2002). *A framework for activity-specific human identification.* Paper presented at the Acoustics, Speech, and Signal Processing.

Kang, H.-B., & Ju, M.-H. (2006). Multi-modal feature integration for secure authentication. *Proc. International Conference on Intelligent Computing* (pp. 1191–1200).

Kantz, H., & Schreiber, T. (2008). Nonlinear time series analysis. *The Economic Record, 84*(266), 396–397. doi:10.1111/j.1475-4932.2008.00502.x

Kasukawa, M., Mori, Y., Komatsu, K., Akaike, H., & Kakuda, H. (1992). An evaluation and improvement of user authentication system based on keystroke timing data. [in Japanese]. *Transactions of Information Processing Society of Japan, 33*(5), 728–735.

Kim, D., Seo, Y., Kim, S.-H., & Jung, S. (2008). Short term analysis of long term patterns of heart rate variability in subjects under mental stress. In *Proceedings of the 2008 International Conference on BioMedical Engineering and Informatics (BMEI 2008),* (vol. 2, pp. 487–491). Washington, DC: IEEE Computer Society.

Kisku, D. R., Sing, J. K., Tistarelli, M., & Gupta, P. (2009). *Multisensor biometric evidence fusion for person authentication using wavelet decomposition and monotonic-decreasing graph.* 7th IEEE International Conference on Advances in Pattern Recognition, (pp. 205—208).

Klosterman, A., & Ganger, G. (2000). *Secure continuous biometric-enhanced authentication.* Technical Report CMU-CS-00-134, Carnegie Mellon University.

Koenig, P. (2004). Personal identification method and apparatus using acoustic resonance analysis of body parts. *Acoustical Society of America Journal, 116*(3), 1328–1328. doi:10.1121/1.1809922

Kong, W. K., Zhang, D., & Li, W. (2003). Palmprint feature extraction using 2-D Gabor filters. *Pattern Recognition, 36,* 2339–2347. doi:10.1016/S0031-3203(03)00121-3

Kong, A., & Zhang, D. (2004). *Competitive coding scheme for palmprint verification.* International Conference on Pattern Recognition, 1, (pp. 520 – 523).

Korotkaya, Z. (2003). Biometric person authentication: Odor . In *Advanced topics in information processing: Biometric person authentication* (p. 16). Department of Information Technology, Laboratory of Applied Mathematics, Lappeenranta University of Technology.

Korpipää, P., Koskinen, M., Peltola, J., Mäkelä, S.-M., & Seppänen, T. (2003). Bayesian approach to sensor-based context awareness. *Personal and Ubiquitous Computing, 7*(2), 113–124. doi:10.1007/s00779-003-0237-8

Kotani, K., Norioka, Y., & Horii, K. (2005). Construction and evaluation of keystroke authentication system using the numerical keypad. [in Japanese]. *The Transaction of Human Interface Society, 7*(1), 149–156.

Krumm, J., & Horvitz, E. (2006). Predestination: Inferring destinations from partial trajectories . In Dourish, P., & Friday, A. (Eds.), *UbiComp 2006: Ubiquitous Computing* (*Vol. 4206*, pp. 243–260). Berlin / Heidelberg, Germany: Springer. doi:10.1007/11853565_15

Kumar, S., Sim, T., Kanakiraman, R., & Zhang, S. (2005). Using continuous biometric verification to protect interactive login sessions. *Proceedings of the 21st Annual Computer Security Applications Conference* (ACSAC 2005).

Kung, S. Y., Mak, M. W., & Lin, S. H. (2004). *Biometric authentication, a machine learning approach* (pp. 1–20). Prentice Hall.

Kwang, G., Yap, R. H. C., Sim, T., & Ramnath, R. (2009). An usability study of continuous biometrics authentication. *ICB 2009* . *LNCS, 5558*, 828–837.

Lalor, E. C., Kelly, S. P., Finucane, C., Burke, E., Smith, R., Reilly, R. B., & McDarby, G. (2005). Steady-state VEP-based brain-computer interface control in an immersive 3D gaming environment. *EURASIP Journal on Applied Signal Processing, 19*, 3156–3164. doi:10.1155/ASP.2005.3156

Lane, T., & Brodley, C. E. (1999). Temporal sequence learning and data reduction for anomaly detection. *ACM Transactions on Information and System Security, 2*(3), 295–331. doi:10.1145/322510.322526

Larsen, P. K., Simonsen, E. B., & Lynnerup, N. (2008). Gait analysis in forensic medicine. *Journal of Forensic Sciences, 53*(5), 1149–1153. doi:10.1111/j.1556-4029.2008.00807.x

Lee, T. S. (1996). Image representation using 2D Gabor wavelets. *IEEE Transactions on Pattern Analysis and Machine Intelligence, 18*, 959–971. doi:10.1109/34.541406

Lee, C.-Y., & Lee, J.-J. (2002). Estimation of walking behavior using accelerometers in gait rehabilitation. *International Journal of Human-friendly Welfare Robotic Systems, 3*, 32–36.

Lee, S.-W., & Mase, K. (2002). Activity and location recognition using wearable sensors. *IEEE Pervasive Computing / IEEE Computer Society [and] IEEE Communications Society, 1*(3), 24–32. doi:10.1109/MPRV.2002.1037719

Leggett, J., & Williams, G. (1988). Verifying identity via keystroke characteristics. *International Journal of Man-Machine Studies, 28*(1), 67–76. doi:10.1016/S0020-7373(88)80053-1

Leggett, J., Williams, G., & Umphress, D. (1988). Verification of user identity via keyboard characteristics . In Carey, J. M. (Ed.), *Human factors in management Information Systems*. Norwood, NJ: Ablex Publishing.

Lenzenwenger, M. F., Mclachlan, G., & Rubin, D. B. (2007). Resolving the latent structure of schizophrenia endophenotypes using expectation-maximization-based finite mixture modeling. *Journal of Abnormal Psychology, 116*(1), 116–129.

Lester, J., Choudhury, T., & Borriello, G. (2006). A practical approach to recognizing physical activities . In Fishkin, K., Schiele, B., Nixon, P., & Quigley, A. (Eds.), *Pervasive computing* (*Vol. 3968*, pp. 1–16). Berlin / Heidelberg, Germany: Springer. doi:10.1007/11748625_1

Li, J., Zheng, R., & Chen, H. (2006). From fingerprint to writeprint. *Communications of the ACM, 49*(4), 77–82. doi:10.1145/1121949.1121951

Li, X. (2006, January). Modeling intra-class variation for non-ideal iris recognition. *Springer International Conference on Biometrics, LNCS 3832* (pp. 419-427).

Liao, L., Fox, D., & Kautz, H. (2007). Extracting places and activities from gps traces using hierarchical conditional random fields. *The International Journal of Robotics Research, 26*(1), 119–134. doi:10.1177/0278364907073775

Liu, Y.-C. (2001). Comparative study of the effects of auditory, visual and multimodality displays on drivers performance in advanced traveller Information Systems. *Ergonomics, 44*(18), 425–442. doi:10.1080/00140130010011369

Liu, J., Yu, F. R., Lung, C.-H., & Tang, H. (2007). *Optimal biometric-based continuous authentication in mobile ad hoc networks*. 3rd IEEE International Conference on Wireless and Mobile Computing, Networking and Communications (WiMob 2007).

Liu, X., Chen, T., & Vijaya Kumar, B. V. K. (2002, May). *on modeling variations for face authentication*. In *the Proceedings of the International Conference on Automatic Face and Gesture Recognition 2002*, (pp. 369-374).

Looney, C. (1997). *Pattern recognition using neural networks – Theory and algorithms for engineers and scientists* (pp. 124–126). Oxford University Press.

Lopes Machado, E. Z., de Souza Crippa, J. A., Cecdio Hcdlak, J. E., Quimarcies, F. S., & Zuardi, A. W. (2003). Electrodermically nonresponsive schizophrenia patients make more errors in the stroop color word test, indicating selective attention deficit. *Schizophrenia Bulletin, 28*(3), 459–466.

Lunt, T. F., Tamaru, A., Gilham, F., Jagannathan, R., Neumann, P. G., & Javitz, H. S. … Garvey, T. D. (1992). *A real-time intrusion detection expert system IDES - Final report*. Technical Report SRI-CSL-92-05, SRI Computer Science Laboratory, SRI International.

Luo, Y.-C. (1995). Sex determination from the pubis by discriminant function analysis. [Forensic Anthropology Around the World.]. *Forensic Science International, 74*(1–2), 89–98. doi:10.1016/0379-0738(95)01739-6

Mansfield, A. J., & Wayman, J. L. (2002). *Best practices in testing and reporting performances of biometric devices*. Deliverable of the Biometric Working Group of the CESG Gov. Communication Headquarters of the United Kingdom. National Physical Laboratory, Report CMCS 14/02. Teddington, United Kingdom. Retrieved from www.cesg.gov.uk/technology/biometrics/media/Best%20Practice.pdf

Mantyjarvi, J., Lindholm, M., Vildjiounaite, E., Makela, S.-M., & Ailisto, H. A. (2005). *Identifying users of portable devices from gait pattern with accelerometers*. IEEE International Conference on Acoustics, Speech, and Signal Processing (ICASSP '05), 2, (pp. 973-976).

Marcel, S., & Millan, J. R. (2007). Person authentication using brainwaves (EEG) and maximum a posterior model adaptation. *IEEE Transactions on Pattern Analysis and Machine Intelligence, 29*(4), 743–752. doi:10.1109/TPAMI.2007.1012

Maricopa Association of Governments. (2006). *Vehicle occupancy study*. Technical report. Retrieved December 28, 2010, from http://www.mag.maricopa.gov

Matey, J. R., Naroditsky, O., Hanna, K., Kolczynski, R., Lolacono, D. J., & Mangru, S. (2006). Iris on the move: Acquisition of images for iris recognition in less constrained environments. *Proceedings of the IEEE, 94*(11), 1936–1946. doi:10.1109/JPROC.2006.884091

Mathie, M., Coster, A., Lovell, N., & Celler, B. (2003). Detection of daily physical activities using a triaxial accelerometer. *Medical & Biological Engineering & Computing, 41*(3), 296–301. doi:10.1007/BF02348434

Mathie, M., Coster, A., Lovell, N., & Celler, B. (2004). Accelerometry: Providing an integrated, practical method for long-term, ambulatory monitoring of human movement. *Physiological Measurement, 25*(2), R1. doi:10.1088/0967-3334/25/2/R01

Matyas, V. Jr, & Riha, Z. (2003). Toward reliable user authentication through biometrics. *IEEE Security & Privacy Magazine, 1*(3), 45–49. doi:10.1109/MSECP.2003.1203221

Maxion, R. A., & Townsend, T. N. (2004). Masquerade detection augmented with error analysis. *IEEE Transactions on Reliability Analysis, 53*(1), 124–147. doi:10.1109/TR.2004.824828

McCraty, R., Atkinson, M., Tiller, W. A., Rein, G., & Watkins, A. D. (1995). The effects of emotions on short-term power spectrum analysis of heart rate variability. *The American Journal of Cardiology, 76*, 1089–1093. doi:10.1016/S0002-9149(99)80309-9

McHugh, J. (2000). Testing intrusion detection systems. *ACM Transactions on Information and System Security, 3*(4), 262–294. doi:10.1145/382912.382923

Mehta, S. S., & Lingayat, N. S. (2007). Comparative study of QRS detection in single lead and 12-lead ECG based on entropy and combined entropy criteria using support vector machine. *Journal of Theoretical and Applied Information Technology, 3*, 8–18.

Mendes, W. B. (2009). Assessing the autonomic nervous system. In Harmon-Jones, E., & Beer, J. (Eds.), *Methods in social neuroscience* (pp. 118–147). Guilford Press.

Mészáros, A., Bankó, Z., & Czúni, L. (2007). Strengthening passwords by keystroke dynamics. *IEEE International Workshop on Intelligent Data Acquisition and Advanced Computing Systems: Technology and Applications*. Dortmund, Germany

Micheli-Tzanakou, E. (1999). *Supervised and unsupervised pattern recognition – Feature extraction and computational intelligence* (pp. 265–267). CRC Press.

Middleton, L., Buss, A. A., Bazin, A., & Nixon, M. S. (2005). *A floor sensor system for gait recognition*. Paper presented at the AUTOID '05: Proceedings of the Fourth IEEE Workshop on Automatic Identification Advanced Technologies, Washington, DC, USA.

Mirsky, A. F., Yardley, S. L., Jones, B. P., Walsh, D., & Kendler, K. S. (1995). Analysis of the attention deficit in schizophrenia: A study of patients and their relatives in Ireland. *Journal of Psychiatric Research, 29*, 23–42. doi:10.1016/0022-3956(94)00041-O

Mohammadi, G., Shousttari, P., Ardekani, B. M., & Shamsolhani, M. B. (2006). Person identification by using AR model for EEG signals. *Proceedings of WASET, 11*, 281–285.

Monrose, F., & Rubin, A. (2000). Keystroke dynamics as a biometric for authentication. *Future Generation Computer Systems, 16*(4), 351–359. doi:10.1016/S0167-739X(99)00059-X

Monrose, F., & Rubin, A. D. (1997). Authentication via keystroke dynamics. In *Proceedings of the 4th ACM Conference on Computer and Communications Security CCS97*, (pp. 48-56). Zurich, Switzerland.

Monrose, F., Reiter, M. K., & Wetzel, S. (1999). Password hardening based on keystroke dynamics. In *Proceedings of the 6th ACM conference on Computer and Communications Security CCS99*, (pp. 73-82). Singapore.

Morris, S. J. (2004). *A shoe-integrated sensor system for wireless gait analysis and real-time therapeutic feedback*. Division of Health Sciences and Technology, Harvard University-MIT.

Mostayed, A., Kim, S., Mazumder, M. M. G., & Park, S. J. (2008). *Foot step based person identification using histogram similarity and wavelet decomposition*. Paper presented at the ISA '08: Proceedings of the 2008 International Conference on Information Security and Assurance (isa 2008), Washington, DC, USA.

Myles-Worsley, M. (2007). P50 sensory gating in multiplex schizophrenia families from a Pacific Island isolate. *The American Journal of Psychiatry, 159*, 2007–2012. doi:10.1176/appi.ajp.159.12.2007

Nazar, A., Traoré, I., & Ahmed, A. A. E. (2008). Inverse biometrics for mouse dynamics. [IJPRAI]. *International Journal of Artificial Intelligence and Pattern Recognition, 22*(3), 461–495. doi:10.1142/S0218001408006363

Ng, J., Sahakian, A. V., & Swiryn, S. (2003). *Accelerometer-based body-position sensing for ambulatory electrocardiographic monitoring* (vol. 37). Arlington, VA: ETATS-UNIS: Association for the Advancement of Medical Instrumentation.

Niinuma, K., Park, U., & Jain, A. K. (2010, December). Soft biometric traits for continuous user authentication. *IEEE Transactions on Information Forensics and Security, 5*(4), 771–780. doi:10.1109/TIFS.2010.2075927

Nisenson, M., Yariv, I., El-Yaniv, R., & Meir, R. (2003). Towards behaviometric security systems: Learning to identify a typist. In *Proceedings of the 7th European Conference on Principles and Practice of Knowledge Discovery in Databases (ECML/PKDD)*. Berlin, Germany: Springer-Verlag.

Nixon, M. S., Carter, J. N., Shutler, J., & Grant, M. (2002). New advances in automatic gait recognition. *Elsevier Information Security Technical Report, 7*(4), 23–35. doi:10.1016/S1363-4127(02)00404-1

Nixon, M. S., Tan, T. N., & Chellappa, R. (2005). *Human identification based on gait*. Springer.

Nixon, M. S., & Carter, J. N. (2004). On gait as a biometric: Progress and prospects. In *Proc. EUSIPCO 2004*, Sept, Vienna, (pp. 1401-1404).

Niyogi, S. A., & Adelson, E. H. (1994). *Analyzing and recognizing walking gures in XYT*. In Conference of Computer Vision and Pattern Recognition.

Nygårds, M., & Sörnmo, L. (1983). Delineation of the QRS complex using the envelope of the ECG. *Medical & Biological Engineering & Computing, 21*(5), 538–547. doi:10.1007/BF02442378

Obaidat, M. S., & Sadoun, S. (1997). A simulation evaluation study of neural network techniques to computer user identification. *Information Sciences, 102*, 239–258. doi:10.1016/S0020-0255(97)00016-9

Obaidat, M. S., & Sadoun, B. (1997). Verification of computer users using keystroke dynamics. *IEEE Transactions on Systems, Man, and Cybernetics. Part B, Cybernetics, 27*(2), 261–269. doi:10.1109/3477.558812

Obaidat, M. S., & Sadoun, B. (1999). Keystroke dynamics based authentication . In Jain, A. K., Bolle, R., & Pankanti, S. (Eds.), *Biometrics: Personal identification in networked society* (pp. 213–230). Springer.

Obaidat, M. S. (1995). A verification methodology for computer systems users. In *Proceedings of the 1995 ACM Symposium on Applied Computing*, (pp. 258-262). Nashville, Tennessee, United States.

Olden, M. (2009). *Biometric authentication and authorisation infrastructures*. Phd Thesis, University of Regensburg, Germany. Retrieved December 28, 2010, from http://epub.uni-regensburg.de/12680/

Oliver, N., & Pentland, A. (2000). Graphical models for driver behavior recognition in a Smartcar. In *Proceedings of the IEEE Intelligent Vehicles Symposium*, (pp. 7–12).

Ong, C., & Lai, W. (2000). Enhanced password authentication through typing biometrics with the k-means clustering algorithm. In *Proceedings of the Seventh International Symposium on Manufacturing with Applications*. Hawaii, USA.

Palaniappan, R. (2005). Multiple mental thought parametric classification: A new approach for individual identification. *International Journal of Signal Processing, 2*(1), 222–225.

Palaniappan, R., & Mandic, D. P. (2007). Biometrics from brain electrical activity: A machine learning approach. *IEEE Transactions on Pattern Analysis and Machine Intelligence, 29*(4), 738–742. doi:10.1109/TPAMI.2007.1013

Paranjape, R. B., Mahovsky, J., Benedicenti, L., & Kolesapos, Z. (2001). *The electroencephalogram as a biometric*. Canadian Conference on Electrical and Computer Engineering, (pp. 1363–1366).

Pärkkä, J., Ermes, M., Korpipää, P., Mäntyjärvi, J., Peltola, J., & Korhonen, I. (2006). Activity classification using realistic data from wearable sensors. *IEEE Transactions on Information Technology in Biomedicine, 10*(1), 119–128. doi:10.1109/TITB.2005.856863

Pearsall, J., & Trumble, B. (2001). *The Oxford English reference dictionary*. Oxford University Press.

Phenice, W. T. (1969). A newly developed visual method of sexing the Os Pubis. *American Journal of Physical Anthropology, 30*, 297–302. doi:10.1002/ajpa.1330300214

Philips, P. J., Martin, A., Wilson, C. L., & Przybocki, M. (2000). An introduction to evaluating biometric systems. *IEEE Computer*, 56–63. National Institute of Technology.

Pilia, G., Chen, W.-M., Scuteri, A., Orrúm, M., Albaim, G., & Dei, M. (2006). Heritability of cardiovascular and personality traits in 6,148 Sardinians. *PLOS Genetics, 2*(8), 1207–1223. doi:10.1371/journal.pgen.0020132

Polemi, D. (2000). *Biometric techniques: Review and evaluation of biometric techniques for identification and authentication, including an appraisal of the areas where they are most applicable*. Technical report, Report prepared for the European Commission DG XIII - C.4 on the Information Society Technologies, (IST) (Key action 2: New Methods of Work and Electronic Commerce). Retrieved from www.cordis.lu/infosec/src/stud5fr.html

Prado, M., Reina-Tosina, J., & Roa, L. (2002). Distributed intelligent architecture for falling detection and physical activity analysis in the elderly, (vol. 3, pp. 1910–1911).

Pusara, M., & Brodley, C. (2004). User reauthentication via mouse movements. *Proceedings of the 2004 ACM Workshop on Visualization and Data Mining for Computer Security*, (pp. 1-8).

Rainville, P., Bechara, A., Naqvim, N., & Damasiom, A. R. (2006). Basic emotions are associated with distinct patterns of cardiorespiratory activity. *International Journal of Psychophysiology, 16*, 5–18. doi:10.1016/j.ijpsycho.2005.10.024

Raj, S. B. E., & Santhosh, A. T. (2009). A behavioral biometric approach based on standardized resolution in mouse dynamics. *International Journal of Computer Science and Network Security, 9*(4), 370–377.

Ramesh, K., & Rao, K. (2009). Pattern extraction methods for ear biometrics - A survey. In *2009 NaBIC World Congress on Nature Biologically Inspired Computing, 2009* (pp.1657–1660).

Rashed, A., & Santos, H. (2010). Odour user interface for authentication: possibility and acceptance: Case study. *Proceedings of the International MultiConference of Engineers and Computer Scientists (IMECS 2010)*, March 17-19, Hong Kong, I:4. ISBN: 978-988-17012-8-2

Reiter, M. K., Monrose, F., & Wetzel, S. (1999). Password hardening based on keystroke dynamics. In *Proceedings of the 6th ACM Conference on Computer and Communications Security*, (pp. 73–82). Singapore. New York, NY: ACM.

Reschovsky, C. (2004). *Journey to work: 2000.* (Technical Report C2KBR-33), U.S. Department of Commerce, Economics and Statistics Administration, U.S. Census Bureau.

Revett, K., Jahankhani, H., de Magalhães, S. T., & Santos, H. M. D. (2008). A survey of user authentication based on mouse dynamics. *Communications in Computer and Information Science, 12*(4), 210–219. doi:10.1007/978-3-540-69403-8_25

Revett, K. (2008). *Behavioral biometrics: A remote access approach. (2008)*. Colchester, UK: Wiley & Sons.

Revett, K. (2008). *Multimodal biometric systems*. John Wiley & Sons, Ltd.

Revett, K., Magalhães, S., & Santos, H. (2005). Enhancing login security through the use of keystroke input dynamics. In *Advances in Biometrics, Lecture Notes in Computer Science, 3832*. Berlin, Germany: Springer.

Revett, K. (2009). Behavioral biometrics: A biosignal based approach . In Wang, L., & Geng, X. (Eds.), *Behavioral biometrics for human identification: Intelligent applications*. Hershey, PA: IGI Global Publishers. doi:10.4018/978-1-60566-725-6.ch005

Revett, K. (2009). A bioinformatics based approach to user authentication via keystroke dynamics. *International Journal of Control, Automation, and Systems, 7*(1), 7-15. ISSN: 1598-6446

Revett, K., Magalhaes, P. S., & Santos, H. D. (2005). *Developing a keystroke dynamics based agent using rough sets*. The 2005 IEEE/WIC/ACM International Joint Conference on Web Intelligence and Intelligent Agent Technology Compiegne, (pp. 56–61).

Riener, A. (2010). *Sensor-actuator supported implicit interaction in driver assistance systems,* 1st ed. Wiesbaden, Germany: Vieweg+Teubner Research. ISBN: 978-3-8348-0963-6

Riener, A., & Ferscha, A. (2007). Driver activity recognition from sitting postures. In T. Paul-Stueve (Ed.), *Workshop on Automotive User Interfaces and Interactive Applications (AUIIA'07),* September 2–5, 2008, (p. 9). Weimar, Germany: Verlag der Bauhaus-Universität Weimar. ISBN: 978-3-486-58496-7

Riener, A., & Ferscha, A. (2008). Supporting implicit human-to-vehicle interaction: Driver identification from sitting postures. In *Proceedings of the 1st International Symposium on Vehicular Computing Systems (ISVCS 2008)*, July 22-24, 2008, Trinity College Dublin, Ireland. ACM Digital Library.

Rimsley, B. G. (2003). *Vehicle occupancy survey: US 52, Harrison, SR 26, US 231. Survey, Tippecanoe County, 20 North Third Street, Lafayette, Indiana 47901*. Retrieved December 28, 2010, from http://www.tippecanoe.in.gov

Rodrigues, R., Yared, G., Costa, C., Yabu-Uti, J., Violaro, F., & Ling, L. (2005). Biometric access control through numerical keyboards based on keystroke dynamics . In *Advances in Biometrics, Lecture Notes in Computer Science, 3832*. Berlin, Germany: Springer.

Rong, L., Jianzhong, Z., Ming, L., & Xiang, H. (2005). *Identification of individual walking patterns using gait acceleration*. In 1st International Conference in Bioinformatics and Biomedical Engineering, (pp. 543-546).

Rong, L., Jianzhong, Z., Ming, L., & Xiangfeng, H. (2007). *A wearable acceleration sensor system for gait recognition*. Paper presented at the Industrial Electronics and Applications, 2007. ICIEA 2007.

Ross, A. K., Nandakumar, K., & Jain, A. K. (2006). *Handbook of multibiometrics*. Springer Verlag.

Rowe, R. K., Uludag, U., Demirkus, M., Parthasaradhi, S., & Jain, A. (2007). A multispectral whole-hand biometric authentication system. IEEE Biometrics Symposium (pp. 1 – 6).

Samura, T. (2008). A Web-based typing learning system that supports Japanese text. [in Japanese]. *Journal of Education in the College of Technology, 31*, 471–476.

Samura, T., & Nishimura, H. (2008). Performance analysis of personal identification by keystroke data in free text typing. [in Japanese]. *Proceedings of SICE Symposium on Systems and Information, 2008*, 59–64.

Samura, T., & Nishimura, H. (2009a). Personal identification by keystroke dynamics in Japanese free text typing. *Transactions of the Institute of Systems* [in Japanese]. *Control and Information Engineers, 22*(4), 145–153. doi:10.5687/iscie.22.145

Samura, T., & Nishimura, H. (2009b). Keystroke timing analysis for individual identification in Japanese free text typing. *Proceedings of ICROS-SICE International Joint Conference, 2009*, 3166–3170.

Samura, T., & Nishimura, H. (2010a). A hybrid model for individual identification based on keystroke data in Japanese free text typing. [in Japanese]. *Transactions of the Society of Instrument and Control Engineers, 46*(11), 676–684.

Samura, T., & Nishimura, H. (2011). Keystroke dynamics for individual identification in Japanese free text typing. *SICE Journal of Control . Measurement and System Integration, 4*(2), 172–178.

Sang, Y., Shen, H., & Fan, P. (2004). *Novel imposters detection in keystroke dynamics using support vector machines* (pp. 666–669). Berlin/Heidelberg, Germany: Springer. ISSN 0302-9743

Savvides, M., & Vijaya Kumar, B. V. K. (2003). Efficient design of advanced correlation filters for robust distortion-tolerant face recognition. *Proceedings IEEE Conference on Advanced Video and Signal Based Surveillance* (pp. 45-52).

Sazonov, E. S., Bumpus, T., Zeigler, S., & Marocco, S. (2005). *Classification of plantar pressure and heel acceleration patterns using neural networks*. Paper presented at the International Joint Conference on Neural Networks, IJCNN '.

Schmidt, A. (2000). Implicit human computer interaction through context. *Personal and Ubiquitous Computing, 4*(2), 191–199. doi:10.1007/BF01324126

Schneiderman, H., & Kanade, T. (2000). *A statistical method for 3D object detection applied to faces and cars* (pp. 746–751). Proc. Of IEEE Computer Vision and Pattern Recognition.

Schonlau, M., DuMouchel, W., Ju, W.-H., Karr, A. F., Theus, M., & Vardi, Y. (2001). Computer intrusion: Detecting masquerades. *Statistical Science, 16*(1), 58–74. doi:10.1214/ss/998929476

Schulz, D. A. (2006). *Mouse curve biometrics*. Biometric Consortium Conference, 2006 Biometrics Symposium, (pp. 1-6).

Schumm, J., Setz, C., Bächlin, M., Bächler, M., Arnrich, B., & Tröster, G. (2010). Unobtrusive physiological monitoring in an airplane seat. *Personal and Ubiquitous Computing . Special Issue on Pervasive Technologies for Assistive Environments, 14*, 541–550.

Setz, C., Arnrich, B., Schumm, J., La Marca, R., Tröster, G., & Ehlert, U. (2010). Discriminating stress from cognitive load using a wearable EDA device. *IEEE Transactions on Information Technology in Biomedicine, 14*(2), 410–417. doi:10.1109/TITB.2009.2036164

Shafie, S. A. M., Vien, L. L., & Sadullah, A. F. M. (2008). *Vehicle occupancy in malaysia according to land use and trip purpose*. In EASTS International Symposium on Sustainable Transportation incorporating Malaysian Universities Transport Research Forum Conference 2008 (MUTRFC08), (p. 8).

Shavlik, J., Shavlik, M., & Fahland, M. (2001). Evaluating software sensors for actively profiling Windows 2000 users. *Proceedings of the Fourth International Symposium on Recent Advances in Intrusion Detection.*

Shen, C., Cai, Z., Guan, X., Sha, H., & Du, H. (2009). feature analysis of mouse dynamics in identity authentication and monitoring. *Proc. of IEEE International Conference on Communications (ICC '09)* (pp. 1-5). Dresden, Germany.

Silva, H., Gamboa, H., & Fred, A. (2007). Applicability of lead V2 ECG measurements in biometrics. *Proceedings of Med-e-Tel 2007*, Luxembourg, April 2007.

Sim, T., Zhang, S., Janakiraman, R., & Kumar, S. (2007). Continuous verification using multimodal biometrics. *IEEE Transactions on Pattern Analysis and Machine Intelligence, 29*(4), 687–700. doi:10.1109/TPAMI.2007.1010

Sminchisescu, C., Kanaujia, A., Li, Z., & Metaxas, D. (2004). *Learning to reconstruct 3D human motion from Bayesian mixtures of experts. A probabilistic discriminative approach.*

Smit, D. J. A., Posthuma, D., Boomsma, D. I., & De Gues, E. J. C. (2005). Heritability of background EEG across the power spectrum. *Psychophysiology, 42*, 691–697. doi:10.1111/j.1469-8986.2005.00352.x

Sprager, S., & Zazula, D. (2009). *Gait identification using cumulants of accelerometer data.* Paper presented at the SENSIG'09/VIS'09/MATERIALS'09: Proceedings of the 2nd WSEAS International Conference on Sensors, and Signals and Visualization, Imaging and Simulation and Materials Science, Stevens Point, Wisconsin, USA.

Stewart, T. D. (1954). Sex determination of the skeleton by guess and by measurement. *American Journal of Physical Anthropology, 12*, 385–392. doi:10.1002/ajpa.1330120312

Streitz, N., & Nixon, P. (2005). The disappearing computer. *Communications of the ACM, 48*(3), 32–35. doi:10.1145/1047671.1047700

Subramanya, A., Raj, A., Bilmes, J., & Fox, D. (2006). Recognizing activities and spatial context using wearable sensors. In *Proceedings of Uncerntainty in Artificial Intelligence.*

Sun, Y. H. Z., Tan, T., & Ren, C. (2008). *Multi-spectral palm image fusion for accurate contact-free palmprint recognition.* IEEE International Conference on Image Processing, (pp. 281-284).

Sung, H., Lim, J., Park, J., & Li, Y. (2004). *Iris recognition using collarette boundary localization.* In International Conference on Pattern Recognition (pp. 857-860).

Sung, K. S., & Cho, S. (2006). *GA SVM wrapper ensemble for keystroke dynamics authentication.* International Conference on Biometrics, (pp. 654–660). Hong Kong.

Sutton, S., Braren, M., Zubin, J., & John, E. R. (1965). Evoked-potentials correlates of stimulus uncertainty. *Science, 150*, 1187–1188. doi:10.1126/science.150.3700.1187

Swets, J. A., & Pickett, R. M. (1992). *Evaluation of diagnostic systems: Methods from signal detection theory.* New York, NY: Academic Press.

Tapiador, M., Sigenza, J. A., & Tcnica, E. (1999). Fuzzy keystroke biometrics on Web security. *IEEE AutoID '99 Proceedings Workshop on Automatic Identification Advanced Technologies,* (pp. 133–136).

Tappert, C. C., Villani, M., & Cha, S. (2009). Keystroke biometric identification and authentication on long-text input . In Wang, L., & Geng, X. (Eds.), *Behavioral Biometrics for Human Identification: Intelligent Applications* (pp. 342–367). Medical Information Science Reference. doi:10.4018/978-1-60566-725-6.ch016

Tessendorf, B., Arnrich, B., Schumm, J., Setz, C., & Troster, G. (2009). *Unsupervised monitoring of sitting behavior.* In Annual International Conference of the IEEE Engineering in Medicine and Biology Society (EMBC 2009), (pp. 6197–6200). IEEE.

Thorpe, J., van Oorschot, P. C., & Somayaji, A. (2005). Pass-thoughts: Authenticating with our minds. *Proceedings of the 2005 Workshop on New Security Paradigms,* (pp. 45-56).

TimesOnline. (2006). *Aiming to catch criminals redfooted.* Retrieved from http://business.timesonline.co.uk/tol/business/law/article685365.ece

Trivedi, M. M., Gandhi, T., & McCall, J. (2007). Looking-in and looking-out of a vehicle: Computer-vision-based enhanced vehicle safety. *IEEE Transactions on Intelligent Transportation Systems, 8*(1), 108–120. Retrieved December 28, 2010, from http://escholarship.org/uc/item/2g6313r2

Turk, M. A., & Pentland, A. P. (1991, June). Face recognition using eigenfaces. *Proceedings of IEEE International Conference on Computer Vision and Pattern Recognition*, (pp. 589-591).

U.S. Department of Transportation. (2009). *2009 National household travel survey: Report, Federal Highway Administration*. Retrieved December 28, 2010, from http://nhts.ornl.gov/publications.shtml

u-blox. (2010). *Automotive GPS chips and chipsets*. Retrieved December 28, 2010, from http://www.u-blox.com/en/gps-chips/automotive-gps-chips.html

Umbaugh, S. E. (2005). *Computer imaging: Digital image analysis and processing* (pp. 239–245). CRC Press.

Umphress, D., & Williams, G. (1985). Identity verification through keyboard characteristics. *International Journal of Man-Machine Studies*, *23*(3), 263–273. doi:10.1016/S0020-7373(85)80036-5

Van Beijsterveldt, C. E. M., Molenaar, P. C. M., de Geus, E. J. C., & Boomsma, D. I. (1996). Heritability of human brain functioning as assessed by electroencephalography. *American Journal of Human Genetics*, *58*, 562–573.

Veeraraghavan, H., Atev, S., Bird, N., Schrater, P., & Papanikolopoulos, N. (2005). Driver activity monitoring through supervised and unsupervised learning. In *Proceedings of the 2005 IEEE Intelligent Transportation Systems*, (pp. 580–585).

Vijaya Kumar, B. V. K., Mahalanobis, A., & Juda, R. (2005). *Correlation pattern recognition*. Cambridge University Press. doi:10.1017/CBO9780511541087

Vijaya Kumar, B. V. K., Savvides, M., Venkataramani, K., & Xie, C. (2002). *Spatial frequency domain image processing for biometric recognition*. International Conference on Image Processing (vol. 1, pp. 53-56).

Vildjiounaite, E., Mäkelä, S.-M., Lindholm, M., Riihimäki, R., Kyllönen, V., Mäntyjärvi, J., & Ailisto, H. (2006). *Unobtrusive multimodal biometrics for ensuring privacy and information security with personal devices*. Paper presented at the Pervasive Computing Conference 2006.

Villani, M., Tappert, C., Ngo, G., Simone, J., St. Fort, H., & Cha, S.-H. (2006). Keystroke biometric recognition studies on long-text input under ideal and application-oriented conditions. *Proceedings of the 2006 Conference on Computer Vision and Pattern Recognition Workshop*, C3-1.

Viola, P., & Jones, M. (2004). Robust real-time face detection. *International Journal of Computer Vision*, *57*(2), 137–154. doi:10.1023/B:VISI.0000013087.49260.fb

Vista Medical Ltd. (2010). *Pressure mapping, pressure imaging and pressure sensing*. Retrieved December 28, 2010, from http://www.pressuremapping.com/

VizSec/DMSEC'04. Washington, DC, USA.

Volokh, E. (2000). Personalization and privacy. *Communications of the ACM*, *43*(8), 84–88. doi:10.1145/345124.345155

Waller, A. D. (1887). A demonstration on man of electromotive changes accompanying the heart's beat. *The Journal of Physiology*, *8*, 229–234.

Wang, Y., Agrafioti, F., Hatzinakos, D., & Plataniotis, K. M. (2008). Analysis of human electrocardiogram for biometric recognition. *EURASIP Journal on Advances in Signal Processing*, *2008*, 1–11. doi:10.1155/2008/148658

Wang, L., Tan, T., Hu, W., & Ning, H. (2003). Automatic gait recognition based on statistical shape analysis. *IEEE Transactions on Image Processing*, *12*(9), 1120–1131. doi:10.1109/TIP.2003.815251

Wayman, J. L. (1999, April). *Fundamentals of biometric authentication technologies*. Paper presented at the CardTech/SecurTech Conference. Bethesda, MD.

Wayman, J. L. (Ed.). (2000). *National Biometric Test Center: Collected works 1997-2000*. Biometric Consortium of the U.S. Government interest group on biometric authentication. San Jose State University, CA. Retrieved from www.engr.sjsu.edu/biometrics/nbtccw.pdf

Weiss, A., Ramapanicker, A., Shah, P., Noble, S., & Immohr, L. (2007). *Mouse movements biometric identification: A feasibility study*. Pace University. doi:10.1.1.88.7902

Wildes, R., Asmuth, J. C., Hanna, K. J., Hsu, S. C., & Kolczynski, R. J. Matey, J. R., & McBride, S. E. (1996 and 1998). *Automated, non-invasive iris recognition system and method.* (U.S. Patent No. 5,572,596 and 5.751,836).

Wong, Y. W., Seng, K. P., Ang, L.-M., Khor, W. Y., & Liau, F. (2007). *Audio-visual recognition system with intra-modal fusion.* International Conference on Computational Intelligence and Security, (pp. 609 – 613)

Woodward, J. D., Horn, C., Gatune, J., & Thomas, A. (2003). *Biometrics – A look at facial recognition. Documented Briefing 396, RAND Public Safety and Justice.* RAND.

Wübbler, G., Stavridis, M., Kreiseler, D., Bousseljot, R.-D., & Elster, C. (2007). Verification of humans using the electrocardiogram. *Pattern Recognition Letters, 28,* 1172–1175. doi:10.1016/j.patrec.2007.01.014

XSENSOR Technology Corporation. (2010). Pressure imaging systems for sleep, patient safety and automotive testing. Retrieved December 28, 2010, from http://www.xsensor.com/

Yao, P., Li, J., Ye, X., Zhuang, Z., & Li, B. (2006, August). *Iris recognition algorithm using modified log-gabor filters.* In International Conference on Pattern Recognition, (pp. 461-464).

Yap, R. H. C., & Ramnath, R. (2008). *Physical access protection using continuous authentication.* IEEE.

Young, J. R., & Hammon, R. W. (1989). *Method and apparatus for verifying an individual's identity.* (Patent Number 4,805,222). Washington, DC: U.S. Patent and Trademark Office.

Yubico. (2010). *The Yubikey.* Retrieved December 28, 2010, from http://www.yubico.com/yubikey

Zhang, D. (2004). *Palmprint authentication.* Kluwer Academic Publishers.

Zhang, D., Kong, W. K., You, J., & Wong, M. (2003). Onine palmprint identification. *IEEE Transactions on Pattern Analysis and Machine Intelligence, 25,* 1041–1050. doi:10.1109/TPAMI.2003.1227981

Zhang, L., & Zhang, D. (2004). Characterization of palmprints by wavelet signatures via directional context modeling. *IEEE Transactions on SMC-B, 34,* 1335–1347.

About the Contributors

Issa Traoré obtained a PhD in Software Engineering in 1998 from Institute Nationale Polytechnique (INPT)-LAAS/CNRS, Toulouse, France. He has been with the faculty of the Department of Electrical and Computer Engineering of the University of Victoria since 1999. He is currently an Associate Professor and the Coordinator of the Information Security and Object Technology (ISOT) Lab (http://www.isot.ece.uvic.ca) at the University of Victoria. His research interests include biometrics technologies, computer intrusion detection, network forensics, software security, and software quality engineering. He has published over 90 technical papers in computer security and software engineering and supervised 23 Master and PhD graduate students in the last 10 years. He is currently serving as Associate Editor for the International Journal of Communication Networks and Distributed Systems (IJCNDS). Dr. Traoré is also a co-founder and CEO of Plurilock Security Solutions Inc. (http://www.plurilock.com), a network security company which provides innovative authentication technologies, and is one of the pioneers in bringing continuous authentication products to the market.

Ahmed Awad E. Ahmed is a Senior Scientist at the Electrical and Computer Engineering Department, University of Victoria. He is a member of the Security and Object Technology (ISOT) Research Laboratory at the University of Victoria and the principal investigator of Biotracker, a new intrusion detection system based on biometrics (http://www.isot.ece.uvic.ca/projects/biotracker). Dr. Ahmed worked as a Software Design Engineer, Project Manager, and Quality Assurance/Security Consultant in a number of leading firms. He is currently the CTO of Plurilock Security Solutions Inc. Dr. Ahmed received his PhD in Electrical and Computer Engineering from the University of Victoria, Victoria, BC, Canada in 2008. His PhD dissertation introduces new trends in security monitoring through human computer interaction devices. Dr. Ahmed completed his BSc and MSc degrees at the Electrical and Computer Engineering Department, Ain Shams University, Cairo, Egypt in 1992, and 1997 respectively.

* * *

Robert B. Batie Jr. has over 20 years of experience in communication security and information assurance. He is a Senior Principal Systems Security Engineer at Raytheon NCS, in St. Petersburg, FL. He is a Raytheon Author, Inventor and Technical Honoree, adjunct Instructor as well as a contributing author for the Official Guide to the CISSP-ISSAP CBK. He has published articles in the CSI Journal, and presented at Raytheon Symposiums, the CSI Conferences, and the International Biometric Conference. Robert has a Master of Science in Computer Systems Management from the University of Maryland, and is currently working on a PhD at Nova Southeastern University. He holds the following information security certifications: CISSP-ISSEP, ISSAP, ISSMP, CISM, and CAP.

Sérgio Roberto de Lima e Silva Filho was born in Boituva, São Paulo, Brazil, in 1980. He received the Bachelor of Science (BSc) and Master of Science (MSc) degrees in Computer Science from the Informatics and Statistics Department, Federal University of Santa Catarina, Brazil, in 2002 and 2005, respectively. His research interests include network and Internet security, behavioral and physical biometrics systems, intrusion detection systems and artificial intelligence, having completed his Master's degree thesis mixing these topics to authenticate users in computers. Currently, he works in a company that develops cryptographic systems, including digital signature, timestamp, encryption, and digital certificates.

Davrondzhon Gafurov received his Diploma in Computer Engineering from Technological University of Tajikistan in 2000 and his PhD in Computer Science from University of Oslo (Norway) in 2008. Previously he worked as a programmer at the Computer Center of Technological University of Tajikistan, and at the same time he was a part-time lecturer at the department of Programming and Information Technology at TUT (2000-2004). Dr. Gafurov also had visits at International Institute for Software Technology, United Nations University (Macau, China) in 2001 and at the department of Electrical and Computer Engineering of University of Calgary (Canada) in 2002. He is researcher at Norwegian Information Security Laboratory, Gjøvik University College (Norway) and actively participated in a number of national and international research and development projects in biometrics (e.g. TURBINE project, www.turbine-project.eu). Dr. Gafurov has more than 35 publications in international conferences and journals; most of them are in the area of biometrics.

Mohammad Omar Derawi received his diplomas in Computer Science engineering from the Technical University of Denmark where he received both a BSc (2007) and MSc (2009) degree. In addition he received the title as the youngest engineer of Denmark in 2009. Derawi is currently pursuing his PhD in information security at the Norwegian Information Security Laboratory (NISLab), Gjøvik University College (Norway). In the beginning of his PhD studies, he was a visiting researcher at the "Center for Advanced Security Research Darmstadt" (CASED, www.cased.de), Germany for an 8 month period. His current research interest includes biometrics with specialization on gait recognition in mobile devices and currently active in the 7th Framework European project "TrUsted Revocable Biometric IdeNtitiEs" (TURBINE, www.turbine-project.eu). Other main interests of areas include keystroke dynamics and fingerprint recognition.

Patrick Bours has studied Mathematics at the Eindhoven University of Technology in the Netherlands where he received both an MSc (1990) and a PhD (1994) degree. After that he worked for almost 10 as a senior policy member in the area of cryptology for the Dutch Government before he moved to Norway. In 2005 he started working at the Norwegian Information Security Laboratory (NISlab), which is a part of Gjøvik University College. Initially he worked in the area of general authentication, but he rapidly specialized himself in biometrics, and in particular in behavioral biometrics. His main areas of interest include gait recognition, both static and continuous keystroke dynamics, and also mouse dynamics. He has supervised many Master and PhD students in topics related to gait and keystroke dynamics. He currently holds an Associate Professor position and is Director of NISlab.

Daniele Gunetti has a Master's degree and a PhD in Computer Science, and he currently holds a permanent position as Associate Professor at the Department of Computer Science of the University of Torino, Italy. His main research interests are in the area of behavioral biometric measures. In particular he works to the analysis of the typing rhythms of free text, and to its application to computer security, especially in the fields of intrusion detection, user authentication and identity tracing over the Internet. In the past he has also conducted extensive research in the areas of machine learning and inductive logic programming, as well as in automated theorem proving.

Phalguni Gupta received the Doctoral degree from Indian Institute of Technology Kharagpur, India in 1986. Currently he is a Professor in the Department of Computer Science & Engineering, Indian Institute of Technology Kanpur (IITK), Kanpur, India. He works in the field of biometrics, data structures, sequential algorithms, parallel algorithms, and image processing. He is an author of 2 books and 12 book chapters. He has published more than 200 papers in international journals and international conferences. He is responsible for several research projects in the area of biometric systems, image processing, graph theory, and network flow. Prior to joining IITK in 1987, he worked in Space Applications Centre Ahmedabad, Indian Space Research Organization, India.

Michael S. Hsiao received the BS degree in computer engineering (highest honors) and the MS and PhD degrees in electrical engineering from the University of Illinois at Urbana-Champaign in 1992, 1993, and 1997, respectively. Currently, he is a Professor in the Department of Electrical and Computer Engineering at Virginia Tech. He and his research group have published more than 200 refereed journal and conference papers. He has served on the program committee for more than sixty international conferences and workshops, in addition to serving as associate editor on ACM Trans. Design Automation of Electronic Systems, and on editorial boards of several journals. He was a recipient of the Digital Equipment Corporation Fellowship, the McDonnell Douglas Scholarship, the National Science Foundation CAREER Award, and is recognized for most influential papers in the first ten years of Design Automation and Test Conference in Europe (DATE).

Aaron Jaech is a student at Carnegie Mellon University graduating with the class of 2011 with a Bachelor of Science in Mathematical Sciences and a Bachelor of Science in Computer Science. He is a research assistant at the Carnegie Mellon Biometrics Center where he works on continuous authentication, face and iris biometrics. He selected to be an IC Scholar of the ODNI's Center of Excellence in Identity Sciences (CASIS). Aaron is also exploring novel biometrics through a CMU spin-off company, BiometriCore.

Harini Jagadeesan completed her BE in Electronics and Communication Engineering at PSG College of Technology (India) in first class with distinction from Anna University in 2007. From 2007 to 2009, she pursued Master of Science degree in Computer Engineering at Virginia Tech. A member of PROACTIVE lab, her research interests include software testing and verification, biometric authentication and security, etc. She currently works at Microsoft in the Core Windows Operating Systems group and concentrates on software verification of networking and security related features for future Windows OSs. She is also interested in music, classical dance, reading, and debates.

Dakshina Ranjan Kisku received the BE and ME degrees in Computer Science and Engineering from Jadavpur University, India in 2001 and 2003, respectively. Currently he is an Assistant Professor in the Department of Computer Science & Engineering, Asansol Engineering College, Asansol, India and also pursuing PhD in Engineering at Jadavpur University, India. He works in the field of biometrics, computer vision, and image analysis. He was a researcher in the Computer Vision Laboratory, University of Sassari, Italy in 2006. He is an author of 5 book chapters, and he has published more than 35 papers in International Journals and International Conferences. He has vast experience in teaching in different engineering colleges. Prior to joining Asansol Engineering College in June 2010, he was a Senior Lecturer and Project Associate at Dr. B.C. Roy Engineering College, India and at IIT Kanpur, India in 2008 and 2005, respectively.

Claudia Picardi is a researcher at the Department of Computer Science of the University of Torino, Italy. She has a MS and a PhD in Computer Science. Besides keystroke dynamics and behavioral biometric measures, her research is currently focused on intelligent user interfaces and semantic reasoning, applied to interactive digital storytelling in the social Semantic Web. In the past she has worked on automated reasoning and knowledge representation, with a focus on model-based monitoring and diagnosis, in the automotive, aerospace and Web service domain. She has participated in several international projects on these topics, and is currently vice-coordinator of an Italian project on the social Semantic Web and augmented reality.

Kenneth Revett is a member of the informatics and computer science department at the British University in Egypt. His undergraduate degrees are from the University of Maryland, College Park, and earned his doctorate in Computational Neuroscience from the same institution in 1999. He specialises in computational biology, with an emphasis in biometrics. He has over 50 publications in the field, is author of the first text on behavioral biometrics (Behavioral Biometrics: A Remote Access Approach, Wiley & Sons), and holds a patent in keystroke dynamics. In addition, Dr. Revett is also the editor of the journal Cognitive Biometrics, published by Inderscience. He runs several workshops in biometrics at a variety of international conferences, promoting the deployment of cognitive biometrics.

Andreas Riener carried out his PhD at the Institute for Pervasive Computing, Johannes Kepler University Linz, Austria from which he received his PhD degree in 2009. In his PhD thesis he has confirmed driver-vehicle interfaces as complex configurations of technological system components and services, and implicit interaction therein as a major research challenge. In a substantial part of his thesis he dealt with implicit interaction modalities based on vibrotactile sensations and notifications affecting the driver-vehicle feedback loop. From March 2006 to July 2009 he was also an employee at the Research Institute for Pervasive Computing (RIPE) in Hagenberg. In June 1999 he received an "Excellence Scholarship" from the technical and natural scientific faculty, JKU Linz. In Autumn 2008 he was awarded the "Talent Funding Award for Science" from the Upper Austrian Federal State Government as honor for his performance in research. Since 2009 he is a Postdoctoral research fellow at the same institute. Andreas Riener is and was engaged in several EU-and industrial-funded research projects, for instance in cooperation projects with Siemens AG or in the FP7 project "SOCIONICAL." His research interests include multimodal sensor and actuator systems with a focus on implicit human-computer interaction. Furthermore, he is interested in driver vital state recognition from embedded sensors and context-sensitive data processing. His core competence and research focus is context-aware computing and implicit interaction influencing the driver-vehicle interaction loop.

Haruhiko Nishimura graduated from the Department of Physics, Shizuoka University in 1980, completed the doctoral program at Kobe University, and received the PhD degree in 1985. After working in the Faculty of Medicine of Hiroshima University, he joined Hyogo University of Education as an Associate Professor in 1990 and became a Professor in 1999. Since 2004, he has been a Professor in the Graduate School of Applied Informatics, University of Hyogo. His research field is intelligent systems science by several architectures such as neural networks and complex systems. He is also presently engaged in research on biomedical, healthcare, and high confidence sciences. He is a member of the IEEE, IEICE, IPSJ, ISCIE, JNSS, and others and was awarded ISCIE paper prize in 2001 and JSKE paper prize in 2010.

Mauro Roisenberg is an Associate Professor at the Informatics and Statistics Department at Federal University of Santa Catarina where he coordinates the Connectionism and Cognitive Sciences Laboratory. He obtained his undergraduate degree in Data Processing Technology in 1984 and Mechanical Engineering degree in 1988 both from the Federal University of Rio Grande does Sul. He received his M.Sc. degree in Computer Science from Federal University of Rio Grande do Sul in 1988 and his PhD in Electrical Engineering from Federal University of Santa Catarina in 1998. He is an active reviewer for several periodicals such as IEEE Transactions on Systems, Man, and Cybernetics Part B, Information Systems and Journal of Petroleum Science and Engineering. His main research interests are in artificial intelligence, neural networks, hierarchical neural networks, prediction intervals for neural networks, robotics, and behavior based agents.

Toshiharu Samura received the PhD degree in science from Kobe University in 1994. He joined the department of Management Information Science of Fukui University of Technology as a lecturer in 1996. Since 2000, he has been an Associate Professor of Department of Electrical and Computer Engineering of Akashi National College of Technology. His research interests include keystroke dynamics, XML database, computer network, and computer education. He is a member of ISCIE, IEICE, IPSJ, DBSJ, and JPS.

Marios Savvides is the Founder and Director of the Biometrics Lab at Carnegie Mellon University. He is also an Associate Research Professor at the Electrical & Computer Engineering Department as well as CMU CyLab. He is one of the four chosen researchers to form the Office of the Director of National Intelligence (ODNI), 1st Center of Academic Excellence in Science & Technology (CASIS). His research is mainly focused in developing algorithms for robust face and iris biometrics as well as pattern recognition, machine vision, and computer image understanding for enhancing biometric system performance. He is on the program committee on several biometric conferences such as IEEE BTAS, SPIE Biometric Identification, and IEEE AutoID. He has authored and co-authored over 130 journal and conference publications, including several book chapters in the area of biometrics and an served as an area editor of the Springer's Encyclopedia of Biometrics. His achievements include leading the R&D in CMU's past participation at NIST's Face Recognition Grand Challenge (CMU ranked #1 in Academia and Industry at hardest experiment #4) and also in NIST's Iris Challenge Evaluation (CMU ranked #1 in Academia and #2 against iris vendors). He is listed in Marquis Who's Who in America and in Marquis Who's Who in Science & Engineering. He has filed 5 patent applications in area of biometrics and is the recipient of CMU's 2008 Carnegie Institute of Technology (CIT) Outstanding Research Award.

Jamuna Kanta Sing received his B.E. degree in Computer Science & Engineering from Jadavpur University in 1992, M.Tech. degree in Computer & Information Technology from Indian Institute of Technology (IIT) Kharagpur in 1993, and Ph.D. (Engineering) degree from Jadavpur University in 2006. Dr. Sing has been a faculty member of the Department of Computer Science & Engineering, Jadavpur University since March 1997. He has done his Post Doctoral research works as a BOYSCAST Fellow of the Department of Science & Technology, Govt. of India, at the University of Pennsylvania, and the University of Iowa during 2006. He is a member of the IEEE, USA. His research interest includes face recognition/detection, medical image processing, and pattern recognition.

Massimo Tistarelli was born on November 11, 1962 in Genoa, Italy. He received a degree in Electronic Engineering from the University of Genoa, Italy in 1987 and the PhD in Computer Science and Robotics in 1991 from the same university. Since 1986 he has been involved as project coordinator and task manager in several projects on computer vision and image analysis funded by the European Community. During 1986, 1991, and 1996 he visited the Department of Computer Science, Trinity College, Dublin Ireland, where he developed methodologies aimed at the investigation of low-level visual processes. In 1989 he was a visiting scientist at Thinking Machines Co. and MIT in Cambridge, Massachusetts, developing parallel algorithms for dynamic image processing on the Connection Machine system. His main research interests cover biological and artificial vision (particularly in the area of recognition and dynamic scene analysis), biometrics, robotic navigation, and visuo-motor coordination. He is author of more than 80 papers in scientific conferences and international journals. Massimo Tistarelli is currently Full Professor in Computer Science at the Department of Architecture and Planning at the University of Sassari, Italy. He is fellow member of IAPR and senior member of IEEE.

P. Daphne Tsatsoulis is a student at Carnegie Mellon University. She will graduate with a Bachelor of Science in Electrical & Computer Engineering and a joint degree in Mathematical Sciences in May 2011. Daphne is a research assistant in the Carnegie Mellon Biometrics Center. She is a member of the HKN honor society and Women in Electrical and Computer Engineering at Carnegie Mellon University.

Index

Symbols

2-graphs (digraphs) 14, 45, 195-196, 198-200, 235, 239-244, 246-247
4-graphs (quadgraphs) 198-199
3-graphs (trigraphs) 198

A

absolute distance 200
action count 26-27, 33-34
activity identification 184
activity period 25-26, 30-36
activity recognition 139, 165, 171-172, 179-181, 184, 188
adaptive enrollment 5
adaptive learning 3
analysis engine 49, 55-56
anatomical biometrics 106, 124, 135
anomaly detection 16, 20, 38, 65, 205-206
ant colony optimization (ACO) 90, 92, 98-99, 101-103
application independent 40, 45-46, 58, 61-63
array disorder (AD) 20-21, 38-39, 212-213, 215-218, 222-225, 228-229
arrival rate 27, 33, 35
artificial neural network (ANN) 19, 64, 234, 237-239, 244-245, 248
attack attribution 17
authentication confidence level 6, 9
authentication mechanism 1, 41-43, 57, 63, 110, 126, 186-187, 233
authentication methodology 232
automatic driver authentication 150, 155
autonomic nervous system (ANS) 111-112, 124, 159, 165, 167

average cycle method (ACM) 20-21, 38, 64-65, 134, 165, 177, 179, 188, 191, 208-211, 230, 249
average vehicle occupancy rate (AVO) 139-140

B

base attributes 46-47
behavioral authentication 43, 62
behavioral biometric characteristic 232, 234-235
behavioral biometrics 11, 19-20, 40, 63, 132-133, 181, 183, 193, 195, 231
behavioral pattern 40, 48
biometric authentication 21, 38, 43, 65, 68-69, 85, 89, 103-104, 110, 135, 163, 165, 211
biometric characteristic 11, 41, 91, 141, 152, 167, 171, 191, 232-235
biometric data 3, 11-13, 21, 39, 71, 74, 181-184, 192
biometric hand-off 68-69, 81, 83, 85
biometric hand-off scheme 68
biometric identification 66, 88, 121, 126, 139, 141, 148-150, 231, 249
biometric measure 163, 212
biometrics 2, 9-15, 18-21, 37-40, 63-66, 68-69, 85-89, 102-112, 116-118, 121, 124, 126-133, 135-136, 138, 141, 149-150, 155, 164-167, 170-172, 177, 181, 183-184, 188, 191, 193-195, 203, 209-211, 230-231, 250-252
biometric sample 11, 71, 191-192
biometric system 8, 10-13, 69, 88-91, 101, 129, 141, 165, 171, 181-183, 191-192, 205, 209, 234, 236, 240, 243-244, 246-248, 252
biometric technology 1, 63, 248
biometric template 11-12
biosignals 105, 108, 111, 120, 126, 128-129, 135, 163
blood pulse volume (BPV) 126

C

cardiac activity 159

cardiac repolarization 115

car-to-car (C2C) 140

car-to-infrastructure (C2I) 140

cognitive biometrics 105-111, 117, 121, 124, 126-130, 135

combiner threshold 243-247

comma separated values (CSV) 148, 160

committee machines 20, 38, 232, 234, 238, 240-241, 244-248

conative response 109

conative state 105-106, 108-109, 128

continuous authentication (CA) 1-10, 12-28, 30-34, 37-43, 46, 48-49, 54, 57, 62-64, 68-72, 74-75, 80, 85, 87-90, 101-103, 106, 126-127, 129, 134, 137, 149, 170-172, 174, 179, 182-187, 193, 205, 211, 232-234, 239, 248

continuous authorization 7, 186

continuous biometric authentication 21, 38, 68-69, 85, 89, 103

continuous enrollment 5

continuous identity authentication system (CIAS) 25

count-based model 27

covariance matrix 77, 81

current-user 41, 59

cyber piracy 208

D

data analysis 8, 20, 48, 103, 143, 145, 147, 164, 176-179, 183-184, 209

deoxyribonucleic acid (DNA) 41, 139

derived attributes 47-48

detection error trade-off (DET) 114, 182

digital signature 235

digraph latency 45, 49, 195-196, 240, 243, 251

discrete cosine transform (DCT) 113-114

discrete wavelet transform 97, 113-114

distance function 178

distance to face space (DFFS) 77

dizygotic 115, 122, 125

driver assistance systems (DAS) 137, 149, 155, 161, 165

dynamic false acceptance rate (DFAR) 29

dynamic false rejection rate (DFRR) 29

E

eigenface 77

eigenvalues 77, 81

electrocardiogram (ECG) 105, 108-109, 111-117, 121, 123-124, 126, 128-137, 139-142, 146-151, 155, 158-159, 163-165, 168

electrodermal response (EDR) 105, 108-109, 111, 117, 124-129, 131, 135-136

electroencephalogram (EEG) 105, 108-109, 111, 117-124, 126-130, 132-136

environment block 56

equal error rate (EER) 101, 110, 114, 117, 120, 126-127, 182, 191, 203, 206

European data format (EDF) 147-148

event related GSR (ERG) 126, 136

event related potential (ERP) 119, 121, 123, 131

F

face biometric 13

false acceptance rate (FAR) 11, 13-14, 16-18, 23, 28-29, 45, 56, 61, 81, 83, 98, 109-111, 116-117, 119-121, 126, 141-142, 149, 173, 177, 184, 195-196, 200-206, 228, 232, 234-236, 243, 245-248, 252

false match rate (FMR) 114, 117, 181-182, 187

false non-match rate (FNMR) 114, 117, 181-182, 187

false reject (FR) 71, 100-101, 141, 163, 210

false rejection rate (FRR) 16-18, 28-29, 45, 61, 63, 110, 120-121, 142, 195-196, 200-206, 228, 232, 234-236, 245-248, 252

feature extraction 65, 73, 77, 91, 93-94, 103, 114, 129, 174, 177, 179, 184

feature index extraction 213, 216

feedforward neural network 240

fiducial points 160

fisher linear discriminant analysis (FLDA) 70, 78-79, 83

fixed sentence 240, 245-246, 248

fixed text 14, 195, 235, 240, 245-248

fixed time interval 3, 30

floor sensor based (FS) 172-173

force sensor arrays (FSA) 144-145, 151, 156

free text 14, 20, 37-38, 193-196, 198, 205, 208-209, 230-231, 240, 245-249

frequency distribution 236, 239

fuzzy controller 25

fuzzy logic 64, 236, 250-251

G

Gabor filter 73, 96-98, 103
Gabor function 96
Gabor kernel 97
Gabor wavelet 90, 92, 96, 101-103
gait authentication 133, 179, 184-185, 187-188
gait biometric 13-14, 170, 172, 177, 179, 181
gait cycle 171, 177
gait recognition 13-14, 20, 38, 133, 139, 170-174, 178-179, 184-185, 187-191
galvanic skin response (GSR) 124-126, 129, 136, 148, 163
Gaussian function 96
Gaussian mixture model (GMM) 120
global pheromone update 98
global positioning systems (GPS) 138, 142, 148-149, 155-156, 159-160, 164, 166, 168, 175, 179, 190
global principal component analysis (GPCA) 70, 76-78, 82-83
ground reaction force (GRF) 14, 173

H

Hamming distance 73, 94, 152
hand geometry 91, 139
hand-off strategy 68-69, 81, 83, 85, 88
hardware authentication 43, 63
hardware-independent 44
heart rate variability (HRV) 116, 132, 146, 148-150, 160-161, 164, 168
hidden Markov model (HMM) 25
high frequency (HF) 95-96, 116, 160-161, 175
hybrid methods 217, 222-223, 225

I

identity assurance (IA) 1
identity tracing 194, 207
impostor pass rate 202
individual principal component analysis (IPCA) 70, 77, 82-85
insider detection application 17
intelligent driver assistance systems 155
interaction quotient (IQ) 47-48, 51, 56, 59
interaction ratio 47-48
intra-modal biometric 90
intrusion detection 2, 14-19, 21, 39, 64-66, 193-194, 205-206, 208, 210
intrusive period 27

J

Japanese long-text 212

K

kernel function 79, 100-101
keystroke analysis 20-21, 38, 71, 193-196, 199, 205-209, 230, 235, 249-251
keystroke data 206, 212-214, 218-219, 228-231
Keystroke digraph latency 45
keystroke dynamics 8, 11-15, 20-21, 24, 37-38, 65-66, 103, 106-107, 126-127, 129-130, 132, 134, 139, 195, 208-213, 229-232, 234-236, 238, 240, 247-252
Keystroke dynamics biometric 8, 14
keystroke pattern 194, 245, 250
Keystroke recognition 71-72
keystroke sequence threshold 243-247
keystroke timing 64, 209, 212-213, 230-231, 249
k-nearest neighbor algorithm 45, 52
k-nearest neighbor (k-NN) 45, 49, 52-53, 56, 114
knowledge and data discovery (KDD) 2

L

latency time 236, 239-243
learning algorithm 74, 238, 244
linear discriminant analysis (LDA) 70, 78-79, 87-88, 113
linear time interpolation 175
local pheromone update 99
logged-in user 41-42, 44, 56, 59
login session 1, 9, 22-24, 26-29, 39, 193-194, 205
long-text input 87, 212-213, 228-231
low frequency (LF) 95, 160-161

M

machine learning 13, 64-65, 87, 105, 115, 118, 123, 127, 132, 178, 195, 209
masquerade attacks 1, 18, 41, 43
masquerading 5, 17, 40-44, 62-63
maximum a posterior (MAP) 52, 99, 120, 123, 132, 164, 237
mean time-to-authenticate (MTTA) 31-37
minimum average correlation filters (MACE) 70, 79-83, 85
monitoring periods 26-29
monitoring session length 27, 36-37
monozygotic 115, 122, 125

motion recording sensor (MRS) 174, 189
mouse dynamics biometric 14
mouse-to-keyboard interaction ratio 47-48
multilayer perceptron (MLP) 237
multi level security (MLS) 186
multimodal biometric 13, 20, 25, 37, 68, 103, 165
multimodal biometric hand-off 68
multispectral palmprint 89-90, 92-93, 102-103

N

neural networks (NN) 40, 45, 48-52, 56, 64-65, 79,
    133-134, 191, 209, 232, 234-238, 241, 243,
    247, 249-251
n-graph time 197-198
normalized correlation (NC) 73, 77-78, 100-102

O

on board diagnostics (OBD) 149, 155-156

P

palmprint 89-97, 102-104
palmprint authentication 95, 102, 104
password recovery 194, 207
pattern analysis 20-21, 38, 85-88, 103-104, 132,
    209, 234-235, 249-251
pattern recognition 20, 45, 50, 64-66, 80, 85-88,
    103, 131, 133-134, 137, 148, 151, 164, 167,
    191, 210, 231, 234, 239, 249-250, 252
peak-to-sidelobe ratio (PSR) 80
periodic detection 30
personal identification 64, 91, 135, 164, 212, 217,
    230
physiological biometrics 64, 106, 110
pressure seat images 137

R

radial basis function (RBF) 100-102
re-authentication 6, 14, 21, 40-48, 54, 56-59, 61-64,
    71-72, 74-76, 81, 129, 207
receiver operating characteristic (ROC) 29-30, 82-
    84, 100
recognition accuracy 93, 179, 222-223, 225-227,
    229
region of interest (ROI) 92-95
relative distance 197-198
retinal patterns 139

S

session hijacking 1-2, 18, 22-23, 39
session identifier 1
silence period 25-26, 32-34, 36
skin conductance level (SCL) 124
skin conductance responses (SCR) 124-125
soft-biometric indicators 71
spatial-frequency response array 73
static authentication 1-3, 7, 23, 28, 43, 181-183,
    185-187, 235
static authorization 7
static enrollment 5
statistical analysis 10, 48-50, 52, 153, 156
statistical heuristics 40
stimulus-response paradigm 105, 111, 127
support vector machines (SVM) 64-66, 70, 79, 83,
    86-87, 90, 92, 99-103, 115, 251
synaptic connections 237
system under design (SUD) 46-49, 52, 56-58

T

thermal imaging 13, 139
time-based model 27
time-to-alarm (TTA) 23, 27, 31-32
time-to-authenticate 23, 27, 31-35
time to correct rejection (TCR) 80
time-to-recognize 24
total errors (TE) 101
traditional authentication 18, 41-42, 57, 63, 193-
    194
training phase 45, 51-52, 54, 62

U

ubiquitous computing 166-167, 180, 189-190
user authentication 9, 20-21, 24, 38, 41, 44-45, 56,
    63-65, 70, 86, 103, 105, 107, 111, 123, 129,
    131-132, 134-136, 170-171, 187-189, 193, 201,
    203, 205, 209, 213, 227-230, 232-235, 238,
    240, 249-251
user re-authentication 6, 14, 21, 40-46, 54, 56, 58,
    61-64
user-resource authentication 9
user-resource-system authentication 9
user-resource-system-transaction authentication 9

V

Vapnik Charvonenkis (VC) 99-100
vehicle context 149

vein patterns 139
verification phase 45, 54, 195
very low frequency (VLF) 160
video sensor based (VS) 2, 59-62, 85, 141, 172, 197
virtual code 240-241
virtual keyboard 194
voice patterns 139

W

wearable sensor based (WS) 171-172, 184, 189
weighted euclidean distance (WED) 212-213, 215-218, 222-225, 228-229
wireless electrocardiograms 137

Y

YubiKey 138, 166